WOMEN, WAR, AND REVOLUTION

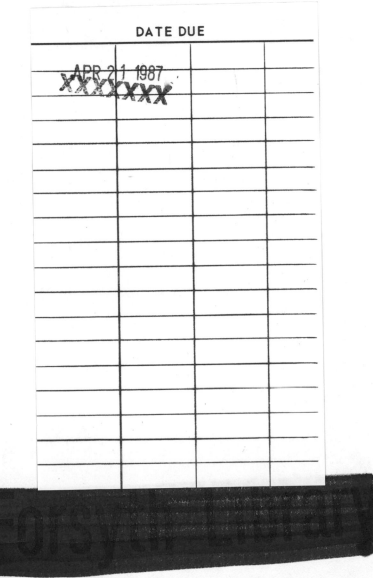

WOMEN, WAR, AND REVOLUTION

Edited by
Carol R. Berkin
and
Clara M. Lovett

HOLMES & MEIER PUBLISHERS, INC.

New York ● London

First published in the United States of America 1980 by
Holmes & Meier Publishers, Inc.
30 Irving Place
New York, N.Y. 10003

Great Britain:
Holmes & Meier Publishers, Ltd.
131 Trafalgar Road
Greenwich, London SE10 9TX

Library of Congress Cataloging in Publication Data

Main entry under title:

Women, war, and revolution.
   Bibliography: p.
   Includes index.
    1. Women in politics—History—Congresses.
2. War—Congresses.   3. Revolutions—Congresses.
4. Women and peace—Congresses.   I. Berkin, Carol.
II. Lovett, Clara Maria
HQ1236.W65 1979   301.41′2   79-26450
ISBN 0-8419-0502-9
ISBN 0-8419-0545-2 pbk.

Manufactured in the United States of America

We dedicate this book to
Richard Brandon Morris and Emiliana Pasca Noether,
who have made a difference in our professional lives.

Contents

Acknowledgments

This book could not have been written without the cooperation of many people who gave generously of their ideas, knowledge, and energy.

Our thanks go, first of all, to the colleagues whose essays appear in this book. Their hard work and their patience with the many demands we made on their time more than offset the inevitable problems and drudgery we as editors had to face. Second, we wish to thank the panelists and participants in the May 1978 conference from which this volume resulted. For a variety of good reasons, some of the panelists did not contribute essays to this volume. But the ideas they and many participants expressed at the conference were invaluable to the contributors and to us as we wrote the introductory essays.

In the absence of outside funding for the conference, we leaned heavily on the support of the Baruch College administration and of our colleagues in the History Department. We gratefully acknowledge the assistance of the Baruch College Alumni Fund and the sympathetic cooperation of President Joel Segall and of Dr. Matthew Goldstein. To our colleagues Stanley Buder and Thomas R. Frazier we owe special thanks for their willingness to help with both intellectual and menial tasks.

At every stage in our project, we had the benefit of Margaret Crahan's expert advice and of Janet Asteroff's organizational efforts. When we were selecting, evaluating, and editing the essays to be included in this book, we received invaluable encouragement and assistance from two devil's advocates with sharp minds and sharp pencils, Benjamin F. Brown and John P. Harper. Our sincere thanks to them, to our three young research assistants, Nancy Friedman, Lisa Master, and Linda Woodman, all of Barnard College, and finally to our gracious and enthusiastic editor, Joyce Seltzer.

C.R.B. & C.M.L.
New York, June 1979

Preface

The raison d'être of academic departments and of professional organizations such as those of which we are members is that they provide opportunities for intellectual exchange and for ongoing dialogue. This in theory. All too often in practice they perform tasks and meet needs that have little to do with intellectual discourse. They are surrogate unions, social clubs, and, not infrequently, battlefields on which ideological and personal rivalries are fought out. As such, they breed opportunism and cynicism more often than new knowledge.

We are, therefore, particularly pleased to report, uncynically, that this book originated from an informal exchange of ideas between two colleagues in an academic department. The idea of a conference on the theme "Women, War, and Revolution," of which this book is a product, began to emerge some two years ago, when we told each other of exciting things we had read, or discovered through original research, in our respective fields. One of us was then involved in two projects: a book on the Loyalists in the American Revolution, and another on the history of American women. The other of us, long interested in the European revolutionary tradition, had just read Judith Howard's doctoral thesis on women after the Italian national revolution of the nineteenth century.

As we compared the state of our respective fields, we began to realize that much original work was being done on women in revolutionary movements and wars. But we also found that much of this new work was developing either within the old straitjacket of national histories or, more frequently, within the new straitjacket of women's history. In either case it obviously suffered from lack of exposure, of comparative perspective, and of integration into a larger body of historical knowledge.

We shared our excitement and concern with several colleagues within and outside of our own department. Their response prompted us to organize a conference that was held at Baruch College, The City University of New York, in May 1978. The invited participants were scholars, many nationally known, some just beginning their careers, who were actively engaged in research and writing on the general theme of women in revolution and war. Pioneers, all of them, regardless of chronological age and professional status, for they were exploring a subject—women—seldom treated in histories of revolutionary movements and wars. But pioneers, above all, because in exploring women's experience they were looking from a wholly new perspective at events that had shaped the Western world since the eighteenth century. In the process they were reinterpreting such well-known episodes as the French Revolution, the Nazi regime in Germany, and the impact of wartime mobilization on American society.

During the late spring and summer of 1977 we made plans for the conference to be held the following year. The task of organizing sessions and of securing commitments by invited participants proved surprisingly easy. We wrote to about twenty-five specialists in American and in modern European history whose work on the general theme of the conference we had read and found especially deserving of exposure and debate. Not all of them answered our inquiry, of course, and among those who did, not all were willing or able to participate. But the twelve scholars who ultimately contributed papers or comments responded most enthusiastically, and we went ahead with plans for three sessions followed by a plenum discussion.

We paid no attention to the fact that only women scholars had submitted proposals for papers. In retrospect, the kinds of responses we got simply reflected the state of the field: more women than men were at work on the topic we had chosen. At any rate, in sending out inquiries we had followed the only appropriate and relevant criteria: the subject and the quality of research. These were also the only criteria we used in deciding which papers were acceptable and which were not. Certainly it never occurred to us to choose the participants on the basis of irrelevant criteria such as, for instance, geographical origin, academic affiliation, or ethnic background.

With plans for sessions already laid out, we began to investigate potential sources of funding. The amount we needed was very small but crucial to our undertaking, for our department has neither staff nor graduate students and our college is not known for its physical amenities. We applied to the one agency—a branch of the federal government—that had a program appropriate to our needs. There were initial assurances of cooperation by officials apparently satisfied with our proposal. Then months of silence, and finally the news that a review panel had recommended against funding our proposal. Informed that we could, however, revise and resubmit the proposal to the same agency, we requested a summary of the review panel's comments. To our astonishment, the reviewers had criticized the lack of "sexual balance" in the composition of the proposed panels and the "feminist emphasis" of the conference.

Weeks of dialogue with the agency by letter and even face-to-face with one official failed to resolve our difficulties. But the denial of funding, based on what appeared at best a misunderstanding of the scholarly purpose of our undertaking, increased our determination to proceed with our plans. Months of intense labor during which we did everything from negotiating with interested publishers to licking stamps and making coffee were amply rewarded by two days of intense and enriching dialogue among the participants and between them and the audience.

When we moved from organizing the conference to preparing this volume, we found that not all of the papers were in a form suitable for publication. Others were, but they were already scheduled to appear elsewhere. Thus, we sought new contributions, which we selected according to exactly the same criteria used for the conference. A call for additional contributions enabled us, among other things, to break out of our own Western intellectual provincialism and to include in our book two essays on women in the Third World. Admittedly, much more than this historiographical tokenism is needed for comparative purposes. But this tokenism reflects more the state of the field than our own cultural biases or unwillingness to look further.

Again, among those invited to contribute to this book were both women and men, both feminists and nonfeminists. Paying no heed to the gender or the ideological preferences of potential contributors, we sought essays that combined original research, fresh interpretation, and felicitous style. Although these qualities seem to be in short supply, at least in the academic world, we believe that our quest has been successful. Readers and critics must judge whether this is so.

We offer no apology for the inevitable lack of uniformity of our book with regard to the literary style and the structure of its component parts. Style and structure are the result of a particular interaction between the author and his or her material. We see no compelling reason for interfering in that process. We have, however, sought to emphasize some important common themes that emerge from the individual contributions. This is why we have organized the book into three sections, each preceded by an introductory essay. The first section deals with the theme of women's emerging political consciousness and increased visibility during revolutionary movements and wars and with the rising expectations that ensue among them. The second and longer section deals with the impact of rising expectations and with the resulting tension in postrevolutionary societies between patriarchal and egalitarian values. Finally, the last three essays discuss the development in very different historical contexts of one particularly interesting mechanism for resolving that tension: the ideal of civic motherhood.

PART ONE

POLITICAL PARTICIPATION
AND ECONOMIC MOBILIZATION

Part One: Introduction

The three essays in this section deal neither with wartime heroics nor with women as individual contributors in national crises. In part, the decision not to focus on this type of women's activism reflects the maturation of our field of inquiry. For, after almost a decade of scholarship in women's history, the patriotic contribution of women in wars and revolutions is a twice-told tale. Such portraits of women martyrs, soldiers, propagandists, and patriots have often marked the birth of women's history within a national specialty. They served to rectify those sins of omission in traditional accounts of wars and revolutionary efforts, and, thus, to educate scholars and lay people alike. They raise consciousness, promote pride, and restore a fullness to the historical event. But such studies of activism and heroism are often descriptive rather than analytical, and valuable as they remain, they reinforce a sense that women deserve notice only when they are active and heroic. The implicit contrast is to a passive, nonpolitical, timid sex—and thus praise is built upon disdain.

The scholars contributing to this section approach women's mobilization and participation from a very different perspective, and a provocative one. Although their specific topics range from the French Revolution to World War II, they share a unifying theme: each asks what expectations were raised in women by the exigencies of war and revolution; what were the explicit promises made by the leadership who sought their cooperation, or by the ideology they were asked to embrace; and, finally, what were the implicit promises of the transformations at work during these national crises? Discovering, isolating, and clarifying these expectations and evaluating the extent to which they were realized are the tasks these scholars have set for themselves. Each essay documents the remarkable fluidity of circumstances and the innovative quality of the experience that characterized these national crises; yet each also attests to the resiliency of traditional roles and structures and to the fragility of egalitarian reform. It is within this contradiction between the promise of change and the restoration of tradition that the experience of women is to be located.

In "Women of the Popular Classes in Revolutionary Paris, 1789–1795," Levy and Applewhite trace the growing sophistication and institutionalization of political activism among the lower-class women of eighteenth-century Paris. The Revolution carries these women from a "subsistence mentality" to an identity as "participating citizens"; the former a political consciousness appropriate to the paternalism of monarchical France, the latter a response to the egalitarian possibilities in the years 1789–1795. Levy and Applewhite show us that the Revolution did not create *de novo* a political awareness in these Parisian women. Rather, it provided them an opportunity to create political organizations and to do so within the context of a reform agenda that made such organizations meaningful. With remarkable speed and skill, patterns of spontaneous protest were transformed into effective, structured, revolutionary activity. Indeed, one tribute to the effectiveness of organizations such as the Society of Revolutionary Republican Women is the speed and force with which both the Jacobin and the Thermidorian governments moved to destroy them. By 1794, the society was dismantled, its class-conscious demands and its relentless exposure of "unfulfilled constitutional promises" silenced. Without a forum in which to debate political issues, without an institutional base for political activity, the Parisiennes returned to the more narrowly focused "bread and butter" protests. But these protests, so similar in appearance to the older "subsistence mentality" era, were not proof that political consciousness had been a temporary impulse for a naturally unpolitical sex and class. Instead, Levy and Applewhite argue, they represented a defeat of maturing structures for democratic participation in national politics.

Levy and Applewhite stress the importance of organizations for effective political activity. But their argument that women, even within a traditional culture like that of pre-Revolutionary France, are not without political consciousness is a most important one. For women, like workers or minority racial groups, have often been assumed to be imprisoned by their own "psychic unreadiness," by their inability to perceive their own interests or, at the least, by an unreadiness to translate desires into effective organizational form. The culture, it is argued, may have so incapacitated them, but the incapacity makes them unable to grasp the liberating opportunity when it arises. Thus, even in the midst of revolution, they capture no brass ring. The history of women in the American Revolution has frequently been written in such a way. But Levy and Applewhite suggest that the extent of women's political participation and organizational activity should be used as a barometer for measuring the democratic character of the French Revolution, not the psychic readiness of the women themselves. Such a view, supported in their own research, may shed more light on the true nature of revolutions than those that lay the blame on the victims themselves.

It is significant to note that the women of the Levy and Applewhite study identified themselves by class rather than sex in formulating their political demands. Their Revolutionary Society was exclusively female, but its aims were not feminist. Historians must take care not to confuse the two. Like these Parisiennes, the women of Leila Rupp's study responded to wartime mobilization as their social class rather than their sex dictated. As Rupp shows, both the methods chosen by the Nazis to promote female employment and the response of the population to it raise interesting questions about the meaning of wartime mobilization for women in our century. Despite its totalitarian potential, the Nazi state did not coerce mass female economic mobilization. Patriarchal attitudes persisted even among Nazi leadership: woman's place was the home, and thus her forced entry into the workplace was repeatedly delayed. This patriarchal reluctance revealed a class bias in the leadership as well, for even before the war over two million German women of the lower classes were working outside the home. Even had Nazi leaders been free of patriarchal bias, a significant segment of their political base was not. The fear of alienating middle-class men—still patriarchs within their own homes—led Nazi officials to delay enactment of universal mobilization laws and undermined enforcement of the laws. Bourgeois women were thus protected by traditional attitudes, a protection they appear to have readily embraced. Their acquiescence in the privileges of class and gender role is subject to multiple interpretations. But, as Rupp notes, one point is worth consideration: the Nazi mobilization program was more punitive than promising in nature; sacrifice, not incentives, was its theme. There was little to motivate women to choices that might carry an implicit challenge to patriarchy.

Rupp's exposure of the Nazi government's sensitivity to class concerns is an important one, for official Nazi ideology proclaimed the death of class and class conflict in Germany. In fact, such conflict was very much alive, as the response of working-class women to mobilization policy attests. They recognized that the Nazi policy discriminated against them, and they protested it. These women had no illusions as to the opportunities factory work promised under Nazi mobilization. Here it is the absence of expectations, and the refusal to internalize a rhetoric of patriotic sacrifice, that is most striking. What working-class women do appear to have entertained was an expectation that the Nazi government would make good its commitment to "social justice" by demanding equal sacrifice from women of all classes. Thus these women did not oppose mobilization; they demanded that it be universal. It is perhaps ironic that Nazi mobilization goals were defeated by the unintended sisterhood of bourgeois resistance and working-class complaint and protest.

For the historian of women, the Nazi experience calls into question the cherished notion that homefront mobilization in the twentieth century always meant gains for women. More importantly, Rupp's essay points to the dangers of attributing to ideology what properly belongs to concrete realities. The women of Nazi Germany do not seem to have embraced the elevating role of Nazi womanhood, with its glorification of sacrifice, nor was their choice between working or remaining at home based on any ideology of women's proper sphere. It was the absence of material incentives that made patriarchal protection attractive to the women of the middle classes and eliminated any advantages to employment that might have won the cooperation of the women of the working class. Neither feminist consciousness nor a heartfelt commitment to domesticity motivated German women of World War II; we should not confuse the consequences of entering or avoiding the workplace with its causes.

Unlike the Nazi government, American business relied on incentives to

draw women into its factories during World War II. The American government aided this recruitment program, not simply with standard patriotic
propaganda, but with a support system to ease women's entry into the work
force. Thus day-care centers sprang up across the country, funded by
federal and local agencies. The success of this mobilization has been a
striking fact in American history, but its meaning is ambiguous. The figures
alone draw our attention: six million women who had never been employed
joined the wartime payrolls. Within five years women increased from 25
percent to 36 percent of the work force. "Rosie the Riveter" was in her glory,
for not only did millions more women work, they worked at jobs traditionally
associated with a masculine affinity for heavy machinery. In her essay on
working-class women in the Portland shipyards during World War II, Karen
Skold offers a vivid and detailed portrait of women in one such industry. She
shows the speed with which the Kaiser Corporation moved to recruit and
train women after Pearl Harbor. By 1942, women once confined to menial
and marginal jobs within the peacetime economy found themselves earning
high wages and working within a union structure. Many factors seemed to
work to women's advantage in the shipyards. First, a small craft industry was
transformed, almost overnight, into a major component of military production. One result was an absolute shortage of labor in the shipbuilding
industry. Second, Portland was an isolated location and offered a limited
male recruitment pool. Finally, the urgent production demands and the
potential profits lifted most restraints on both recruitment and incentive
policy.

Yet, despite these advantages for women, work and employment patterns
soon revealed discriminatory practice and policy. Hierarchies based on sex
took shape within the shipyards. Skold has subjected this apparent revolution
in work patterns to a careful scrutiny and offers several explanations for the
swift re-creation within this novel work situation of old inequalities. But
Skold's study suggests that war mobilization crises in modern industrial
nations are less favorable for women than might be expected. In America, at
least, such a crisis was carefully contained in both time and ideological space;
despite the accommodations made to women's dual role as workers and
mothers, despite the swift and uncontested entry of women into craft union
occupations, despite the incentives of equitable pay and hours, both government and private industry viewed women's employment in heavy industry as
a temporary phenomenon. The adjustment to a peacetime economy meant
the reintegration of soldiers into the work force and the rapid return of women
to their marginal employments or to the home. No government policy for full
employment was ever formulated, although this alone might not have pre-
served for the women welders and the factory workers what the war had given
them. The lack of such a policy is not surprising, for the availability of a
cheap and flexible labor pool was as essential to the American economic
structure as it was traditional. After World War I and the end of mass
immigration into the country, women constituted that labor pool. Ironically,

that female pool would soon be mobilized again, but not for jobs on assembly lines or in factories. The postwar period was the era of the secretary and file clerk, but it was the middle-class woman who filled this sex-segregated and poorly paid role in the new American bureaucracies. Not the war but the shift from production to service industries insured new employment slots for women.

It is important to note that here, too, class is a significant factor in the process under study. Minority and working-class women were the members of their sex whose expectations rose during World War II, but it was their middle-class white sisters who found employment in peacetime. In evaluating the meaning of war mobilization and of the office-employment revolution which followed, historians must take care to identify the participants. It is not enough to know only their sex.

The essays that constitute this section raise as many questions for us as they answer. And this is as it should be. The archaeology of women's experience requires a slow and complex peeling away of layers: new stereotypes often cover old ones, and the well-intended polemics of feminists, like the sexist history they deplore, often prevent the reconstruction of the past as it was rather than as it should have been. Frequently the source of women's failure to snatch egalitarian victories from the jaws of defeat has been sought, not in the larger configurations of a society or in the fate of a revolutionary reform agenda itself, but in the naiveté, the lack of sisterhood, or the "natural" passivity of women themselves. These three studies escape these traps. And, although they offer neither prescriptions for the future nor excuses for the past, they fulfill the historian's first duty: to reconstruct the past as objectively as possible and to interpret its dynamics without prejudice.

1/Women of the Popular Classes in Revolutionary Paris, 1789-1795

Darline Gay Levy
Harriet B. Applewhite

Colorful descriptions abound of common women in revolutionary Paris: market women marching with loaves of bread and bouquets to thank Sainte Geneviève for alleviating hunger in August and September, 1789; fishwives milling about the meeting hall of the National Assembly during the October Days, chastising its president, Joseph Mounier, for supporting M. le Veto; laundresses petitioning the Jacobin Club to demand the death penalty for hoarders and speculators in foodstuffs and bleach; red-pantalooned sword-wielding Républicaines-Révolutionnaires guarding escape routes and chasing Girondin deputies from the Convention in May 1793. All these and many others—cooks, actresses, lacemakers, charcoal-carriers—appear to be part of the supporting cast, adding color and drama, but not performing lead roles in the Revolution.

Common women did indeed have a significant impact on the men and institutions involved in revolutionary power struggles, and their participation was a departure from traditional forms of collective feminine activity and a step in the direction of participatory democratic politics. They were not feminists, and their goals were often the age-old concerns of wives and mothers for the survival of their families, but they learned to use revolutionary institutions and democratic tactics to secure political influence.

This essay questions certain assumptions about women's involvement in revolutionary politics that appear in recent historical writing. Some historians, especially those concerned with feminism, stress the failure of women's political efforts. Scott Lytle and Marguerite George in articles on the Society of Revolutionary Republican Women both state that the ultimate disbanding of the society was a defeat for feminism, and deemphasize the society's political influence during its half-year existence.[1] Two general surveys of women in revolution, by Jane Abray and Olwen Hufton, similarly emphasize the defeat of feminists and disasters for working women.[2] Hufton goes

---

Unless otherwise indicated in the footnotes, all eighteenth-century documents quoted in English in this paper are our translations, cited from our book with Mary D. Johnson, *Women in Revolutionary Paris, 1789-1795* (Urbana, Ill.: University of Illinois Press, 1979).

furthest in underlining the political annihilation, physical hardship, and psychological guilt and devastation that Parisian women experienced after 1795. This emphasis on failure and defeat distracts the historian from investigating the network of political institutions that made possible a successful, though briefly tolerated, experiment in locally based democratic government, in which nonelite women were fully participating citizens.

This study draws upon documentary evidence which places women of the people in the political context of revolutionary Paris and shows the evolution in their political sophistication and influence that ultimately led to repression at the hands of Thermidorian officials fully cognizant of the implications of feminine political activities.

It is also concerned with clarifying disagreement among certain historians concerning the nature of political changes in the Revolution. The dramatic extent of revolutionary political mobilization in Paris has been well documented, but some historians of popular movements, notably George Rudé and Jeffrey Kaplow, have argued that the spring of 1789 marked a dramatic break with traditional popular manifestations in the Old Regime.[3] The laboring poor, accustomed to riot recurrently but apolitically when hardships became intolerable, now acquired an understanding of the consequences of their actions for national politics; a political rhetoric from pamphlets, journals, and speechmakers; and, later on, a base for their efforts in popular societies and Section assemblies.

An alternative viewpoint places emphasis on the continuity of popular movements throughout the entire period of state-building and transition to preindustrial capitalism within a predominantly agrarian economy. These interpretations center on the problems of food supply, urban provisioning, and popular protest in times of high prices and shortages. The urban poor are not "prepolitical," but motivated by a "subsistence mentality," an ethic of "moral economy," which stipulates that government officials—local, regional, national, and even the king—are obligated to intervene in the grain markets to police the people's food supply and protect their livelihood and security when shortages occur.[4] Since women managed their family's meager income, shopped in the markets, and purchased bread, the dietary staple, they were often central figures in food riots and market disturbances.[5]

The behavior of eighteenth-century food rioters bears out the contention that they knew what they were about. The disciplined limits they often observed; their skill in frightening those who profited from the grain trade; their choices of targets for protest, whether bakers, grain merchants, customs houses, or the Parlement—all this evidence suggests political motivation, political awareness, and a certain modicum of political skill. The popular classes had no political power, except in their ability to threaten public order, but they understood how political power operated to affect their livelihoods.

Political change in eighteenth-century France affected political institutions in Paris and touched the lives of common women, foreshadowing the revolutionary experiences of their daughters and granddaughters. The administrative centralization of such governmental concerns as taxes, justice, police public works, and natural resources that occurred during the long period between the seventeenth century and the Revolution had complicated and contradictory impacts on people's lives: their religious practices, their work, and their subsistence. A dramatic example concerned the cult of François de Pâris, which developed after 1727 when miraculous cures were alleged to have occurred at the tomb of Pâris, a saintly mystic whose charity had endeared him to his neighbors in the faubourg Saint-Marceau. The cult of convulsionaries was especially attractive to laundresses and other working women in the faubourg, who were allowed important roles in rituals and were considered the equals of male adherents. When a government order closed the tomb in 1732, women joined protests and denunciations of despotism. These confrontations led to a "vague, but potentially important, political consciousness" among humble residents of the faubourg Saint-Marceau.[6] A second example from the 1720s links women, government subsistence policy, and the Church. In the year 1725–26 the Paris police began organizing grain stocks to be stored (as sources of emergency supplies) in hospitals and religious institutions; in an account of January 1729, twenty-three regular female convents and seven secular female houses were listed as having stockpiles. The program created rumors of speculative hoarding and suspicion of government involvement in conspiracies to create artificial shortages and drive up prices; the linking of such fears to religious institutions was one root origin of revolutionary anticlericalism among the popular classes.[7]

In the 1760s and 1770s, the government reform effort marked a radical departure from government's expected role as protector of livelihood. Turgot's suppression of the guilds in 1776 was greeted enthusiastically by some newly liberated workers, but violently protested by others, who demanded a reinstatement of controls on trade. There were many fewer exclusively female guilds than male guilds and only limited inclusion of widows in certain others, but those women who had guild protection feared its removal.[8] The government's attempts to free the grain trade in the 1760s were seen as disastrous repudiations of government's traditional responsibility to provision the cities and feed the hungry. All these examples show that, whether resented as oppressor or demanded as protector, government was increasingly experienced by Parisians as a systematic and rationalized intervention in their lives.

On the eve of the Revolution, women of the people were subjects of a government whose officials at both the local and national level were trying sporadically to rationalize their fiscal, judicial, and provisioning operations. Sometimes women coped with these changes, sometimes they protested, and sometimes they rioted. They were not "prepolitical." They knew how to operate within the confines of their world: their parishes and churches, their priests and employers, their shops and guilds, and their marketplaces. But their power was ephemeral. The Revolution in Paris provided them with opportunities to evolve from subjects, sometimes passive, sometimes protesting, into participating citizens. On some occasions women made traditional subsistence demands for plentiful food at acceptable prices, but also adopted new tactics of democratic participation in a framework of revolutionary institutions along with extrainstitutional protest. Incidents of *taxation populaire* (setting the price of commodities by crowd intervention) might be combined with drafting and presenting petitions to the Commune, the national legislative assemblies, or the Jacobin Club. At other times, women combined subsistence demands with broader demands for public recognition of their rights as democratic citizens. Not only did women claim redress of individual grievances, but they also made occupational group claims and claims based on patriotic or republican interests. The principal agencies of these transformations in women's political roles were political journals, clubs, elected assemblies, and popular societies, all functioning to mobilize women for political activities.

What follows is a chronological examination of revolutionary events involving women, presented to document the thesis that the processes of nationalization of politics in a revolutionary setting generated and sustained a matrix in which women of the people evolved from subjects into participating citizens.

What was unique about the French experience in the age of democratic revolution was the dramatic mobilizing effect of events that began in 1788 with the decision to convoke the Estates-General for the first time since 1614. The procedure for electing deputies involved an extremely broad suffrage and, for men at least, the stirring experience of meeting together in electoral assemblies. Similarly, the process of drafting *cahiers de doléances* for the deputies to take to Versailles involved many Frenchmen in drawing up preliminary grievance lists. In the first year of the Revolution, other events drew ordinary people into the turmoil of national politics: the national circulation of revolutionary pamphlets, like the Abbé Siéyès's *Qu'est-ce que le Tiers Etat?*; the proliferation of revolutionary journals after June 1789; the Réveillon riots in Paris in April and the subsequent fraternizing between royal troops and Parisians in the cafés and stalls of the Palais Royale; the resistance of some of the upper two orders to the demands of the Third Estate for the vote by head in the Estates; the ultimate decision to create the National Assembly; the rumors in early July of a coup d'état by the king against the deputies; the conquest of the Bastille; the Great Fear in the countryside outside Paris; the decrees of August 4; and the food shortages and movements of people into Paris leading up to the women's march on October 5 to Versailles. The result of these complex and dramatic events was to mobilize Parisians for the national power struggle and to confront them with new or transformed institutions through which that struggle would be carried out.

In January 1789, as the hope of regeneration took hold of an entire nation, women identifying themselves as "women of the Third Estate" published their petition to the king. They explained that they were excluded from "national assemblies" by laws which they had no hope of reforming; they were not requesting extraordinary permission to send deputies to the Estates-General because they thought the electoral process could be manipulated. They accepted their roles as subjects, entrusting their king with the full responsibility of representing their interests and satisfying their needs. However, when they asked for royal guarantees that certain trades and positions would be reserved exclusively for them and that free public schools would be established offering practical and moral training to prepare them for honorable places in a transitional economy and society, these subjects of modest means, with trade-specific interests, revealed their awareness of needing new strategies and special government protection in order to cope with dignity and with a fair chance of success in a highly competitive marketplace.[9]

In August and September 1789, following the popular insurrection which culminated with the fall of the Bastille and the reorganization of municipal government in Paris, the women of the people were participating in almost daily processions of thanksgiving to Sainte Geneviève, patron saint of Paris.

Jennifer Dunn Westfall has presented impressive evidence in an unpublished Mount Holyoke honors thesis that there were at least three discrete populations of these women marchers—fishwives from the individual market districts of the city; women representing trades, for example the city's laundresses; and women who came from a particular parish and who were accompanied by their parish clergymen.[10]

These processions followed a prescribed route. Typically they took the women first to the église Sainte-Geneviève, where they offered bouquets and breads to the patron saint; one report noted that the women "thanked Heaven for the conquest of liberty"; another report noted that they implored the saint "to serve as the protectress in Heaven of our brothers who perished, sacrificing themselves for the fatherland."[11] From the église Sainte-Geneviève the marchers sometimes moved to Notre Dame Cathedral, and from there to the Hôtel de Ville, where they presented Lafayette, commander of the newly formed bourgeois National Guard, with loaves of bread and bouquets. Westfall cites one report of a young woman representing the female second-hand clothes dealers of the Halles and vendors from the Cimitière des Innocents as having lauded the Commander-General in these words: "We have come to offer you the homage which you most like, that of our hearts. It is to your sublime virtue, to your profound wisdom that we owe our safety. We can only look upon you as an angel that was sent from Heaven to save his people. We are confident that you, as the common father of so large a family, will find a way to replace scarcity with abundance, arbitrary despotism with enlightened justice, troubles and disorders of which we have so long been the victims with calm and peace."[12]

What is so interesting about the processions is that these marchers, who expressed both their subsistence concerns and their new interest in "justice" and "liberty," were accompanied by contingents from the newly organized bourgeois National Guard. Apparently the women were not protesting, they were not petitioning—only participating in acts of thanksgiving. However, it is clear that at the same time they were making their organized physical presence felt in alliance with a militia which was under the direct authority of the new bourgeois municipal government, and which had been organized with the express purpose of defending bourgeois interests against the double menace of a repressive royal military force and uncontrollable urban crowds.

Some of the best evidence concerning the women's processions of August and September—and in an appendix to her study Westfall counts and categorizes thirty-four between August 18 and September 23—comes from the diary of Siméon-Prosper Hardy, the Parisian bookseller. On Wednesday, August 22, Hardy observed:

> Towards the hour of noon, a kind of procession of girls and women is seen once again passing along the rue Saint-Jacques, [a procession] which one would say came from the quartier Saint-Eustache, accompanied by soldiers from the bourgeois militia and by musical instruments; these girls and these women returned from Sainte-Geneviève to drumbeat with two consecrated breads, five large brioches, bouquets, and two branches of vines decorated with bunches of grapes which they were going to offer to the Holy Virgin in the metropolitan church, having to go afterwards to the Hôtel de Ville. Several people were heard criticizing and censuring these multiplied and daily gatherings of *citoyennes*, who appeared, however, to have no object other than that of giving solemn thanksgiving to the supreme being for the visible protection he had just accorded to Parisians.[13]

Three and a half weeks after this entry, Hardy's tone had changed markedly. Reporting on a celebration in the faubourg Saint-Antoine for the anniversary of the conquest of the Bastille—a celebration by members of the National Guard of Saint Antoine with young virgins of the district—Hardy noted: "Many people found there was something terrifying in [the procession's] arrangement, composition, and immensity. Sensible persons found these public acts, which could not be interrupted and of which piety was unfortunately not the entire motive, ridiculous. They thought that it would have been infinitely wiser for each citizen to thank the Almighty privately."[14]

Peaceful but highly organized and conspicuously escorted by the National Guard (which may have been reaching down to the women of the people for a popular base even as the women reached up and out to this bourgeois militia for support), these processions of thanksgiving, with the people's church and the new bourgeois municipal government as targets, can be read as dress rehearsals for the October Days.

The women who sounded the tocsin of alarm on October 5, 1789, and who gathered at the Hôtel de Ville demanding that Lafayette lead them to Versailles to get bread, came from some of the same market districts and faubourgs which had supplied marchers for the summer thanksgiving processions. When Lafayette hesitated, the crowds of women recruited sympathetic National Guardsmen and set off in the rain to march to Versailles.

What they did when they got to Versailles provides us with evidence that some among these thousands of women acquired a political education—in addition to assurances from Louis XVI that Paris would have bread and a king in residence.

Women who later insisted that they marched under coercion from armed furies nevertheless told the Châtelet Commission investigating the march how they had taken the initiative, how they had made their demands known to deputies and other authorities. Marie-Rose Barré, a laceworker, testified to the Châtelet Commission investigating the October Days that although pressured to go to Versailles, she ended up as one of the four women selected to have an audience with the king. Not only did her delegation ask the king for bread for Paris, but it made specific requests that he provide escorts for four transports to be sure that they would arrive there. The king provided them the escorts.[15]

Madelaine Glain, a forty-two-year-old *faiseuse de ménage*, testified that she was "forced, as many other women were, to follow the crowd that went to Versailles last Monday, October fifth." But she also reported that she "went with the other women to the hall of the National Assembly, where they entered, many strong. Some of these women having asked for the four-pound loaf at 8 sous, and for meat at the same price, she, the declarant, called for silence, and then she said that they were asking that they not be lacking bread, but not [that it be fixed] at the price these women were wanting to have it at." Later, she returned with a National Guardsman and "two other women to the Hôtel de Ville in Paris to bring back the decrees they were given at the National Assembly." And finally, under escort of the National Guard, she was led to the district of l'Oratoire to "convey this good news."[16] So this "involuntary participant" in the October Days also turned out to be a woman who, having forced her way into the National Assembly meeting at Versailles, communicated the marchers' objectives to the deputies, and was part of a delegation which conveyed back to the bourgeois government in Paris the news that the marchers' demands had been met, and more.

In one account of the October Days, a journalist noted that women occupying the meeting place of assembly voted with the deputies on motions and amendments relating to legislation on the circulation and distribution of grains, and "exercised . . . the function of the legislative power and the executive power."[17] This essay has suggested that the summer processions in Paris can be looked upon retrospectively as dress rehearsals for the march to Versailles; but the playacting at Versailles shows that women were fulfilling an impressive number of roles for which there had been, apparently, no rehearsal. There had long been a French tradition of festivals when common folk put on the clothing and played the roles of mayors, judges, and other town authorities. In October 1789, the women comprehended that the deputies at Versailles were their representatives, not their rulers, and that they could playact at being their own representatives. They were holding a dress rehearsal for their performance as the sovereign people.[18]

The thousands of women who marched to Versailles on October 5 were only loosely organized; but their alliance with the National Guard and their impressive numbers gave them the leverage that contributed so heavily to their success: they conquered in their demands for bread; and they conquered a king for Paris. The thousands of women who returned in triumph to Paris on October 6 had become part of a complicated political struggle for control of the Revolution. When they played legislators for a night, served as representatives to the king, formed part of delegations to the City Hall, and served as emissaries to their Sections, these women were learning through experience how their traditional roles in insurrectionary movements could be combined with new roles as citizen-participants to yield impressive results—to begin with, the satisfaction of immediately pressing demands for protection, security, and subsistence.

On the Champ de Mars in Paris in July 1791, two years after the events of the October Days, women of the people are again prominent among the crowds gathered there to sign a petition calling for a referendum on the future of the king's executive role. During the years 1789–1791, small numbers of common women had been admitted to popular societies; they were spectators in the galleries of radical clubs which espoused openly republican ideas.

In the winter and spring of 1791, members of the Cordeliers Club in Paris used correspondence, delegations, and petitions linking the growing number of popular societies founded to instruct the people and oversee the conduct of officials. In May, representatives from the Cordeliers and fraternal societies formed a central committee led by François Robert to protest against the restrictive suffrage laws for election to the national legislature and to support strikes of carpenters, typographers, and iron merchants.[19]

In late June 1791, as the Constitution was being completed, Louis XVI, who had resisted some of the National Assembly's earlier legislation, fled Paris with the royal family; he returned escorted by civilian and military revolutionaries unable to renounce a monarch who was at the center of the new constitutional arrangement. Now, republican voices among club members became stronger; political clubs, led by the Cordeliers Club, carried their call for a national referendum on the issues of monarchical executive authority into the fraternal societies. In this way, significant numbers of common men and women were alerted to the urgency and centrality of an issue—the legitimacy of monarchical executive authority—that was not directly related to traditional bread-and-butter issues that typically brought people into the streets.

A call went out from the radical clubs for a rally at the Champ de Mars to sign a petition calling for the popular referendum. Women were deputized by fraternal societies; they took part in the Cordeliers Club debates, and in debates in other clubs.

On July 14, 1791, women were prominent among members of the Cordeliers Club and the popular societies who gathered on the Champ de la Fédération and signed and delivered a petition to the National Assembly. Forty-one women, "women, sisters, and Roman women," signed that petition—the petition "of the hundred." It read in part: "The citizens present here come therefore with this [character] which they hold from the Romans; with this character of liberty which they will preserve until they die; to ask of the Nation's representatives that they not legislate anything definitive concerning the fate of Louis XVI until the desires of the commoners [les communes] of France have been expressed and until the voice of the mass of the people has been heard."[20]

Another participant in the petition signing, a young shopwoman and member of a fraternal society, was designated and deputized by her society to present the petition to the National Assembly. While engaged in this mission, the shopkeeper was menaced by the mayor and a member of the bourgeois National Guard, whom she accused of threatening to kidnap her and close and raze her shop. The following day, when she joined another deputation "of thousands" which presented a petition to the Jacobin Club requesting that its members sign the Champ de Mars petition individually, this woman was in a position to ask that the president of the Jacobin Club protect her from menaces coming from the highest echelons of the revolutionary establishment. She had learned to identify personal and political enemies and the institutions that could be expected to guard her against abuses of power.[21] She might well have been following a pattern of patron-client relationships—between servant and employer, or parishioner and *curé*—that was customary in the Old Regime, but she understood that the Revolution had transformed her source of aid into a public and impersonal institution.

When crowds numbering in the tens of thousands gathered on the Champ de Mars on July 17 to sign the final petition demanding the referendum, Lafayette called out the National Guard to disperse them. The petitioners tarried and the Guard opened fire, killing about fifty persons. Following the *journée* of the Champ de Mars, members of the Cordeliers Club were arrested or forced to flee; women were arrested as well; among them were not only leading feminists, including Etta Palm d'Aelders, but also the wife of a butcher who was active in Section politics, the wife of a wine merchant, and the owner of Hébert's print works.[22]

Among those who marked the petition were women unable to sign their names. An eleven-year-old boy who testified at an inquiry into the Champ de Mars incidents noted "that we saw many people go up to sign, among them, with her children, [was] an old woman, who, not knowing how to write, had one of her children sign for her."[23]

Louise Evrard, a cook, was arrested on July 17 because she insulted the wife of a National Guardsman who had participated in the events at the Champ de Mars that day. George Rudé has paraphrased her cross-examination by the police commissioner of the Section Fontaine de Grenelle. That cross-examination reveals that Evrard, who was present at the Champ de Mars "[to] sign a petition 'comme tous les bons patriotes,' " as she puts it, also knew very well what the issues were. "She understood its aim was 'à faire organiser autrement le pouvoir exécutif.' " She acknowledged that she was frequently at the Palais Royal and at the Tuileries—centers for the communication of political news; that she had attended Cordeliers Club meetings, although she was not a member. She acknowledged that her expression of grief at the death of the radical journalist Loustalot had found its way into the *Révolutions de Paris*; and finally, she stated that she read Marat's journal, along with Audouin's and Desmoulins', and frequently the *Orateur du peuple* as well.[24]

By the summer of 1791, then, women of the people in Paris had begun to institutionalize their political activities within clubs and popular societies. There, and especially in the wake of the king's flight to Varennes, they became sensitized to issues of royal legitimacy and the extent of suffrage at a critical moment in revolutionary history. In fact, the participation of radicalized women in petition signing at the Champ de Mars indicates that they were looking critically not only at royal authority but also at the Constituent Assembly, which had failed to withdraw support of the monarch. Women who gathered at the Champ de Mars were willing to take a stand on revolutionary political issues that were not bread-and-butter issues. The extent of their participation may never be known—much of the critical evidence burned in the great fire of 1871—but the fact of it cannot be ignored: in the summer of 1791, women of the people combined petition signing with club attendance, the study of newspapers, the formation of delegations and deputations—a whole panoply of political role-playing within re,olutionary institutions that signals to us the expansion of their awareness of the potency of their political influence. Finally, the *journée* of the Champ de Mars may have alerted the people of Paris—artisans, shopkeepers, men and women of the laboring poor—to the serious and tragic implications of the split between their needs and interests and the goals of the revolutionary leadership.

Nonetheless, once the Constitution was completed (September 1791) it was generally accepted, notwithstanding the tragic incident at the Champ de Mars. The legitimacy crisis which that incident illuminated and exacerbated was reactivated in 1792–1793. Under the impact of critical events during the period January 1792–February 1793—the overthrow of monarchy; new and intensified economic hardship; the creation or strengthening of Section assemblies and societies and new clubs dominated and led by *sans-culottes*; and the formation of a new national legislature, the National Convention— the common women, the *femmes sans-culottes*, stepped up the pace of their political activity and focused it principally on subsistence concerns.[25]

The events of the *journées* of February 1792 and February-March 1793 illustrate the rich, complex combinations of legal and marginally legal politics of the *femmes sans-culottes* and allow us to measure their progress as citizen-participants.

The Sugar Crisis of January-February 1792 occurred as civil war raged between royalists and patriots in the French West Indies. Capitalizing on the crisis, speculators hoarded their stores of colonial products, especially coffee and sugar, in expectation of soaring prices. Working-class women, for whom sugar had become a necessity—they used it with coffee in the mornings and at lunchtime, as an energizer—protested the price hikes in petitions to the Commune and the Legislative Assembly; finally, when the Assembly failed to act on their complaints, they resorted to a traditional form of crowd violence, *taxation populaire*, in the capital's faubourgs and central markets.[26]

In February of the following year, with a republic proclaimed, the *sans-culottes* were in a position to articulate, from their strengthened organizations in the Sections, the common people's demands: political and economic terror against the people's enemies and laws against hoarders. In a period of exacerbated subsistence crisis, *femmes sans-culottes* once again organized. They sent deputations to the Jacobin Society, to the Paris Commune, and to the National Convention to demand fixed grain prices and severe punishment for the nation's domestic and foreign enemies. On February 24, 1793, at the Commune, the revolutionary municipal government, "a large deputation of *citoyennes*" asked for authorization to go before the Convention to demand that prices on subsistence commodities be reduced, and to denounce hoarders. Commune officials informed them that the Commune's authorization was not necessary; but they also urged the women to return home, and assured them that Commune authorities were preparing an address to the Convention demanding a strict law against hoarders.[27]

On February 22, 1793, at the Jacobin Society, "a deputation of *citoyennes* from the Section des Quatre-Nations" requested the use of the Jacobin meeting hall to discuss the hoarding problem. Robespierre the Younger objected "that repeated discussions about foodstuffs would alarm the Republic"; the president declared that "the Jacobins no longer were free to dispose of their meeting room during the day; and were absolutely unable to offer it for use"; Dubois-Crancé declared that the revolutionaries had priorities: "first liberty must be conquered, that afterwards foodstuffs would be cheap"; another member voiced his fear "that if the *citoyennes* were allowed to use the meeting room, 30,000 women might foment disorder in Paris"; Jeanbon Saint-André added that the solution "would be to exclude from the popular societies any person who instigated discussion on this subject with the intention of breaking the peace."[28]

On February 24, 1793, several delegations of *citoyennes* appeared at the National Convention. The petition of a deputation of *citoyenne* laundresses read as follows:

> Legislators, the laundresses of Paris have come into this sacred sanctuary of the laws and justice to set forth their concerns. Not only are all essential foodstuffs being sold at excessive prices; but also the price of the raw materials used in bleaching have gotten so high that soon the least fortunate class of people will be unable to have white underwear which it cannot do without. It isn't that the materials are lacking; they are abundant; it's hoarding and speculation which drive up the price. You have made the blade of the laws bear down on the heads of these public bloodsuckers. We ask the death penalty for hoarders and speculators.

The president of the Convention responded to this demand with the observation that nothing drove prices up more certainly than cries of hoarding.[29]

Another deputation of *citoyennes* from a "fraternal society meeting in the locale of the former Jacobins" (probably the nexus of the future Society for Revolutionary Republican Women) expressed its concern that the price of subsistence goods be forced down and asked for the report on "the law which makes silver negotiable." A deputy, backed by the president, informed this deputation that the committees of the Convention were working on the problem and would report the following day.[30]

A day later, having met with delaying tactics at the Convention, women took the matter of their subsistence into their own hands. The journalist Prud'homme reported on the crisis in his *Révolutions de Paris* for February 25. Noting that hoarding, lack of bread, and high soap prices had evoked complaints and protests from the *citoyennes* of Paris, Prud'homme observed:

> Already bitter complaints were being heard in the spectator galleries of the General Council of the Commune. It [the Council] replied: "Go take your complaints to the bar of the Convention." The advice was heeded. Sunday, among the petitioners, several cried out: "Bread and soap!" These cries were supported outside the hall by large and very agitated groups. The Convention took all that in with considerable coolness and adjourned until Tuesday, when the matter was to be taken up. Far from calming and satisfying [them], this resolution embittered them still more, and upon leaving the bar [of the Convention] the women in the corridors said aloud, to whomever was willing to listen: "We are adjourned until Tuesday; but as for us, we adjourn ouselves until Monday. When our children ask us for milk, we don't adjourn them until the day after tomorrow."[31]

Police reports on the *journées* of February 1793 describe the women's alternative to adjournment, insurrection: their instigation, leadership, and support of numerous expeditions of *taxation populaire*, raids on warehouses, bakeries, and groceries, and sales at an enforced "just price."

The commissaire who filed his report on damages at the warehouse of Citizen Command on February 25, 1793 noted that women dominated the crowds; Command attested that "a considerable number of men and a larger number of women appeared at the door of his house." Command also testified that the women were there to remove soap, and then sugar, once they understood that Command had no soap in stock:

> First, several of these women asked him whether he had any soap, to which he replied, no. Seeing that a portion of them were taking a stand against him personally, he went back in. Neighbors and other good citizens approached these women. They assured them that there wasn't any soap, and in fact, he hadn't had any at his place for a year. One of these women, letting it be seen that she was pregnant by slapping her stomach, said, "I need sugar for my little one." Immediately, all the women said, "We must have sugar."

Furthermore, the commissaire's report shows that the women were not embarked on pillages; they had organized and were executing an expedition of *taxation populaire*: "Then all the women streamed into the warehouse, and seized the sugar, brown sugar, and coffee that was stored there. Several insisted on paying, as follows: 20 sous a livre for sugar; 10 sous a livre for brown sugar; and 20 sous a livre for coffee." Finally, the commissaire's report provides evidence of the magnitude of these operations: Citizen Commard's total losses, as he calculated them, were 25,458 livres, 11 sous.[32]

The commissaire's report on the events of February 24, 25, and 26 in the Section de l'Arsenal provides other examples of women's *taxation populaire*. Describing his midafternoon tour of a grocery on the quai des Armes, where men and women forced him to accompany them on an inspection of the grocer's house and then returned to his shop, where they mounted an operation of *taxation populaire*, the commissaire noted:

> And finally, there was a woman, of fairly good appearance, unknown to me, but whom we would recognize perfectly. She was about five feet one inch tall, thirty years old, with blond hair, white skin, and slightly red eyes. She wore her hair in a demi-bonnet to which a rose-colored ribbon was attached. She was dressed in a *déshabillé* made out of linen, with a blue background and a standard design on it. She wore a mantlet of black taffeta and a gold watch on a steel chain. . . . This woman did everything in her power to add to the sedition. She had gone on the inspection. And once they returned, it was she who set the price for soap at 12 sous per livre; and for sugar at 18. After which, the aforementioned merchandise on hand at the aforementioned Rousseau's place was handed over with an unbelievable impetuosity. Everyone wanted to pay, to be waited on, and to get out, all at the same time. We were compelled to take in the cash in order to prevent a total loss. The aforementioned woman took the aforementioned goods, for which she paid us, and we barely had the time to take in the money, hand over the goods, and put the money in the drawer.

Later in the afternoon, the commissaire returned to the quai des Armes, in response to reports of new disturbances:

> We saw a *citoyenne* there, well dressed, who was influencing people, and stirring up trouble. Having listened to her during a period allowed for this moment, we apprehended her calling upon constituted armed force for support. *Another perilous moment*, given that the people were opposed to her being taken away. Finally, we brought her before the Committee where we drew up a *procès-verbal*, and we sent this *citoyenne* to the commissaire of police of the Section de la Maison Commune so that whatever the laws dictate might be done.[33]

The events of February 1792 and February 1793 provide insight into the complex ways in which Parisian *femmes sans-culottes* worked within and on the margins of revolutionary institutions, fusing tactics like petitioning, which they had mastered and practiced within their popular societies, Section assemblies, and as members of organized trades, with *taxation populaire*, insurrectionary demands invoking the people's right to subsistence commodities at a just price.

The response of authorities to the feminine politics of violence changed over the course of the year. In February 1792, the Legislative Assembly listened to reports by the mayor of Paris on popular disturbances. The mayor told the deputies that he had confronted the protesting crowds, who assured him that they were not gathered to pillage. The mayor suggested that they try petitioning, and they did. The Legislative Assembly blamed counterrevolutionary hoarders for inciting the people, but recommended nothing more than voluntary boycotts of colonial products. The following year, the National Convention again blamed the popular violence on aristocrats, but moved beyond calls for voluntary abstinence to vote new sums of money to the Commune for provisioning Paris. The Convention also authorized the municipality to sound the general alarm; one deputy, Chaumette, urged laws against hoarders and regulations governing the issuing of *assignats*.* He insisted that wages must be coordinated with the price of necessities if liberty was to mean anything at all to poor people.[34]

In the popular societies, Section assemblies, and radical clubs where women of the people frequently gathered—as members or as spectators—during the radical phase of the revolution (1793–1794), leadership and control had typically devolved to their friends, brothers. fathers, and husbands, an articulate *sans-culotte* elite. It was not, however, until February 1793, at a critical stage in the power struggle pitting Girondin moderates against Jacobin radicals, that the common women of Paris succeeded in establishing their own institutional base, the Society of Revolutionary Republican Women.[35] The society allowed for the most complete institutionalization of the *femmes sans-culottes'* revolutionary political activity. The society had its own regulations, with carefully elaborated procedures for meeting, for election of officers, for membership, correspondence, and deputations. It had its own meeting place. The society's known leaders, Pauline Léon and Claire Lacombe, were women with socially marginal occupations; Léon was a chocolate-maker, a trade undermined by sugar shortages and the departure of the aristocrats, and Lacombe was an actress from the provinces. Both had been active in revolutionary events before 1793. Perhaps most central to their real influence on revolutionary politics was their close contacts and effective working alliances within Sections controlled by *sans-culottes*.[36] They formed a close liaison with the *Enragés*, spokesmen on the far left for the *sans-culottes'* interests. The Revolutionary Republicans had proven their loyalty to the Jacobins during the critical *journées* of May–June 1793: they joined with Jacobins, Section chiefs and residents, the National Guard, members of popular societies, and *Enragés* to oust Girondin deputies from the Convention. They also enjoyed important contacts with the Cordeliers Club.

By September 1793, the society, which numbered several hundred members, campaigned actively for the implementation of a political program

---

*Paper certificates backed by confiscated ecclesiastical or aristocratic property.

which the Montagnard establishment, along with market women and even some members of the society itself, found massively threatening.

In the autumn of 1793, the society, in combination with the *Enragés* and other radical democratic factions, applied heavy pressure on Sections, popular societies, Jacobin clubs, and Convention deputies to support a full program of protective and repressive measures for the safety of the people. Their tactic paid off. The Convention legalized the Terror on September 5; voted an *armée révolutionnaire* on the ninth; passed a law of suspects on the seventeenth. On the twenty-ninth, the Convention passed a law of the "general maximum," providing for uniform price controls on necessities. On September 21, again acceding to pressure from the society, the Convention voted to require all women to wear the revolutionary tricolor cockade in public. The society's members were aggressive and relentless in pressing the revolutionary authorities to enforce this legislation energetically.

Despite these efforts, the society met with defeat, defeat at the hands of Montagnards as well as women in the district where the society was holding its meetings. Market women, former servants, and religious women opposed the price controls the society supported and were critical of legislation meting out harsh punishments for suspect aristocrats and former clergy. They resisted the new legislation on the tricolor cockade. Even more critical, Montagnard authorities at all levels were also threatened by the Revolutionary Republicans. Along with the *Enragés*, the society's members represented the most coherent opposition in revolutionary Paris to critical proposals in the Montagnard political program. The society was one of the very few remaining fighting fronts for a *sans-culotte* population which persisted in waging war for the complete realization of a democratic society of liberty, equality, fraternity, and virtue.

The Revolutionary Republicans conspicuously opposed Jacobin policies of compromise with moderate revolutionaries whose support, in fact, the Jacobins needed to supply the armies and to maintain themselves in power. The women relentlessly exposed the Jacobins' unfulfilled constitutional promises; they demanded enforcement of the law of the general maximum, the surveillance of merchants, and the use of *sans-culotte* vigilante forces to control revolutionary officials.[37] On September 16, 1793, at a meeting of the Jacobin Society, members who a few weeks earlier had offered the Society of Revolutionary Republican Women its meeting hall, greeted its deputations warmly, and supported its members' views on terror and subsistence, exposed and denounced the Revolutionary Republican leader Claire Lacombe along with Théophile Leclerc, the *Enragé* journalist. The Jacobins charged that Républicaines-Révolutionnaires had spoken scornfully of "M. Robespierre who dared to treat them as counter-revolutionaries"; one member reported that "Citoyenne Lacombe meddles everywhere"; at one assembly meeting, "she asked for the constitution, the whole constitution, only the constitution . . . . after which she wanted to sap the foundation of the constitution and overturn all kinds of constituted authorities"; motions were entertained which would have called for the revolutionary women to "rid themselves by a purifying vote of the suspect women who control the Society" and requesting that word be sent to the Committee of General Security to "have suspect women arrested"; first of all Citoyenne Lacombe. In the end, Lacombe did appear before the Committee of General Security; her papers were sealed, but when inspected, were found to contain no incriminating evidence.[38]

In October 1793, when the Républicaines-Révolutionnaires attempted to enforce the law on the cockade, outraged and threatened market women attacked the society's members in the streets.[39] At the end of October—newly dated 7 Brumaire, Year II—market women, aided and abetted by hostile authorities, stormed a meeting of the Revolutionary Republicans and abused and beat society members with impunity. When the society's vice-president called upon the Section Revolutionary Committee to draw up a *procès-verbal* of the incident, the committee deliberately delayed; women suspected of assault and battery were brought to the committee, but they were released. When the Revolutionary Republicans persisted in their demands for a *procès-verbal*, a troop officer, in collusion with committee members, persuaded them to desist, to abandon their *procès-verbal*, and to make their escape from what the officer falsely assured them was a huge, angry crowd crying "Vive la République! Down with the *révolutionnaires!*"[40]

The following day, 8 Brumaire, a delegation of market women filed a formal complaint against the Revolutionary Republican Women with the Convention. And on the ninth André Amar reported to the Convention on behalf of the Committee of General Security.

He questioned the patriotism of the Républicaines-Révolutionnaires, intimating that they were counterrevolutionaries. He went further, addressing himself to two general considerations: "Should women exercise political rights and meddle in affairs of government?" and "Should women meet in political associations? . . . Can women devote themselves to these useful and difficult functions?" His answer was that women were physiologically, psychologically, and intellectually incapable of governing.

One deputy asked whether it made sense to invoke higher principles to justify dissolving popular societies, even if it could be shown that some members had committed indiscretions. Another deputy argued that the Convention had already "thrown a veil over principles out of fear that they might be abused to lead us into counter-revolution. Therefore, it is only a question of knowing whether women's societies are dangerous." The Convention decreed: "The National Convention after having heard the report of its Committee of General Security, decrees: Article 1: Clubs and popular societies of women, whatever name they are known under, are prohibited. [Article] 2: All sessions of popular societies must be public."[41]

When women appeared at the Convention during a session of 15 Brumaire with a petition protesting the radical revolutionary leadership's liquidation of the Society of Revolutionary Republican Women, the deputies refused to hear them: "The women petitioners leave the bar hurriedly," the *Moniteur* reported. When a deputation of women wearing the red caps of the Revolutionary Republicans appeared before the General Council of the Paris Commune on 27 Brumaire, Chaumette, a council member who had tangled earlier with the Revolutionary Republicans, reminded the deputation that physiological and cultural considerations indicated to women: "Be a woman. The tender cares owing to infancy, household details, the sweet anxieties of maternity, these are your labors." Chaumette also reminded the petitioners of the fate of La Roland and "the impudent Olympe de Gouges who was the first to set up women's societies, who abandoned the cares of her household to get mixed up in the republic and whose head fell beneath the avenging knife of the laws. Is it the place of women to propose motions? Is it the place of women to place themselves at the head of our armies?" Chaumette's demand that the woman's deputation not be heard, that no future female deputation be received, except on an ad hoc basis, was warmly applauded and unanimously adopted.[42]

The Revolutionary Republicans institutionalized political roles for *femmes sans-culottes* more fully and more successfully than any other body in revolutionary Paris. Radical revolutionary authorities responsible for repressing this society, whose leaders and members had crystallized and successfully implemented a political program to satisfy the needs of the *menu peuple* for protection and subsistence, had taken a fateful step that would lead inexorably to the liquidation of the organizational bases for the democratic revolution in Paris.

By the time that Robespierre and the Montagnards proclaimed the revolutionary government on October 30, 1793, a day after the dissolution of the Society of Revolutionary Republican Women, they had undermined the political power of the *Enragés* and the Revolutionary Republicans, among the last groups capable of exerting programmatic efforts on behalf of the common people. The Jacobins did not want to risk being exposed by organized censors and critics continually demanding that they fulfill their constitutional guarantees and promises. Women did continue to contact authorities but generally to petition for the satisfaction of personal demands and not to represent larger issues, in part because the organizational bases from which such confrontations would normally come had been eroded by the government of the Terror. During the Terror, wives petitioned on behalf of husbands in the army or in jail; teachers asked for help in collecting unpaid salaries; workers attested to the revolutionary patriotism of their employers. Despite the problems of provisioning the city in wartime, the Montagnards maintained steady, reassuring supplies of subsistence goods at controlled prices.

In July 1794, government authority shifted suddenly back to better-off people—the Thermidorians—who undermined both the political institutions which had given power to the *menu peuple* and the economic legislation which had protected their livelihood. In October 1794 new laws prohibited petitions, affiliations, and correspondence among clubs. Price supports were curtailed in favor of free trade, which brought back hoarding, speculation, and inflation—and food shortages and long bread lines. The last great popular revolutionary insurrections, the *journées* of Germinal and Prairial, broke out in response to these deprivations. Over a three-month period, in a series of collisions with authorities, women once again used the strategies which they had mastered in the course of the Revolution. They led protest marches, they carried petitions to the Section committees and the National Convention; and they engaged in their traditional *taxation populaire*. However, they operated without benefit of formalized revolutionary organizations: popular societies, sympathetic Section officials, and strategic allies among journalists and deputies. The organization they could use was conspiratorial. When these conspiracies were uncovered, women who had further strategies at hand had no option except to submit.

Interrogations and police reports show that the authorities felt threatened by calls for a return of the institutions that had been the bases of popular influence the previous year. One witness during a police interrogation on the night of 29 Germinal recalled overhearing the remarks of a woman during a conversation on a street corner: " 'Yes, I see women who, when they receive a quarter-pound loaf, not having gotten any the night before, are really satisfied and very happy. If you go to present a petition about it to the National Convention, you are arrested. The popular societies have been closed. That was in order to plunge us back into slavery. We are all suckers.' "[43]

Officials also feared crowds of women as the most serious threat to public order. For example, on 7 Floréal, Year III, a police investigator reporting on "the mood of the public" stated:

> The women, above all, seemed to be playing the principal role there [in the squares, streets, public places, and at the bakers']; they were taunting the men, treating them as cowards and seemed unwilling to be satisfied with the portion that was offered to them. A large number of them wanted to rush into insurrection; even the majority appeared to be determined to attack the constituted authorities and notably the government Comités, which would have happened were it not for the prudence and firmness of the armed troops.[44]

Women led marches from Section headquarters to the Convention, mobilizing women along the route; they seized flour wagons, violently protested to the Comité civil that they would not allow the flour to be distributed to the bakers; in the end they took the law into their own hands, arresting members of the Comité civil "in the name of the sovereign people."[45]

Finally, it required an armed force from the Section, reinforced by troops from other Sections, to end the disturbance.

After 1795, Parisian women did not again rise in insurrection until 1848. We want to question whether there is any progression in the nature, extent, and significance of female political participation moving from the spring of 1789 to the spring of 1795.

Women began as subjects who reacted to elite initiatives by zealously guarding traditional prerogatives, but they learned to operate as citizens working through revolutionary institutions to demand the satisfaction of needs as rights which were abstract and sophisticated and which included political power. Real life seldom progresses with theoretical neatness, but there is documentary evidence for such a transition. This essay is concerned not only with describing how women came to work through organizations for revolutionary goals, but also with explaining why they did so and whether their efforts had political significance. Such an explanation must link the nature of people's demands, the collective actions they take, the organizational bases from which they operate, and the responses of governmental authorities.

In the late summer of 1789, the processions of women in Paris represent a fascinating mix of a traditional harvest festival and a show of force by a vigilant citizenry. During the October Days, women demonstrated to demand that the king resume his medieval role as provider, but their actions imply a vague recognition of current political issues, such as the royal veto clause in the Constitution and the roles of deputies as representatives of the popular will. This awareness increased as revolutionary activists published journals, harangued public gatherings, and founded clubs and popular societies. The petition on royal executive powers of July 1791 represents many of the elements of modern collective political action: a deliberate, planned gathering on the Champ de Mars, petitions to the Jacobins and the National Assembly spelling out specific demands for a referendum, and the participation of organized associational groups, including the Cordeliers. The demonstration lacked tight organization and control. The violent retaliation by authorities, coupled with the Assembly's restoration of full executive authority to the king, ended any further large-scale collective action until the sugar crisis of February 1792.

The food riots of 1792 and 1793 differed in scale and in the reaction of authorities. Both represented, again, a mix of traditional ad hoc demands that government protect the food supply and participatory tactics of petitioning local and national government. By 1793 protestors were adding demands for permanent protection, enforceable laws against hoarding, and the regulation of currency.[46]

The activities and tactics of the Républicaines-Révolutionnaires are indications that women had come to understand how to corner a share of political power: purging the Convention, policing the markets, arguing for the harsh prosecution of suspects, petitioning for specific laws to control the marketplace both economically and physically.

In the spring of 1793, women had linked their subsistence grievances to their constitutional rights. What is striking in these events is the evidence of the authorities' tactics of relying upon neighborhood groups to control behavior by using spies, setting tradeswomen against their customers, or urging men and women in street gatherings or bread lines to implicate one another.

Clearly, the popular associational institutions such as Section assemblies of the Year II and popular societies were not sufficiently large, tightly organized, or supported to prevent the Thermidorians from using centralized and controlled police networks and local and national government to destroy the women's political power.

Female political leaders often emerged from marginal social positions—actresses, former practitioners of the undermined luxury trades—or from occupations such as printing and publishing that put them at the center of political communication. When dramatic events, uncertain power struggles, or economic scarcity were great enough, as in the summer of 1791 and the spring of 1793, more women became involved. Women signed petitions, marched and demonstrated, attended meetings, formed deputations, and persuaded, frightened, or coerced political authorities to accede to their demands. When police and other agents of government threatened them, or when they felt their security undermined by aristocrats, hoarders, and speculators, they joined forces in popular societies and Section assemblies.

The crucial variable determining the nature and extent of women's political influence is the availability of political institutions geographically proximate, sympathetic to women's interests, and open to women as spectators, petitioners, delegates, and members. Women who had earlier joined up with loosely organized and somewhat incoherent groups rooted in the parish, the market, and the trade and occupational structures in Paris were able to move during the revolutionary mobilization into popular societies, the Section assemblies, and the galleries of the Commune and the national legislatures. These popular organizations did not last sufficiently long to enable their participants to overcome their rivalries and to integrate their interests. Government officials were aware of these rivalries and exploited them, in addition to using tactics of repression, to regain and perpetuate control over the city. Two generations later, the granddaughters of the women of the Revolution would emulate them as heroines, remembering that they had been among those who began the fight for popular control of political power.

What is unique about the French Revolution, compared to other revolutions in the eighteenth-century world, is that it was a democratic revolution which not only enlightened but engaged an entire nation of French men and French women in the struggle for influence and power as citizen participants. Government repression, targeting *femmes sans-culottes*—sometimes along with men and sometimes as especially threatening insurgents—brought this democratic experiment to an end.

Notes

1. Scott H. Lytle, "The Second Sex (September, 1793)," *Journal of Modern History* 27 (1955): 14–26; Margaret George, "The 'World Historical Defeat' of the *Républicaines-Révolutionnaires,*" *Science and Society*, 40 (1976–77): 410–437.

2. Jane Abray, "Feminism in the French Revolution," *American Historical Review*, 80 (1975): 43–62. Olwen Hufton, "Women in Revolution, 1789–1796," *Past and Present*, 53 (1971): 90–108. See also Hufton, *The Poor of Eighteenth-Century France, 1750–1789* (Oxford, 1975), and "Women and the Family Economy in Eighteenth-Century France," *French Historical Studies* 9 (1975): 1–22.

2. "The laboring poor were essentially prepolitical": Jeffrey Kaplow, *The Names of Kings* (New York: Basic Books, 1972), p. 153. George Rudé, *The Crowd in History* (New York, 1964), chap. 6, especially pp. 93, 94.

4. The term "subsistence mentality" is used in Steven L. Kaplan, *Bread, Politics and Political Economy in the Reign of Louis XV*, 2 vols. (The Hague, 1976), p. 680. On "moral economy," see E. P. Thompson, "The Moral Economy of the English Crowd in the Eighteenth Century," *Past and Present,* 50 (1971): 76–136.

5. Olwen Hufton, "Women in Revolution, 1789–1796," *Past and Present* 53 (1971): 90–108; Louise A. Tilly, "The Food Riot as a Form of Political Conflict in France," *Journal of Interdisciplinary History*, 2 (1971): 23–57.

6. B. Robert Kreiser, *Miracles, Convulsions, and Ecclesiastical Politics in Early Eighteenth-Century Paris* (Princeton, 1978), p. 396, and see also pp. 244–254; Kaplow, *Names of Kings*, pp. 122–126.

7. Steven L. Kaplan, "Lean Years, Fat Years: The 'Community' Granary System and the Search for Abundance in Eighteenth-Century Paris," *French Historical Studies*, 10 (1977): 197–230.

8. Kaplow, *Names of Kings*, pp. 37, 56.

9. *Pétition des femmes du Tiers-Etat au Roi, 1er janvier 1789* (n.p., n.d.).

10. Jennifer Dunn Westfall, "The Participation of Non-Elite Women in the Parisian Crowd Movements of the Opening Year of the French Revolution," (unpublished honors thesis, Mount Holyoke College, 1976), pp. 79–80.

11. Westfall, "The Participation of Non-Elite Women," p. 81, citing Lebois, *Récit exact de ce qui c'est passé hier à Sainte-Geneviève* (Paris, 1789).

12. Westfall, "The Participation of Non-Elite Women," pp. 81–82, citing *Procession solennelle de femmes fripières de la Halle, et les Marchandes du Cimetière des Innocents* (Paris, 1789).

13. Siméon-Prosper Hardy, *Mes Loisirs*, 8, fol. 443, in Bibliothèque Nationale (BN), MSS, no. 6687.

14. Westfall, "The Participation of Non-Elite Women," p. 83, citing Hardy, *Mes Loisirs*, 8, fol. 475.

15. *Procédure criminelle instruite au Châtelet de Paris* (Paris, 1790), Deposition 343, as reprinted in Philip Dawson, ed., *The French Revolution* (Englewood Cliffs: Prentice-Hall, 1967), pp. 66, 67.

16. *Réimpression de l'Ancien Moniteur, seule histoire authentique et inaltérée de la Révolution française, depuis la réunion des Etats Généraux jusqu'au Consulat*, 32 vols. (Paris, 1847), 2 (May 1789–Nov. 1799), pp. 542–44, testimony 83.

17. *Révolutions de Versailles, Dédiées aux dames françoises*, no. 1 (n.p., n.d. ["du samedi 3 octobre au—(deletion in text) du mê mois"]), p. 18.

18. Natalie Zemon Davis, "The Reasons of Misrule: Youth Groups and Charivaris in Sixteenth-Century France," *Past and Present,* 50 (1971): 41–75.

19. Albert Mathiez, *Le Club de Cordeliers pendant la crise de Varennes et le massacre du Champ de Mars* (Paris, 1910), pp. 30–34; Isabelle Bourdin, *Les Sociétés populaires à Paris pendant la Révolution de 1789 jusqu'à la chute de la royauté* (Paris, 1937), chap. 4.

20. Albert Mathiez, *Le Club des Cordeliers,* pp. 112–115, reprinting text of petition to National Assembly of July 14, 1791, with signatures, from Archives Nationales (A.N.), cahier 75, no. 737.

21. *Mercure universel,* as reprinted without indication of date in Marcel Reinhard, *La Chute de la royauté* (Paris, 1969), p. 482.

22. Mathiez, *Le Club des Cordeliers,* pp. 198, 199, 203, 211, 266, 267.

23. A testimony from a copy of the procedure of inquiry into the Champ de Mars incidents, A.N., F⁷ 4622; copy made by the lawyer Buirette de Verrières, one of the accused, and reprinted in Mathiez, *Le Club des Cordeliers,* p. 247.

24. Archives, Préfecture de Police, Paris, Aa 148, fol. 30, xx, as paraphrased by George Rudé, *The Crowd in the French Revolution* (London, 1959), pp. 86–87.

25. Rudé, *The Crowd in the French Revolution,* p. 105.

26. Rudé, *The Crowd in the French Revolution,* chap. 8.

27. *Moniteur universel, réimpression,* report of Feb. 24, 1793, in 15, 555.

28. Procès-verbal, meeting of the Jacobin Society, Feb. 22, 1793, as reprinted in F. A. Aulard, ed., *La Société des Jacobins,* 6 vols. (Paris, 1889–97, vol. 3, p. 37.

29. Minutes, session of the National Convention, Feb. 24, 1793, as reprinted in P. B. Buchez, B. C. Roux, eds., *Histoire parlementaire de la Révolution française,* 40 vols. (Paris, 1834–38), 24, 328–33.

30. Ibid.

31. Prud'homme, *Révolutions de Paris,* no. 190 (Feb. 23–March 2, 1793), reprinted in Buchez and Roux, eds., *Histoire parlementaire de la Révolution française,* 24, 333–35.

32. Commissaire's report on damages committed at the warehouse of Citizen Commard, Feb. 26, 1793, Section des Gardes-françaises, in Archives, Préfecture de Police, AA 153, nos. 73 ff.

33. Commissaire's report on events of Feb. 24, 25, and 26, 1793, Section de l'Arsenal, in Archives, Préfecture de Police, Paris, AA 69, nos. 296–97.

34. *Archives parlementaires,* ed. M. J. Mavidal and M. E. Laurent, vol. 37 (1891): 604–10; 59 (1901): 189–91, 301–02.

35. R. B. Rose and Scott Lytle date the founding of the society as May 1793, but documents refer to women requesting the Jacobin's hall in February 1793. See Levy, Applewhite, and Johnson, *Women in Revolutionary Paris, 1789–1795* (Urbana, Ill.: University of Illinois Press, 1979), chap. 4.

36. R. B. Rose, *The* Enragés: *Socialists of the French Revolution* (London, 1959).

37. Margaret George, "The 'World Historical Defeat' of the Républicaines-Révolution-naires," citing *Moniteur,* 18-IX-93, 9-X-93, 27-X-93, Alexandre Tuetey, *Répertoire général des sources manuscrits de l'histoire de Paris pendant la Révolution française,* 11 vols. (Paris, 1890–), vol. 9, p. 1388.

38. A.-F. Aulard, *La Société des Jacobins: Recueil de documents pour l'histoire des Jacobins de Paris,* 6 vols. (Paris, 1889–97), vol. 5, pp. 406–09; to compare with *Rapport fait par la Citoyenne Lacombe à la Société des républicaines-révolutionnaires* [sic] *de ce qui s'est passé le 16 septembre à la Société des Jacobins concernant celle des Républicaines-révolutionnaires* [sic]. *Séante à S. Eustache; et les dénonciations faites contre la Citoyenne Lacombe personnellement* (n.p., n.d.).

39. Pierre Caron, ed., *Paris pendant la Terreur; Ministère de l'Intérieur, Rapports des agents secrets du ministre de l'intérieur* (Paris, 1810), vol. 2, report of Latour-Lamontagne, pp. 154–164.

40. Prud'homme, *Révolutions de Paris,* 17, no. 215 (du tridi 23 brumaire, au decadi 30, an deuxième de la République française, une et indivisible), 207–10.

41. *Moniteur, Réimpression,* vol. 18, 298–300.

42. Ibid., 350, 450, 451.

43. Archives, Préfecture de Police, Paris, AA 216, Section Pont Neuf, 29 Germinal, Year III.

44. F.-A. Aulard, ed., *Paris pendant la réaction thermidorienne et sous le Directoire, Recueil des documents pour l'histoire de l'ésprit publique à Paris,* 3 vols. (Paris, 1898–99), vol. 1, pp. 683–85.

45. Extrait du Registre des délibérations du Comité civil de la Section du Bonnet de la Liberté, Séance du 11 Floréal, an 3ème de la République française une et indivisible, printed in B.N., LB40 1747, and reprinted in Walter Markov and Albert Soboul, eds., *Die Sans-Culotten von Paris, Dokumente zur Geschichte der Volksbewegung, 1793–1794* (Berlin, 1957), pp. 466–480.

46. R. B. Rose, "Eighteenth Century Price-riots, the French Revolution, and the Jacobin Maximum," *International Review of Social History,* 4 (1959): 432–445.

Suggestions for Further Reading

Well in advance of contemporary women's studies, historical research on women in the French Revolution had yielded a considerable literature. We call attention to Jules Michelet, *Les Femmes de la Révolution* (Paris, 1854); Edmond and Jules de Goncourt, *La Femme au dix-huitième siècle,* 2 vols. (Paris, 1882); Baron Marc de Villiers, *Histoire des Clubs de Femmes et des Légions d'Amazones, 1793–1848–1871* (Paris, 1910); Léon Abensour, *La Femme et le féminisme avant la Révolution française* (Paris, 1923); Léopold Lacour, *Les Origines du féminisme contemporaine: Trois Femmes de la Révolution: Olympe de Gouges, Théroigne de Méricourt, Rose Lacombe* (Paris, 1900). Jeanne Bouvier, *Les Femmes pendant la Révolution* (Paris, 1931), includes a most interesting essay and some very valuable revolutionary documents.

More recent accounts of women in the Revolution are, for the most part, based upon these earlier studies. In our opinion, these descriptive studies emphasize the ultimate failure of women's political efforts; the reader is left with the impression that women's roles were marginal and that their participation was narrowly focused on the subsistence issue. Jane Abray's article, "Feminism in the French Revolution," *American Historical Review* 80

(February 1975): 43–62, is the most complete brief survey of women in the Revolution for the English reader. Abray treats both the consciously feminist demands of educated women and the principal concerns of women of the popular classes with issues involving their livelihoods, their welfare, and their security. The first modern "interest group" for nonelite women is the Society of Revolutionary Republican Women of 1793, treated by Scott Lytle, "The Second Sex (September, 1793)," *Journal of Modern History* 26 (1955): 14–26; and Margaret George, "The 'World Historical Defeat' of the Républicaines-Révolutionnaires," *Science and Society* 40 (1976–77): 410–37. The most thoroughgoing account of this society is Marie Cerati, *Le Club des citoyennes républicaines révolutionnaires* (Paris, 1966). Women journalists and printers served as a critical link between educated women involved in revolutionary events and nonelite Parisian women who were shopkeepers, workers, market women, and wives of *sans-culottes*. See Evelyne Sullerot, *La Presse féminine* (Paris, 1963). Jennifer Dunn Westfall has traced the neighborhood origins and the revolutionary expressions of Parisian women's crowd activities in the late summer and the fall of 1789: "The Participation of Non-Elite Women in the Parisian Crowd Movements of the Opening Year of the French Revolution" (unpublished honors thesis, Mount Holyoke College, 1976).

More broadly focused recent studies of women in revolution have helped us to formulate our themes. A French study, Paule-Marie Duhet, *Les Femmes et la Révolution, 1789–1794* (Paris, 1971), contains a useful chronology of women's activities and good material on attitudes about women's public roles through the Year II; however, the close interweaving of Duhet's commentary with excerpts from documentary sources makes it difficult to follow. Of fundamental importance for our understanding of the lives of common people is the work of Olwen Hufton, a close student of provincial archival sources. Our general impression is that provincial women experienced the Revolution as trauma and disruption of their already insecure lives and were not mobilized for autonomous political activity as were their Parisian counterparts. See Olwen H. Hufton, "Women in the French Revolution," *Past and Present,* 53 (1971): 90–108; "Women and the Family Economy in Eighteenth Century France," *French Historical Studies* (Spring 1975): 1–22; and *The Poor of Eighteenth-Century France, 1750–1789* (New York: Oxford University Press, 1975).

Two recent books which take the long view of women in history present closely reasoned discussion of the Marxist and feminist approaches to understanding the nature and extent of the oppression of women. Roberta Hamilton makes excellent use of research in religious and social history, mainly of England, France, and the United States in *The Liberation of Women: A Study of Patriarchy and Capitalism* (London: Allen and Unwin, 1978). Elise Boulding, *The Underside of History* (Boulder, Col.: Westview, 1977), rejects a theory of biological determinism in accounting for the perpetual subjugation of women, but does not offer an alternative explanation.

Ultimately, the history of women cannot be written separately from the history of men. What is needed is a sensitive awareness of whether, when, and how men and women experience historical events differently, suffer or benefit from the distribution of power in societies, and contribute to the lives of others and the times they live through. We have found a number of books and articles extremely suggestive as we sought to understand the roots of revolutionary activism and the impact of revolution on working-class women. George Rudé's work on revolutionary crowds must be the point of departure for any study of women of the popular classes. Rudé has calculated the numbers and proportions of men and women involved in different categories of popular movements and has offered insightful explanations of the ways in which cultural and institutional differences affect the public roles of men and women. See George Rudé, *The Crowd in the French Revolution* (New York: Oxford University Press, 1959); *Paris and London in the Eighteenth Century: Studies in Popular Protest* (New York: Viking, 1969). We do find less than convincing Rudé's point that the spring of 1789 marked the beginning of political consciousness among the Paris crowds. Jeffrey Kaplow follows the same interpretation in his colorfully descriptive account of the Parisian poor, *The Names of Kings* (New York: Basic Books, 1972). Evidence for prerevolutionary political consciousness concerning subsistence issues is found in Steven L. Kaplan, *Bread, Politics and Political Economy in the Reign of Louis XV,* 2 vols., (The Hague, 1976); and Louise A. Tilly, "The Food Riot as a Form of Political Conflict in France," *Journal of Interdisciplinary History* 2 (1971): 23–57. The connection between politics and religion was made for the Parisian *menu peuple* during the reign of Louis XV. B. Robert Kreise's monograph on religious cults, *Miracles, Convulsions, and Ecclesiastical Politics in Early Eighteenth-Century Paris* (Princeton: Princeton University Press, 1978), describes the reaction to government intervention in cults particularly attractive to women. Kaplan's report on a program for emergency grain reserves uncovered data on the use of female convents and secular houses as storage depots during the 1720s; see Kaplan, "Lean Years, Fat Years: The 'Community' Granary System and the Search for Abundance in Eighteenth-Century Paris," *French Historical Studies* 10 (1977): 197–230.

Although Albert Soboul does not look at gender differences, his history of the *sans-culottes* and their network of political institutions in the Year II offers a framework to guide archival research on women in the popular classes. Richard Cobb's neighborhood-based studies are particularly important for understanding the Paris police and their tactics, although again there is no direct consideration of variations in the policing of men and women. See Richard Cobb, *The Police and the People: French Popular Protest, 1789–1820* (New York: Oxford University Press, 1970); Cobb, *Reactions to the French Revolution* (New York: Oxford University Press, 1972), and *A Second Identity: Essays on France and French History* (New York: Oxford University Press, 1969).

Our ideas on collective behavior were particularly stimulated by Natalie Zemon Davis's discussion of symbolism and playacting in sixteenth-century Lyons, "The Reasons of Misrule: Youth Groups and Charivaris in Sixteenth-Century France," *Past and Present* 50 (1971): 41–75; and by E. P. Thompson's evidence for reasoned, purposive actions by which English crowds manifested popular demands and values, "The Moral Economy of the English Crowd in the Eighteenth Century," *Past and Present* 50 (1971): 76–136. Finally, there is a goldmine of hypotheses concerning revolutionary festivals in Jean Ehrard and Paul Viallaneix, eds., *Les Fêtes de la Révolution* (Paris, Société des Etudes Robespierristes, 1977); see especially M. Ozouf, "La fête révolutionnaire et le renouvellement de l'imaginaire collectif." Using official minutes of revolutionary festivals, Ozouf has uncovered a tension between the organizers' intentions to use festivals to educate and inspire, and the participants' choice of symbols and performances to co-opt the festival and transform it to express their own concerns.

We have relied upon three sources to reconstruct the institutional network which at least initially facilitated women's political participation. Our evidence for the influence on women of revolutionary journals is supported by indications of a fairly high literacy rate for Parisian women. See Michel Fleury and Pierre Valmary, "Les Progrés de l'instruction élémentaire de Louis XIV à Napoléon III d'aprés l'enquête de Louis Maggiolo (1877–1879)," *Population* 12 (1957): 71–92. Rich descriptions of the activities, membership, recruitment patterns, and ultimate fate of popular societies in Paris are found in Isabel Bourdin, *Les Sociétés populaires à Paris pendant la Révolution de 1789 jusqu'à la chute de la royauté* (Paris, 1937). These were key institutions for communicating political issues to women, inspiring their patriotism, connecting their public roles to men's and organizing their political activities. The most radical Parisian women—Rose Lacombe, Pauline Léon, and the Society of Revolutionary Republican Women—were linked personally, ideologically, and politically to the *Enragés*, whose careers are examined in a thoroughly researched monograph by R. B. Rose, *The* Enragés: *Socialists of the French Revolution?* (Melbourne: Melbourne University Press, 1965).

One of the basic questions underlying the roles of Parisian women in revolutionary France is the extensiveness of revolutionary change. Upon what base of feminine political involvement did the events and the leaders of the Revolution build, and how extensively did the Revolution politicize women of the popular classes? Answers to these questions require further archival research, especially into the history of the local, neighborhood-based institutions: the parish, the market, the workplace, and the shop. In our opinion, Charles Tilly and his collaborators have offered the most suggestive insights into larger questions of the relations between economic development, government intervention into production and distribution, the keeping of public order, and popular movements—questions basic to understanding the transformation of eighteenth-century Parisian politics and economics into a national Revolution, and the roles of women in this process. See Charles Tilly, ed., *The Formation of National States in Western Europe* (Princeton: Princeton University Press, 1975); Charles Tilly, *From Mobilization to Revolution* (Reading, Mass.: Addison-Wesley, 1978); Charles Tilly, Louise Tilly, Richard Tilly, *The Rebellious Century, 1830–1930* (Cambridge, Mass.: Harvard University Press, 1975).

The documentary evidence we drew upon for this paper has been taken from our book with Mary D. Johnson, *Women in Revolutionary Paris 1789–1795* (Urbana, Ill.: University of Illinois Press, 1980).

The following list includes the basic printed sources for documents relevant to the roles of women: F.-A. Aulard, *Le Culte de la raison et de l'Etre suprême, 1793–1794: Essai historique* (Paris, 1892); Aulard, *Paris pendant la réaction thermidorienne et sous le Directoire*, 5 vols. (Paris, 1898–1902); Aulard, *Recueil des Áctes du Comité de salut public, avec la correspondance officielle des représentants en mission et le registre du Conseil executif provisoire*, 28 vols. (Paris, 1881–1951); Aulard, *La Société des Jacobins: Recueil de documents pour l'histoire du Club des Jacobins de Paris*, 6 vols. (Paris, 1889–1897); P. B. Buchez and B. C. Roux, eds., *Histoire parlementaire de la Révolution française ou Journal des Assemblées nationales depuis 1789 jusqu'à 1815* (Paris, 1834); Pierre Caron, *Rapports des agents secrets du ministre de l'Intérieur*, 4 vols. (Paris, 1910–1949); Charles L. Chassin, *Le génie de la Révolution*, 2 vols. (Paris, 1863–1865); Philip Dawson, ed., *The French Revolution* (Englewood Cliffs, N.J.: Prentice-Hall, 1967); Albert Mathiez, *Le Club des Cordeliers pendant la Crise de Varennes et le Massacre du Champ de Mars* (Paris, 1910); Marcel Reinhard, *La Chute de la Royauté* (Paris, 1969). Kare Tønneson, *La Défaite des Sans-Culottes: Mouvement populaire et réaction bourgeoise en l'an III* (Oslo and Paris, 1959); Alexandre Tuetey, *L'Assistance publique à Paris pendant la Révolution*, 4 vols. (Paris, 1895–1897); Tuetey, *Répertoire général des sources manuscrites de l'histoire de Paris pendant la Révolution française*, 11 vols. (Paris, 1890–1914); Walter Markov and Albert Soboul, eds., *Die Sans-culotten von Paris. Dokumente zur Geschichte der Volksbewegung, 1793–1794* (Berlin and Paris, 1957).

2/"I Don't Call That *Volksgemeinschaft*": Women, Class, and War in Nazi Germany

Leila J. Rupp

Nazi Germany—a fascist society that glorified masculinity and male authority while simultaneously undermining patriarchy by intervening in the family to an unprecedented extent—provides a particularly fascinating case in which to explore the relationship between war and women's situation. Often the major question asked about this relationship is whether war liberates women, but in dealing with Nazi Germany it is impossible to think in terms of liberation. In this case we can learn more about women and war by placing women themselves in the forefront and concentrating on the impact of the war effort on women's responses to government policy. That women's responses, differentiated according to class, did have an important impact on the Nazi war effort forces us to question some traditional assumptions about the nature of totalitariansim under Nazism. In addition, significant questions are thus raised about the ways in which women have exercised power, albeit indirectly, even in a hostile authoritarian regime, even in wartime.

The role that women's responses to mobilization policies played in the ultimate failure of German society to engage in total war is the first issue to be considered. That the female population remained only partially mobilized throughout the war can no longer be disputed.[1] The female labor force increased by a mere 1 percent during the war, and this tiny increase was not a result of a high level of mobilization in the prewar period: in 1943, the female participation rate (the percentage of the female population in the labor force) was 35.6 percent, the same as in 1925.[2] Nor was it the result of an adequate supply of labor, for the regime faced increasingly serious labor shortages that even the importation of foreign workers and prisoners of war could not solve. The regime grappled with the problem of mobilizing women throughout the war, yet never effectively implemented conscription, despite the impression of early observers that Germany possessed "a system of regimentation of labor in scope and intensity such as the world has never seen."[3] Nazi officials had available a number of measures with the potential to mobilize women even before the outbreak of war. A 1935 law introduced the Labor Book, a

Research for this paper was made possible by a grant from the National Endowment for the Humanities.

required permanent record of an individual's employment designed to control and mobilize labor.[4] Legislation a few months later made a term in the Labor Service, originally a public works program designed to ease unemployment during the Depression, compulsory, although this did not become binding on women until the outbreak of war in 1939 (and even then its numbers never increased beyond 150,000).[5] In 1938, the Office of the Four-Year Plan introduced the Duty Year, a compulsory year of labor in agriculture or domestic service for young single women seeking jobs for the first time.[6] More direct measures included an unpublished Defense Law, drawn up in 1935, that called for the service of all German women and men in case of war, and a 1938 decree providing for the conscription of women and men for a limited period of time for specific tasks.[7] A final decree with the potential for mobilizing women, issued in February 1939, empowered the employment offices to conscript individuals for work of national importance.[8]

Despite the existence of these measures, the Nazi leadership decided early in the war not to mobilize women en masse. The employment offices called up women in certain limited categories, almost exclusively women who had previously worked but were currently nonemployed. The Labor Ministry specifically instructed the employment offices *not* to call up women who had never worked.[9] By June 1940, only 250,000 women had been called up, and most of these had Labor Books (that is, had been employed sometime after 1935).[10]

In this atmosphere of hesitation, party and state officials debated the desirability of a general service obligation. Despite widespread support for such a measure, Hermann Göring, in accordance with Hitler's wishes, refused to sign the proposed decree.[11] Instead, legislation in 1941 specifically empowered the employment offices to call up women who had left work since the outbreak of the war.[12]

The leadership waited until January 1943 to enact the much-discussed general registration measure. The Law for the Defense of the Reich ordered the registration of women seventeen to forty-five and men sixteen to forty-five.[13] It granted exemptions for those who already worked at least forty-eight hours a week, employers of five or more persons, those employed in agriculture or health services, students, pregnant women, and women with one child under six or two children under fourteen. Further legislation extended the provisions of the registration decree, but as is already clear, it never resulted in successful mobilization. Hitler, whose personal intervention had delayed the introduction of the registration decree until 1943, had communicated his opposition to the conscription of women to his Plenipotentiary General for Labor Supply, Fritz Sauckel, when Sauckel took office in 1942.[14] Advocates of total mobilization, especially Albert Speer, complained repeatedly, even after the 1943 registration law, of the lack of mobilization.[15] In February 1944, the government, despite the 1943 decree, called once again for the voluntary mobilization of women.[16] Joseph Goebbels' appointment as Plenipotentiary for Total War in July 1944 and his desperate attempt to shut down all inessential activities came too late. Despite the extension of the age limit to fifty for women in the registration order, the situation did not improve.[17] German retreat and defeat, combined with Allied bombing, created such chaos that evaluation of this last period of the war is difficult.[18] In spite of Speer's warnings, Germany went down to defeat with a partially mobilized female labor force.

No simple explanation can make comprehensible the Nazi failure to mobilize enough women to keep up the strength of the civilian labor force while the armed forces consumed men at an increasing rate. The decision early in the war not to conscript women reflected the strength of traditional attitudes held by some of the Nazi leaders, especially Hitler.[19] In addition, Hitler's conviction that the war could be won without an all-out effort, without demanding of the German population too great sacrifices, helps to explain the initial reluctance to conscript women. Hitler decided in 1941 that it would be necessary to mobilize women only if the United States entered the war, but even after the German declaration of war on the United States, Hitler continued to oppose conscription.[20] The chaotic bureaucratic structure of government and the lack of clear allocation of responsibility for labor supply permitted the blocking of implementation at several points, so that even after the passage of the registration decree of January 1943, local officials responsible for enforcement sometimes ignored the order out of personal conviction or fear of antagonizing sections of the population.[21] The reluctance of the regime to implement measures unpopular with the middle and upper classes meant that the government, rather than enforcing the registration of women, settled on a policy of threat and encouragement through propaganda.[22] The Nazi leadership made this decision explicit in 1941 by launching a major propaganda campaign as an alternative to enacting a registration decree.[23]

The propaganda designed by the regime to persuade women to go to work made use of the Nazi image of the dedicated woman, willing to sacrifice her own interests for the good of the state. Propaganda made clear that work for women in wartime meant sacrifice, not benefits. Just as Nazi ideology before the war compared mothers to soldiers—both risking their lives to do their duty to the Fatherland—so propaganda during the war made mothers on the assembly line the analogue of men at the front. Sacrifice, which the Nazi leadership had been extolling long before the war, rather accurately described the situation of women at work. That is not to suggest that women took up employment in a spirit of sacrifice—the propaganda effort failed to persuade women to go to work in any case—but rather that the conditions of employment were grim enough that women avoided work if privileged enough to do so. Women received low wages and worked long hours under poor conditions, despite Nazi rhetoric on the "beauty of work." Women who could afford to do so—largely middle- and upper-class women—avoided employment whenever possible. Since the government ultimately pinned its hopes on the expectation that women would conform to the Nazi image of the dedicated woman, the failure of mobilization can be attributed to the lack of response from women to the demands made upon them by the regime.

Women's responses take on enormous significance in the history of the war, yet it is not a simple case of women opposing conscription and thus crippling the war effort. Middle- and upper-class women stayed out of employment and even evaded the registration decree, as the regime well knew. The nature of women's responses depended on class. As Timothy Mason points out in his most recent book on the working class under Nazism, classes did not cease to exist because the Nazis proclaimed that they had.[24] The Nazi leadership ruthlessly suppressed working-class opposition while proclaiming that the Third Reich had achieved the harmony of class collaboration. As we know, the Nazis failed entirely, despite brutal and vigorous measures, to stamp out working-class resistance. But it was not working-class opposition that kept the Nazis from conscripting women, althouth working-class dissatisfaction with the social injustice of Nazi mobilization policies played a significant role in the failure of mobilization. While middle- and upper-class women avoided employment, working-class women favored a general conscription measure, since women already employed or threatened with a limited conscription policy would only benefit from a law that would force nonemployed middle- and upper-class women to share the burden—the "sacrifice," in Nazi rhetoric—of the war effort. The extensive public opinion reports collected by the regime make clear that women already working under strict legal controls bitterly resented the lack of a general conscription measure. The regime's failure to mobilize women must be understood as a failure to mobilize women *not of the working class*. This revealed and deepened class conflict, making a mockery of the Nazi idea of *Volksgemeinschaft*, a classless people's com-munity. Women of all classes responded negatively, if differently, to Nazi mobilization policies, presenting a kind of challenge, if indirect and limited, to Nazi authoritarianism.

We know about women's responses to mobilization policies because the Nazi government stayed remarkably well-informed about public opinion. The Security Service (SD) of the SS, in particular, collected and compiled reports on the attitudes of the population, circulating these reports to government agencies every few days.[25] The information in the SD reports came from voluntary reporters as well as full-time paid informers and attempted to include material on all classes. The reliability of these reports is suggested by the picture they present, not one the government would have chosen had it dictated the results in advance. One historian who used these reports exten-sively in a book on public mood and attitude during the war indicates that a comparison of local reports and the final reports shows some moderation in the final products, so that the rather grim situation emerging from the reports may even be understated.[26] But, probably most telling of all, the truth ulti-mately seemed dangerous to the Nazis, so in 1944 Martin Bormann and Robert Ley forbade all functionaries of the party and the Labor Front to cooperate with the SD.[27] As a result, the last regular SD report appeared in July 1944. The SD, however, was not the only government agency interested in public opinion, and in conjunction with the scattered records of other branches of both party and state, the SD reports provide a clear picture of the responses of German women to labor mobilization policies.

The voluntary recruitment of German women was, as discussed above, a disastrous failure. As early as February 1940, the SD reported that it was no longer possible to recruit the women needed in agriculture, domestic service, and industry through voluntary means, and the failure of voluntary mobilization provided a constant theme in the population reports.[28] Nonemployed middle- and upper-class women ignored the appeals directed at them by Nazi propaganda and opposed the introduction of conscription, while women called up by the employment offices and women already working under strict legal controls, as well as nonemployed working-class women, expressed resentment of the social injustice of Nazi policies.

The Nazis aversion to Marxist terminology and inclination to euphemism led to the development of an odd vocabulary, one that obscures the real status of individuals described in the Nazi documents. The SD reports, for example, referred to the resentment of women of "the simple circles" toward the "so-called better circles" or the "socially better placed women." Because of this vocabulary, it is difficult to be sure whom the Nazis meant. Most often the reports talk about the "working population," which probably means the working class. Sometimes they use the terms "poorer circles" or "lower occupational levels," which almost certainly refer to workers. This terminology, added to the special relationship women have to the class structure—that is, identification with class through a husband's or father's relationship to production as well as through their own—creates a great deal of ambiguity. Occasionally the reports identify a section of the middle class as sharing the resentment of the working class toward wealthier women. It is clear that employed women resented nonemployed women of whatever class, and that nonemployed women of the working class and lower-middle class refused to go to work while upper-middle and upper-class women flaunted their wealth and leisure. It is unfortunately impossible to be precise about the status of the anonymous individuals quoted in the population reports; one would like to know more about their social background, and especially something about their political affiliation before 1933. Of course not all working-class women worked, nor were all employed women working class. But in general it seems clear that working-class women, whether employed or not, favored conscription as a measure of social justice, while middle-class and certainly upper-class women opposed conscription and often avoided employment. Keeping in mind the difficulties, what is clear beyond question is that the responses of women to mobilization policies depended on, and reveal to us, the existence of class conflict.

Why did nonemployed women fail to respond to the appeals for voluntary mobilization? A major reason that emerges from the sources is lack of financial incentive. Women complained about low wages from the first months of the war, and they complained, too, about receiving less than the men they replaced had earned.[29] The support of the Frauenschaft, the Nazi women's organization, for an equal pay policy meant little in a state that organized women but gave them no real power.[30] Despite the SD's insistence that women should receive equal pay, women continued to earn very little, sometimes a third of what men earned.[31] The regime established strict wage controls in an attempt to control inflation, and so refused to increase women's pay. To make matters worse, Nazi policy toward allowances for dependents of men in the armed forces created disincentives for employment during the first years of the war. Allowances were quite generous, inducing women actually to quit their jobs at the outbreak of war since they could live on their allotments without working.[32] Even worse, the government originally reduced the allowances of women who worked.[33] The SD repeatedly recommended that the government revise its policy toward dependents' allowances in order to avoid penalizing women who kept working or entered employment for the first time. In 1941 the government followed this advice, amending the legislation to end the practice of subtracting a portion of a woman's wages from her allowance; the new legislation even reduced a woman's allowance if she refused to work, an action that met with reports of mixed results.[34]

Lack of financial incentive and, in the case of women receiving dependents' allowances, actual disincentive kept women out of the labor force. So too did women's traditional "second shift" at home which the regime did little to alleviate when it failed to provide services for working women. Despite day nurseries and the provision of special services for large families, women complained that they could not work because they had no way to care for their children.[35] Women objected to the long hours of work, prompting the SD to recommend a shortening of the work day and the institution of part-time work to allow women to discharge their domestic duties.[36] Other complaints included long commutes to and from work as well as shopping difficulties.[37] The resentment of working women emerged in the complaints about nonemployed women, who had all day to shop, unnecessarily and unfairly crowding the stores during the only hours when working women could shop. The regime's concern for this problem, typically, resulted in propaganda urging nonemployed women to "be comrades" and shop early in the day.[38] The regime that prided itself in its propaganda on the introduction of social institutions to benefit workers did not succeed in easing the burden of women who worked.

Women who could afford to do so stayed out of the labor force because there was little financial incentive to take a job and their traditional double burden made employment difficult. In addition, some women who had never worked expressed fear of factory work—for middle-class women, a decidedly proletarian form of employment—and fear of the Labor Book system, which they suspected could keep them in the labor force even after the war emergency.[39]

As a result, nonemployed women avoided employment, using ingenuity to escape from the various measures designed to bring them into the labor force. Reports indicated that young women of "known" families evaded their Duty

Year obligation by arranging to "work" in the homes of acquaintances.[40] Gertrud Scholtz-Klink, the head of the Nazi women's organization, criticized mothers who tried to spare their daughters the rigors of the Duty Year (designed to help large families) by advertising for positions with conveniences and without children.[41] Most importantly, women continued to avoid employment even after the 1943 registration order. They sought medical excuses, took up "fake work" with friends or relatives, and even, reportedly, hurriedly conceived in order to avoid having to register.[42] One woman, the SD reported, wrote to her soldier husband to urge him to come home quickly on leave in order to conceive a child so that she could be exempt from registration.[43] The number of women leaving on trips with unknown destinations increased rapidly, according to the population reports.[44] If none of the evasion techniques worked, women demanded easy office jobs—anything to stay out of the factories. One individual wrote to the government complaining about women who entered the universities in order to avoid war work: "There are young girls who, in wartime, studied first art history, then law, and now psychology."[45] The SD reported that the registration decree caused great discontent in Vienna among "society women" who declared that they would not be forced to work and criticized the measure as "Bolshevist."[46]

Why nonemployed middle- and upper-class women would oppose conscription, then, is not difficult to understand. (Such indifference to Nazi propaganda is certainly significant, however, and worth noting.) When we turn to working-class women, we find a different but also easily understandable situation. From the early months of the war, the SD reported complaints from women of the "poorer circles" that they were forced to carry the entire burden of the war effort.[47] The SD, in fact, explicitly attributed the failure of voluntary mobilization to the resentment of women of the working population, citing complaints from such women that the women of the "so-called better circles" still had servants, frequented cafes, visited the beaches, played tennis, and lounged in their gardens.[48] Disapproving citizens called the attention of the employment offices to classified newspaper advertisements placed by women looking for companions with free time.[49] The SD even reported criticism of the Duty Year on the grounds that it only applied to young women who planned to enter employment, not to all women.[50] Nonemployed wives of artisans and middle-level officials with no children reported promised to take jobs only if the wives of prominent men in similar situations did.[51] The 1941 decree designed to bring back into the labor force women who had quit work since the beginning of the war provoked an angry outburst in Dortmund: "We agree that it is necessary for us to return to work. It will mean a great deal of inconvenience for us, but it is wartime and so we want to help. But why is Frau Direktor S. with her servants not called up? She could certainly put her four-year-old son in the NSV [National Socialist Welfare Organization] kindergarten for the day just as we do. . . . What has happened to the equal treatment of all folk comrades?"[52] The lifestyles of wealthy families irritated employed women; the SD reported, for example, that suntanned young women in winter resort areas angered the working population.[53]

Voluntary mobilization, and especially talk of the desirability of avoiding compulsory labor, seemed hypocritical to women working under strict legal controls. Women already at work could be punished—even imprisoned—for minor infractions of work discipline. The SD reported popular criticism of cases in which women went to prison for missing work due to illness or domestic difficulties. For example, the courts sent a Wuppertal woman to prison for three months in 1941 for leaving her job for a week for domestic reasons, a sentence the population considered unnecessarily harsh.[54] Employers sometimes threatened employed women with the Gestapo.[55] Despite popular disapproval of such tactics, ignoring women who broke their contracts could be just as bad from the government's point of view, since it might encourage other women to follow suit.

Men as well as women responded bitterly to what they perceived as social injustice. The SD reported that front soldiers in particular objected to the calling up of their wives while other women remained idle, warning that dissatisfaction on the front could be extremely dangerous for the regime.[56] Soldiers on leave angrily criticized women crowding the trains on vacation and flaunting their idleness in cafes and in shopping districts.[57] One soldier summed up what the reports indicated many felt: "I have forbidden [my wife] to work as long as the rich women and girls are not called up to work as well. I am fighting abroad not only for my family, but for them as well. . . . The wife of a worker is just as valuable to the state as the wife of a manufacturer."[58] Some soldiers even wrote hostile and bitter letters directly to the employment offices that tried to call up their wives.[59] One, for example, wrote forbidding his wife to work and asking the head of the employment office if his own wife was working, adding: "I bet she isn't, because then you would not have an orderly house in which to recuperate from your *hard* work. . . . Certainly there are men in your office whose wives have no children and who don't go to work. If I were in your place I would be ashamed to summon to work a soldier's wife who has a six-month-old child. But there is no point in writing you in this way, because you sit there always warm and dry. . . . You are only a bureaucrat, not a human being."[60] Hostility toward the men safe at home in their office jobs, as well as the conviction that men at the front were more than adequately fulfilling the family's duty to the state, were common themes in the complaints from soldiers. Another letter made explicit the class hostility only implied in the slurs on bureaucratic selfishness: "There are probably enough women in Niesky who have not known for a long time what they should do, but who must still keep a servant so that they won't lose any of their acquired beauty and congenital laziness. . . . As long as there is not a fairly implemented obligation requiring every woman without regard to status to satisfy her national obligation for six or eight weeks in the sense of a people's community, it is out of the question for my wife."[61] Complaints from men were not limited to soldiers and workers; the SD reported that men of the "upper circles" contacted the employment offices to object to the idea of their wives working.[62]

There is, of course, more involved in these complaints from men than class resentment. Dörte Winkler, in her recent book on women in the labor force in the Third Reich, makes a distinction between petit bourgeois resentment and proletarian consciousness expressed in the letters of soldiers, but I am not convinced that such a distinction is meaningful.[63] All of the men, whether expressing hostility toward wealthy women or toward bureaucrats, shared a recognition of unjust treatment, but also a patriarchal assumption of their right to dictate what their wives should or should not do. Gertrud Scholtz-Klink noted that men opposed the idea of their wives working not only because it was a mark of status to have a nonemployed wife, but also because employed women could not devote themselves as fully to providing domestic comfort for their men. In words that conjure up the bureaucrat in his orderly house, Scholtz-Klink told men that they could wait a moment for their meals or warm up the food themselves while their wives went out to work.[64]

The bitterness at obvious injustice continued as the war dragged on. What legislation did exist seemed to working women to put the entire responsibility for the war effort on their shoulders. As early as 1940, while the top party leaders debated the desirability of a general service obligation, the SD reported that the population knew and approved of the expected order.[65] When it did not appear, party leaders and propagandists, forced to justify patently unjust policies, grew increasingly nervous. Angry audiences demanded explanations from Labor Front leaders; even the best speakers lost the trust of their listeners by either remaining silent on the question of conscription or giving conflicting answers, creating doubt about the certainty of the leadership.[66] As a result, work morale sank and the population increasingly lost respect for the authorities, according to the SD. Propaganda continued to call for sacrifice for the good of the state, but from 1940 on the SD noted the hypocrisy and resulting ineffectiveness of such appeals.[67]

It was in this atmosphere that the January 1943 registration decree appeared. The SD reported great popular interest tempered by skepticism. Party officials in Vienna warned that if the measure were not fairly implemented, sharp criticism and passive resistance could be expected.[68] In small cities especially, the SD found, people closely observed the wives of prominent men, suspicious that they would not actually go to work.[69] Hitler issued a statement in 1943 expressing his expectation that the wives and offspring of prominent party leaders would take up employment; such prompting suggests a basis for the population's suspicions.[70] Nonemployed working-class and lower-middle-class women explained that they would act when the "fine ladies," often mentioned by name, went to work in the factories.[71] All reports agreed that the success of the registration measure would depend on the fairness of its implementation.[72]

The worst fears of working women were confirmed by the reports of widespread evasion of the registration decree by the "better circles."[73] Given the reluctance of women to register and the apparent ease of landing in an exempted category, only strict enforcement measures could have made this a successful mobilization measure. Despite provisions in the 1943 law for fines and, as a last resort, legal proceedings against women who did not report to the employment offices, the authorities were unwilling to take strong measures.[74] Even before the 1943 decree, a woman who suggested that the army take control of mobilization noted: "There is at present hardly an official prepared to take measures against women unwilling to work or engaged in passive resistance at work."[75] Party records generally admitted the failure of the registration decree, and the statistics make clear that even the successful registration of 2.5 million women by the end of March 1943 had negligible results in terms of actual additions to the labor force.[76]

The introduction of the registration decree did not stem the tide of popular criticism of the social injustice of the regime's mobilization policies. Working women waited for the wives of factory managers, officers in the armed forces, and party leaders to take up factory work and criticized the regime for failing to enforce the registration law.

The complaints reported by the SD and other party and state agencies make clear that it was not opposition to conscription from the working class that caused the party to hesitate on the question of mobilizing women. Nonemployed middle- and upper-class women opposed conscription, as is evident from the reports of widespread evasion. But the working class, or the "working population" of Nazi jargon, favored equitably enforced conscription of women as a measure that would distribute the burden of the war effort more fairly. The complaints about social injustice suggest that perhaps some people took seriously the Nazi promises of *Volksgemeinschaft*. From Breslau, for example, came a report of an individual who insisted: "The word *Volksgemeinschaft* is very nice; for that very reason it seems suitable that the authorities extend this concept as it applies to employment to all circles."[77] In response to the registration decree, the SD reported that "the population— and above all the working circles—expects with the implementation of this order *exceptional justice*."[78] This is just what the regime promised after all: the official party newspaper, for example, carried an article about the registration law entitled "Labor Mobilization According to the Principle of Socialist Justice."[79] The SD quoted a woman worker in a munitions factory who summed up the unfairness of labor mobilization in this way: "I don't call that *Volksgemeinschaft*."[80] It is of course possible that these comments represent cynical manipulation of Nazi ideology by the population. Dörte Winkler adopts this view, arguing that the more people saw through the ideology, the more they used it to advance their own interests.[81] One may argue that it is impossible to know whether the individuals quoted in the SD reports were using the concept of *Volksgemeinschaft* as a weapon against its inventors, but at least a part of the working class, despite its skepticism toward mobilization policies, may have taken the Nazi rhetoric of social justice seriously enough to complain when it was utterly disregarded in practice.

The popular response to the mobilization of women provides a clear indication of class conflict and hostility in the Third Reich. Even Nazi officials broke down in the face of it and occasionally used the word "class" and even "class conflict," which had, according to Nazi ideology and propaganda, been eliminated in the Third Reich. An SD report in 1943 warned that unjust implementation of the registration decree aroused "instincts of class conflict."[82] Internal criticism of Goebbels' famous "total war" speech of February 1943 argued that Goebbels' public condemnation of the attitude of the German population would excite class conflict and mistrust.[83] Sauckel released a manifesto on Hitler's birthday in 1943 that called, among other things, for the elimination of the "last tendencies of class conflict" from the offices concerned with labor mobilization.[84] A regional report also noted "tendencies of class conflict," adding that the "lower occupational levels" took malicious pleasure in the idea of the dependents of higher-status men employed in the munitions industry, especially performing manual labor.[85] And, probably most frightening of all to the Nazi leadership, the SD reported in 1943 that the workers were beginning once again to think in terms of classes and to speak of those who were exploiting them.[86]

Mobilization measures throughout the rest of the war brought no satisfaction to disgruntled working women. And, because the regime ultimately depended on the cooperation of women, the failure of nonemployed women to meet the government's expectations was crucial. The responses of women to Nazi mobilization policies reveal that the theoretically totalitarian regime was unable or unwilling to enforce the conscription of women, despite desperate labor shortages. We are left with a somewhat paradoxical view of the regime: totalitarian enough to collect detailed information about public opinion, but not totalitarian enough to suppress popular discontent or not secure enough to enforce conscription against the wishes of the middle and upper classes, the mainstay of the regime. Working-class discontent with the injustice of mobilization was vocal enough to worry Nazi officials, but the regime was sure enough of its monopoly of force not to fear an organized uprising; the measures taken in the first months of the Third Reich against the Communists, Social Democrats, and trade unions had seen to that.

In order to enforce the registration order, the regime would have had to be willing to imprison women who evaded registration. Although the government risked the population's outrage and punished some working women for absenteeism even before 1943, the population reports make no mention of punishment for women who did not register. The class nature of the Third Reich is here laid bare, as it is in the statements of Hitler and others that women should be spared the rigors of employment, statements made in complete disregard of the millions of women already working. It is important to understand that, in the face of middle- and upper-class women's reluctance to go to work in the factories, only decisive mass action could have succeeded in mobilizing them. This suggests a kind of limit to the power of the authoritarian regime, a limit imposed by the extent of passive resistance to governmental policies.

Looked at from the perspective of the women themselves, the failure of mobilization suggests that women exercised real, if indirect and ultimately limited, power over the fascist regime. It would, however, be a mistake to idealize the passive resistance of middle- and upper-class women, or the resentment of working-class women, as conscious political resistance to Nazism. Women forced by economic need to work for low wages and women subject to unfairly enforced legislation resented the ostentatious leisure of middle- and upper-class women and refused to take seriously talk of sacrifice and *Volksgemeinschaft* unless labor mobilization were justly enforced. This was class resentment, certainly, but not necessarily ideological hostility to fascism. In the same way, the resistance of middle- and upper-class women to the registration decree was not grounded in opposition to Nazism, but represented a response to an unfavorable employment situation. Of course, the responses of women of all classes *do* represent an implicit rejection of Nazism's view of women: simply by refusing to act the dedicated Nazi fanatic, German women expressed their indifference, consciously or not, to at least a part of Nazi ideology and propaganda. Women realized that participation in the war effort was a question of economics and politics: how much they could earn and how they could minimize government control in an authoritarian system with potential totalitarian powers. What the government expected of women depended, before the war and during the war, on the needs of the state. How German women responded to the demands of the regime depended on their perceptions of individual and class interests. Women's responses to mobilization, differentiated according to class, are central to an understanding of the failure of mobilization, and lay bare the Nazi pretense of class consensus in the Third Reich.

That German women did not eagerly seize the wartime "opportunity" to move into areas of employment previously reserved to men suggests that the traditional concept of war's beneficial consequences for women is too simplistic. Entry into the labor force has never been a sufficient condition for the liberation of women, even in situations far more favorable than that of the Third Reich. For women in Nazi Germany, war brought hardship and social injustice but little in the way of benefits.

Notes

1. See Dörte Winkler, *Frauenarbeit im "Dritten Reich,"* Historische Perspektiven 9 (Hamburg: Hoffmann und Campe Verlag, 1977); and Leila J. Rupp, *Mobilizing Women for War: German and American Propaganda, 1939–1945* (Princeton: Princeton University Press, 1978).

2. Calculated from statistics in Statistisches Reichsamt, *Statistisches Jahrbuch für das deutsche Reich,* 1941–1942 (Berlin: Verlag der Reimar Hobbing, 1942), p. 33; U.S. Strategic Bombing Survey (USSBS), *The Effects of Strategic Bombing on the German War Economy,* Overall Economic Effects Division, October 31, 1945, pp. 202–207.

3. Ludwig Hamburger, *How Nazi Germany Has Mobilized and Controlled Labor* (Washington: The Brookings Institution, 1940), pp. 57–58. See also "The Employment of Women in Germany under the National Socialist Regime," *International Labour Review,* 44 (Dec. 1941), 617–659; and Judith Grünfeld, "Mobilization of Women in Germany," *Social Research* (Nov. 1942), 476–494.

4. *Reichsgesetzblatt (RGB),* 1935, I, p. 311; *RGB,* 1939, I, p. 602. A law of 1939 extended the coverage of the Labor Book; see *RGB,* 1939, I, p. 824.

5. *RGB,* 1935, I, p. 769; *RGB,* I, p. 1693. See Frieda Wunderlich, *Farm Labor in Germany 1810–1945* (Princeton: Princeton University Press, 1961) p. 322.

6. *Reichsarbeitsblatt (RAB),* 1938, I, p. 46; *RAB,* 1938, I, p. 48.

7. *RGB,* 1935, I, p. 609; *RGB,* 1938, I, p. 652; *RGB,* 1939, I, p. 206.

8. *RGB,* 1939, I, p. 206; *RGB,* 1939, I, p. 403; *RGB,* 1939, I, p. 444.

9. Bundesarchiv Koblenz (BA), R 41/159.

10. Winkler, *Frauenarbeit,* p. 89; Winkler cites *Deutsche Volkswirtschaft,* 8 (1940), 731, as the source of this information.

11. BA, R 43 II/652.

12. Meldungen aus dem Reich (MadR), No. 210, Aug. 11, 1941, BA, R 58/163; Arbeitseinsatz familienunterhaltsberechtigter Frauen, June 30, 1941, BA, R 43 II/652.

13. *RGB,* 1943, I, p. 67. A second decree appeared in 1944: *RGB,* 1944, I, p. 133.

14. Interrogation of Sauckel, International Military Tribunal, *Trial of the Major War Criminals Before the International Military Tribunal,* (Nuremburg: International Military Tribunal, 1947–49), vol. 14, pp. 621–622; U.S. Chief of Counsel for the Prosecution of Axis Criminality, *Nazi Conspiracy and Aggression* (Washington: U.S. Government Printing Office, 1946–68), vol. 3, p. 53.

15. *Trial of the Major War Criminals* vol. 41, pp. 460, 468, 486, 487, 488. See Albert Speer, *Inside the Third Reich,* trans. Richard and Clara Winston (N.Y.: Avon, 1970), pp. 294–295. On the conflict between Sauckel and Speer, see also Edward L. Homze, *Foreign Labor in Nazi Germany* (Princeton: Princeton University Press, 1957), pp. 204–229.

16. SD-Berichte zu Inlandsfragen (SD-BzI), April 20, 1944, BA, R 58/193.

17. *RGB,* 1944, I, p. 168; Bormann to Lammers, July 29, 1944, BA, R 43 II/654.

18. USSBS, *Effects,* pp. 38–39. See Winkler, *Frauenarbeit,* pp. 142–153.

19. See Rupp, *Mobilizing Women,* chap. 2, for an analysis of Nazi attitudes toward women.

20. Sept. 23, 1941, BA, R 43 II/652. Bormann to Lammers, Sept. 25, 1941, BA, R 43 II/652. On Hitler's belief that total mobilization was unnecessary, see Burton H. Klein, *Germany's Economic Preparations for War* (Cambridge: Harvard University Press, 1959); Clarence D. Long, *Labor Force in War and Transition: Four Countries,* Occasional Paper no.

36 (N.Y.: National Bureau of Economic Research, 1952); Alan S. Milward, *The German Economy at War* (London: Athlone Press, 1965); USSBS, *Effects.*

21. *Trial of the Major War Criminals,* vol. 41, pp. 486, 488–489; Sauckel to Gauarbeitsämter, Nov. 3, 1943, BA, R 43 II/654; Präsident des Landesarbeitsamtes Südwestdeutschland to Reichsarbeitsminister, Aug. 2, 1940, BA, R 41/150.

22. See Rupp, *Mobilizing Women.*

23. *Reichsverfügungsblatt,* March 17, 1941, Ausgabe B, BA R 43 II/652.

24. Timothy W. Mason, *Arbeiterklasse und Volksgemeinschaft* (Opladen: Westdeutscher Verlag, 1975). Mason published a revised version of the introductory essay as *Sozialpolitik im Dritten Reich: Arbeiterklasse und Volksgemeinschaft* (Opladen: Westdeutscher Verlag, 1977). See Molly Nolan's review essay, "Class Struggles in the Third Reich," *Radical History Review,* 4 (Summer-Summer 1977), 138–159; and a comment by David Abraham, "Nazism and the Working Class," *Radical History Review,* 18 (Fall 1978), 161–165.

25.   These reports, called Meldungen aus dem Reich (MadR), are located in the Bundesarchiv Koblenz (BA), R 58/144–194; they are also available on microfilm in the Records of the Reich Leader of the SS of the German Police (T-175), Rolls 258–266, National Archives Microcopy. See Heinz Boberach, *Meldungen aus dem Reich: Auswahl aus den geheimen Lageberichten des Sicherheitsdienstes der SS 1939–1944* (Neuwied und Berlin: Hermann Luchterhand Verlag, 1965); and Ursula von Gersdorff, *Frauen im Kriegsdienst 1914–1945* (Stuttgart: Deutsche Verlags-Anstalt, 1969).

26.   Marlis G. Steinert, *Hitler's War and the Germans: Public Mood and Attitude During the Second World War,* ed. and trans. Thomas E. J. de Witt (Athens, Ohio: Ohio University Press, 1977), pp. 14–18.

27.   Boberach, *Meldungen,* p. xxvii–xxviii.

28.   MadR, No. 55, Feb. 19, 1940, BA, R 58/148.

29.   MadR, No. 27, Dec. 11, 1939, BA, R 58/146; MadR, No. 55, Feb. 19, 1940, BA, R 58/148; MadR, No. 107, July 22, 1940, BA, R 58/152; MadR, No. 162, Feb. 13, 1941, BA, R 58/157; MadR, No. 263, Feb. 26, 1942, BA, R 58/169; MadR, No. 338, Nov. 26, 1942, BA, R 58/177; MadR, No. 373, April 5, 1943, BA, R 58/182; Kreisfrauenschaftsleitung to Kreisleiter, April 7, 1943, Records of the NSDAP (T-81), Roll 75, Frame 86374-86375, National Archives Microcopy.

30.   On the Frauenschaft's support of equal pay for equal work, see *Deutsches Frauenschaffen: Jahrbuch der Reichsfrauenführung,* 1937, p. 50.

31.   See Gerhard Bry, *Wages in Germany, 1871–1945* (Princeton: Princeton University Press, 1960).

32.   MadR, No. 55, Feb. 19, 1940, BA, R 58/148; MadR, No. 107, July 22, 1940, BA, R 58/152; MadR, No. 162, Feb. 13, 1941, BA, R 58/157; MadR, No. 181, Apr. 25, 1941, BA, R 58/159; MadR, No. 189, May 26, 1941, BA, R 58/160; MadR, No. 194, June 16, 1941, BA, R 58/161; MadR, 224, Sept. 29, 1941, BA, R 58/164; MadR, No. 263, Feb. 26, 1942, BA, R 58/169; Letter from Generalbevollmächtigte für die Reichsverwaltung, May 9, 1940, BA, R 43 II/652; Letter from Reichsverteidigungskommissar für den Wehrkreis IV, May 27, 1940, BA, R 43 II/652; Letter from Präsident des Arbeitsamtes Berlin, July 2, 1941, BA, R 41/162; Chef des OKW to Beauftragte für das Vierjahresplan, Feb. 9, 1942, BA R 41/162. See Long, *Labor Force,* pp. 41–43.

33.   Verordnung über Kriegsfamilienunterhalt, Sept. 1938, BA, R 41/160; Kritische Bemerkungen zur Verordnung, May 16, 1939, BA, R 41/161.

34.   MadR, No. 224, Sept. 29, 1941, BA, R 58/164; MadR, No. 253, Feb. 26, 1942, BA, R 58/169; Letter from Reichsminister des Inneren, June 30, 1941, BA, R 43 II/652; Ley to Göring, Sept. 10, 1941, BA, R 43 II/652; Dr. Suren to Göring, Oct. 2, 1941, BA, R 43 II/652; Letter from Reichsminister fü Bewaffnung und Munition, Aug. 21, 1941, BA, R 41/162; Bekämpfung der Arbeitsvertragsbrüche der Frauen, Aug. 27, 1941, BA, R 41/162.

35. MadR, No. 30, Dec. 18, 1939, BA R 58/146; MadR, No. 91, May 27, 1940, BA, R 58/151; MadR, No. 107, July 22, 1940, BA, R 58/152; MadR, No. 162, Feb. 13, 1941, BA, R 58/157; MadR, No. 263, Feb. 26, 1942, BA, R 58/169; MadR, No. 373, Apr. 5, 1943, BA, R 58/182.

36. MadR, No. 30, Dec. 18, 1939, BA, R 58/146; MadR, No. 55, Feb. 19, 1940, BA, R 58/148; MadR, No. 100, June 27, 1940, BA, R 58/151; MadR, No. 107, July 22, 1940, BA, R 58/152; MadR, No. 162, Feb. 13, 1941, BA, R 58/157; MadR, No. 189, May 26, 1941, BA, R 58/160; MadR, No. 263, Feb. 26, 1942, BA, R 58/169; Präsident des Arbeitsamtes Niedersachsen to Arbeitsminister, Nov. 24, 1939, BA, R 41/158.

37. MadR, No. 263, Feb. 26, 1942, BA, R 58/169.

38. Poster in Bundesarchiv collection.

39. Reichsverteidigungskommissar für den Wehrkreis XII to Göring, Feb. 10, 1941, BA, R 41/162. In response to fear of the Labor Book, the Labor Ministry issued an order on June 16, 1941 giving women voluntarily taking up employment during the war an "Ersatzkarte" instead of a Labor Book; BA, R 41/162. Fear of factory work was much commented upon in the SD reports and in the Nazi press; see Rupp, *Mobilizing Women*, p. 111.

40. MadR, No. 120, Sept. 2, 1940, BA, R 58/154.

41. Gertrud Scholtz-Klink, *Tradition Is Not Stagnation But Involves a Moral Obligation: Women's Conference at the National Congress of Greater Germany* (Nuremburg: Deutsches Frauenwerk, 1938), p. 9. See Rupp, *Mobilizing Women*, p. 110.

42. MadR, No. 356, Feb. 4, 1943, BA, R 58/180; MadR, No. 366, Mar. 11, 1943, BA, R 58/181; MadR, No. 373, Apr. 5, 1943, BA, R 58/182; *Reichsverfügungsblatt*, Feb. 17, 1943, Ausgabe B, BA R 43 II/654; "Schluss mit den Scheinarbeitsverhältnissen!" *Deutsches Nachrichtenbüro*, July 28, 1944, pp. 35–36, BA, R 43 II/665; MadReichsgau Oberdonau, Feb. 8, 1943, BA, NS 6/408; Auszüge aus Berichten der Gauleitungen u.s. Dienststellen, Feb. 12, 1943, BA, NS 6/414; Stimmen zu dem Aufruf des GBA . . . March 7, 1944, BA, NS 6/407.

43. MadR, No. 358, Feb. 11, 1943, BA, R 58/180. See also Einfluss der Versorgung mit dem Bedarf zur Kinderpflege auf die bevölkerungspolitische Lage, May 2, 1944, BA, NS 6/244.

44. MadR, No. 366, Mar. 11, 1943, BA, R 58/181.

45. BA, R 43 II/665.

46. MadR, No. 358, Feb. 11, 1943, BA, R 58/180.

47. MadR, No. 55, Feb. 19, 1940, BA, R 58/148. Also MadR, No. 100, June 27, 1940, BA, R 58/151; MadR, No. 189, May 26, 1941, BA, R 58/160; MadR, No. 197, June 26, 1941, BA, R 58/161; MadR, No. 224, Sept. 29, 1941, BA, R 58/164; MadR, No. 263, Feb. 26, 1942, BA, R 58/169; Dr. Naumann to Lammers, Jan. 2, 1943, BA, R 43 II/655; Gauleiter Ost-Hannover to Präsident des Arbeitsamtes Niedersachsen, Apr. 1, 1940, BA, R 41/158.

48. MadR, No. 107, July 22, 1940, BA, R 58/152.

49. BA, R 41/158.

50. MadR, No. 306, Aug. 6, 1942, BA, R 58/174; Kritische Stimmen zur Ableistung des Pflichtjahrs, Nov. 12, 1942, BA, NS 6/243.

51. MadR, No. 146, Dec. 2, 1940, BA, R 58/156. Also MadR, No. 210, Aug. 11, 1941, BA, R 58/163.

52. MadR, No. 210, Aug. 11, 1941, BA, R 58/163.

53. MadR, No. 267, Mar. 12, 1942, BA, R 58/170.

54. MadR, No. 197, June 26, 1941, BA, R 58/161; Also MadR, No. 263, Feb. 26, 1942, BA, R 58/169; MadR, No. 320, Sept. 25, 1942, BA, R 58/175; Schwierigkeiten beim Fraueneinsatz, Nov. 13, 1940, BA, R 41/159; Bekämpfung der Arbeitsvertragsbrüche der Frauen, Aug. 27, 1941, BA, R 41/162; Bekämpfung der Arbeitsvertragsbrüche, Dec. 11, 1942, BA, R 41/237a.

55. MadR, No. 263, Feb. 26, 1942, BA, R 58/169.

56. MadR, No. 162, Feb. 13, 1941, BA, R 58/157; MadR, No. 224, Sept. 29, 1941, BA, R 58/164; MadR, No. 263, Feb. 26, 1942, BA, R 58/169.

57. MadR, No. 263, Feb. 26, 1942, BA, R 58/169.

58. MadR, No. 263, Feb. 26, 1942, BA, R 58/169.

59. Verstärkung des Fraueneinsatzes, BA, R 41/162.

60. Transcript of letter to Arbeitsamt Görlitz, July 27, 1941, BA, R 41/162.

61. Transcript of letter to Arbeitsamt Niesky, Aug. 6, 1941, BA, R 41/162.

62. MadR, No. No. 146, Dec. 2, 1940, BA, R 58/156.

63. Winkler, *Frauenarbeit*, p. 111.

64. "Rede der Reichsfrauenführerin Frau Gertrud Scholtz-Klink im Sportspalast in Berlin am 13. Juni 1940," *N.S. Frauen-Warte*, 9 (July 1940), 24–25. See Rupp, *Mobilizing Women*, p. 107.

65. MadR, No. 107, July 22, 1940, BA, R 58/152.

66. MadR, No. 263, Feb. 26, 1942, BA, R 58/169; MadR, No. 309, Aug. 17, 1942, BA, R 58/174.

67. MadR, No. 107, July 22, 1940, BA, R 58/152; MadR, No. 162, Feb. 13, 1941, BA, R 58/157; MadR, No. 263, Feb. 26, 1942, BA, R 58/169; MadR, No. 309, Aug. 17, 1942, BA, R 58/174; Dr. Naumann to Lammers, Jan. 2, 1943, BA, R 43 II/655; Regierungspräsident Magdeburg to Landrat des Kreises Jerichow II, Dec. 7, 1939, BA, R 41/158.

68. Auszüge aus Berichten der Gauleitungen u.s. Dienststellen, Feb. 12, 1943, BA, NS 6/414.

69. MadR, No. 356, Feb. 4, 1943, BA, R 58/180.

70. Anordnung des Führers über die vorbildliche Haltung der Angehörigen an hervorragender Stelle stehender Persönlichkeiten bei dem umfassenden Kriegseinsatz, May 16, 1943, BA, R 43 II/655a. Also SD-BzI, Dec. 13, 1943, BA, NS 6/244.

71. MadR, No. 362, Feb. 25, 1943, BA, R 58/180.

72. MadR, No. 358, Feb. 11, 1943, BA, R 58/180; MadReichsgau Oberdonau, Feb. 2, 1943, BA, NS 6/408; MadReichsgau Oberdonau, Feb. 8, 1943, BA, NS 6/414; Auszüge aus Berichten der Gauleitungen u.a. Dienststellen, May 1, 1943, BA, NS 6/415.

73. MadR, No. 356, Feb. 4, 1943, BA, R 58/180; MadR, No. 357, Feb. 8, 1943, BA, R 58/180; MadR, No. 358, Feb. 11, 1943, BA, R 58/180; MadR, No. 373, Apr. 5, 1943, BA, R 58/182; *Reichverfügungsblatt*, Feb. 17, 1943, Ausgabe B, BA, R 43 II/654; Sauckel to Gauarbeitsämter, Nov. 3, 1943, BA, R 43 II/654; *Deutsches Nachrichtenbüro*, No. 210, July 28, 1944, BA, R 43 II/665; Verordnung über die Meldungen von Arbeitskräften in Scheinarbeitsverhältnissen, *RGB*, I, 1944, p. 167; MadREichsgau Oberdonau, Feb. 2, 1943, BA, NS 6/408; MadReichsgau Oberdonau, Feb. 8, 1943, BA, NS 6/408; Zum Bericht des SD-Abschnittes Schwerin, Mar. 7, 1944, BA, NS 6/407; Zum Bericht des SD-Abschnittes Schwerin, Mar. 14, 1944, BA, NS 6/244; Zum, Bericht des SD-Abschnittes Schwerin, May 2, 1944, BA, NS 6/244.

74. BA, R 43 II/654. See Verordung über die Meldung von Arbeitskräften in Scheinarbeitsverhältnissen, *RGB*, I, 1944, p. 167; Goebbels' press release, Aug. 25, 1944, BA, R 43 II/666b.

75. Irmgard Schäfer to General v. Bünau, Jan. 26, 1942, BA, R 41/162. See Winkler, *Frauenarbeit*, pp. 96–101, on the punishment of women unwilling to work before the 1943 order. In general, as is clear from the failure of mobilization, women went unpunished and took advantage of that fact.

76. MadR, No. 373, Apr. 5, 1943, BA, R 58/182; Sauckel to Gauarbeitsämter, Nov. 3, 1943, BA, R 43 II/654; Grundfragen der Stimmung und Haltung des deutschen Volkes, Nov. 29, 1943, BA, NS 6/244; SD-BzI, Dec. 13, 1943, BA, NS 6/244.

77. MadR, No. 210, Aug. 11, 1941, BA, R 58/163.

78. MadR, No. 356, Feb. 4, 1943, BA, R 58/180.

79. "Arbeitseinsatz nach dem Prinzip der sozialistischen Gerechtigkeit," *Völkischer Beobachter*, Feb. 5, 1943, BA, R 43 II/654.

80. Zum Bericht des SD-Abschnittes Schwerin, Mar. 14, 1944, BA, NS 6/244.

81. Winkler, *Frauenarbeit*, p. 114.

82. MadR, No. 366, Mar. 11, 1943, BA, R 58/181.

83. Dr. Fritz Michael to Lammers, Feb. 21, 1943, BA, R 43 II/639a.

84. Manifest des GBA an alle Dienstellen des Arbeitseinsatzes und der Reichstreuhander-verwaltung, Apr. 20, 1943, R 43 II/652a.

85. MadReichsgau Oberdonau, Feb. 8, 1943, BA, NS 6/408.

86. Grundfragen der Stimmung und Haltung des deutschen Volkes, Nov. 29, 1943, BA, NS 6/244.

Suggestions for Further Reading

Recently a number of books and articles on women in Nazi Germany have appeared, although few of these cover the war years. The classic work, written before the war, is Clifford Kirkpatrick, *Nazi Germany: Its Women and Family Life* (N.Y.: Bobbs-Merrill, 1938). David Schoenbaum broke new ground with his chapter on women in *Hitler's Social Revolution: Class and Status in Nazi Germany 1933–1939* (Garden City, N.Y.: Doubleday, 1966). Jill Stephenson's *Women in Nazi Society* (N.Y.: Barnes and Noble, 1975), which covers the years 1930 to 1940, is the first book-length study of Nazi policy toward women, and the only one currently available in English. Claudia Koonz's article "Mothers in the Fatherland: Women in Nazi Germany," in *Becoming Visible: Women in European History,* ed. Renate Bridenthal and Claudia Koonz (Boston: Houghton Mifflin, 1977), pp. 445–473, provides a brief overview of the major themes of women's history in the Nazi period. See also Koonz's "Nazi Women Before 1933: Rebels Against Emancipation," *Social Science Quarterly* 56 (March 1976): 553–563. Also important is Timothy Mason's two-part article, "Women in Germany, 1925–1940: Family, Welfare and Work," *History Workshop: Journal of Socialist Historians* 1 (Spring 1976): 74–113; 2 (Autumn 1976): 5–32.

The only book in English that covers the entire war period is my own, *Mobilizing Women for War: German and American Propaganda, 1939–1945* (Princeton: Princeton University Press, 1978). Ursula von Gersdorff edited a collection of documents on German women in war service that includes a lengthy introduction: *Frauen im Kriegsdienst 1914–1945* (Stuttgart: Deutsche Verlags-Anstalt, 1969). More recent, and most relevant, is Dörte Winkler's study of the employment of women in Nazi Germany, *Frauenarbeit im "Dritten Reich,"* Historische Perspektiven 9 (Hamburg: Hoffman und Campe Verlag, 1977).

3/The Job He Left Behind: American Women in the Shipyards During World War II

Karen Beck Skold

During World War II, Portland, Oregon, was one of the major centers of the American shipbuilding industry. Hundreds of Liberty ships, tankers, aircraft carriers, and other vessels were built between 1941 and 1945 by a labor force numbering 125,000 at its peak. What was remarkable about this army of workers was that one-fourth of them were women. They were welders, burners, electricians, and shipfitters, working in jobs once the exclusive domain of men. Climbing scaffolding on the hulls or descending into the ships' holds, they earned the same wages as the men, wages that were the highest of any industry at the time. The importance of women's labor was recognized in the media campaigns recruiting more women, and by the creation of child-care centers at the workplace.

The boom in shipbuilding was short-lived. Yet women gained access during the war years to skilled trades and high wages from which they had traditionally been excluded. What was the meaning of this experience? Was a model of equality between women and men in the labor force briefly created? How much change really occurred in the definition of "women's work" and "men's work" under the pressure of the war emergency?

This essay shows, first of all, how and why women entered the ship-yards, and what the process meant in terms of increased opportunities. Second, it compares the actual work done by women and men. And, finally, it examines women's postwar plans and what happened to them when the shipyards closed.

Women Enter the Shipyards

The sudden, rapid growth of the shipbuilding industry changed Portland from a quiet, provincial city into a wartime boom town. Three huge shipyards built and operated by the Kaiser Corporation dominated the industrial life of the area. Here ships for the U.S. Maritime Commission were built at record-breaking speed. In addition, several local companies built small craft for the Navy. The first of the Kaiser yards, the Oregon Shipbuilding Corporation, was built in 1941, and it absorbed most of the area's supply of unemployed men. Shortly after Pearl Harbor, Kaiser was granted a contract to build a second yard across the Columbia River from Portland in the small town of Vancouver, Washington. Then, in March 1942, a third Kaiser yard began at Portland's Swan Island.[1] The demand for labor thus increased sharply at the same time that the supply of healthy young men was being decreased by the draft.

Beginning in the summer of 1942, Kaiser recruiters sought unemployed men in such cities as Minneapolis and New York, promising to pay their transportation costs as an advance on wages. Before long a housing crisis developed in Portland, as migrants arrived faster than the war housing projects were built. The bottleneck in housing was broken with the construction of Vanport, the "world's largest housing project," built in 110 days by Kaiser and other construction firms on swampland midway between the three Kaiser yards. A year after ground was broken, Vanport was the second largest "city" in Oregon, with 40,000 residents. Between 1940 and 1944, nearly a quarter of a million migrants came into the Portland-Vancouver area.[2] The consequent strain on schools, housing, transportation, and other services was typical of defense-industry centers. War industries were not built with the location of an adequate labor supply in mind. Rather, workers had to move to the jobs, given the inducement of high wages.

Meanwhile, another source of labor had begun to be tapped. Plans were made quite early to hire women in the Kaiser yards. In January 1942, the Vancouver school board learned that women would be used to help "man" the shipyard, barely under construction, and it decided to admit ten women to the school district's defense training classes. In April, when Oregon Ship hired two women as welders on the outfitting dock, it became the first of the nation's Maritime Commission yards to employ women in production work. As word spread, first private, then public welding schools began sending more women to the yards.[3]

The women who began to enter the yards in 1942 were not the only workers new to the industry. The Kaiser company estimated that only 2 percent of its workers had ever built ships before.[4] The incorporation of masses of inexperienced workers, made necessary by the vast expansion of the industry, was made possible by changes in the organization of work. Before the war, shipbuilding had been a small industry; ships were individually built by skilled workers who served long apprenticeships to learn all aspects of their trades. The war brought standardization of products to the industry, and made preassembly of ships practical. Welding replaced riveting as the means of joining steel plates because it was faster and easier to learn. These changes, combined with the specialization of tasks, made possible the use of unskilled labor. Detailed planning by management split apart the forty to seventy skills that made a craft so each could be learned with a brief period of training. Specialization in the preassembly phase meant that a crew of workers built the same section of a ship over and over. But there were limits on skill breakdown in shipbuilding. The basic skills of cutting, shaping, and joining steel could not be learned as quickly as assembly-line jobs. As F. C. Lane notes: "There was still a considerable range of skills in the shipyards even after scientific management had broken down the jobs."[5]

The union did not oppose the dilution of skills because neither wages nor union status were threatened by the change. Craft rules were relaxed to permit workers with limited training to do jobs traditionally reserved for the "first-class mechanic," provided they got the same wages and joined the union. The dues of the new members enriched union treasuries, and closed-shop agreements prevented management from using the job breakdown to undermine the unions. In addition, the old-time craftsmen moved rapidly into foreman and supervisory positions.[6]

Government-funded War Production Training, administered by state and local school boards, enabled new workers to learn specific skills in a short period of time. Free defense training classes were offered by Portland and Vancouver vocational schools. Soon welding schools were opened in all the major shipyards, and paid trainee programs began in March 1943 to help meet the critical need for more welders. At the peak of the training program, government agent Augusta Clawson enrolled in the Swan Island welding school to discover ways of improving training and reducing turnover, especially among women. At her suggestion, an orientation program for the newly hired was started, which included a special session for women workers conducted by the women's counseling department. A few months later, the turnover rate for women production workers dropped to just slightly above that of men.[7] The training program, coupled with the breakdown of crafts into component parts, made it easy for women and other inexperienced workers to enter shipbuilding.

Another barrier to the employment of women fell when unions admitted women to membership. Workers in the Portland yards, as in most West Coast shipyards, were represented by the American Federation of Labor (AFL) craft unions. Even those conservative unions soon recognized that if women had to be hired in the shipyards, it was preferable that they work under union jurisdiction. In September 1942, the Boilermakers Union, which controlled two-thirds of all shipyard jobs, voted to admit women. This decision came a few months after the first women welders were hired in Portland.[8]

Increasing rapidly from dozens to hundreds of thousands, women became a significant part of the overall labor force in the shipyards. Only 3 percent of the total payroll in January 1942 (all office workers at that point), the female labor force grew to 15 percent by January 1943 and to 28 percent a year later. Both total employment and women's employment rose steeply through the end of 1943. During 1944, employment fluctuated due to uncertainty about the future of shipbuilding contracts. The Kaiser yards lost 10,000 workers in the first half of the year, but the percentage of women remained high. A production drive at Oregon Ship and Vancouver in the latter half of the year brought employment up again, and women made up as much as 30 percent of the work force. At this point 28,000 women were working in the Kaiser shipyards and several thousand more in smaller Portland yards.[9]

Women were hired earlier and in greater numbers in Portland than in most of the nation's shipyards. When the U.S. Women's Bureau made visits to forty-one shipyards in the fall of 1943, few had employed women for as long as one year, and six had yet to hire women. But in the three Portland-Vancouver Kaiser yards, 27 percent of the employees were women by April 1944; on Swan Island the figure was 32 percent compared to 18 percent in Kaiser's Richmond, California, yards, and to 8–10 percent at most eastern shipyards.[10] The main reason was that the sudden growth of shipbuilding in a low-population area had created a greater labor shortage than in other areas of the country. Male workers were always the preferred labor force, and women were only hired when it was clear that sufficient men were not available. This point was simply reached sooner in Portland, a small city in a rural state. The eastern shipyards were located near highly populated areas, and they also had most of the nation's trained shipbuilding workers since many of the yards dated from prewar times.

Women entering shipbuilding gained access to high wages, to equal pay, and to jobs from which they had formerly been excluded. Wages in shipbuilding were the highest of any defense industry, averaging $63 a week in September 1943. This reflected the importance of the industry to the war effort. Shipbuilding was also noted for its high ratio of skilled to unskilled workers. Sixty percent of the workers were journeymen, who earned $1.20 an hour as a basic rate. The rest were mostly helpers, earning 95 cents an hour. Wages were set by the job, so women and men in the same job category earned the same pay.[11] Despite the skill breakdown, the crafts that women workers entered involved more interesting and varied work than most other jobs available to them in the past. Even the simplest welding job, that of tacking, required two weeks to learn and longer to master; it could provide a sense of accomplishment greater than cleaning houses, waiting on tables, or filing letters. Workers were not tied to one spot, as on an assembly line, but moved about as the work demanded. In addition, women did not enter the industry at the bottom, as is often the case when they move into a formerly male job. The first women hired were welders; only later did women branch out into unskilled helper and laborer jobs, as well as into other crafts.

Recruitment campaigns stressed high wages and the capabilities of women workers. A major mobilization campaign was held in Portland in June 1943, under the auspices of the U.S. Employment Service, the War Manpower Commission, and the Office of Civil Defense. The mayor declared "Working Women Win Wars Week," and a door-to-door canvass to find women able to take war jobs was publicized by the local media. Women war workers demonstrated their skills on lathes and other machines in the display windows of downtown department stores.[12] The Kaiser employee publication urged shipyard men to "help your yard lick the manpower problem" by recruiting their wives: "If your wife, or any woman of your acquaintance, is between 18 and 35, not employed in essential industry, active, in good physical condition, and not overweight, tell her about these well-paid welding jobs." Starting at 95 cents an hour during training, welders could earn from $62 a week on day shift to $72 on graveyard.[13]

The importance of women's labor to the war effort was recognized by the creation of government-funded child-care centers. Community-based centers, funded through the Lanham Act, were opened in Portland, Vanport, and Vancouver. Of greater importance to shipyard mothers were the two Kaiser child service centers, nationally known for their quality and innovations in workplace child care. Located at the shipyard entrance, so parents could drop off their children on their way to work, the centers operated on all three shifts, and could accommodate up to 350 children each. The best child development experts were recruited to run the centers, which became a showcase proving that young children could thrive in group care for long hours. Meals and snacks were planned by a well-known nutritionist, and an infirmary cared for mildly ill children. Another notable feature was "home-service food," precooked meals which workers could purchase at the child-care centers, take home, and reheat for dinner. High quality child care was made possible by the unusual method of funding: the cost of child care was absorbed by the Maritime Commission when it purchased the ships.[14]

The shipyard child-care centers were a result, not a cause, of the high percentage of women workers. The child-care centers did not open until November 1943, after the period of greatest increase in the female labor force. Though the centers were reputed to be the largest in the world, the number of children cared for was small compared to the total number of women workers. At their peak in the summer of 1944, the Swan island and Oregon Ship centers cared for a total of over 700 children. But there were roughly 16,000 women workers in these two yards. The centers provided much-needed services to many shipyard mothers, but could not have affected the total number of women workers very much.

Women were attracted to shipyard work for a combination of reasons, but high wages was the most important. Many women learned of opportunities for shipyard jobs from their husbands or other friends and relatives already working in the yards. One woman said she worked in the shipyard "to make money. My husband was working there. We hadn't been married too long, and we decided that if I was going to work I might as well work where the pay was a little more."[15] Women who were the sole support of their families were especially interested in the high wages. A divorced mother of two was working on a Work Projects Administration (WPA) job when the program was phased out because of the war. She was given a choice of training for a shipyard job or of working in a child-care center. She inquired about the pay, found that child care paid $35 a week compared to $62 a week in the yards, and said "I'll take the shipyards."[16]

For some women, the chance to do different or more interesting work was as important as the high wages. One young mother of three followed her husband from Nebraska to Portland when he found a railroad job there. Explaining her interest in welding, she said: "Dad had a blacksmith shop. We lived in the country. I was always around metal and fire burning, drills and the whole bit. I really liked it. Even as a child I'd rather be outside than inside."[17] Another woman was working as an egg candler in Portland when she heard from her husband, a welder, that women were being hired for shipyard work. "I just thought I'd like to weld," she said. "That was the reason I went. I just wanted to."[18]

Concern about the war was also a factor, especially for those women who had relatives in the service. A woman from Oklahoma said, "I came out here because I had three sons and a son-in-law in service and I felt like I should be doing something to help." But she also noted that the wages were much higher than in her factory job, and that it was a chance for her to make a change in her life. "I wanted to get away. I was a widow, my family was raised. I thought this would be a good opportunity for me to do something different."[19]

Women's Work in a Man's World

Women's entry into shipbuilding challenged the sexual division of labor and traditional notions of femininity. The first woman office worker at Oregon Ship recalled in a 1944 interview that "for more than a year, no woman was allowed to walk along the ways or in any construction area for fear she would be injured." A cartoon in the shipyard newspaper in the spring of 1942 ridiculed the notion that women might be hired in production work, picturing housewives in aprons and high heels ineptly handling machinery.[20] Although some men had declared they would walk out if women were hired, no one actually did. The first women welders were stared at, whistled at, and then grudgingly accepted as a war necessity.

But uneasiness about women's new work roles remained. Rumors that welding caused sterility in women were persistent, reflecting a concern that women were losing their femininity. Strict dress regulations for women were based as much on "principles of concealment and sexless propriety as on concern for safety," according to Katherine Archibald, a sociologist who worked in a California shipyard for two years. "Like soldiers infiltrating enemy lines, women in the shipyards had to be camouflaged lest the difference in sex be unduly noted and emphasized," she wrote.[21]

Regardless of how men felt about it, women were doing men's work, and doing it quite well. Only six months after the first women welders were hired, a study comparing male and female welders in all seven Kaiser shipyards showed that women nearly equaled men in productivity. In the fall of 1942 the shipyard newspaper described a woman who had outwelded all the men on her crew doing difficult overhead welding on the hull of the ship. Women soon entered other jobs in the yard. By the end of 1942, women at Oregon

Ship were working as burners, crane operators, duplicators, electricians, expediters, machinists, reamers, riggers, shipfitters, laborers, and helpers in eleven different crafts. In June 1943, they were rapidly replacing men as truck and delivery car drivers. Soon there were few job categories without women.[22]

Though barriers were clearly broken, it is necessary to ask a further question: To what extent were women doing the same work as men? Studies have shown the prevalence of segregation by sex in the labor force, and its remarkable persistence over time, despite changes in the occupational structure and in the sex composition of particular jobs.[23] As the shortage of male labor pulled women into the shipyards, were they hired in the same jobs as men? Or were they channeled into some types of work and not others?

The extent of difference between women's and men's jobs can be measured by an index of segregation. This index compares the occupational distribution of the two groups, and tells the percentage of the labor force that would have to change jobs in order to create an equal distribution of jobs by sex. For example, in a situation of equality, if 20 percent of the men were welders, then 20 percent of the women would be welders also. An index of segregation was calculated for each of the three Kaiser shipyards, based on data collected by the War Manpower Commission in 1942 and 1943. The amount of segregation was substantial. Approximately half of all women or all men working in the shipyards would have had to change jobs in order to equalize the occupational distribution of women and men.[24]

In order to understand why this occurred, it is necessary to look at the kinds of jobs women held. A careful examination of the data for all three yards revealed that in general women were overrepresented as welders and underrepresented as journeymen in the other major crafts. Women were overrepresented as helpers and laborers; in some of the unskilled jobs nearly all the workers were women.

The reasons why so many women were welders are fairly clear. As the War Manpower Commission report put it, "Welding is the craft that has absorbed most women—mainly because of the urgent need for thousands of welders in modern shipbuilding, but also because women can be trained for welding more easily than most other shipbuilding jobs."[25] The demand for welders was always high because virtually all joining of steel was done by welders. Speed of production thus depended more on the availability of sufficient welders than on any other group of workers. The skill breakdown and the paid, in-plant trainee program made it easy to recruit and train women in this craft. After two weeks of training, novice welders could be put to work in the yard as tackers, making temporary welds to hold pieces in place until the seams were fully joined by production welders. It was the demand for more welders that first opened shipbuilding work to women, and at first women were hired only for this job. Thus it is not surprising that women were highly concentrated in this craft. Though women were a significant percentage of all welders (over 40 percent at Swan Island in the summer of

1943), welding was never a predominantly female job. A comparison of data for the three yards, collected at different times, shows that the overrepresentation of women as welders decreased as the number of jobs in which women were employed increased.[26]

When women entered crafts other than welding, they remained a small percentage of their craft and of all women workers. The reasons for this are less clear-cut, but some examples of women working in crafts which remained overwhelmingly male suggest possible explanations. It was very easy for women to become welders, but to enter other crafts sometimes required a great deal of persistence and initiative on the part of the woman, and in some cases, the cooperation of male co-workers.

The first full-fledged "loftlady," promoted to her job in December 1943, was an example of persistence as well as special ability. A former housewife, she went to shipfitting school and did so well that she was encouraged to take courses in loft training. After one day in the mold loft (where templates, or patterns for pieces of the ship, were made) she decided she needed more training. After 200 additional hours of training at Vancouver High, she went back to work in the loft. The superintendent assigned her to the office for some time, where she checked detail prints with structural changes. She showed such ability that she was promoted. It was almost unheard of for a woman to become a loftsman, according to the shipyard newspaper, because "not one woman in a thousand has become interested enough in mechanical craftsmanship to equal her ability."[27]

The only woman who did wiring atop the fifty-foot masts of the Liberty ships came to the yard as an electrician's helper. She asked for the job climbing the masts, agreeing that if she failed to do the job as well as a man they could replace her. She was still on her job, and liked it, over a year later. This confident young woman lived on a ranch with her parents, and hoped for a career in aviation after the war. An article entitled "Slender Blonde Does Good Job as Rigger" told the story of another atypical woman, one of only three who had successfully tackled that job. Riggers were usually "husky ex-lumberjacks," and their job was to attach loads to cranes and then guide the crane operator with hand signals. She attributed her success to the cooperation of a fellow worker. "I never could have made the grade if it hadn't been for Joe Harris, the other crew member. He taught me a lot of tricks in rigging to take the place of the brawn a woman rigger doesn't have."[28] Presumably, women not fortunate enough to work with a "good Joe" had a more difficult time.

Hierarchies of pay and responsibility may also have played a part in limiting women's access to certain jobs. While most journeymen earned a basic rate of $1.20 an hour, in some crafts, presumably those requiring greater skill, the pay was $1.33. Loftsman was one such job, and as the example cited above shows, only a woman of exceptional ability and persistence was able to break the barrier to this craft. A similar job was layer-out in the mold loft, which also paid $1.33 an hour. The account of one woman who was finally able to transfer from welding to layout suggests that it was not a lack of ability that kept women out, but a desire to maintain a male monopoly on a good job. She described the work as follows: "They have patterns and you lay them out on steel, then trace around them to cut out parts for the ship. It's just like making a dress." She needed no extra training to do this job well, because she found her high school home economics background in pattern-making sufficient. As she put it, "patterns are patterns." The mold loft would have been a logical place for the shipyards to make use of women's traditional skills. But few women worked there. The reason, according to this woman, was that "the men who were qualified layout people felt that they should get the jobs because they were men."[29]

Even when there was no wage differential, the work relationships between crafts may have influenced the placement of women. In her book based on her work experience at Swan Island, Augusta Clawson noted that welders had a "strange status" in the shipyard: "Shipfitters and shipwrights often cannot go on with their jobs until a spot has been fixed by a chipper, burner, or welder. The consequence is that they are always yelling for us. 'Come and tack this!'—or 'Burn that'—or 'Chip this.' It gives the impression that we are working *for* them although we are really on the same pay and job."[30] Frequently the welders and burners were women. Chipping was not done by women, but it was often done by black men. In contrast, only 10 percent of the shipfitters at Swan Island were women, and there were no women shipwrights. Jobs which involved directing the work of others may have been considered more appropriate for men. And women may have shared this attitude. Clawson recorded her experience of working with a woman ship-fitter whom she described as a "slave-driver."

Basically, however, in all crafts where the supply of men was sufficient, barriers to the employment of women journeymen remained. Because welders were needed, the shipyards made it easy for women to enter that craft; paid trainee programs were located right in the shipyard. But training in many other crafts was less conveniently located, lasted longer, and was not paid. Women with an immediate need for income preferred entering the yards as helpers or trainees. Many women learned of job possibilities in other crafts only after they had become welders, and it was often difficult to transfer. To enter other crafts often took special efforts, skills, or good luck.

Aside from welding, there was a concentration of women in helpers' jobs. Forty-two percent of all women at Swan Island and 50 percent at Vancouver were helpers. In both these yards, the occupational data were collected at a time when the number of women employed was approaching its peak. The data from Oregon Ship, in contrast, represented an earlier phase. At the end of 1942, only 8 percent of Oregon Ship's production workers were women, and the majority of them were welders. At the other yards in 1943, there were more women in the helper than in any other category. Thus the expansion of job opportunities for women took place in large part in the unskilled categories. While a greater variety of skilled jobs were held by women in 1943 than in 1942, most women entered unskilled jobs.

Why were so many women helpers? The reason is suggested by a quote from the War Manpower Commission report, which noted that "women have been filling gaps in increasing numbers where men are not available or not willing to accept this kind of employment."[31] Apparently, as the labor shortage grew more severe, it was difficult to find male workers for the low-wage, unskilled jobs. One woman who worked as a tank cleaner commented that "the men didn't want to do menial jobs anyway. They wanted money. They'd go for electrician or welding."[32]

Some of the unskilled job categories were filled almost entirely by women. In an industry in which all work had previously been done by men, and in which women were a minority of the labor force, the existence of any job category that was predominantly female is significant. It suggests that such jobs were now identified as "women's work." For example, laborers were 80 percent female at Vancouver and 90 percent female at Swan Island. A detailed job breakdown for Vancouver, in which helpers were identified by crafts, revealed eleven jobs that were over 60 percent female, and three in which women constituted over 90 percent of the workers. Fully one-quarter of all women workers were found in these three "women's jobs": painter helper, tool checker, and shipwright helper.[33]

Why were women channeled into some unskilled jobs rather than others? Sometimes the nature of the work, not always reflected in the job title, lent itself to sex stereotyping. The job of sweeper, for example, did not appear in any occupational classification. Sweepers were hired as laborers, shipwright helpers, and boilermaker helpers. The reason nearly all laborers at two of the yards were women, and most shipwright helpers were women in another, may have been that their actual job was sweeping. Sometimes women ended up sweeping regardless of their job title or training: "In the plate shop all new women employees start with the crew of 150 women who sweep up and clean up in that area. Regardless of experience or ultimate job desired, if the new employee is a woman, her first job is sweeping."[34]

Older women were often found in these unskilled jobs. The division of labor by age may have intensified the division based on sex, since older men were more likely to have had access to some skills or training that could be useful in the shipyards. The preferred age for women welder trainees was 18–35, so women over 35 often found themselves in helper or laborer jobs. While less skilled than welding, these jobs were not necessarily light and easy. Augusta Clawson noted that a number of women in her welding class had started as laborers. "Apparently they were terribly overworked," she wrote. "They were paid 88 cents an hour and had to pick up and carry heavy metal all day. Lots of women have quit such jobs."[35] Other women, accustomed to hard work and chores considered menial by others, were proud of their endurance. A 65-year-old woman who "picked up used rod and emptied skiffs on the ways" didn't miss a day's work during the hard winter of 1943–44. "I came here from my own farm in Idaho that I worked myself," she said, "and I guess I'm used to hard work and cold weather."[36] Another woman, who worked as a scaler, scraping welded seams smooth, said: "When you bring up ten children, you work hard and you do a lot of things that aren't pleasant. This job is helping to win the war, and I feel I'm doing my bit."[37]

The separation between men's work and women's work in the shipyards may have been greater than is indicated by the data on occupational distribution. Evidence suggests that within the same job categories, women and men were doing different types of work, with the women concentrated in the less skilled, more routine aspects of the job. This is most clear in the case of welding, where the distinction between tackers and welders lent itself to a sex-based division of labor. Frequent references to tackers as women in a variety of sources suggest that women were more likely to be tack-welders, never moving on to more skilled types of welding. Most women electricians were probably wiring lights in the electrical shops, rather than installing them on the ships.[38]

There are other indications that women and men in the same jobs were doing different work. A report on labor requirements listed workers needed both by craft and by sex. Why did Swan Island need 215 *male* welders and 166 *female* welders that week, unless they were to be assigned to different types of work?[39] Women were typically pictured in all-women crews in the shipyard newspapers, and most women interviewed said they had worked in all-female crews. While this practice sometimes contributed to women's solidarity as they entered a male-dominated work place, it may also have reflected a difference in the type of work done by women.

Traditional distinctions between the sexes were maintained in the matter of promotion to supervisory positions. Though there was an acute shortage of supervisory personnel, women were rarely considered suitable for promotion. The War Manpower Commission report noted that "the increase in the proportion of marginal and women workers due to the draft and other causes had materially reduced the supply of leader material."[40] Helper and laborer leadwomen were the main exception. All 45 leadwomen and the only forewoman at Swan Island were supervising helpers or laborers. At Vancouver, 68 percent of helper leadmen were women. The probable reason why there were leadwomen over helpers and laborers crews is that they earned less than the average journeyman's wage—labor leadmen, for example, earned $1.15 at the most.[41] In addition, they were supervising mostly women in those jobs.

Sometimes women were promoted in the crafts. Welding was the obvious job where leadwomen might be expected, since women had begun welding earlier than any other craft. A woman pictured in the shipyard newspaper in the fall of 1942 was identified as a welder leadwoman. But by the time the occupational data for the War Manpower Commission reports were collected, there were no welder leadwomen. A former welding leadman said that men objected when several women were promoted, even though they were on all-women crews. "There was quite a little friction over that," he said. "The men resented it very much. Some of them were old-time welders and had to take a back seat to these women."[42] Other women who were interviewed recalled no leadwomen on welding crews. "There was absolutely no hope of a woman going in as a leadman," said one former welder. "That was strictly male."[43] One exception was a crew of women welders at one of the smaller shipyards which had a leadwoman and a female welding instructor. But that was not until mid-1944, and it was the first such crew in that yard.[44]

Even more exceptional was a machinist leadwoman, since few women were even journeymen in that craft. She and her crew of eight men and five women were responsible for installing locks on steel doors, and other similar tasks. The shipyard newspaper pointed out that she was probably the only woman on the West Coast to hold down a job of that kind. Not surprisingly, she liked her job, and said, "If there is any place for me after this war is over, I'd like to continue in this type of work."[45]

In general, the pattern of job segregation may be summarized as follows: women were overrepresented as unskilled workers, and in some of these jobs, nearly all of the workers were women. Women were underrepresented as journeymen, except in welding. Women were promoted to leadman only over helpers and laborers, with a few exceptions. In addition, women and men in the same job categories may have been doing different types of work. The barriers that channeled women into some jobs rather than others were not rigid, however, and women with exceptional talent or persistence could gain access to most shipyard jobs.

The labor shortage broke the barrier to employment of women, and women entered welding because of the critical demand for workers in this craft. In general, women were hired to fill gaps where the supply of men was insufficient. The gaps increasingly were in the unskilled, lower-wage jobs, some of which became "women's jobs." The skill breakdown and the training programs, which made it easy to utilize women's labor, also facilitated the development of sex-based segregation in shipyard jobs.

Despite the opportunities that shipbuilding offered to women, in the form of high wages (even as helpers) and access to new jobs and skills (even diluted skills), the pattern of men's work and women's work reasserted itself. While women welders challenged traditional conceptions of appropriate work for women, the principle that men and women are fundamentally different kinds of workers was maintained in the organization of shipyard work.

Postwar Plans and Realities

How did women feel about their shipyard jobs? Surveys showed that half of them wanted to keep their war jobs. In September 1943, one shipyard newspaper asked women to fill out "coupons" stating whether or not they wanted to keep their present jobs after the war. The results, reported in a Portland newspaper, revealed that "Women welders were 60 percent for staying in overalls. Other women workers, ranging from electricians to tarp sewers, were 50 percent for staying on the job." A sheet-metal worker interviewed by a reporter said, "I hate to think of leaving $65 a week to come back to dishes and diapers."[46] This expressed the feelings of many women. However, neither the number nor the percentage of women workers who responded to the voluntary survey was recorded.

A comprehensive survey of workers at the Kaiser shipyards, conducted in January 1944, produced a similar finding. Nine-tenths of the yards' 91,000 workers were interviewed concerning their postwar plans. Of the women, 53 percent said they wanted to continue in industrial work, 8 percent were undecided, and the rest planned to seek other jobs or to return home. That fall, the women's counseling department at Oregon Ship found that 45 percent of the women wanted to continue in the same type of work after the war. They had interviewed 872 women, maybe one-tenth of the total. Did the 8 percent drop represent a real change of opinion? It is difficult to know. The shipyard newspaper pointed out that the figure was quite high, considering that the yard had been on a seven-day week for the past three months. In any case, it is more important that three different types of surveys at three different times produced roughly similar results.[47]

Despite their desire to continue in industrial work, it soon became clear that there would be no place for women in "men's jobs" after the war. Shortly after VE-Day, an article in the shipyard newspaper proclaimed "The Kitchen—Women's Big Post-War Goal." What women really wanted, the article stated, was to "put aside the welder's torch" and to give it back to the men. They wanted to get out of their "unfeminine" work clothes and look for a "vine-covered cottage," where they could put up frilly curtains and grow geraniums. The message was emphasized by a drawing of a woman in work clothes and tin hat racing home, reappearing dressed in ruffled apron and high heels, washing dishes and singing gaily while two angry children fought at her feet. The article was supposedly based on interviews with 100 women in the yards. Of the sixty-five women who were working in nonclerical jobs, only seven "stated flatly that the home life had no appeal for them and that they would stay in industry if given half a chance." This drastic change of opinion is understandable, however, given the conditions of the interviews. The article noted that men kept interrupting the questions to insist, "They ought to go home. Women haven't any business trying to do men's work," and that many women agreed with these remarks because it was "a time-honored way of satisfying the male ego." In general, the women were reported to be "philosophical about the fact that there will probably be no place for them in industry doing the tasks ordinarily performed by men after the war."[48]

When the war with Japan ended in August 1945, shipyard production declined rapidly. Cancellations of Navy and Maritime Commission contracts for ships led to heavy layoffs. From 65,000 workers on August 1, the shipyards were down to 25,000 by October. A year later, only 4,500 remained. Ship repair, conversion, "moth-balling," and scrapping operations kept some shipyard workers employed for a while. But these jobs were reserved for men. The last three women welders at Oregon Ship got their "quit-slips" at the end of October 1945. A few women remained in unskilled jobs. A tank cleaner worked at oregon Ship until it closed, then worked at a small shipyard through December 1946. "I was the last housekeeper there," she said.[49]

Women's work in the shipyards had come to an end. The child-care centers at Oregon Ship and Swan Island closed abruptly on September 1, 1945. The enrollment had been declining for several months, reflecting layoffs of women before the war ended. One of the centers became an elementary school, but a proposal to keep a small preschool program was vetoed by the school board. As a result of a national campaign, government-funded centers got their support extended to March 1946. But the purpose of child-care funding was to aid production for the war effort, and the emergency was over.[50]

In the job market, old lines were redrawn. Job opportunities were clearly differentiated by sex, age, and race, and skills acquired in the shipyards were discounted. Employers were becoming choosy. Once willing to hire anyone because of the labor shortage, many now specified "not over 45 years, male, and white."[51] There was a demand for skilled mechanics, but employers were interested in prewar skills. "The quickly acquired skills of the lush shipyard days are a drug on the market. Inside electricians who pushed a yellow or red wire through a hole, or [those] who sprayed paint on a ship or were emergency welders are not considered skilled according to the yardstick of employers."[52] This automatically excluded women, whose only access to the skilled trades had been in the shipyards.

The jobs available to women were in traditionally female areas, at wages considerably lower than those in the shipyards. The governor's postwar planning commission noted that the war had ended at a good time, when Oregon's seasonal industries could absorb many of the unemployed: "Fruit and vegetable canneries especially favor female help." A year later, women on the night shift in the canneries earned 85 cents an hour, while men earned $1 for "harder duties." In December 1945, there were few job openings in the higher-paid brackets, but there were plenty of jobs for 65 cents an hour. At the end of 1946, women trained as stenographers, nurses, and office workers were needed. "An equal demand is for domestics and laundry workers, with few accepting those jobs."[53]

Women's unemployment after the war was dismissed as unimportant because of the convenient belief that all women were "housewives" who didn't really need to work. In September 1945, 60 percent of Oregon's unemployment claims were filed by women. As late as March 1946, it was noted that "more women than men from the shipyards are filing claims each week. This was anticipated, for housewives who worked in the shipyards or aircraft industries have returned to their domestic affairs, but they are not over-looking any checks that may be coming to them."[54] In fact, no more than 40 percent of shipyard women listed their previous occupation as housewife, and many of these needed to continue working after the war.[55] Statistics showed that "84% of American working women in 1944 and 1945 were employed because of economic necessity and were self-supporting and/or financially responsible for other members of their family."[56]

What actually happened to women shipyard workers after the war? No systematic records were kept. Unions, which lost thousands of members in a few months, did not make any checks on what had happened to their former members. It was assumed that these people had left the state, or in the case of women, had "returned to their household duties." But the pattern is clear: women were pushed back into "women's work," whether in the home or in traditionally female-employing industries.[57] Examples from interviews illustrate the process. One black woman, who had been a scaler in the shipyard, was unemployed for several months after the war. She finally found seasonal work picking chickens and turkeys in a poultry factory, then worked in a laundry for the next nine years. A young mother of three had to quit welding when the night shift at her yard shut down. She and her husband had managed child care by working on different shifts. For the next five years, she was mostly at home, and had several more children, but she managed to work off and on in a restaurant, in a knitting mill, and in a department store. Then she found full-time work as a meat-wrapper, a job she held for the next twenty-two years. A middle-aged widow, who had earned $1.20 an hour as a shipyard electrician, returned to her prewar job as an elevator operator at 25¢ an hour. She had to sell her house in order to survive.[58] The line between women's work and men's work had been reestablished; not until the early 1970s would women have access to those jobs again.[59]

The wartime demand for labor briefly opened new opportunities to women. Barriers to the skilled trades fell, and women entered shipbuilding, the highest paying defense industry. Access to skills and high wages was especially great in the Portland shipyards, which hired women earlier and in greater numbers than most of the nation's shipyards. The importance of women's labor was recognized by the creation of model child-care centers at two Kaiser shipyards, demonstrating that excellent workplace child care was possible, given sufficient resources.

Although women's entry into shipbuilding challenged the sexual division of labor, the basic distribution between men's work and women's work was not altered. To a great extent, women and men in the shipyards were doing different types of jobs. Women filled in where men were unavailable or unwilling to work. Thus women were concentrated in welding and in the unskilled helper jobs. Within the crafts, they were often assigned to the more routine operations. The same skill breakdown and in-plant training programs that eased the employment of women also helped channel them into certain types of jobs. That job segregation by sex persisted even in the midst of dramatic changes in the type of work done by women suggests its importance as a structural feature of the labor force.

Although shipyard jobs were sometimes arduous and routine, many women preferred them to their prewar work. Half of all women shipyard workers hoped to continue in industrial jobs after the war. But employers' preferences for young white men with prewar skills confined women to the low-paying jobs in which they had always been found. Women's unemployment was disguised and discounted by the myth that all women war workers were "housewives" whose husbands could support them. In reality, however, the segregated job market assured a plentiful supply of cheap female labor for seasonal industries like the food-processing plants in Oregon and for the postwar expansion of clerical and service jobs.

While the war did create some preconditions for greater equality between women and men at work, such as equal pay, child care, and access to new skills, the changes were temporary. In an economy in which full employment was possible only during a war, and in the absence of a self-conscious women's movement or of an effective labor movement willing to defend the rights of working women, there was little chance of consolidating these gains.[60] Women were temporary substitutes for men in a labor shortage. Like farm women helping out at harvest time, women in industry could do "men's work" when necessary, but it remained "men's work."

Notes

1. U.S. War Manpower Commission, *A Survey of Shipyard Operations in the Portland, Oregon Metropolitan Area* (Portland, 1943), 3 vols. (WMC I, II, or III.)

2. Kaiser Industries Corp., *The Kaiser Story* (Oakland, Calif., 1968); Vanport City, Oregon Schools, *6000 Kids from 46 States* (Portland, 1946); U.S. Census Bureau, *Population,* Aug. 12, 1944, Series CA-2, No. 6.

3. "Yards to Give Women Jobs," *Oregonian,* Jan. 30, 1942, sec. 3, p. 3; *Bo's'n's Whistle,* May 7, 1942, p. 6. *Bo's'n's Whistle (BW)* was the employee publication for the Kaiser shipyards in Portland. "Kaiser Shipyards Lead U.S. in Employment of Women," *Oregonian,* April 27, 1944, sec. 2, p. 2.

4. Kaiser Industries Corp., *The Kaiser Story,* p. 31.

5. Frederick C. Lane, *Ships for Victory* (Baltimore: Johns Hopkins Press, 1951), p. 239.

6. Ibid.

7. WMC II: 45–46. See also Oregon State Board of Education, Division of Vocational Education, "Descriptive Report of Vocational Training for War Production Workers," 1945; WMC I, II, and III; Augusta Clawson, *Shipyard Diary of a Woman Welder* (New York: Penguin Books, 1944).

8. Paul R. Porter, "Labor in the Shipbuilding Industry," in Colston E. Warne et al., eds., *Yearbook of American Labor* (New York: Philosophical Library, 1945), pp. 345–360; "Boiler-makers to Admit Women in Ranks of Union," *Oregon Labor Press*, Sept. 25, 1942, p. 1.

9. "Employment in the Three Kaiser Yards," *BW*, Jan. 14, 1944, pp. 4–5; "Employment Rolls Stable in 1944: Personnel Nears '43 Peak as Workers Heed War Demands," *BW*, Dec. 29, 1944, p. 3.

10. Dorothy K. Newman, "Employing Women in Shipyards," Women's Bureau Bulletin No. 192–6, 1944.

11. "Ladies in Overalls," *BW*, Sept. 27, 1942, p. 18; Porter, "Labor in Shipbuilding"; Oregon Shipbuilding Corp., "Occupational Codes and Classifications," 1945.

12. "Civilian Defense Leaders Open Women-in-War Drive," *Oregonian*, June 22, 1943, p. 8.

13. "How You Can Help Your Yard Lick the Manpower Problem," *BW*, June 3, 1943, p. 3.

14. Carol Slobodin, "When the U.S. Paid for Daycare," *Day Care and Early Education* (Sept./Oct. 1975), pp. 23–25; Kaiser Corp. Inc., Portland Yards and Oregon Shipbuilding Corp. Child Service Centers, "Final Report, 1943–45."

15. Interview 14, Beaverton, Oregon, May 16, 1976. Interviewees are identified by number only, to protect their privacy.

16. Interview 7, Portland, Oregon, February 14, 1976.

17. Interview 8, Portland, Oregon, February 15, 1976.

18. Interview 22, Lake Oswego, Oregon, June 20, 1976.

19. Interview 6, Beaverton, Oregon, February 14, 1976.

20. "OSC Yard Opening Recalled by Woman," *BW*, Sept. 29, 1944, p. 4; *BW*, March 26, 1942, p. 8.

21. Katherine Archibald, *Wartime Shipyard: A Study in Social Disunity* (Berkeley: University of California Press, 1947), p. 22. Rumors of sterility are mentioned by Clawson, as well as in *BW*, June 3, 1943.

22. Kaiser Co. Inc., Richmond Shipyard No. 3, "Women in Shipbuilding," Jan. 1, 1943; "Mabel Can't Do That to Us," *BW*, Nov. 5, 1942, p. 9; WMC I, p. 26; "Womanpower in the Three Kaiser Shipyards," *BW*, June 17, 1943.

23. For example, see Edward Gross, " 'Plus Ca Change. . . ?' The Sexual Structure of Occupations Over Time," *Social Problems* (Fall 1968), pp. 198–208.

24. Data from WMC I, II, and III. Index based on 18 major job categories, excluding office workers. Results were: Oregon Ship, 55%; Swan Island, 48%; Vancouver, 57%. For expla-nation of index of segregation, see Gross, " 'Plus Ca Change. . . .'"

25. WMC I, p. 51.

26. Comparing the percentage of all women welders with the percentage of all workers who were welders, women were overrepresented as welders by 28% at Oregon Ship in December 1942, by 11% at Swan Island in August, 1943, and by only 2% at Vancouver in October, 1943.

27. "Loftlady," *BW*, Dec. 23, 1943, p. 12.

28. "Slender Blonde Does Good Job as Rigger," *BW*, Sept. 29, 1944, p. 4. The wirer is described in "High Climber," *BW*, Jan. 28, 1944, p. 13.

29. Interview 10, Portland, Oregon, May 14, 1976.

30. Clawson, *Diary*, p. 123; see also " 'Gus' Comes Back; Welder-Author Visitor," *BW*, May 12, 1944, p. 2.

31. WMC II, p. 29.

32. Interview 23, Portland, Oregon, July 11, 1976.

33. WMC III, p. 22.

34. "The Story of 130 Dozen Brooms," *BW*, May, 20, 1943, pp. 10–11.

35. Clawson, *Diary,* p. 48.

36. "Hard Job 'Natural' for Idaho Woman," *BW,* Sept. 29, 1944, p. 4.

37. "These and All Shipbuilding Mothers Honored May 14," *BW,* May 12, 1944, p. 1.

38. References to women as tackers from interviews, Clawson, *BW;* to women as inside electricians from Interview 5, Portland, Oregon, Feb. 13, 1976 and Postwar Readjustment and Development Commission, "Progress Report," Nov., 1945 (PRDC).

39. WMC II, p. 28.

40. WMC I, p. 63.

41. Oregon Shipbuilding Corp., "Occupational Codes and Classifications," 1945.

42. Interview 23.

43. Interview 7.

44. "All-Women Welding Crew," *Stem to Stern,* June 1, 1944, p. 7.

45. "Machinist Leadwoman Position Unusual Job for Woman," *BW* (Vancouver), Dec. 15, 1944.

46. Ellen Mills Ewing, "Postwar Poser: Pants or Aprons?," *Oregonian,* Nov. 21, 1943, mag. sec., p. 7; see also "Women at WISCO," *Stem to Stern,* Sept. 9, 1943.

47. Two-thirds of all shipyard workers hoped to continue in industrial work. "Workers Shy Postwar Plans," *BW,* March 10, 1944, p. 7; "Many Women Plan to Stay in Industry," *BW,* Nov. 24, 1944, p. 3.

48. *BW,* May 11, 1945, p. 7.

49. Interview 23; see also PRDC Aug. 1945, Oct. 1945; Oregon State Employment Service, "Analysis of Oregon Labor Market," Oct., 1947; "Women Welders Out," *BW,* Nov. 2, 1945, p. 8.

50. Child Service Centers, "Final Report," Minutes and Reports of the Day Care Committe, Portland Council of Social Agencies, 1945; Howard Dratch, "The Politics of Child Care in the 1940s," *Science and Society* (Summer 1974), pp. 167–204.

51. PRDC Oct. 1945.

52. PRDC Dec. 1945, p. 5.

53. PRDC Aug. 1945, p. 3; PRDC Sept. 1946; PRDC Nov. 1946, p. 3.

54. PRDC March 1946, p. 6; see also PRDC Sept. 1946.

55. PRDC Nov. 1946. The figure of 40% former housewives was deduced from previously cited reports that by 1944 28 percent of shipyard workers were women and from a report in *BW* of March 10, 1944, indicating that 11 percent of all shipyard workers listed "housewife" as previous occupation. Other listed occupations were not broken down by sex.

56. Lyn Goldfarb, *Separated and Unequal: Discrimination Against Women Workers After World War II* (Washington: Union for Radical Political Economics, n.d., probably 1976), unpaginated, quote from eleventh page.

57. PRDC Nov. 1945.

58. Interview 12, Portland, Oregon, May 15, 1976; Interview 8; Interview 5.

59. Several women interviewed had returned to welding in Portland shipyards in the early 1970s.

60. Even a progressive union like the UAW did not defend the jobs of its women members. See Goldfarb, *Separated and Unequal.*

Suggestions for Further Reading

Chafe, William H. *The American Woman: Her Changing Social, Economic, and Political Role, 1920–1970.* New York: Oxford University Press, 1972. Part II of this book is a good introduction to the impact of World War II on women's lives and work. Chafe documents both the opportunities opened by the labor shortage—access to better jobs, higher wages, and unionized industries—and the continuing inequality between the sexes: failure to implement equal pay for equal work, inadequate child care and other community services, and the exclusion of women leaders from manpower policy decisions. He argues that despite limited progress toward equality, the war permanently expanded the accepted role of married women to include work outside the home. Whether this change was a result of the war or of long-term economic trends, and whether it represented a step toward equality, are debatable questions.

Dratch, Howard. "The Politics of Child Care in the 1940s." *Science and Society,* 38 (Summer 1974), 167–204. An in-depth analysis of the political struggle over federal funding of child care during the war. Dratch shows how the conflicting interests and ideologies of different federal agencies, as well as those of industry, organized labor, child welfare officials, and women workers, shaped the development and subsequent dismantling of the wartime child care program. Of particular interest is his documentation of union efforts (Congress of Industrial Organizations and United Engineers) on behalf of child care and evidence of grassroots protest against the cut-off of funds at the end of the war. For Dratch, the politics of child care illustrate the priorities of capitalism, and he contrasts the meager and temporary support for child care with the massive government subsidies to industries involved in war production.

Goldfarb, Lyn. *Separated and Unequal: Discrimination Against Women Workers After World War II.* Washington, D.C.: Union for Radical Political Economics Political Education Project, n.d., prob. 1976. A valuable case study showing how women were pushed out of the Detroit auto industry as it reconverted to peacetime production. Even a progressive union like the United Auto Workers (UAW) failed to protect the job rights of its women members. Of special interest are the examples of grievances filed by women protesting discriminatory layoffs, reclassification of jobs, etc. Local union officers more concerned with men's jobs, ignored the complaints of the women. The UAW principle of equal treatment for all members was frequently violated in practice. Goldfarb argues that the misleading identification of women workers as "housewives" allowed the employers to get rid of large numbers of workers without protest by the union. This weakened the union and the position of workers as a whole.

Gregory, Chester W. *Women in Defense Work during World War II: An Analysis of the Labor Problem and Women's Rights.* Jericho, N.Y.: Exposition Press, 1974. Describes the work done by women in various defense industries and their successful performance in traditionally male jobs. The author assumes that women's war work lead to greater equality between the sexes but does not present evidence in support of this view. He ignores postwar layoffs of women from industrial jobs, as well as other forms of discrimination.

Pierson, Ruth. "Women's Emancipation and the Recruitment of Women into the Labour Force in World War II." In *The Neglected Majority: Essays in Canadian Women's History,* edited by Susan M. Trofimenkoff and Alison Prentice. Toronto: McClelland and Stewart, 1977, 125–145. The experience of women in Canada provides a useful comparative perspective. Pierson disputes the idea that the war brought great gains for women. She shows that the government viewed women as a labor reserve to be tapped as needed for the war effort. Women's place remained in the home, and their increased employment was justified as a necessary sacrifice for the war. Child care and other special provisions for women workers were inadequate and temporary. Aspects of the Canadian experience which differed from that of the United States are also of interest: the registration of all women who were potential workers, a tax law which encouraged wives to work, and a campaign to recruit women as part-time workers.

Quick, Paddy. "Rosie the Riveter: Myths and Realities." *Radical America* 9 (July–Oct. 1975): 115–131. A Marxist interpretation of the rise and fall of women's labor force participation during and after World War II. The author criticizes attempts to explain women's entry and exit from wage labor in terms of changes in their attitudes, men's attitudes, or the image of working women in the media. She stresses the importance of basic economic factors such as the supply of male labor, the availability of high wages, and changes in the birth rate. (This issue of *Radical America* is devoted to "American Labor in the 1940s" and contains other articles of interest. In particular, see the reprinted excerpts from Augusta Clawson's *Shipyard Diary* and Katherine Archibald's *Wartime Shipyard.*) See also Alan Clive, "Women Workers in World War II: Michigan as a Test Case," *Labor History,* Winter 1979: 44–71.

Slobodin, Carol. "When the U.S. Paid for Day Care." *Day Care and Early Education* (Sept.–Oct. 1975): 23–25, 49. On the Kaiser child-care centers. The author describes how they were funded, how the program was developed, and what services were offered. Includes material from recent interviews with child-care experts who developed the program.

Straub, Eleanor F. "United States Government Policy Toward Civilian Women During World War II." *Prologue* 5 (Winter 1973): 240–254. A well-researched article showing that women had little voice in shaping the nation's manpower policies, despite the importance of women's labor to the war effort. Overall policy concerning women workers was fragmented and disorganized, and the expertise of women leaders was ignored. The case of the Women's Advisory Committee to the War Manpower Commission illustrates how women were sidelined from decision-making. The author attributes this to the fact that women as a group were not an effective power bloc.

Tobias, Sheila and Lisa Anderson. "What Really Happened to Rosie the Riveter? Demobilization and the Female Labor Force, 1944–47." *MSS Modular Publications*, Module 9 (1973). This article is important for the issues it raises. The authors argue that women did not retire voluntarily from their high-paying war jobs, but were "forcibly laid off" and not rehired after reconversion because of discrimination by both employers and unions. They stress that most women workers during the war were working-class women who had been employed before Pearl Harbor and whose primary motivation was financial necessity. Mechanisms such as separate seniority lists, reclassification of jobs, and reintroduction of protective legislation were used to push women out of industrial work after the war. Women had to find employment in low-wage "women's jobs" or go on welfare, the authors suggest. Their arguments were based on an investigation of the Detroit auto-aircraft industry, and Goldfarb's later study of the UAW (cited above) offers more documentation on many points, though from a different perspective.

Trey, Joan Ellen. "Women in the War Economy—World War II." *Review of Radical Political Economics* 4 (July 1972): 40–57. Points out the connection between changing needs of the economy and changes in ideology. Trey argues that women were used as a reserve labor force during the war, pulled into the work force when there was a shortage of men, and then pushed out to provide jobs for returning servicemen. She shows how the media image of women changed dramatically from the war to the postwar period and suggests that women were manipulated in and out of the labor force by changes in ideology about working women. Different interpretations are offered by Quick, cited above, and by Leila Rupp in her essay, "Woman's Place Is in the War: Propaganda and Public Opinion in the United States and Germany, 1939–1945," in Carol Ruth Berkin and Mary Beth Norton, eds., *Women of America: A History* (Houghton Mifflin, Boston, 1979), pp. 342–359. Also, Trey's assumption that women left the labor force after the war is inaccurate.

PART TWO

PERSISTENT PATRIARCHY AND REVOLUTIONARY CHANGE

Part Two: Introduction

The essays in this section deal with the impact on women of five major revolutionary movements that were unusually successful both in achieving their stated goals and in providing models for future generations in the never-ending human quest for political and social change.

Although they occurred over the span of two centuries and were rooted in very different social and political circumstances, these five revolutions had much in common. They fought against one or more common enemies: despotism in its various forms, ascriptive privilege, hereditary political power, and theocracy. Above and beyond specific programs for change at the institutional or cultural level, they proclaimed a common goal as ambitious as it was abstract: to rearrange society along egalitarian, national, and secular lines. And finally, these five revolutions were characterized by mass participation. Even the earliest and most conservative of them, the American Revolution, could not have succeeded if the signers of the Declaration of Independence and the Minutemen had not enjoyed widespread support in their communities.

Although women were rarely found among the leaders of these revolutions, they did participate in a variety of more or less active roles. The essays in this section deal in part with the forms, the significance, and the consequences of that participation. In so doing, they meet, with distinction, one of the vital requirements of historical scholarship: to shed light on heretofore little-known aspects of the human past. But if individually these essays enrich our understanding of the past, together they add up to something different and perhaps more important than a contribution to historical knowledge. Taken together, in fact, these essays have as much to offer the present-minded reader as they do the student of history.

Most obviously, these essays point to the dichotomy between the egalitarian rhetoric of the revolutions in question and the reality of women's continued subservience and powerlessness in postrevolutionary societies. This dichotomy is most evident in Marylynn Salmon's essay on the legal status of American women. The decisions and attitudes of judges in postrevolutionary South Carolina gave little indication that they had internalized the egalitarian impulse of the Revolution. To the extent that they had internalized that impulse at all, they applied it selectively to the realm of government institutions, but not to the realm of family relationships and certainly not to the economic system. Hence their belief in and their defense of patriarchy and slavery. Hence the contradictory (to us) character of the early republic, in which the most egalitarian and flexible political system of the late eighteenth century coexisted with a social and economic system built upon oppression and segregation by gender and by race.

The *sans-culottes* of Mary Johnson's essay and the Russian Communists discussed by Beatrice Farnsworth were much less reluctant than their American counterparts to accept the extension of egalitarian principles to marriage and family relationships. Thus, for instance, the French revolutionary legislation accorded both women and men the right to initiate divorce proceedings. And in postrevolutionary Russia, women won unprecedented legal freedoms. Yet even in revolutionary France and Russia, the gap between women's legal emancipation, on the one hand, and their political marginality and economic dependence, on the other, was but briefly narrowed during the years of turmoil. It remained open and grew very wide in the immediate postrevolutionary period.

Thus, through their analysis of women's experience, the following essays offer important clues to the nature of certain major revolutions. At the very least, they caution the student of revolutions past and present to look at major upheavals from more than one perspective and to distinguish between revolutionary ideology and practice. There are lessons to be learned here not so much by historians as by policymakers. Joan Maloney's essay, for instance, shows a Chinese Communist leadership committed to radical change, yet forced to come to terms with traditional values and social relationships not amenable to such change. One such value was the belief that governing and political organizing are man's work. One such social relationship was that between women and men, particularly within the family. Departures from these norms could and were made in the China of the 1960s and early 1970s, as they had been during the other revolutionary upheavals described in this section. Yet in every case a return to relative political and social stability was marked by an at least partial retreat by women from the political sphere and by a renewed emphasis on the importance of the family.

The extent of this retreat (if indeed it was that) and the significance of this emphasis on the family are discussed in Part Three. A different sort of question must be raised here. Do the essays in this section tell a story of disappointed hopes, of betrayed trust, of oppression? Were the Parisian *femmes du peuple*, the Russian and Chinese Communist women, the Mercy Otis Warrens of the American Revolution manipulated and used by male leaders for as long as their energies were needed for the success of the revolution, then cast aside and denied a share of power? Should one conclude, as Renate Bridenthal and Claudia Koonz have, that "revolutionary men attempting to establish a liberated new order [cling] to patriarchal values . . ." and therefore try to reimpose those values as soon as possible in the postrevolutionary period?

Yes. Read on one level, these essays do indeed tell a story of thwarted hopes, of politically sophisticated women denied authority, if not always influence, in the postrevolutionary society. They also suggest that male revolutionaries were suspicious of women's political activism, especially if they could not control or direct it. Clearly they were not unhappy to see women activists channel their energies into such seemingly peripheral organizations as the Women's Section of the Russian Communist Party. Yet any statement about the persistence or the reassertion of patriarchy in postrevolutionary societies needs to be carefully qualified. For an interpretation of revolutionary and postrevolutionary history from the perspective of women-as-victims can ultimately lead to distortions.

This interpretation is based on three assumptions. First, that male revolutionary leaders were in a position to reimpose patriarchal values threatened *by their own actions* much more than by women's actions against the existing social order. Second, that it was in their interest to do so. And third, that the women activists bowed to male pressure as they abandoned the political sphere altogether or redirected their energies exclusively toward women's issues. Not the least important intellectual contribution of these essays is that they point to the persistence even in the midst of cataclysmic changes of patriarchal values and social arrangements unfavorable to women. Yet they go well beyond the history of women-as-victims, opening the door to hypotheses about and investigations of the reasons for persistent patriarchy. And they clearly demonstrate the importance, indeed the necessity, of a comparative perspective before valid generalizations can be made about women's position in postrevolutionary societies.

For instance, the first assumption mentioned above, that male revolutionary leaders have both the will and the power to reimpose patriarchy in postrevolutionary societies, is supported by evidence from the history of the American Revolution. Gerda Lerner has written : "Neither during nor after the American Revolution . . . did women share the historical experience of men. On the contrary, they experienced in both periods status loss and a restriction of options as to occupations and role choices." But evidence from the other, more radical revolutions discussed in this section calls for a more sober assessment of men's power and women's status.

That women's experience of the revolution was different from men's might also be said, for instance, of Mary Johnson's *femmes du peuple*. What cannot be said of them is that they experienced "status loss and a restriction of options as to occupations and role choices." Rather, during the revolution they experienced roughly the opposite: a rapid, dramatic, stressful expansion of the responsibilities to which they were accustomed and the burden of new, ill-defined responsibilities to their class and their country. At first they felt the pressure of having to perform their traditional economic functions under conditions of instability and scarcity. Later on in the revolution, they were called upon to defend the French republic on the homefront while the men of their class defended it on the battlefields of Europe. To be sure, the women's growing political consciousness as they performed traditional roles in altered form or took on new ones kept the male leaders of *all* social classes and factions nervous and on edge. Nonetheless, it was not male revolutionaries in general who cracked down on women's protest demonstrations. Nor were all

male revolutionaries responsible for that quintessential reassertion of patriarchal values in a postrevolutionary society, the Napoleonic Civil Code.
Other aspects of the Napoleonic regime, particularly its political structures,
destroyed for most men as well as for all women the options opened up by the
Revolution.

These essays indicate that women's revolutionary activism arose mostly
out of their traditional roles as wives, mothers, and providers of food and
services. Even the highly politicized women in the Bolshevik leadership,
Farnsworth writes, usually had male sponsors. And Maloney points out that
first-generation Chinese Communist women were often the wives of male
leaders. In this light, it is perhaps time for historians of women to revise (or
discard) their notion of conflicting traditional (i.e., basically domestic) and
nontraditional (e.g., political) roles.

With a few exceptions, women revolutionaries do not seem to have
perceived such a conflict any more than did men. On the contrary, the
behavior of Parisian women on the bread lines and of Russian leaders like
Smidovich and Liubatovich suggests that in their view revolutionary change
would enable them to function better as wives, mothers, and providers. If this
was indeed their self-perception (and further research is needed on this issue),
the preservation of patriarchal values and their rapid postrevolutionary
resurgence reflected something more complex than a deliberate and callous
exercise of power by male leaders over their female allies. Perhaps it reflected
the belief of revolutionaries of both sexes that the effective performance of
traditional duties, especially child raising, by women was no less vital to the
functioning of postrevolutionary society and to the consolidation of some
revolutionary gains than was the actual direction of public policy. Two essays
in the third section of this volume do, in fact, illustrate how nineteenth-
century French and Italian women, while excluded from political power,
performed an important civic function within the family. The introduction to
Section Three shows this to have also been the case in the early years of the
American republic.

Farnsworth, Maloney, and Casal, however, show that such separate and
unequal spheres continued to exist even in times and in societies where the
traditional economic functions of the household had become obsolete and
where the state had taken charge of the civic education of the young. In
postrevolutionary Russia, China, and Cuba, women were not only given full
civil and political rights, they were also expected to participate in political
activities, at least if they were party members. And they were expected to
contribute to the economic development of their countries by taking jobs
outside the home. The consequences of these policies are implicit in the
essays themselves.

For women, the revolution in those and other countries in the twentieth
century has meant liberation, but also a double burden that has effectively
discouraged their political activism and their individual career ambitions. But
what of male revolutionaries? The economic and social conditions of the

twentieth century, even in backward countries, have made it difficult to rationalize the persistence of patriarchal arrangements and of separate spheres for men and women on the basis of larger societal needs or of a necessary division of labor. And so, while women grow increasingly restive under their double burden, men have to face up to a thorny and long-avoided dilemma. They can try to cling to patriarchal arrangements, at least within the family. But if they do, they can expect to be challenged by women who are subject to the worst of the old society and of the new. Or they can carry their egalitarian ideology—stripped of any qualifications and rationalizations—to its logical conclusion. But if they do, they must be prepared, at the very least, to plan along with women and to accept alternatives to the autonomous household, to the nuclear family, and so forth. The essays by Salmon and Johnson illustrate the compromises that were made in different societies to resolve the tension between persistent patriarchy and revolutionary change. Those by Farnsworth, Maloney, and Casal raise the question whether lasting compromises of this sort are still possible in this century.

4/"Life, Liberty, and Dower": The Legal Status of Women After the American Revolution

Marylynn Salmon

In the years following the Revolution, American jurists groped to apply new republican standards to their knowledge of the law. They sought to reduce their dependence on English law, which—along with all other English-based institutions—had become suspect. As they pondered the suitability of various legal principles to their newly formed governments, these men stood in a unique position in the history of Western jurisprudence. For, during that brief period in the late eighteenth and early nineteenth centuries, American lawyers were free to shape a new series of legal precedents.[1] They planned to reject those principles of the English law that were inapplicable to a democratic nation and to retain those that seemed to be supportive.

The fact that the American legal community rejected little of its heritage during the early national period says a great deal about the nature of the Revolution. It shows that the dominant element in American society—middle- and upper-class white males—was steeped in English tradition and wary of any innovation in the law which might change social relationships. The groups in power were satisfied with the class, racial, and sexual structure of the country.

The basic conservatism of the American Revolution becomes apparent when comparing what might have happened to American law with what did happen; when one considers the possibilities for change and sees instead the continued dependence of the courts on English precedents. This is certainly true of those areas of the law that affected women's rights. No radical changes alleviated the basic position of dependency occupied by married women.[2] The courts retained their paternalistic, protective attitudes and did little to help women achieve independence or equality.

This does not mean that the law was static, for during the quarter century 1775–1800 women did move forward in regard to their legal rights. But the changes were gradual, conservative, and frequently based upon English developments. Only a few changes occurred as a direct result of the Revolution. When debates reigned concerning which of England's laws should apply in the republic, they did not include discussions of how to alter those laws to give women equal legal rights. The courts wanted to protect women in their dependency; they did not consider making them independent. In some cases, liberal attitudes fostered by revolutionary philosophies did promote and augment beneficial legal developments for women. It must be emphasized, however, that many of these improvements were under way before America's separation from the mother country.

This essay investigates several areas of the law that affected the status of women in postrevolutionary society. Particular attention is paid to women's property rights: their use of marriage settlements, support systems for widows, and the development of a law of alimony and divorce. The amount of economic independence a woman exercises in society denotes her position in that society. A culture that approves of independent, aggressive women gives them control over their own property. One that prefers passsive or subservient women places their property in the hands of others—fathers or husbands. By studying the degree of control that American women were allowed to exercise over their own financial well-being, a better understanding of the ideal republican woman can be reached. The degree of financial control reveals the amount of independence she was expected to demonstrate, as well as the boundaries of her normal, dependent condition.

Since nothing is uniform in American law, it is almost impossible for a legal historian to generalize accurately. Each colony and state had its own judicial system; each followed its own set of precedents. For the purposes of this study the law of one jurisdiction—South Carolina—is discussed. Examples from other areas serve to support the general statements.

Marriage Settlements

In 1794 two South Carolina attorneys debated the wisdom of enforcing marriage settlements in republican nations. One counselor stated that these contracts, which allowed married women to own property separately from their husbands, were unadaptable to the American situation.[3] His opponent denied that contention, claiming that historically republics had supported the rights of married women to control their own estates: "Settlements produce a conformity to the laws of Rome and others, where women had rights: not as according to the English laws where the woman's existence is supposed to be annihilated."[4]

American judges, like their English counterparts, gave strong support to marriage settlements in the postrevolutionary decades. They viewed these financial arrangements as unavoidable evils, destructive of family unity but necessary to provide women with minimal economic security. In fact, the validity of separate estates for married women was so widely accepted by eighteenth-century American jurists that not even the effects of the Revolutionary War could shake them.[5] Throughout the war the wives of Loyalists were allowed to retain their own properties, in spite of their husbands' traitorous activities and of the virulent feelings that ran against opponents of the American cause.[6] In South Carolina this support of settlements is particularly evident.

South Carolina's 1782 confiscation act specifically recognized the claims of persons holding mortgages, valid bills of sale, and marriage settlements.[7] Therefore, although the act ordered confiscation of all property belonging to Loyalists, some wives found protection from the rigors of the law under the words of this settlement clause. They employed it successfully to secure for themselves at least a portion of their family property. According to the South Carolinian statesman Stephen Bull, Mrs. Wright, Mrs. Russell, Mrs. Jenkins, "and many other ladies" relied on their marriage settlements for protection during this difficult period.[8]

Cases disputing the rights of Loyalists' wives to hold property under trust estates appeared shortly after the Revolution. In fact, Stephen Bull understood the situation well when he uttered the remark just noted. At the time he was embroiled in an attempt to overthrow the trust of his own aunt, Hannah Bull, wife of the former lieutenant governor of South Carolina. She and her staunchly pro-English husband executed a deed of their property to trustees for her use in 1777. Clearly they anticipated the danger a proposed confiscation act would pose to their own situation and thus created the trust estate in an attempt to avoid the consequences of their Loyalist leanings. Stephen Bull, who hoped to obtain the large estate of his aunt and uncle for his own use, argued that such an intention made their settlement illegal. But the court ruled against his argument. As a matter of policy the court supported Hannah Bull's deed of settlement.[9]

Another case demonstrates even more clearly the tendency of South Carolina judges to support all marriage settlements, even those made under questionable circumstances. In *Wilson* v. *Wilson* (1791) a woman attempted to utilize the settlement loophole in the confiscation act by arranging for her separate estate after the act was passed. While in *Bull* v. *Bull* the judges could hide their lenient attitudes behind the fact that the deed was executed before 1782, that excuse was not possible in the case of Winifred Wilson.

During the Revolution, Mrs. Wilson lived alone with her young child on the land that she and her husband John farmed. The property was hers. She had inherited it from her first husband, but there was no settlement for her benefit. To the commissioners of confiscated estates, then, it appeared to be John Wilson's property, and when he joined the British army in New York they placed it on their confiscation list. Fearful that everything she had was about to be taken from her, Winifred wrote to John, asking that he sign an antedated marriage settlement. She explained that she thought the 1782 act exempted lands held as women's trust estates and reasoned, "If they will admit of marriage settlements, I will shew mine under the deed . . . if not, I will say I have no claim."[10]

John agreed to the settlement, executed the deed, and sent it back to his wife, who employed it to save the farm from confiscation. But after the war he regretted the action and his loss of the land titles. In Wilson's 1791 suit brought to annul the conveyance, counsel argued that since the deed had been created with a clear intention of avoiding the law, it was illegal and invalid. The attorney angrily denounced the custom of marriage settlements in general, stating that they were deviant contracts and "dangerous instruments of domestic unhappiness, by *imperium in imperio.*"[11] Courts of law should always be wary of carrying them to extremes, he argued, especially in cases where they represented an attempt to thwart the law or defraud the state.

In *Wilson* v. *Wilson* the Supreme Court of South Carolina chose not to rule in favor of the husband's marital rights. Instead it recognized the woman's makeshift settlement as legitimate and rationalized the decision by saying: "The commissioners of confiscated estates had taken possession of the estate—the wife, to save it, implored her husband to execute the bond, and protect the property for her and her child." In the judges' opinion this was a "laudable" motive and "no crime" because, as they said, "The bond was [not] given merely to cover the property from confiscation in evasion of the law; it was also to make provision for the wife and child."[12]

Mrs. Wilson's recovery of her estate in this case is surprising, for any property that a wife brought into a marriage was subject to strict definitions of ownership at the time of the Revolution. Under the common law provisions for handling women's property, everything that Winifred possessed before her marriage to John became his at their union. Her slaves and other personal property were his absolutely. He held the real property under a life estate title, as tenant by curtesy.[13] There is no doubt that the state Supreme Court could have declared the settlement void, the property the husband's and sold the slaves and lands for a valuable profit. Instead they supported the deed and claimed to admire the motives which forced its creation.

The intention of the chancellors is clear. They recognized the injustice of Winifred Wilson's position and sought to protect her as much as possible by stretching the law of marriage settlements to cover her particular case. American judges were fully cognizant of the delicate position of married women. They could not help feeling the cruelty of the law in cases such as these. Their response, full support for the few legal procedures that did protect women, indicates a basic attitude of paternalism. They wanted child-like dependency from women, and knew they could achieve it only by acknowledging the importance of procedures such as trust estates, which obviated the need for complete self-sufficiency.

Another procedural safeguard for married women—the right to separate examinations as to their consent to land conveyances—was also the subject of debate in South Carolina during the postwar period.[14] Once more the courts of that state demonstrated their concern for women's rights, by supporting a protective policy against the weight of English precedents. In *Ewing* v. *Smith* (1811) the courts discussed the validity of a mortgage deed created by a wife to satisfy her husband's creditors. Could they allow her to convey her separate estate for the payment not of her own debts, but of her husband's?[15]

Ann Smith inherited considerable property from her father. Some of it was secured to her separate use by a trust deed which stipulated that it was not to be held liable for Roger Smith's debts or encumbrances. But when Roger became indebted for large sums, he asked his wife to mortgage her trust estate as security. She agreed. The couple was ultimately unable to meet their payment schedule, and when Roger died his creditors sued for possession of the trust property.

This case posed an interesting problem for South Carolina jurists. The only available authorities on the issue were English; few American cases had dealt with it. But in the wake of the Revolution, jurists were uncomfortable in relying exclusively on English precedents. In addition, the judges on the court of appeals did not agree with English practice on the subject. The known precedents maintained that a married woman's powers of disposition over her separate estate were unlimited. She could do anything she pleased with the property just as though she were a *feme sole,** provided there were no limitations specified in the settlement. South Carolinians disapproved of this open policy, and at first glance their position appears to be regressive.

On closer examination, however, the decision in *Ewing* v. *Smith* is understandable. The judges' belief in the efficacy of a husband's coercion caused them to limit the ability of a wife to execute conveyances, for if a woman could legally alienate her separate estate, her husband might coerce her into doing so for his benefit. This danger undermined the primary purpose of marriage settlement—the protection of a *feme covert*'s own property. The limitation imposed by the court was a very minor one: they simply required a separate examination of a woman any time she executed a deed of her property, in order to discover her true wishes regarding sale or conveyance. It was no more than they demanded of all married women in the normal conveyancing procedure, as they explained in deciding the case of Ann Smith.[16]

Mrs. Smith's settlement was designed to provide her with financial security in the event that she outlived her husband. By her own action she had destroyed this security, and her right to do so formed the basis of an extensive legal discussion in South Carolina. The Circuit Court of Chancery determined that she could legally make a disposition of her own property without a separate examination. Chancellor Desaussure, who wrote the court's opinion, studied the English precedents with care and decided accordingly. Separate estates gave women unlimited powers, he wrote, and while it was unfortunate that wives might be subjected to the coercion of their spouses, the courts could do little to protect them. If they were to hold separate estates, they had to be regarded as *femes soles* in administering those estates.[17]

The court of appeals reversed Chancellor Desaussure's decision. In his opinion on the case, Judge Waties agreed that a married woman who owned

*A *feme sole* was an unmarried woman, a *feme covert* a married woman.

separate property should be free to alienate it as she pleased, either to her husband or to any other person. But he disagreed with Desaussure's opinion that the courts had no obligation to protect her from her husband's potential coercion. He believed that an absolute right of ownership required an absolute right of disposition; but the rule, he noted "is only applicable to persons of full legal capacity." Women were not such persons in the early nineteenth century, and Waties found it strange "that English judges should have ever lost sight of the common law so far as to apply it [the rule] to a married woman."[18] In executing conveyances, he wanted all women to submit to separate examinations, as a means of providing at least some form of protection.

Judge Waties believed that he was fully justified in determining this case against the authority of English decisions. In his mind, they placed women in an unfair, dangerous position by removing what slight protection the law could offer them. South Carolina had no obligation to adhere to such a policy. In fact, the Judge wrote, "I should feel that I was not fulfilling the purpose for which my country has been pleased to place me here, if instead of exercising my own judgment in the best manner I could in construing and applying any principle to cases as they occur, I should implicitly follow the construction given to it in similar cases by the Judge of a foreign court."[19]

This South Carolina development in the law of marriage settlements was made possible by the Revolution. It produced what for those times was viewed as a benefit for married women, by strengthening the procedural safeguards designed for their protection. It would be an exaggeration, however, to claim that this manner of change in the law indicated a meaningful change in the status of women. The development is more indicative of a pervasive attitude of paternalism than of a desire to promote women's economic independence. The attitudinal barometer here is not the particular legal innovation of the court, but its continued and increasing support of marriage settlements, a protection for women that began long before the Revolution and lasted long after it.

The law of marriage settlements in Maryland substantiates this point. Although courts in that state also recognized the rights of married women to own property separately from their husbands, they did not follow the South Carolina precedent of separate examinations. Instead they ruled that women holding property under deeds of trust had full powers to sell or mortgage, just as though they were unmarried. No private examinations were necessary when settlements recognized active rights of management.

Maryland reached this decision in *Tiernan* v. *Poor* (1829), a case in which a wife mortgaged her separate estate to provide security for her husband's $600 debt, and lost it to his creditors.[20] Under her settlement Deborah Poor possessed the right to dispose of the trust estate, but her counsel maintained that as a *feme covert* she could convey her property only through the medium of a private examination. None had been taken in this case. Opposing counsel objected to the argument, citing the English precedents that South Carolina rejected. The reasoning was that with regard to her separate estate a woman was a *feme sole*, that such a condition gave her all rights of management, and that courts of law had no authority to restrict her by requiring separate examinations.

The Maryland judges supported English precedent in *Tiernan* v. *Poor*. In their case opinion they wrote that women possessed unrestricted powers over their own property. If a wife chose to convey her property to pay her husband's debts or to otherwise support him, that was her decision and the court would recognize its validity. They noted, "She was never intended to be placed in a state of pupilage with regard to her property, but left free to act as she pleased, with regard to it."[21]

When the Maryland and South Carolina decisions are examined together, it becomes clear that the mode of enforcing *feme covert* conveyances was not the key issue. One state rejected its English legal heritage to provide added safeguards for women and the other did not. But both maintained strong support systems for settlements, in recognition of their importance to women. Both before and after the Revolution, separate estates functioned to alleviate the dependent position of *femes coverts*. The end of English rule in America brought no radical change in the right of women to own property, either progressive or regressive. As these cases demonstrate, the courts were concerned primarily with guaranteeing existing rights, not with developing new ones. That concern did not surface until the middle of the nineteenth century, when legislatures began to pass married women's property acts.[22] For the time being states such as South Carolina and Maryland contented themselves with continuing policies that promoted joint property ownership between husband and wife. The concept of marital unity was firmly entrenched in American law; it would take more than a change in political allegiance to shake it.

Inheritance Rights

Dower was the common law right of a widow to support from the proceeds of her deceased husband's estate. South Carolina judges of the revolutionary period were just as careful to preserve the dower rights for widows as they were to protect the marriage settlements for wives.[23] This was true even for those women whose husbands fought against independence. Since state law kept women bound into a dependent, subservient position, jurists considered themselves obliged to support the few legal rights they did have. Dower was one of the most important of these, and it was supported consistently for Loyalists' wives.

In the cases of *Mongin and Wife* v. *Baker and Stevens* (1789) and *Wells* v. *Martin* (1796), widows of banished Loyalists applied to the state for their dower rights in confiscated property. The husbands in both cases were listed as traitors in the confiscation act of 1782. As a result, the state had seized their property and sold it at a public auction under the provisions of the act. Stevens, Baker, and Martin, the defendants in these two dower cases, had purchased the lands from the state at full price and supposedly free from all encumbrances. They disputed the widows' dower claims to one-third value of the estates, stating that the 1782 act did not include dower as a legal encumbrance on Loyalists' properties in the same way that it did mortgages, prior judgments, and marriage settlements. Great inconveniences to the state would result from allowing widows to make dower claims against property that had already been conveyed to new owners. The defendants' attorneys pointed out that the state had warranted the titles "against all claims and demands whatsoever"; a decision against those titles would produce endless suits at law for compensation.[24]

Counsel for the complainants argued in both cases that the widow's right to dower was favored by the law.[25] English law denied it only to the wives of men who were tried and convicted of treason. They then noted that treason trials were never held in South Carolina. Instead, Loyalists were banished by an act of the assembly. Although the act specifically prohibited Loyalists from owning property in the state, it did not bar widows' dower claims, and therefore the court had no power to do so at a later date. This argument prevailed in the minds of the judges, who wrote in their opinion: "The court is not bound to give, nor will they ever give such a harsh construction to the act, as to deprive a widow of a common law right, when the act itself is silent upon the subject."[26]

Had the 1782 act barred dower, the South Carolina judges would have been forced to rule against the women in these cases. Since it did not, they chose to rely upon a common law definition that denied widows' dower only when their husbands were convicted traitors. Their reading of the statute in this regard was lenient, indicating a desire on the part of the judges to protect widows' rights. As Judge Baker wrote, the dower right of a widow was one of the highest rights known to the law, "and one which the courts of justice have ever held sacred." They could not refuse it to innocent women who needed the allowance for their maintenance, and therefore decided against the claims of purchasers from the state.[27]

The postrevolutionary period saw improvements for women in the laws governing dower and the distribution of intestates' estates. In 1777 "An Act for the more easy and expeditious obtaining the admeasurement of dower to widows of the lands of their deceased husbands" passed the General Assembly. Through this statute South Carolina lawmakers sought to alleviate one of the hardships in the common law system for widow support. For the first time they gave statutory recognition to an option that had previously been used on an informal basis by widows and heirs-at-law: the replacement of dower in real property with a cash payment to the widow of one-third the value of her husband's estate.[28]

Under the prerevolutionary dower statute in South Carolina, a widow received one-third the value of her husband's lands. In some cases she acquired an actual percentage of his total holdings and in others she received lands that produced one-third the profits of the whole estate. John Rogers' wife, for example, was granted lands that were estimated to yield a third of his total annual production. When Rogers died, he owned three tracts of land, "Two hundred and Fifty Acres near the Wexsawa, Two hundred and fifty Acres on Sawney Creek and Five hundred Acres on the High Hills." His heir gave one of the smaller tracts to the widow and she accepted it "tho not the Number of Acres equal in Quantity to the Third of the Whole" because it appeared to her an equal share of the total value of the lands.[29]

This was the best and easiest way to admeasure Mrs. Rogers' dower. But such a simple solution did not present itself in every case. Sometimes a man owned several totally disproportionate parcels of land and it was impossible to assign a woman only one of them. This was the case for Mary Pawley Rollins, whose husband owned neighboring tracts of 80, 809, and 163 acres.[30] Here the commissioners in dower divided each individual tract into thirds and gave the widow one part of each. It was a fair division, but a complicated and time-consuming one for the courts. In addition, women found it difficult, if not impossible, to support themselves from the proceeds of small sections of various tracts of land. For this reason they may have preferred a cash provision in lieu of dower and perceived the legal change as a liberating one.[31]

There is no doubt, however, that the legislature was thinking beyond the question of widows' rights when they gave statutory recognition to this procedure. They were also considering the rights of creditors, whose interest in lands was damaged by the encumbrance of a widow's life estate. It appears that after the Revolution the growing commercial emphasis of South Carolina favored creditors over widows in land disputes. A woman who desired to retain ownership of a portion of her husband's real property increasingly found herself overruled when creditors also established claims to the estate. In fact, by 1791 widows were effectively denied traditional dower rights in all cases involving creditors.

In the case of *John Scott's Creditors* v. *Sarah Scott* (1795) the estabment of a new dower policy in South Carolina can be seen. Here the commissioners named in a writ of dower assigned the widow a lot on Broad Street in Charleston with its house and store, a lot on East Bay Street with its appurtenances, the family pew in Saint Philip's Church, and a house with outbuildings in the village of Greenwich as her share of her husband's property holdings. It was a division similar to that made for the wife of John Rogers, but in this case the interests of creditors caused the court to disallow the assignment. They claimed that the commissioners had assigned the most valuable lots in the estate to Mrs. Scott as dower. The value of the whole, they reported, was "much impaired" and rendered "unsaleable" by the nature of the distribution, and their rights in the property were consequently endangered.[32]

Mr. Pinckney, counsellor for the creditors, claimed "that the commissioners ought to have assigned the dower out of each tract, and not to have taken *the most valuable part of the estate,* and given that in lieu of the whole." He demanded that dower be assigned in one of two other manners: as a third part of each piece of property comprising the estate, or a third of the value in cash "if they found the other to be inconvenient." He pointed out that South Carolina's custom of allowing dower in whole tracts of land was not supported by the common law unless all parties, including creditors, consented. Otherwise dower was assignable by "metes and bounds" only, that is, as one-third of each individual piece of land.[33]

The court recognized Pinckney's arguments, and as a result Mrs. Scott was forced to accept a cash sum in lieu of her dower share in the real estate. Freed from the encumbrance of a life estate interest, the various parcels of land could now easily be sold for the benefit of Mr. Scott's creditors. In his discussion of the issue, Judge Rutledge noted that it was a peculiar situation of South Carolina that fortunes were easily damaged by the division of plantations. In his opinion the assembly had confirmed the right of commissioners in dower to assign widows cash sums "not to vary the right of dower, but to institute a more easy and certain mode of obtaining it."[34]

The case of *Scott's Creditors* v. *Scott* formed a precedent for similar cases in the early nineteenth century.[35] After 1791, when an estate was insolvent and the creditors pressed their demands, a South Carolina widow was not entitled to hold undivided pieces of family property. The type of dower assignment accorded to Mrs. Rogers was possible only when an estate was clear of debts and when the heir or heirs agreed to such an arrangement. Otherwise, the widow took a third share in each part of the estate or a cash sum in lieu of dower.

It is difficult to determine how women perceived this shift in the law of dower. Some may have preferred their traditional settlement and saw this development as a regression in their legal rights. But at least one benefit was recognized by all: the provision for absolute ownership. Even when an estate was totally insolvent, the wife and her heirs retained part of its value forever. They no longer held it during the life of the widow only, as they had under dower estates. This change in the law created a new atmosphere of self-respect for the wives of debtors by removing the stigma of charity from women who relied on dower as their only means of financial support. What they possessed was now their own, to manage and devise as they pleased, free from restrictions against waste or alienation.

This development in the law reflects a recognition of widows' rights to possess their own estates. While there is no evidence that the Revolution had a direct effect on these attitudes, it is clear that postrevolutionary courts felt a strong obligation to promote the interests of widows. This is demonstrated by another change in inheritance law, the abolition of the rights of primogeniture.

At the Constitutional Convention of 1790, South Carolinians moved to end an ancient English custom that controlled the distribution of intestate estates. By prerevolutionary law, when a man died without making a will, the bulk of his property descended to his eldest son rather than to all of his children equally. For the men of the revolutionary generation this custom smacked of royalism. After the war they worked quickly to end it. The state Constitution of 1790 directed the legislature "as soon as might be convenient" to pass a law abolishing primogeniture and replacing it with a more "equitable" mode of distribution. The result was an act which admitted the equal rights of all children, regardless of age or sex. It also contained provisions outlining the rights of widows to support from the estates of their deceased husbands.[36]

In line with the 1777 dower law allowing absolute ownership to widows, the 1791 Primogeniture Act gave wives of intestates fee simple rights in real property.[37] The proportion of a woman's share was unchanged—one-third to one-half the real and personal property—but the legislature removed the dower restriction to a life estate. Now what she inherited was her own. Similarly, a husband became entitled to the same share of his intestate wife's estate, when she held property under a marriage settlement. The result of these changes was an increased equality between the spouses with regard to their inheritance rights.

In fact, one of the most significant features of the act was its emphasis on equality. Several provisions worked not only to increase women's property rights but also to reduce the rights of men to control their wives' estates. For example, before the passage of this act a husband could legally claim all of his wife's *choses in action* when she died intestate. The courts assumed that the property was his by virtue of the marital rights. After 1791, however, he was entitled to only one-third. This provision grew out of the new assumption that the property was hers, and it demonstrates a growing recognition of a married woman's right to own property. Justice Nott's opinion on the development is representative of juridical attitudes in the early nineteenth century. He wrote:

> [I] am very well satisfied with the construction which has been given to the act of 1791. The old law which subjected both the person and property of the wife to the absolute dominion of the husband: which even permitted his *flagellis et fustibus acriter verberare uxorem,* was the offspring of a rude and barbarous age. The progress of civilization has tended to ameliorate the condition of women, and to allow even to wives, something like personal identity. I never could see any good reason why they should not retain all their interest in personal as well as real estate. I am sensible of the mischiefs which might result from a divided empire. But the right of property is not necessarily connected with the right of sovereignty. I am disposed, therefore, to protect and preserve the rights of the wife, as far as we can consistent with the rules of law, and the decisions of our courts, provided we do not invade the prerogatives of the husband.[38]

Many South Carolina judges would have added another phrase to the end of Judge Nott's sentence, making it read, "provided we do not invade the prerogatives of the husband or the husband's creditors." For as was noted, even as courts moved to extend women's property rights, they also moved to protect the interests of creditors. A final example will illustrate this point more fully.

According to the words of the Primogeniture Act, a widow was entitled either to her fee simple interest in her husband's lands or to a traditional dower estate. Since a woman could not have both, she chose between the two according to her best interests. In some instances, of course, there was no practical choice involved; this was true for the wives of insolvent debtors. Only dower protected these women from the claims of creditors. If they claimed absolute rights of ownership to family property, it could be seized to pay debts.

It did not take long for problems to arise regarding this policy. At times a woman chose her fee simple interest under the 1791 statute because she assumed her husband had died in solvent circumstances. When it later appeared that his estate was not solvent, and that the property a widow held as her own was now made liable for unpaid debts, the courts were faced with a delicate problem. What property could they subject to the creditors' demands?

The courts never questioned a widow's right to support from some part of her husband's estate. Thus they developed a procedure of substitution for cases such as these. If a woman's income were threatened or destroyed by an honest error in judgment, the courts did not hold her to that damaging decision. They recognized her right to reapply for a dower share, even years after the original settlement was made.[39]

It is significant to note that courts did not enforce the obverse principle to this policy. That is, a woman who chose dower under the assumption that her husband's estate was insolvent could not later reverse her decision if the debts proved to be smaller than she had supposed. She was forced to rely on a life estate interest only.

This policy appears inconsistent with the courts' attitudes toward widows. It denied to a certain class of women the major benefit of the Primogeniture Act. But it actually did follow the contemporary judicial thoughts on dower. Widows were still guaranteed a share in their husband's estates, and although they did not acquire as much property as they would have under a different assignment, contemporary judges believed that they were receiving fair treatment. Lawmakers viewed a small difference in property values as a minor problem, granted the assumption that women still enjoyed their share in family property under traditional dower law. In other words, women were protected, and the judges could claim that they had done their duty. For in the words of Judge Brackenridge of the Pennsylvania Supreme Court, the law favored three things: life, liberty, and dower.[40] Although South Carolina women had years to wait for full rights to own property, at the end of the eighteenth century their needs were beginning to be recognized and supported as fully as contemporary attitudes would allow.

Divorce

In the decade before the American Revolution, several colonies passed private divorce bills that were subsequently disallowed by the English Privy

Council.[41] English policy opposed the dissolution of marriages during this period, although the rich could sometimes procure divorces from Parliament by private bill. The Privy Council maintained that colonists, like other English citizens, should apply to Parliament for their divorces, and in 1773 colonial governors received instructions from the king to that effect. They were not to approve the bills of divorce that colonial assemblies passed.[42]

As a result of this order, divorces stopped in colonies such as Pennsylvania and New York before the Revolution. Immediately afterward, they were resumed; Pennsylvania passed a divorce statute in 1785 and New York in 1787. Maryland allowed its first absolute divorce (*divortium a vinculo matrimonii*) in 1790.[43] Clearly the new freedom from English precedents produced a significant change in this area of the law for many jurisdictions.

This, however, was not the case in South Carolina, which retained its conservative attitude toward divorce for another hundred and fifty years.[44] In 1848 Chancellor Durgan wrote proudly, "The policy of this state has ever been against divorces. It is one of her boasts that no divorce has ever been granted in South Carolina."[45] But while absolute divorces were unheard of in South Carolina, courts of chancery did grant separations from bed and board (*divortium a mensa et thoro*) to women whose husbands treated them with physical cruelty. This was not a postrevolutionary development—the first such case occurred in 1726, and others appear throughout the colonial period.[46]

Although each state handled divorce differently, similar attitudes governed the administration of the law in all jurisdictions. They all claimed to abhor divorce and to grant separations only as a last resort, "to prevent the open contamination of the morals of society."[47] Such contamination occurred either when a couple was totally unfit to cohabit, or when they abused each other physically, or committed unforgivable crimes such as adultery or desertion. In many court opinions, the judges grappled with the question of degree—what conduct was abusive enough to warrant a separation; alternatively, what was a spouse expected to tolerate? Judge Nott defined the degree of cruelty necessary for a separation in his state in the case of *Rhame* v. *Rhame,* tried in 1826. He wrote that the danger of "life, limb, or health" was usually given as the ground on which the court granted divorces from bed and board. "What merely wounds the mortal feelings," he continued, "is, in few cases, to be admitted, where they are not accompanied with bodily injury, either actual or menaced."[48]

South Carolina courts of law in the early nineteenth century were solicitous of the physical safety of married women. They understood the dangers of their dependent state and sought to protect them from the worst of its consequences. Women who could prove ill treatment at the hands of their husbands received separation decrees from the courts, and alimony rights, providing their own conduct was blameless. For the paternalism of the courts extended only to innocent women. A wife who provoked or encouraged her husband's abuses was not considered to be worthy of the court's concern. Again, there is evidence of debate over the kind or degree of provocation that a woman was permitted to display. Surely, some judges argued, a woman could not continually remain passive against threats and blows. At times her temper must show itself.

In *Taylor* v. *Taylor* (1811) there was evidence that Mrs. Taylor scolded her husband and disobeyed him when he ordered her not to visit her relations.[49] They quarreled frequently, and witnesses testified that their arguments were instigated by her as well as by him. But in spite of these infractions against the rules of proper conduct, the court supported Mrs. Taylor when she petitioned for a separation. The judges' opinion noted, "The dragging of her up stairs by the hair of her head, and imprisoning her all night; the flinging a knife and fork across the table at her, and knocking her down with a stool before his own father, have all been fully proved, and are instances of outrageous conduct, seldom witnessed in civilized society. That she was at fault is not sufficient excuse."[50]

Margaret Gilliam was not as fortunate as Mrs. Taylor in eliciting the assistance of the South Carolina Chancery Court. Although the judges admitted that Mr. Gilliam's behavior was "beyond description exceptionable," they did not order a separation because there was clear evidence that Mrs. Gilliam had provoked his abuses. Rather than comporting herself as a meek and properly obedient wife, she encouraged his fits of temper in the hopes of eventually procuring a separation. Such evidence of design the court would not tolerate. In spite of the fact that she was the object of physical abuse, Margaret Gilliam was ordered to return to her husband, or find some way of supporting herself without him.[51]

Although the end of British rule in South Carolina did not produce a radical change in divorce policy, changing attitudes toward women and the family in the early nineteenth century did promote an important legal development. Beginning in 1809 women who received separation decrees from the courts were also sometimes granted custody over their young children. This was an unknown privilege in the colonial period. The change indicates a shift in attitudes toward familial relationships, a new desire to leave children in the care of their mothers against the wishes of fathers. It demonstrates the growing importance that was placed on motherhood as the ideal feminine role; from roughly the turn of the century, women were acknowledged to be the more important influence over the development of their children.

In South Carolina the first child custody case that favored a woman occurred in 1809.[52] Jennet Prather petitioned the Chancery Court for a separation from her husband, asking as well for custody of their five children on the grounds that her husband, whom she charged with gross abuse, was incompetent to care for them. The court awarded her a separation with alimony, for there was no question about the ill treatment she received from William Prather. But the question of child custody was a difficult one. The court noted that witnesses produced no evidence to indicate child abuse. Without such evidence, the father must be recognized as the natural and proper guardian of his children's welfare.

The judges determined that they could not give Jennet her children to care for; they must remain with William, with one signficant exception. For the first time in South Carolina a court ignored the traditional rights of a father and gave a woman custody over her infant daughter. Although the chancellors perceived their decision as an innovation, stating that they were treading "new and dangerous" ground, they could not remove a baby from the care and comfort of its mother. And as for the four older children, the court voiced in strong terms a mother's right to visit them: "The mother has her right also. She has a right to the comfort of her children's society occasionally; and the Court will protect her in the enjoyment of it." They ordered William to permit his wife to see her children "at all reasonable times," and to allow them to visit her occasionally.[53]

Other, later cases in South Carolina confirmed the rights of women to custody of their children. In *Williams* v. *Williams* (1811) the court appointed a mother guardian of her three daughters when she proved that their father had brought his mistress into the house to live with them. It is interesting to note that the sons in this case remained with their father, and although the judges did not give a reason for their decision to keep them at home, the move is clearly indicative of a double standard of sexual morality.[54]

In *Threewits* v. *Threewits* (1815) the Chancery Court also granted a mother's request for the guardianship of her youngest children. Once more an older son remained with the father. He was no longer of such a "tender age" as to need the ministrations of a mother, although the court stipulated that she was to have access to the child whenever he was ill.[55]

The recognition by Chancery Court of a mother's right to her children was a significant advance for South Carolina women. It coincided with a growing emphasis on a domestic sphere for women. If the domestic was to be defined as the female domain, society had to acknowledge women's right to rule within it. Those rights included child custody, and there is no doubt that women regarded it as one of their most significant victories over male supremacy in the first half of the nineteenth century. As Catherine Beecher and other women's leaders noted, there were important advantages to a separation of the sexual spheres, and, for women, this was one of them.

Femes coverts in South Carolina were not as fortunate in other aspects of their state's divorce code. Conservatism reigned on the issue until the twentieth century, a fact which demonstrates the strict adherence of this southern state to its doctrine of paternalism. Echoing the needs of society, judges wanted docile, home-oriented women who suffered the ill humor of their spouses in silence and sought separations only as a last resort, to protect themselves from physical abuse. Ideal women accepted the domestic sphere as the only proper and fulfilling one for them, leaving the wider world of finance and business to their independent, aggressive husbands.[56]

The evidence in this essay shows that the end of British rule in America produced no immediate change in legal perceptions of women. Some developments indicate new differences between English and American practice—the recognition of divorce in some jurisdictions or the enforcement of private examinations in *feme covert* land conveyances—but conservative attitudes governed even these advances. The aim of the law in South Carolina was to protect women from the dangers of the doctrine of marital unity. There was no commensurate movement to revise the doctrine or to release women from their dependence upon the common law. This is demonstrated by even the most radical of South Carolina postrevolutionary legal changes, the abolition of the rights of primogeniture and the accordance of fee simple inheritance rights to widows. The advance was an important one, but it was circumscribed by courtroom interpretations of the statute that favored creditors' rights over those of widows. Thus, the law in the early national period was beginning to recognize women's rights to property, but its progress was halting and labored. The motives behind these changes were unclear. But in the South they seem to have stemmed from a desire to maintain female dependency more than from a new democratic impulse to promote sexual equality.

It is tempting to compare Southern judicial attitudes toward *femes coverts* with those held toward slaves, for in both cases the judges were concerned primarily with protection. Of course, Southern white women were the objects of much greater solicitude than were black slaves, but the tone of judicial decisions in cases involving women and blacks is often strikingly similar. For instance, Judge Nott wrote that courts should protect the rights of wives so long as they did not "invade the prerogatives of the husband." In *State* v. *Negro Will* (1834) a North Carolina slave heard his attorney make a similar argument in his behalf:

> [Courts] have of late frequently announced from the bench, the progression of humanity in the relation, and the clear conviction, that the condition of the slave was rapidly advancing in amelioration, under the benign influence of Christian precepts and the benevolent auspices of improving civilization. . . . In a popular government, we can nowhere look for more correct information of the state of the public mind, upon a subject deeply interesting to the people at large, than in their laws. The history of the legislation of the State for the last century on this subject, during which more than a dozen principle acts have been passed at intervals, is a history of the gradual progression in the improvement of the condition of the slave, in the protection of his person, his comforts, and those rights not necessary to be surrendered to his master.[57]

For both the white woman and the black slave, Southern paternalism served similar ends. It promoted their subservience while soothing the consciences of white men. For both women and slaves, paternalism faded with the century, although its vestiges are still apparent in our modern lives.

Notes

1. For a full discussion of this issue see Perry Miller, *The Life of the Mind in America* (New York, 1965), pp. 127–130.

2. For a previous attempt by this writer to define the husband/wife relationship under colonial American law in the case of Pennsylvania, see "Equality or Submersion? *Feme Covert* Status in Early Pennsylvania," in Carol Ruth Berkin and Mary Beth Norton, eds., *Women of America: A History* (Boston, 1979), 92–113. For the traditional interpretation that colonial women were favored by the law, see Richard B. Morris, *Studies in the History of American Law* (Philadelphia, 1959).

3. Under the Anglo/American legal system of this period, everything that a woman possessed before marriage automatically became her husband's afterward. The law favored a policy of marital unity which called for the couple's joint ownership of family property, management rights belonging to the husband. This policy was obviously a dangerous one for women whose husbands were poor businessmen, dishonest, or unfaithful. Under a branch of the law termed equity, some women were able to protect themselves from the hardships of property law. A woman placed her own estate in the hands of trustees who held the lands, etc., for her benefit, paying to her the rents of the real estate or the profits from investments.

4. *Ward* v. *Wilson et al.,* 1 Desaussure 405–406 (South Carolina, 1794).

5. Salmon, "Equality or Submersion?" 98–101; Tapping Reeve, *Domestic Relations* (New Haven, 1816), 162–163; see also e.g., *Bethune* v. *Beresford,* 1 Desaussure 174–183 (South Carolina, 1790); *Givens* v. *Branford,* 2 McCord's Law Reports 152–157 (South Carolina, 1822).

6. We can safely assume that if Loyalist women were allowed to retain property under marriage settlements, patriot women would have enjoyed equal or greater property rights. Thus my use of cases involving Loyalist women demonstrates the minimal protections that the law offered to women of the revolutionary generation.

7. "An Act for disposing of certain Estates, and banishing certain persons, therein mentioned," Thomas Cooper, ed., *The Statutes at Large of South Carolina* IV (Columbia, South Carolina, 1838), 516–523.

8. *Bull* v. *Bull* (October 1, 1788), Charleston District, Court of Equity, Case Papers, in the South Carolina State Archives, Columbia.

9. Ibid.

10. *Wilson* v. *Wilson,* 1 Desaussure 235 (South Carolina, 1791).

11. Ibid., 234.

12. Ibid., 236.

13. A man who had a child born alive of his wife became "tenant by the curtesy of England" and gained strong rights to her real property. He was entitled to the rents and profits of the state, and was free to manage the property as he pleased during his life. When he died, the property descended automatically to the child or children of the marriage. These rights were accorded to the husband as guardian of his child. The law assumed that he would protect the property and manage it well for the heir's benefit.

14. Throughout this period wives joined their husbands in all land conveyances. At the time of executing the deed, a circuit court judge or justice of the peace took the women aside and questioned her privately about her true wishes regarding the sale or mortgage. The law required this examination on the assumption that a man could be coercing his wife into a transaction that she opposed.

15. *Ewing* v. *Smith,* 3 Desaussure 417–465 (South Carolina, 1811).

16. Reeve, *Domestic Relations,* 108–115.

17. *Ewing* v. *Smith,* 446–450.

18. Ibid., 455–462.

19. Ibid., 459.

20. *Tiernan* v. *Poor,* 1 Gill and Johnson 216–230 (Maryland, 1829).

21. Ibid., 229.

22. For an excellent discussion of the beginnings of law reform in regard to married women's property in New York, see Peggy Rabkin, "The Origins of Law Reform: The Social Significance of the Nineteenth-Century Codification Movement and its Contribution to the Passage of the Early Married Women's Property Acts," *Buffalo Law Review* 24 (1974–75), 683–760.

23. Under the common law, a widow's dower share consisted of one-third the value of all the real property that her deceased husband had possessed during the marriage. He could not defeat the dower right by selling the property during his lifetime, for unless a woman joined in the conveyance and renounced her rights in the property, she could claim dower in it at the death of her husband. Dower consisted of a life interest only. That is, the widow could use and enjoy the property during her lifetime but it descended to her husband's heirs at her death. She could not sell, mortgage, or devise the estate, nor could she commit waste upon it during her life tenure (i.e., work mines, sell timber, or otherwise reduce the value of the lands). Dower was designed as a means of support for widows; it did not give them economic freedom.

24. *Mongin and Wife* v. *Baker and Stevens,* 1 Bay's Reports 73–80 (South Carolina, 1789); *Wells* v. *Martin,* 2 Bay's Reports 20–23 (South Carolina, 1796).

25. *In Graff* v. *Smith's Administrators,* 1 Dallas 484 (Pennsylvania, 1789), Judge Shippen noted that the right of a woman to dower was "so sacred a right that no judgment, recognizance, mortgage or incumbrance whatever, made by the husband after the marriage, can at common law affect her right of dower: even the king's debt cannot affect her."

26. *Mongin and Wife* v. *Baker and Stevens,* 80.

27. *Wells* v. *Martin,* 22.

28. In section one of the act, it is ordered that commissioners in dower are to assess for the widow her third share in her deceased husband's estate, "Provided always, that the said commissioners shall have power, and they are hereby authorized, in the admeasurement aforesaid, to have relation and regard to the true value of the lands in question; and when the same cannot be fairly and equally divided, without manifest disadvantage, then to assess a certain sum in money, in lieu of dower, to be paid by the heir at law." Cooper, ed., *The Statutes at Large,* IV, 385–387. The legislature revised this statute in 1786, and creditors became liable with heirs at law for the widow's dower: "And where the same cannot in the opinion of a majority of them [the commissioners], be fairly and equally divided, without manifest disadvantage, then they, or a majority of them, as aforesaid, shall assess a sum of money to be paid to the widow in lieu of her dower by the heir at law, or such other person or persons who may be in possession of the said land." "An Act for the more easy and expeditious obtaining the admeasurement of Dower to Widows, of the Lands of which their deceased husbands were seized in fee at any time during their Marriage," Cooper, *Statutes,* IV, 742–743.

29. Elizabeth Woodroof Petition, 1784, Petitions and Writs for Dower, Charleston District, in the South Carolina State Archives, Columbia. I would like to thank Charles H. Lesser for alerting me to this source and allowing me to use the records before processing was completed.

30. Mary Pawley Rollins Petition, 1778, Petitions and Writs for Dower, Temporary Box 2, South Carolina State Archives, Columbia.

31. For an interesting discussion of the problems widows encountered in supporting themselves out of dower estates see Alexander Keyssar, "Widowhood in Eighteenth-Century

Massachusetts: A Problem in the History of the Family," *Perspectives in American History,* 8 (1974), 83–119.

32.   *Creditors of Scott* v. *Scott,* 1 Bay's Reports 504–509 (South Carolina, 1795). See also Sarah Scott Petition, 1791, Petitions and Writs for Dower, Charleston District, in the South Carolina State Archives, Columbia. The schedule was a complicated one and demonstrates why Mrs. Scott did not receive a third of each piece of her husband's land. In time the courts came to realize that they were being overly generous to widows in making the one-third provision. They then began to assess dower shares according to the interest values of the property rather than according to its full purchase value. This meant that a 75-year-old widow received a smaller dower share than a 30-year-old. See *Heyward* v. *Cuthbert,* 2 Brevard's Law Reports 482–488 (South Carolina, 1814); *Williams' Case,* 3 Bland 264–283 (Maryland, 1827).

33.   *Creditors of Scott* v. *Scott,* 504–505.

34.   Ibid., 507.

35.   Out of 92 existing petitions for dower submitted to the Charleston County Court of Common Pleas between 1783 and 1834, 82 resulted in a judgment giving widows one-third the value of their husband's estates in cash. Ten women received one-third the acreage of their husbands' property.

36.   "An Act for the abolition of the Rights of Primogeniture, and for giving an equitable distribution of the Real Estate of Intestates; and for other purposes therein mentioned," Cooper, ed., *The Statutes at Large,* V, 162–164. For a discussion of the legislature's motives in passing this statute see *Means* v. *Evans,* 4 Desaussure 247 (South Carolina, 1812).

37.   Cooper, ed., *Statutes at Large,* V, 162–164.

38.   *Sturgineger et al.* v. *Hannal et al.,* 2 Nott and McCord's Law and Equity Reports 148–149 (South Carolina, 1819).

39.   See the Chancery Court decision in *Snelgrove* v. *Snelgrove,* 4 Desaussure 292–303 (South Carolina, 1812), and *Quarles* v. *Garrett,* 4 Desaussure 145–148 (South Carolina, 1810).

40.   *Kirk* v. *Dean,* 2 Binney 355 (Pennsylvania, 1810).

41.   See Nancy F. Cott, "Divorce and the Changing Status of Women in Eighteenth-Century Massachusetts," *William and Mary Quarterly,* 33 (1976), 591, and sources there cited.

42.   Leonard Woods Labaree, ed., *Royal Instructions to British Colonial Governors, 1670–1776,* I (New York and London: D. Appleton-Century, 1935), 154–155.

43.   "An Act concerning divorces and alimony," *Laws of the Commonwealth of Pennsylvania,* I (Philadelphia, 1810), 343–349; "An Act directing a Mode of Trial, and allowing of Divorces in Cases of Adultery," *Laws of the State of New York,* I (New York, 1792), 428–429; "An Act for annulling the marriage of John Sewell, of Talbot County, and Eve his wife," William Kilty, ed., *The Laws of Maryland,* II (Annapolis, 1799), n.p.

44.   Paul H. Jacobson, *American Marriage and Divorce* (New York: Rinehart, 1959), 109–112; J. D. Sumner, Jr., "The South Carolina Divorce Act of 1949," *South Carolina Law Quarterly* 3 (March, 1951), 253–302.

45.   *Hair* v. *Hair,* 10 Richardson's Equity Reports 174 (South Carolina, 1858).

46.   Anne King Gregorie, *Records of the Court of Chancery of South Carolina, 1671–1779* (Washington, D.C., 1950), 328, 330, 360, 381–382.

47.   2 Bland 561 (Maryland, 1818).

48.   *Rhame* v. *Rhame,* 1 McCord's Chancery Reports 205–206 (South Carolina, 1826).

49.   *Taylor* v. *Taylor,* 4 Desaussure 167–174 (South Carolina, 1811).

50.   Ibid., 174.

51.   *Gilliam* v. *Gilliam* (1812), Washington District Equity Court Decrees 1807–1821, 51, in the South Carolina State Archives, Columbia.

52. *Prather* v. *Prather,* 4 Desaussure (South Carolina, 1809).

53. Ibid., 39, 44.

54. *Williams* v. *Williams,* 4 Desaussure 183 (South Carolina, 1811).

55. *Threewits* v. *Threewits,* 4 Desaussure 560–578 (South Carolina, 1815).

56. The age of the child involved was obviously of great concern in these cases. Infants and very young children were more likely than older children to be left under the care of their mothers. See *The Commonwealth* v. *Addicks and Wife,* 5 Binney 520–522 (Pennsylvania, 1813), and *The Commonwealth* v. *Addicks and Lee,* 2 Serjeant and Rawle 174–177 (Pennsylvania, 1815).

57. *State* v. *Negro Will,* 1 Devereux and Battle's Law Reports 142 (South Carolina, 1834).

Suggestions for Further Reading

It is currently difficult for students of early American legal history to locate adequate general studies of their subject. When they do read the available essays and books, they often find them prejudiced by outdated historical perspectives or marred by legal verbiage. Two useful historiographical essays will help students understand the context in which legal history is now being written: Stanley Katz, "Looking Backward: The Early History of American Law," 33 *University of Chicago Law Review* 867 (1966), and Morton Horwitz, "The Conservative Tradition in the Writing of American Legal History," 17 *American Journal of Legal History* 275 (1973).

Lawrence Friedman has produced the only comprehensive history of American law, *A History of American Law* (New York: Simon and Schuster, 1973). For a critical review of Friedman, see M. V. Tushnet, "Perspectives on the Development of American Law," 1977 *Wisconsin Law Review* 81 (1977). Other useful attempts at synthesis include studies of the legal profession such as Maxwell Bloomfield's *American Lawyers in a Changing Society, 1776–1876* (Cambridge, Mass.: Harvard University Press, 1976), and G. Edward White's *The American Judicial Tradition* (New York: Oxford University Press, 1976). Two valuable studies of legal change over time are William Nelson's *Americanization of the Common Law: The Impact of Legal Change on Massachusetts Society, 1760–1830* (Cambridge, Mass.: Harvard University Press, 1975), and Morton Horwitz's *The Transformation of American Law, 1760–1860* (Cambridge, Mass.: Harvard University Press, 1977).

For a better understanding of American law at the time of the Revolution, see Robert Boden, "The Colonial Bar and the American Revolution," 60 *Marquette Law Review* 1 (1976); James Ely, "American Independence and the Law: A Study of Post-Revolutionary South Carolina," 26 *Vanderbilt Law Review* 939 (1973); Stanley Katz, "Republicanism and the Law of Inheritance in the American Revolutionary Era," 76 *Michigan Law Review* 1 (1977); Dennis Nolan, "The Effect of the Revolution on the Bar: The Maryland Experience," 62 *Virginia Law Review* 969 (1976); and Gordon Wood, *The Creation of the American Republic* (New York: W. W. Norton, 1972), especially 259–291.

When students of American history try to find discussions of women under the law they encounter significant problems. Little has been written on women's legal status, especially in the years prior to the beginning of the women's rights movement. Several older studies on the political status of women are still useful, however. See Sophie Drinker, "American Attorneys of Colonial Times," 56 *Maryland Historical Magazine* 335 (1961), and "Votes for Women in Eighteenth-Century New Jersey," 80 *New York Historical Society Proceedings* 31 (1962). On the latter subject see also Mary Philbrook, "Woman's Suffrage in New Jersey prior to 1807," 57 *New Jersey Historical Society Proceedings* 87 (1939), and Eleanor Boatright, "Political and Civil Status of Women in Georgia, 1783–1860," 25 *Georgia Historical Quarterly* 301 (1941).

Women's property rights have been the subject of several discussions. See most recently Marylynn Salmon, "Equality or Submersion? *Feme Covert* Status in Early Pennsylvania," in Carol Ruth Berkin and Mary Beth Norton, eds., *Women of America: A History* (Boston: Houghton Mifflin, 1979). My discussion there is a reinterpretation of older works such as Richard Morris, *Studies in the History of Early American Law* (New York: Columbia University Press, 1930) and Mary Beard, *Woman as Force in History* (New York: Macmillan, 1946). For critiques of Beard, who emphasized equity over the common law in her discussions of women's property rights, see Carl Degler, "*Woman as Force in History* by Mary Beard," 103 *Daedalus* 67 (1974) and Berenice Carroll, "On Mary Beard's *Woman as Force in History:* A Critique," in Berenice Carroll, ed., *Liberating Women's History* (Urbana: University of Illinois Press, 1976), 26. For excellent studies of widows' property rights, see Lois Carr and Lorena Walsh, "The Planter's Wife: The Experience of White Women in Seventeenth-Century Maryland," 34 *William and Mary Quarterly,* 3rd series, 542 (1977) and Alexander Keyssar, "Widowhood in Eighteenth-Century Massachusetts: A Problem in the History of the Family," 8 *Perspectives in American History* 83 (1974). Nineteenth-century changes in property law are discussed by Peggy Rabkin in "The Origins of Law Reform: The Social Significance of the Nineteenth-Century Codification Movement and Its Contribution to the Passage of the Early Married Women's Property Acts," 24 *Buffalo Law Review* 683 (1974). An older but still provocative essay is Joseph Warren, "Husband's Right to Wife's Services," 38 *Harvard Law Review* 421 (1925).

Perhaps more has been written on the history of divorce than on any other area of the law affecting women. In two excellent articles Nancy Cott has outlined the early divorce code of Massachusetts: "Divorce and the Changing Status of Women in Eighteenth-Century Massachusetts," 33 *William and Mary Quarterly*, 3rd series, 596 (1976), and "Eighteenth-Century Family and Social Life Revealed in Massachusetts Divorce Records," 10 *Journal of Social History* 20 (1976). On Connecticut divorce see Henry Cohn, "Connecticut's Divorce Mechanism: 1636–1969," 14 *American Journal of Legal History* 35 (1970), and for New York, Matteo Spaletta, "Divorce in Colonial New York," 39 *New York Historical Quarterly* 422 (1955). There are two studies of Pennsylvania divorce: William Riddell, "Legislative Divorce in Colonial Pennsylvania," 57 *Pennsylvania Magazine of History and Biography* 175 (1933); and Thomas Meehan, " 'Not Made Out of Levity': Evolution of Divorce in Early Pennsylvania," 92 *Pennsylvania Magazine of History and Biography* 441 (1968).

Several contemporary works on women's rights are generally available to students of legal history and serve as valuable guidelines to juridical attitudes. See in particular Tapping Reeve, *Law of Baron and Feme* (New Haven: Oliver Steele, 1816), Zephaniah Swift, *A System of Laws for the State of Connecticut* (New Haven: Thomas and Samuel Green, 1796), and James Kent, *Commentaries on American Law*, Vol. 2 (New York: O. Halsted, 1826).

5/Old Wine in New Bottles: The Institutional Changes for Women of the People During the French Revolution

Mary Durham Johnson

The Napoleonic state that emerged from the French Revolution reasserted the patriarchal values that had existed for centuries in French society. For women the institutional changes of the revolutionary decade were more apparent than real. Throughout the numerous political upheavals and changing revolutionary institutions, the definition of women's roles remained as it had been in the *Ancien Régime*. Napoleon's reforms regarding women did not distort the French heritage but provided a more efficient means for controlling women's behavior than preceding regimes had ever accomplished. This can be seen by tracing the institutions most responsible for defining the place of the common women of Paris.

The *femmes du peuple* occupied the lowest strata in the society of pre-revolutionary Paris. This had always been their place in the hierarchical social structure and in the patriarchal culture of Bourbon France. The *femmes* represented many social groups, from female relatives of petit bourgeois shopkeepers to destitute spinsters and widows living on alms. The privileged and wealthy order of the *Ancien Régime* tended to disregard these gradations of status; they referred to common Parisiennes as the *canaille,* or riffraff, and they believed it was fitting and natural for such social scum to remain subservient and respectful of their social superiors. Even men of the lower orders thought it improper for their female counterparts to act independently, and they exercised psychological and physical restraints to remind women of "their place." Not uncommonly, small artisans and wage earners abused their wives after frustrating workdays or drinking bouts in the local wineshops. Enterprising merchants were known to make handsome profits by charging male clients for the chance to peek at the most intimate parts of young women on display in their boutiques.[1] Common soldiers, male domestic servants, and unmarried journeymen made sport of domestic servant girls and female apprentices, rarely bothering to assume financial and legal obligations toward women who became pregnant.[2] Engravings of street life in eighteenth-century Paris graphically sum up the demeaned lot of the common women: marketwomen sit amid the filth of cluttered courtyards; along the bridges coachmen knock down female pedestrians without even stopping to help their victims; and in the cheap cabarets women are intoxicating themselves to forget the monotony of their lives.[3]

A variety of economic realities in prerevolutionary Paris narrowed women's opportunities to alter their ascribed roles. Most conspicuous was the sex division of labor that assured men a monopoly of the skilled occupations. Female access to the privileged artisans' corporations was restricted. Several Parisian corporations allowed widows of deceased members to assume their husbands' masterships, but these women did not enjoy the full prerogatives of male members and were often required to work with a male advisor.[4] Journeymen's associations also excluded female members. Although the *"mères"* who kept lodgings for the journeymen received high accolades for their services, the brethren strictly forbade them from participating in their rituals and deliberations.[5] In the late seventeenth century the royal government had attempted to augment women's economic prospects by insuring them a monopoly of the dressmaking and flower-selling corporations, but a reorganization of the corporations in 1776 opened them to membership of both sexes. Thus women had to compete with better-trained men in the traditional male professions as well as in those formerly reserved for women.[6]

The great majority of *femmes* had to seek their livelihood in the less remunerative semiskilled and unskilled occupations. Women predominated in the marketplaces as ambulatory merchants of foodstuffs and of used clothing. They were also prevalent in the textile and luxury industries that catered to the expensive tastes of the bourgeoisie and the aristocracy, and thousands of younger women worked as domestic servants or as actresses and dancers in the booming entertainment industry of the late eighteenth century.[7] Most women workers labored either at home or in small shops, but by the latter half of the eighteenth century a few thousand of them filled the unskilled positions in larger establishments with more than fifty employees. Wages for women were typically half of what men in similar occupations earned; those who worked on piecework rates at home or in small ateliers scarcely made enough for their daily needs.[8] Female peddlers faced keen competition from their male counterparts, who were not only physically stronger but were also better organized to exact favors from royal inspectors supervising the marketplace.[9]

A corollary to the sexual division of labor was the fact that women's economic survival depended to a considerable extent on male relatives or employers and "friends" in the upper social orders. Petites bourgeoises often assisted in family boutiques; those operating their own shops or rooming houses were usually widows who were carrying on family concerns. Wives of journeymen and wage earners supplemented family incomes with part-time work as hawkers or seamstresses and occasionally by prostitution, but they did not earn enough to maintain themselves, let alone any dependents. Unmarried women employed as apprentices or domestic servants frequently had to resort to prostitution, since the slightest disagreement with employers could result in dismissal.[10] Indigent women relied on public or private charity dispensed by royal officials, by the religious orders, and by philanthropic organization. Only a fractional minority of Parisiennes achieved a modicum of economic independence. These included the skilled seamstresses and dressmakers who ran their own ateliers, successful artists, and marketwomen with their own stalls.[11]

Occupational rivalries also circumscribed women's economic horizons. Women affiliated with corporations bitterly resented their sisters in the free labor market who tried to encroach on their commerce.[12] Female stallkeepers distrusted female domestic servants, since it was widely assumed that domestics associated with the criminal underworld. Most intense were the struggles among female hawkers who constantly vied with one another over places to dispense their wares.[13] Internal dissensions such as these made it difficult for women to unite in protest against their marginal situation.

The only issue that the *femmes* could agree on was that they needed to be able to have bread at reasonable prices. When there were poor harvests, a proverbial fear among Parisiennes was that a conspiracy of aristocrats and brigands would cut off the city grain and flour supplies, exposing the people to misery and death.[14] Hence the slightest rumor of bread shortages in the markets could foment disorder on bread lines and discontent with bakers unable to serve their clientele. In times of prolonged bread shortages during the *Ancien Régime* the *femmes* went directly to the king to demand bread.[15]

Yet the political environment discouraged such militance among women. Finally law in the *Ancien Régime* clearly defined women as legal minors, wards of their fathers and husbands; and the Church, which claimed jurisdiction over marital laws, held firmly that marriage was a sacrament not to be broken by human intervention. Woman's role in the absolutist state was to perform her conjugal duties and to bear healthy children. Quite deliberately the Bourbons promoted this notion among the *femmes du peuple* by bequeathing dowries to indigent young women during royal festivals and by allocating special funds for charities that helped mothers during confinement and breast-feeding.[16]

Parisiennes came into more direct contact with the patriarchal monarchy than their sisters in the provinces. Because Paris was the center of royal justice and the major commercial entrepôt for the realm, monarchs took a personal interest in its government. The monarchs also attempted to regulate Parisian behavior, manners, language, and religious and social mores. The royal institutions which exerted the greatest control over the *femmes du peuple* were the police of Paris, the Parisian courts located in the fortress of the Châtelet, and the public hospitals. The personnel of these institutions were men from the privileged orders who had purchased their posts from the monarchy and had an obvious vested interest in preserving the status quo.

The police authority in prerevolutionary Paris affected all the activities of the common women,[17] its chief being one of the most powerful royal administrators. Assisted by a complex bureaucracy of commissioners, inspectors and secret agents, the lieutenant-general of the Paris police supervised supply and distribution in the markets, arbitration of disputes between artisans' corporations, registration of peddlers and of hoteliers and brothel-keepers, maintenance of public hygiene and lighting, control of vagrancy, mendicants, and prostitution, censorship of printed matter and public language, and recommendation of individuals for admittance to public hospitals and charity workshops. In addition to these comprehensive administrative tasks, the lieutenant-general presided over a court that dealt with minor infractions of public manners such as prostitution and vagrancy.[18]

During the daytime, the greatest amount of contact between police and women occurred in les Halles, the central marketplace of Paris, and in the smaller markets where thousands of marketwomen earned their livelihood and where housewives, female domestics and apprentices, women workers, and dayworkers from the suburbs regularly procured their basic necessities. From the Middle Ages the kings had taken the responsibility of directing commerce in the Parisian markets. In theory, royal justice subscribed to the popular concept of the "just price," which held that goods in the public market, grain and flour for bread in particular, should be sold at their real value and not at inflated prices caused by profiteering.[19] By the eighteenth century, however, the traditional moral economy was disintegrating. Provisioning les Halles with sufficient foodstuffs and raw materials for Parisian trades and manufactures was a large-scale business, and major wholesalers kept their central warehouses there. Les Halles had been enlarged so it spanned much of the space in the central districts; separate market areas for each commodity were being constructed to increase the efficiency of marketplace transactions.[20]

Monitoring the behavior of Parisiennes in the eighteenth-century markets was a particularly arduous chore for the police. The *femmes* felt threatened by the changing market conditions and identified the police as enemies who were placing the interests of profit above the interests of the poor. Omnipresent was the uneasy tension between women who tried to evade the regulations and police who were assigned to maintain order. The police habitually concentrated their inspection on the petty merchants, often women, whose illicit affairs were easier to detect, but they tended to disregard infractions committed by the more sophisticated and influential traders and wholesalers.[21] Irritating to marketwomen and consumers alike was the police repression of complaints about dishonest merchants. In minor squabbles between shopkeepers and women, the police employed verbal reprimands to silence obstinate women; in larger disturbances they did not hesitate to wield their canes and whips to restore peace.

Police ordinances on public health produced additional aggravations. Many of these reforms interfered with marketplace customs and impeded the efforts of marketwomen to earn their living. The police ban on the use of copper vessels for the sale of milk, for example, meant hardship for milkmaids, who traditionally used copper urns; similarly, regulations on the sale of meat and fish often left *tripières* and *poissardes* with excess supplies that had to be sold immediately at much reduced rates.[22] Demolition of the Cemetery of the Innocents, located in les Halles, was the cause célèbre during the decade preceding the Revolution. Founded in the late Middle Ages, by the 1780s it contained the remains of over a million cadavers. After the hygienist Cadet de Vaux reported that foul odors issuing from the grave-yard endangered public health, the lieutenant-general ordered that the Innocents be razed and a flowermarket be erected on the site.[23] Removal of the cemetery dislocated hundreds of marketwomen who had found ready-made stalls in its crenelated walls and hiding places from the police among the charnels and tombs inside its confines. The new flowermarket with its more open and airy spaces benefited the police in marketplace inspection more than the marketwomen, who had to pay to rent umbrellas for use in the market.

Police surveillance of the Parisiennes did not abate at night, when the streets of prerevolutionary Paris were notoriously dangerous; swarms of pick-pockets, criminal gangs, and unruly soldiers and servants mingled with crowds in public places.[24] To preserve the public tranquillity the police com-missioners conducted night patrols in every quarter. Prostitution was a major preoccupation of these patrols. The term prostitute loosely designated any woman who did not appear to have a permanent abode or a respectable occupation. Even if women claimed to be seamstress-workers, actresses, dancers, or domestic servants, the police were likely to presume they were *filles publiques* and treat them accordingly. For centuries kings had tried to eradicate the oldest profession with repeated statutes ordering the incar-ceration or banishment of prostitutes and brothel-keepers, but such regu-lations became impossible to enforce in the eighteenth century, when the prostitute community approximated twenty thousand. From the mid-eigh-teenth century the general tendency among police commissioners had been to acknowledge prostitution as a necessary evil and try to regulate it by restricting solicitation to certain redlight zones and ordering the *filles* and their matrons to register with the police.[25] Although registration procedures were inconsistently applied, policing of prostitutes was a potent means for preserving the patriarchal stereotype of women as inherently evil beings.

The magistrates of the Criminal Chamber of the Châtelet handled the majority of offenses committed by commoners of both sexes from Paris and its surrounding suburbs, while the Parlement attended to matters involving persons of higher social standing. Only in rare instances could individuals convicted at the Châtelet appeal its decision before the Parlement, and when such appeals were made, the decision of the Châtelet was usually upheld.

So harsh and arbitrary was Châtelet justice that men and women of the lower orders referred to the fortress of the Châtelet as the people's Bastille. Proceedings of the tribunal took place in great secrecy and were often unfair to the accused. At no time before or during the interrogations was the accused permitted defense counsel, and during and between interrogations the judges reserved the right to prescribe torture as a means of extracting a confession.[26]

Punishments ranged from the severest mode of execution (burning the convict alive before hanging) to its milder forms (breaking the convict's neck prior to exposure on the wheel) as well as permanent or temporary detention. Whatever the sentence, guilty parties of both sexes received the "mark," a letter signifying the nature of the offense which was branded with a hot iron on the right shoulder. Whenever a person was detained at the Châtelet, medical inspectors could thus determine if he was a repeater. Sentences of detention were often preceded by public exposure at the stocks in one of the public squares.[27]

To a limited extent patriarchal values of the *Ancien Régime* shielded the Parisiennes from the full impact of royal justice. An a priori assumption among magistrates was that the second sex lacked either the intelligence or the physical fortitude to perpetrate premeditated acts of violence and complicated fraud. Consequently, only about 20 percent of all cases considered by the Châtelet in the last decades of the *Ancien Régime* involved female suspects. The overwhelming majority (87 percent) of female offenses were classified as petty larceny. Domestic theft from masters, deception in marketplace sales, reception of stolen property, complicity with male pickpockets or criminal gangs, and theft of clothing and household items from neighbors were the most common charges against women. They were rarely accused of premeditated homicides, violent assault, housebreaking, or the use of skeleton keys to commit robberies, typical male crimes in eighteenth-century Paris.[28] The difficulties of verifying the commission of abortion or infanticide (capital offenses) discouraged prosecution of such crimes, and the majority of domestic and cabaret quarrels involving Parisiennes fell under the immediate jurisdiction of the police commissioners.[29] Female reproductive functions also helped to mitigate the effect of Châtelet justice. A pregnant convict could not be executed until the birth of her infant, and such delays could be advantageous in providing time to plan escapes. Also, magistrates never sentenced women to the galleys (a typical sentence for men), but dispatched them to the public hospitals of Salpêtrière to learn honest professions and a disciplined style of life.

Treatment of prisoners at the Châtelet reflected the social and sexual values of the *Ancien Régime.* The same inquisitorial procedure applied to both sexes, but, out of respect for moral propriety, matrons inspected female prisoners for the mark. Penalties for both sexes were often inconsistent with the gravity of the offenses.[30] Theft of an inexpensive item such as a sheet could warrant banishment or the death penalty, while a mere sentence of detention could be awarded a convicted murder. Usually the social status of the victim rather than the sex of the accused determined the severity of punishment: as a general rule of thumb, the higher the social status of the victim, the harsher the verdict. Judges were particularly hard on servants who stole from their masters or who abused children of higher social standing.[31] Female accomplices of criminal gangs and female fences were sentenced as harshly as the principal authors of the crimes if they were uncooperative in divulging information on their male connections.

On the other hand, sentencing patterns for moral offenses revealed that the double standard of morality was embedded in Châtelet justice. Judgments in conjugal murder trials elucidated the sexist biases of the era. Husbands charged with murdering their wives in adultery cases were frequently absolved on grounds that their wives had been unfaithful; wives accused of attempting to poison or strangle their husbands for abusive treatment or neglect normally received death sentences.[32] In the late eighteenth century the double standard was most apparent in verdicts for youthful offenders. Fearing that detention in the galleys condemned young men to a life of crime after their experience among hardened criminals, magistrates tended to render mild decisions in cases of rape or physical assault on women, often prescribing a fine for damages rather than detention.[33] Conversely, judges believed that it was salutary for young prostitutes to spend time at Salpêtrière. Moreover, the eighteenth-century magistrates revived the long discarded custom of sentencing brothel-keepers to the public humiliation of being dragged through the streets on the back of an ass in order to curtail the scourge of prostitution.[34]

Parisian hospitals played as critical a role in preserving public order as did police and magistrates by performing many of the functions entrusted to social welfare agencies in modern states. Administering health care to the poor, caring for orphans and the aged, setting up charity workshops for the able-bodied poor, and distributing alms and free soup in times of social hardship were within their purview. Several dozen small parish hospitals and charities were run by the clergy and by female religious orders. Orphanages for girls, workshops for women, rehabilitation centers for prostitutes, rest homes for elderly widows and breast-feeding mothers dotted the Parisian parishes in the final decades of the *Ancien Régime*. The *femmes* were grateful for these services and felt deep attachments for their local *curés* and *religieuses* who seemed to evince such concern for the plight of the poor.[35] Also beneficial were several private charities supported by philanthropic men and women who wanted the poor to learn ways to help themselves. Of special significance for Parisiennes was the Maternal Charity, which provided help for poor mothers during their confinement and instructed them in breast-feeding and infant care.[36]

Space and equipment in the religious and private institutions only accommodated small numbers of patients, and the governing boards restricted admissions to the "honest poor" of their respective parishes. The public hospitals, Hôtel-Dieu and Salpêtrière, served a much larger sector of the *femmes du peuple*. Hôtel-Dieu, which did not discriminate in admissions against non-Parisians, became the refuge for thousands of Parisian and provincial unwed mothers. These outcasts had no other recourse, for the Maternal Charity required applications to show proof of their legal marriage, a recommendation from their *curé*, and evidence of having breast-fed previous children.[37] The hospital of Salpêtrière doubled as a prison. Most inmates had been committed either by the police, the Châtelet, or families who could not care for them. Female orphans who were raised in the public orphanage until the age of five were automatically transferred to Salpêtrière for vocational and religious instruction until they reached their maturity. In all, by the late eighteenth century there were about 5,600 inmates at Salpêtrière, including five hundred "insane" patients.

In contrast to the local hospitals and charities which sought to inculcate women with the virtues of obedience, passivity, and maternal love, the physical and moral atmosphere of Hôtel-Dieu and Salpêtrière degraded women's views of themselves and left them with such a sense of helplessness that they could not even perceive a better life. The maternity ward of the Hôtel-Dieu, for instance, crowded five or six expectant mothers in the same bed. Unsanitary conditions created frighteningly high rates of maternal and infant mortality. According to Tenon, an attending physician on the ward, approximately 85 percent of the newborns of provincial mothers died in the first month and about 7 percent survived until their fifth year; maternal mortality ran as high as 25 percent.[38] Rates were only slightly better with native Parisiennes who had been spared long uncomfortable journeys prior to their confinement. New mothers typically turned their infants over to the public foundling home since they had no means of keeping them.

There were similarly low standards at Salpêtrière, with no separation of criminals from indigent widows and orphans. The insane merited no special treatment and often incurred abuse from male orderlies and other female inmates. Shrewd prostitutes and pimps used their periods of detention to corrupt the morals of younger inmates so they could not learn a useful occupation in the hospital workshop. Among the criminal population, those without family or friends had no way of knowing how long their incarceration would last.[39]

The triad of police, courts, and hospitals seemed to work sufficiently well at keeping the *femmes* in their place. The regular constabulary was able to localize the majority of marketplace disputes, and during food riots the lieutenant-general could rely on the royal regiments of the French Guards and Swiss Guards to subdue the crowds.[40] But a major defect in the absolutist state was the conflict of jurisdictional claims between aristocracy and Church. Parisian nobles, for instance, had a number of private residences immune from royal jurisdiction where prostitutes and mendicants could seek asylum from the police.[41] The clergy often violated statutes pertaining to parental control of minors. According to royal legislation, minors (females under twenty-five and males under thirty) needed parental permission to marry as a guarantee against mésalliances. The clergy, however, were wont to ignore this law, since they maintained that canon law had complete authority over the marriage sacrament.[42] Clerical control of the registers of births, deaths, and marriages, the *état civil*, also created loopholes that women could use to their advantage. Record-keeping procedures for these documents were not standardized, and it was relatively easy to acquire forged certificates. Thus, for instance, a number of female bigamists went undiscovered for many years because they had used false identities on their marriage licenses.[43] Religious charity, which so many *femmes* appreciated, countered the efforts of the royal administration to compel all able-bodied poor to earn their livelihood in workhouses.

Flaws in the royal institutions themselves furnished women additional opportunities to manipulate the absolutist environment. Since offices were venal, officials wanted to extract as much as possible from their positions. Subordinate police officers were known for taking bribes, and police inspectors granted immunity from supervision to their female marketplace spies who reported marketing infractions and counterfeit operations.[4] At the Châtelet, poor female prisoners could not only ameliorate the physical conditions of their detention by satisfying the jailers' greed with sexual favors, but they could improve their chances for escape by becoming pregnant in the course of their incarceration.[45]

These survival tactics, however, only entrapped women more in their servile status, and their dependency was only accentuated in the months just prior to the outbreak of the Revolution because they were living through the worst famine of the century. Thousands of Parisian poor managed to endure the debacle only by eating at free soup kitchens run by the *religieuses* and by pawning all their meager possessions at the public pawnshop.[46]

The advent of the Revolution in 1789 greatly raised the expectations of the *femmes,* so long relegated to the most precarious and marginal roles in Parisian society. Revolutionary leaders promised to create a society of freedom and equality for all. Having disavowed the theory of Divine Right and the privileged society of absolutist France, they embraced the concept that only laws emanating from the French nation were the sovereign authority. All citizens were to be equally subject to the majesty of the law, which would guarantee each individual's right to private property, freedom, and equal justice.

Paris was at the very heart of the revolutionary enthusiasm, and every district of the city held its assembly to elect delegates to the Estates-General at Versailles. Politics was the paramount topic in markets, workshops, and public squares. In July 1789 the revolutionary bourgeoisie, helped by the people of Paris, wrested their city from royal tutelage and proclaimed an autonomous municipality dedicated to serving the interests of the people rather than those of the privileged orders. The Parisian National Guard, a civic militia of 12,000 volunteer citizens, replaced the apparatus of the royal police, and the office of the lieutenant-general was suppressed. The Parisiennes therefore assumed that they were a part of the new political nation. This proved to be a false assumption.

The October Days of 1789 was the event primarily responsible for bolstering the Parisiennes' optimism about revolutionary promises. After months of near famine, inflated prices, and unemployment, the *femmes* exploded in a spontaneous protest on October 5. Several thousand marketwomen, housewives, and working women marched en masse to Versailles to demand bread from the king and the National Assembly. They were militant and showed little respect for property or the government as they stored into its meeting place chanting "Bread!" and hurling obscenities at the national representatives. The National Guard, which included many former soldiers from the royal French Guards, joined the women's rebellion. On October 6, the *femmes* returned to Paris with wagons filled with grain and with the king's solemn pledge to insure future supplies for Paris. In addition, the royal family and delegates from the National Assembly accompanied the return procession to take up permanent residence in the capital, affording tangible proof for Parisiennes that the royal oath would be honored. The October Women were not summarily arrested and detained at the Châtelet and Salpêtrière but received a heroine's welcome from the municipal dignitaries.[47]

But constitutional crisis rather than women's economics was the key factor determining the outcome of the October Days. Throughout the early autumn, rumors had circulated that the king planned to muster a counterrevolutionary force to dissolve the National Assembly and restore absolutism. Radicals disseminated tracts in the markets informing the people that current economic difficulties were part of a royalist plot to destroy the Revolution and exhorting Parisians to defend their newly won liberties.[48] The women's march merely furnished the occasion for Parisian radicals to pressure the Assembly with their political demands. For Parisian revolutionaries in general, and for the radical movement in particular, the October Days represented a major political triumph. Under the threat of Parisian insurrection, the representatives had voted to enact the first articles of the constitution. Moreover, the installation of the government in Paris enabled Parisians to scrutinize the activities of the Naitonal Assembly and to avert future impediments to the completion of a revolutionary constitution.

The chimera of freedom and equality vanished rapidly for the women. The National Assembly commissioned the Châtelet to conduct a full investigation of the causes of the October uprising and hastily finished the draft of a new penal code which eliminated many of the arbitrary features of royal criminal procedure.[49] However, the revolutionary assembly was not willing to sanction disturbances of the public peace by unruly marketwomen. With bread supplies still unpredictable in the weeks that followed, there were numerous incidents at bakeries, and in late October a mob strung up a baker presumed to be a hoarder. To restore order in the capital, the assembly authorized Lafayette, commander of the National Guard, to take stern measures against troublemakers.[50]

Examination of the political and institutional framework of the municipality in the period of the constitutional monarchy (1789–1792) discloses very few changes for the *femmes du peuple*. Essentially, they exchanged old masters of the aristocracy of birth for those of the aristocracy of wealth. The revolutionary bourgeoisie, men of property, were the "active citizens" entitled to full political privileges and to service in the National Guard; the "passive citizens" were the men of the lower orders, known as the *sans-culottes,* and women of all social stations, who were guaranteed civic but not political rights. The active citizenry elected the municipal officials and the commander of the National Guard; assemblies of each of the administrative wards, called Sections, elected their own local administrative personnel such as commissioners of police, justices of the peace, and clerks.[51]

Patriarchal values remained intact, despite the new faces in the municipal government. The city fathers of all political persuasions viewed the women's part in the October Days as an aberration of nature which had exposed Paris to anarchy. Whether they regarded women as dupes of dissident National Guard elements or of counterrevolutionary agents, their underlying assumption was that women were incapable of taking aggressive action on their own accord. Indeed, during the constitutional monarchy, municipal posters and speeches constantly implored women not to be led astray by subversive individuals. Women were to abstain from public affairs, and they required close supervision by the municipal fathers if the interests of law and order were to be upheld.[52] Police, national workshops, and patriotic societies, which acclimatized Parisiennes to revolutionary laws and mores during these years, all elaborated on women's traditional roles of obedience and dependence.

The police had the most extensive interaction with the *femmes du peuple.* Its prerevolutionary functions had not been substantially revised; however, the reorganization of the new police department was more democratic than before. Elected commissioners supervised policing in their respective Sections. Since the revolutionary police were expected to rely on denunciations from respectable citizens, officers discarded spies and secret agents. Search warrants were required to investigate private residences and written statements of motives had to accompany all arrests.[53] The National Guard carried out the patrol services of the defunct royal gendarmes, and municipal police and correctional tribunals handled minor infractions such as prostitution and vagrancy that had once been within the competence of the lieutenant-general.

Generally speaking, the civic police were milder in dealing with the *femmes* than the royal police had been. The main concern of the police in the constitutional monarchy was to prevent the women from congregating in large spontaneous crowds that could resuscitate the insurgent mood of 1789. Patrols removed women from places where demagogues were advocating a republic to replace the constitutional monarchy and where workers were agitating for their full political rights. Although there were disorders in the markets during late fall of 1789, antagonism between marketwomen and police subsided by early 1790 when marketing conditions stabilized; women on food lines were reportedly orderly through much of the constitutional monarchy. Since the patrols were lenient in pursuing prostitutes and mendicants, friction once engendered by the royal night patrols also dissipated.[54]

Two episodes, however, disillusioned women with the new policing and reawakened many of the hostilities they had felt toward the royal police. The first incident was the demonstration at the Champ de Mars in July 1791, during which thousands of men and women gathered to sign a petition demanding the abolition of the monarchy and the formation of a democratic republic. Women did not initiate the movement, but they participated in a signing ceremony when the National Guard appeared and invoked martial law to break up the crowd. Guards fired on the demonstrators to hasten the dispersion, leaving several hundred men, women, and children dead and wounded.[55] Repression of the Sugar Riots during the winter of 1791–92 was the second incident to diminish the women's confidence in and respect for the revolutionary police. The high prices of sugar and soap triggered an outbreak of riots in which women took over stocks in groceries and shops and dispensed the items equally among themselves at the "just price" determined by the crowd. Numerous scuffles ensued between women and guards, and the riots ended with arrest by the National Guard of several female pillagers along with male apprentices and workers.[56]

The revolutionary promise of public assistance was similarly disappointing to the *femmes*. The revolutionaries envisioned a national system of public assistance to replace the hospitals and charities of the *Ancien Régime*. Rochefoucauld-Liancourt, who chaired the Committee on Medicancy, drafted proposals for a national chain of local clinics, hospitals, and public workshops which would instill in the poor good work habits and a sense of self-worth, as opposed to the lazy habits and feelings of dependence nurtured by the church system of charity and alms.[57] The National Assembly, however, laid these recommendations aside for future consideration. Meanwhile, the *femmes* found themselves more helpless than ever amid the decline of normal services and the disappearance of the *curés* and *religieuses* whom they had relied upon in the *Ancien Régime*. Nationalization of church property and emigration of many former private donors in 1789 had further depleted traditional revenues for the parish and public hospitals. The National Assembly had promised to take over the financial burden of services formerly rendered by the Church, but no concrete plan of reimbursement had matured and the hospitals had to operate on reserve funds.[58]

Personnel problems also interfered with patient care. Priests unwilling to take an oath to the constitution insisted on staying at their posts; the *religieuses* who were permitted to remain engaged in interminable controversies with lay personnel and municipal administrators over their respective functions. Also disrupting normal hospital services was the unprecedented number of unemployed and indigent who sought relief and medical attention. Hôtel-Dieu, with a capacity for 4,800, reported 7,000 patients in 1789, and the smaller hospitals could not keep abreast of the much increased demand for alms and free soup because of declining revenues.[59]

The national workshops opened in Paris in 1790 were the one innovation the revolutionaries introduced to the Parisian welfare system, and the traditional allocation of sex roles was rigidly observed in them. Men's shops were separate from women's shops, and men did outdoor relief work. In the two large women's workshops workers spun yarn and cleaned cloth. Attempts to train workers in new techniques and in the use of machinery miscarried because the women resisted the novel ways and the government found it too expensive to continue these experiments. Wage rates for women were lower than for men.[60] Inside the shops the socialization patterns resembled those in shops formerly under Church auspices. Since municipal administrators considered married women more responsible than single women, they conferred the majority of supervisory posts on married female applicants. The supervisors were indulgent toward nursing mothers and held them up as models for the younger unmarried workers; older workers sharply rebuked their younger colleagues for loose morals, and they did not hesitate to leave the more arduous tasks for the younger women.[61] Not uncommonly, the supervisors employed their favorites in personal domestic work; in some instances, they also took advantage of their posts to augment their own income. If workers protested unfair practices of their supervisors or low wages, the municipality sided with the supervisors and took either economic or penal sanctions against miscreant workers.[62]

The patriotic societies also stressed women's traditional roles. A network of these societies had emerged in the Parisian sections to educate passive citizens of both sexes to their new rights.[63] Men in positions of leadership cautioned female members about the dangers of returning to the religious mores of the past which impaired the success of the new free society. Interestingly enough, the patriotic definition of the ideal woman embodied many of the same feminine attributes that had been emphasized by the state and Church of the *Ancien Régime*. The stereotype of the ideal *patriote* was the loving wife and mother who concentrated on her domestic chores and waited for her husband to return from his public affairs to give him comfort and tranquillity. As the perfect mother, she breast-fed her children, raised them to become law-abiding citizens, and only left her abode to applaud the patriotic deeds of her husband and children. *Patriotes* stood in sharp contrast to the promiscuous aristocratic ladies and courtesans who had corrupted morals in the *Ancien Régime* with their laziness and lack of maternal solicitude.[64]

For the most part, the *femmes du peuple* were content with their traditional roles. In spite of efforts of a group of middle-class women to enlist them in political agitation for a more democratic franchise, the *femmes* did not believe they should take part in the political sphere. Indicative of the political apathy among the common Parisiennes was their response to the democratic campaign of 1791. Male workers in the national workshops became so engrossed in the radical political movement that the municipality decided to close their shops. By contrast, women workers seemed untouched by the attempts of radicals to rally their support. The municipal authorities felt it was safe to leave the women's shops open because it was easier to supervise them there than in the public squares.[65] When the *femmes* did participate in public affairs, it was at the behest of their male relatives; women wanted representation for the *sans-culottes* in the political nation where the social interests of the poor could be pressed.

But women did try to assert their economic interests in times of shortages and inflation. Following the October Days, for example, the widespread unrest among the *femmes* declined significantly as soon as the government was able to insure a regular supply of bread at fixed rates.[66] More surprising was the ease with which the government placated women in the aftermath of the Sugar Riots. The national representative, Louvet, delivered a patriotic appeal for women to emulate their sisters in the American Revolution who had sacrificed luxuries for the public good. In response, the marketwomen rose to give their pledge to be abstinent in the interests of the Revolution and to persuade their children and male relatives to do likewise.[67]

Three factors help explain why the discrepancy between the revolutionary promises and the realities for the *femmes* failed to generate a sustained protest in the years following the October insurrection. First, and perhaps most important, was the relative stability in marketing conditions. Scarcity of bread was the only issue that could unite the *femmes,* as the October Days had so vividly manifested, and for the duration of the constitutional monarchy the government maintained an adequate bread supply at fixed rates so that poorer customers were assured their daily needs. The shortages of soap and sugar most directly affected laundresses who habitually served their workers sugared coffee in the mornings so that they could work all day without a break.[68]

A second factor that contributed to quiescence among the *femmes* was the new government's inefficiency; church reforms are a case in point. In the attempt to nationalize the Church, the government ordered all secular clergy to take an oath to the constitution if they wished to be salaried by the nation; the regular clergy were pensioned and forced to leave their monasteries for secular occupations. On the other hand, the government exempted many of the *religieuses* who worked as nurses and teachers among the poor if they were willing to stay on in their posts. Not until August 1792 were the *religieuses* compelled to pay allegiance to the Constitution and leave their communities. Thus, during most of the constitutional monarchy there were *religieuses* who succeeded in keeping local hospitals and charities open despite the disarray of financing and administration. Another church reform that did not go into effect until the end of the constitutional monarchy was the secularization of the registers of births, deaths, and marriages. While the clergy monopolized control over these records, there were still ways for women to capitalize on the lack of uniform procedures. In fact, a major reason for secularizing the *état civil* was that nonswearing clergy were still performing marriages among the faithful.[69]

The time needed to reorganize the judiciary also softened the impact of revolutionary innovations. Elections for judges in the new network of Parisian tribunals did not occur until the spring of 1791, and the courts were so back-logged with cases that there was a rather lax prosecution of prostitution and vagrancy. Because of overcrowding at Salpêtrière and indiscriminate mixing of youthful offenders with seasoned criminals, there was an effort in 1791–92 to reduce the sentences of first offenders and to release prostitutes who did not have long criminal records.[70] Further, since the municipal administrators did not perceive women as the instigators of social and political turmoil, fewer women than men were prosecuted for involvement in public disorders. The mayor himself pleaded with the magistrates to show mercy for several housewives detained for their part in the Sugar Riots. These women, argued the mayor, had been the victims of subversive forces that had misled them into acts of violence, and they deserved to be restored to their families where they belonged.[71]

Malfunctions in the more democratic police system constituted a third factor that attenuated the effect of the revolutionary reforms. The political cleavages among guards posed perpetual obstacles to law enforcement. The democratically inclined guards disliked taking action against the people. As in the *Ancien Régime,* police and guards focused their attention on the activities of single and unattached women in the more populous districts near les Halles and the chief government buildings. During marketplace disorders, police routinely referred married female troublemakers, especially those with children, to their husbands for reprimands. Throughout the Sugar Riots the government was apprehensive that guards could not be depended upon to break up the crowds. The commander of a battalion in one of the chief troublespots subsequently admitted that he had been reluctant to use coercion against women since he shared their disdain for wholesalers and speculators.[72]

The revolutionary wars hastened the pace of change and broke down the modus vivendi which had existed between the *femmes* and the state in the early Revolution. By 1793 local war between France and Austria had escalated into a much larger confrontation in which France was pitted against a coalition of monarchical states and counterrevolutionary armies. The government requested 300,000 volunteers in February 1793. When recruits were not forthcoming, it prepared to call up by universal conscription half a million men.

Military expediency served as a catalyst for a rapid series of political, social, economic, and cultural reforms, which transformed France into a secular nation-state with a central administration more efficient than preceding administrations of the *Ancien Régime* and the early Revolution. This process did not culminate until the Napoleonic era, but all the necessary reforms were introduced between 1792 and 1795 when the military crisis was most acute for the revolutionary state. The need for reliable patriotic soldiers precipitated the popular uprising of August 10, 1792, which replaced the constitutional monarchy with a republic. The First French Republic granted universal male suffrage and it offered the poorer soldiers and their families a commitment to look after their interests in return for their sacrifices in defense of the nation. Incorporated in the republican Constitution of 1793 were guarantees of the right to work for all able-bodied poor, a national system of free primary school education, and the implementation of a national program of public assistance.

The secular reforms of the Republic were of special significance to women in that they altered the traditional legal status of the second sex. Devotion to the Republic became the official religion, and the Republic swept away the vestiges of traditional Christianity. The state assumed control of the état civil, removing the clergy from competing with secular legislation on family life and social mores, and it intensified the campaign to eliminate the unpatriotic clergy and religieuses from the hospitals. The Republic declared marriage a civil contract and enacted legislation which permitted divorce on an equal basis for both partners, inheritance rights for women and illegitimate children, and the right of youths of both sexes over twenty-one to marry without parental permission.[73] The Republic even softened the stigma against unwed mothers with promises to establish free rest homes for these women with proper medical care and instructions in breast-feeding.[74]

The femmes derived little benefit from their legal emancipation. The years of the first French Republic were trying times for Parisiennes, who were more enslaved than ever by their economic circumstances. Home life underwent dramatic alterations as the enfranchised sans-culottes devoted more time to political and military affairs.[75] The more the government urged these men to proceed to the front lines, the more panicked their women grew. They did not trust the Republic to protect their interests while their principal breadwinners departed for active duty. Government promises of armament workshops to employ needy wives of volunteers in sewing uniforms were slow to materialize.[76] Bread lines lengthened and shortages of market goods left market-women without supplies, while wage earners faced layoffs due to the dearth of raw materials such as soap and hemp. Nor had the government honored its mandate to create a national program of public assistance. The sectional welfare committees, organized in March 1793, had few resources, and the parish hospitals that had managed to survive the early Revolution closed down due to persecution by the secular Republic.[77]

The femmes refused to stay in their old place in these unsettled times. Throughout the tenure of the National Convention (1792–5), the Parisiennes tried to uphold their right to survival, and they challenged local, municipal, and national authorities that hindered women from pursuing their interests. Female protests took the form of spontaneous food riots, market-place disruptions, delegations to political assemblies, and participation in popular societies. Women themselves said that they were "upright," ready to insure the interests of the people, and they definitely viewed themselves as part of the people.

The republican administration felt otherwise. The men of the First French Republic held the same patriarchal values that had prevailed in the society of the Ancien Régime and survived through the constitutional monarchy. They viewed the unorthodox behavior of the Parisiennes as a threat to national security; women belonged in the home performing their domestic chores, sewing uniforms and knitting socks for the soldiers. Several government decrees limited the number of female campfollowers to essential cooks and laundresses, requiring all "excess female baggage" to return home, for their presence in the army disrupted military discipline and the allocation of supplies.[78] Women's aggressive manner in the Parisian markets and assemblies interfered with men's ability to make rational judgments and corrupted public manners. Despite differences among the male leadership as to how to manage the war, there was broad consensus on the place of women. The three groups that dominated the National Convention (Girondins, Jacobins, and Thermidorians) attempted to return women to their place.

Unruly Parisiennes first posed a serious problem of social control in the months between February and September 1793. There were no curbs on the unprecedented turbulence of the marketplace during these months while dissent paralyzed national and local government. In the markets and the vicinity of the National Assembly, Parisiennes bandied radical slogans about and berated magistrates for the deteriorating economy and the drain of Parisian manpower to the front.[79] For several days in late February, laundresses and housewives triggered off a wave of military food riots. Two female deputations brought petitions to the convention, warning the legislators that the women would interfere with military recruitment if the government did not immediately impose price controls on items of prime necessity and exact justice against the political and economic enemies of the urban poor.[80] Again, during June, laundresses and their workers pillaged barges along the Seine, informing the municipal and national officials that they would not respect private property as long as their lives were so endangered.[81] Violence in the markets was endemic through the spring and summer as increasing numbers of housewives, domestic servants, working women, and marketwomen took part in disputes with merchants, revolutionary commissars, police, and National Guard patrols.[82]

The creation of the Society of Revolutionary Republican Women contributed to the summertime anarchy. The Revolutionary Republicans had organized an exclusively female patriotic society with the purpose of pursuing the interests of female consumers and of reporting marketplace aristocrats who violated existing legislation against hoarding and speculation. Politically, these women were dedicated to the overthrow of the Girondins, and they fully supported the coup d'état of 31 May–2 June which placed the Jacobin minority in control of the National Convention. After the coup the Jacobins relied on the Revolutionary Republicans to popularize their regime in the marketplace, but the female allies soon proved more a liability than an asset, prodding the Jacobins to enact harsher methods of marketplace supervision than the Jacobins were willing to sanction.

The insubordination of Parisiennes became most menacing to national security in August. The military situation had steadily deteriorated over the summer as hostile forces impinged on all French borders and civil war still flared in the western departments. Expelled by the assembly during the Jacobin coup, several Girondins returned to their home departments and were mustering a force to overthrow the Jacobins. To meet the emergency, the government proclaimed universal conscription on August 23 and stepped up operations to impose economic controls and political surveillance against external and domestic enemies. Women were frightened by these measures more than they had ever been since the birth of the Republic. Scores of Parisiennes donned male attire and tried to enlist with sectional regiments.[83] Others sought profits in the traffic of military uniforms; prostitutes perfected the art of duping recruits out of the funds allocated by the Sections for their journey to the front lines.[84] The dwindling supplies of bread, meat, vegetables, and fruits aggravated previous tensions and prompted incessant disturbances on food lines. Women in the national workshops complained of inadequate wages, and unemployed ones urged the government to hasten its plans for the formation of armament workshops for women.[85] Translating women's grievances into the political idiom were the Revolutionary Republicans, increasingly dissatisfied with Jacobin direction of the wartime economy and surveillance of counterrevolutionaries in the capital. In the final days of August they threatened insurrection if the soldiers were sent to the front without complementary legislation to help women on the home front.[86]

Paradoxically, the increased momentum and organization of protest among Parisiennes rendered them more vulnerable to governmental retaliation and paved the way for the suppression of women's autonomy in republican France. During the autumn of 1793 the Jacobins consolidated their political power with the assistance of the *sans-culottes* and rewarded their partisans with secure control over sectional assemblies and committees. The invigorated Republic suspended civic rights "until the peace," and entrusted executive authority in the Committee of Public Safety. The linchpin of the Jacobin terrorist legislation was the Law of Suspects, which classified all categories of political offenses and empowered the sectional watch committees to investigate, arrest, and detain all men and women within their respective Sections whose behavior, language, associations, or sympathies endangered the security of the Republic. This law had not been designed to deal specifically with marketplace troublemakers; it was intended to ferret out former aristocrats, refractory clergy, and moderate bourgeoisie hostile to the Jacobin dictatorship. But its wording was sufficiently vague for prostitutes, working women, domestic servants, housewives, shopkeepers, mistresses, and female artisans to be construed as "suspects." Two additional decrees issued in the early autumn enhanced the ability of the *sans-culottes* commissars to cope with deviant marketplace behavior: the decree of the "maximum," which set price controls on fifty items of primary necessity and enumerated fines and sentences for violations; and the decree on public morality, which identified prostitution and insolent marketplace manners with aristocratic mores to be handled by watch committees in conjunction with local criminal tribunals.

The Parisiennes energetically resisted the attempt to close down all their channels of protest. Characteristic of the clash between the Jacobins and the Parisiennes was the "battle of the cockades" which raged in Parisian markets during the last weeks of September.[87] The Revolutionary Republicans, eager to impose republican morality in the marketplace, persuaded the government to decree that all women had to wear the revolutionary tricolor as a badge of their patriotism, and they patrolled the markets to assure that their enemies were conforming with the novel sumptuary legislation. Marketwomen, domestic servants, and small shopkeepers, who resented the new economic decrees and the political persecution of their wealthier clientele, assailed the patriotic women with every available weapon: insults, mud balls, rotten fruit, laundry poles, and brooms.[88] Jacobin police observers could scarcely understand what had provoked the hysteria. One exclaimed that Pitt's agents had undoubtedly instigated the cockade controversy in order to sow discord among patriots.[89]

The revolutionary government patently refused to countenance such unpatriotic behavior. Through late September and October, the Jacobin and *sans-culottes* officials purged the marketplace, chastising all forms of unorthodox language and illicit commerce. The counterpart to the purge was the campaign to inculcate women with the appropriate feminine virtues of *citoyennes* in the Jacobin Republic. The ideal *citoyenne* was described in much the same fashion as the ideal *patriote* of the constitutional monarchy. *Citoyennes* obeyed their male relatives, lauded the Jacobin chiefs, performed their domestic and maternal obligations, and waited patiently on food lines. Prostitutes and former aristocrats and *religieuses* symbolized the debauched manners and fanaticism of the tyrannical days of Bourbon France. The positive reinforcement took place primarily in the public galleries of the sectional and municipal assemblies and local popular societies, where national festivals and republican suppers paid homage to the loyal *citoyennes,* especially mothers and wives of soldiers. The *femmes sans-culottes* became role models for their sisters and took a prominent part in organizing local festivities to commemorate the republican victories and the virtuous deeds of the Jacobin administration.[90]

The Jacobins inaugurated their program for controlling the unruly Parisiennes with a public censure of the Society of Revolutionary Republicans, the center of much of the marketplace chaos. At an evening session in mid-September, the Jacobins disgraced the president of the Revolutionary Republicans, Claire Lacombe, while praising the rank and file who buttressed the government's effort to establish law and order. The Jacobin humiliation of Claire Lacombe explicitly defined women's place in the Republic. Lacombe's major faults were her aggressive manner, eloquent language, criticism of male leadership, and involvement in radical Parisian politics. The official Jacobin press identified her with prostitutes and thieves who carried daggers and pistols.[91] In October the request by the marketwomen for the curtailment of clubwomen who disrupted their commerce gave the National Convention the pretext to order the dissolution of the Society of Revolutionary Republicans and all other female societies. All good *citoyennes* were welcome to join the societies of the patriotic *sans-culottes,* but there were to be no more independent *femmes grenadières.* The government did not immediately imprison the leading Revolutionary Republicans, but Jacobin officials kept them under close vigilance, interrogating them at the least sign of suspicious behavior.[92]

The sectional watch committee followed the Jacobin example. Armed with the authority to enforce terrorist measures, the *sans-cullotes* commissars swept the marketplace of troublemakers, affecting a much broader cross-section of the female population than had previously been the case in revolutionary France. Among the roster of unmarried suspects were working girls, domestic servants, self-employed seamstresses and laundresses; and among married suspects were housewives and widows. Although the highest proportion of arrests took place in the central Sections according to conventional police practice, there was a perceptible increase of arrests in the more distant Sections, where guardsmen and inspectors apprehended domestic servants and dayworkers for hoarding violations and for presumed liaisons with emigrés living in the surrounding communes. Other groups, previously unaffected by revolutionary legislation, were the foreign working girls and servants who had served bankers and entrepreneurs in the vicinity of the Bourse. Technically, working-class foreigners were exempt from the Law of Suspects, but many of these foreign girls attracted the suspicion of watch committees because they had neglected to obtain identification cards from their Sections and written statements from their employers as to their means of livelihood.[93]

The autumnal purge quieted the marketplace without creating widespread alienation among the *femmes.* The majority of suspects received temporary sentences or fines, and the *sans-culottes* showed considerable tolerance toward obstinate housewives and widows whom they usually referred to husbands or employers for reprimand. Only a handful went before the revolutionary tribunal for alleged complicity on conspiracy, and the common women afflicted with the longest periods of detention were those without close relatives to vouch for their good character.[94] The marketplace did not calm down immediately, because it took several months for the Jacobin economic controls to take effect, but by the late winter there was sufficient bread available to prevent the anarchy of the preceding summer. Shortages in meat and vegetables fostered discontent, but without the Revolutionary Republicans the women lacked the means to articulate their grievances in the political forum.

The Hébertist crisis which crystallized in the early spring of 1794 tested the effectiveness of the Jacobins' control of marketplace behavior. Hébertist agitators had sought to rekindle an insurgent mood among the *femmes* by playing on their proverbial fears of famine and of military invasion. The Parisiennes recoiled from challenging the government. Marketwomen, housewives, and working women testified against Hébert and his accomplices at a state trial and corroborated the Jacobin thesis that the current economic difficulties had been intentionally fabricated by the Hébertist scoundrels. Women in the spectator galleries and in the markets applauded the Jacobins for their virulent prosecution of Hébertist "aristocrats."[95] Special precautions prevented marketplace dissenters from misleading their law-abiding sisters. The Committee of General Security issued arrest warrants for former leaders of the Revolutionary Republicans who had allegedly convened clandestinely with Hébertists. The revolutionary tribunal convicted one Widow Padel as an "Hébertist troublemaker" after she had insulted her butcher and local commissar for their inequitable methods of distributing rations.[96]

The structure of the Jacobin administration did not alter in the post-Hébertist months, but it became less flexible and more bureaucratized. Revolutionary justice made little distinction between leftist and rightist critics of the government. Show trials mingled batches of commoners and nobles in the same process, and two or three spectacles included uncooperative *femmes du peuple.* Although common Parisiennes represented less than 1 percent of all Parisian victims, they were stunned by the acceleration of the Terror in which the petit bourgeoisie and *sans-culottes* were daily classified as counter-revolutionaries. Police observers reported overhearing discontent among marketwomen about the despotic Republic and alerted the government to the disturbing fact that marketwomen were holding secret masses for the victims of the Terror.[97]

The watch committees' procedures for isolated troublemakers discouraged a resurgence of the civic unrest characteristic of 1793. In the latter months of the Jacobin administration the greatest number of arrests concerned prostitutes and marketwomen who openly criticized the Terror. The expressions attributed to deviant marketwomen and prostitutes who were detained for uncivic manners suggest the assiduity with which commissars monitored marketplace behavior. Some women called the commissars *petits tyrans* and *despotes*, and a few brazen prostitutes dared to lament the passing of the *Ancien Régime* police, who had not been as ruthless as their republican successors.[98]

Another deterrent to misconduct in the post-Hébertist months was the phenomenon of neighbor denunciations against misbehaving women. Such denunciations by women had been minimal during the fall of 1793, but they became more common in the final months of the Jacobin government. The majority of these collective denunciations singled out women either reputed for their rudeness to merchants or feared as "outsiders." Female residents in one Section charged a longtime neighbor, Mme. Goyon, with uncivic behavior because she carped about prices at the local butchershop. The female denunciators told their local commissars that they deemed it their patriotic duty to expose the bad *citoyennes.* Widow Stalin occasioned disharmony in the Section Faubourg du Nord when she announced that the scarcity of salad and wine at the national meal signified the incompetence of the Republic and its tyrants. Her neighbors duly reported these words to their local commissars, who took the issue seriously since Stalin was a newcomer with no visible means of support.[99] The increased volume of neighbor denunciations suggest that the mechanisms for enforcing revolutionary justice sufficed to preserve law and order without recourse to armed forces or the intervention of national agents. The *femmes du peuple* seemed more inclined to purge their own ranks of nonconformists than to join dissidents who imperilled the harmony of revolutionary Paris.

The Thermidorian coup against the Jacobin leadership in July 1794 coincided with a new approach to curbing feminine dissonance. The Thermidorian majority disparaged the authoritarian revolutionary government and referred to the *sans-culottes* as "cannibals" and "bloodthirsters" for conspiring with the Jacobin "despots" in terrorizing middle-class citizens of both sexes, the *honnêtes gens*. Shortly after securing power, the Thermidorians dismantled the centralized revolutionary government and the apparatus for enforcing terrorist legislation. More gradually, the *honnêtes gens* supplanted the *sans-culottes* in sectional government and the former watch committees dissolved into twelve *arrondissement* committees, each representing four Sections.[100] In the post-Hébertist era the Jacobins had already begun to circumscribe local autonomy in Parisian politics, but the Thermidorians carried the process further by making sectional and *arrondissement* officials responsible to national committees rather than to local assemblies.

The Thermidorians' disdain for the popular democratic institutions of the Jacobin era directly influenced their policy with the *femmes*. They attributed public disorders to the *sans-culottes*, who had purportedly encouraged the *canaille* (common coin in Thermidor for unruly women) to pillage shops and to persecute respectable citizens. In order to control the marketplace, the Thermidorians adopted a program of negative reinforcement designed to discourage public involvement by both men and women of the lower orders. With quasi-official sanction, the Gilded Youth who hated the political and social policies of the austere Jacobin Republic harassed men and women who met in popular societies. They delighted in brandishing canes and whips at the *"tricoteuses,"* women who had allegedly applauded the excess of Jacobin Terror. Inspectors of the public galleries barred poorer women from entry while paying deference to well dressed middle-class and former aristocratic ladies who carried special passes.[101]

The full brunt of the Thermidorians' effort to exclude the populace from public life was not felt among the great majority of *femmes* until a famine in the spring of 1795 reduced the poor to near starvation rations of bread and rice. Although the police kept close watch on the large groups of women angered over declining market goods and job layoffs, they attached little political significance to feminine complaints and restricted marketplace arrests to a small minority of the more vocal female troublemakers. However, the officials evinced much greater consternation about the *sans-culottes* militants who were advocating a restoration of the democratic institutions of 1793. This became most evident in the government's reaction to the Germinal demonstration in April, when Parisians of both sexes marched en masse to the National Convention to insist that the people have bread and their full rights as republican citizens. Not only did officials arrest hundreds of *sans-culottes* participants, but they blamed male rebels for planting women in their processions to mitigate the reprisals of the government against the popular movement.[102]

The armed popular uprising in Prairial (19–23 May), less than six weeks after the Germinal demonstration, compelled Thermidorians to make their policy toward the *femmes* much more explicit. Having eliminated the apparatus of the legal Terror, the Thermidorian government had to convoke a regular armed force to quell the rebellion. When military and civilian eyewitnesses concurred that the *femmes* had been in the vanguard of the popular protest before and during the four-day insurrection, the government realized how seriously it had underestimated the political potential of the *canaille*. A deliberate effort was then made to bring the women within the purview of Thermidorian administration and treat them in the same manner as their male counterparts.[103]

Particularly after Prairial, the Thermidorians were much more methodical than their predecessors in imposing discipline on unruly Parisiennes. The first and most striking aspect of the Prairial proceedings was the absence of a buffer between the women and their government. Even in the final months of the Terror, women had been able to air their grievances before sympathetic commissars, but the Thermidorian regime's middle-class civil servants enforced the laws with little compassion for the *canaille*. In contrast to the marketplace dragnet of 1793 that rounded up so many prostitutes, single working girls, and female servants, sectional investigations after Prairial pinpointed female relatives of *sans-culottes* activists, many of whom had lost their civic rights or faced criminal prosecution for their role in the Jacobin government.[104] These women came predominantly from the more respectable strata of shopkeepers and skilled artisans and often worked in the family business with their male relatives. The Sections opened extensive inquiries into the political careers of their female suspects' previous club affiliations, female associates, and public expressions in spectator galleries and bread lines. No detail was too trivial: rumor that a suspect once sat in the galleries of the Jacobin Club and the revolutionary tribunal was sufficiently incriminating to charge the women with unorthodox political sentiments.[105]

Thermidorian justice against unruly Parisiennes was also harsher than that meted out by the Jacobins. Fifteen women and one hundred and forty-nine men were indicted by an extraordinary military tribunal, and more than half the women received sentences along with male insurgents. Although the court prescribed milder sentences for women than for men, the very fact that the government subjected fifteen common Parisiennes to the trauma of a military trial had a tremendous effect on the populace. Neighbors of the Prairial "furies" drafted collective petitions that attested to the upright character and patriotism of the accused, emphasizing their usefulness to the community as respected mothers and wives.[106] The fifteen "furies" brought before the military tribunal represented only the tip of the iceberg. The sectional registers listed hundreds of women who had pursued National Guards, invaded civil committee meeting rooms, and perpetrated bread line disruptions; at least two women were cited as participants in the assassination of the national representative Féraud. Scores of these marked women managed to evade arrest by moving from their neighborhoods. Verdicts of local courts ranged from indefinite detention for criminal misdemeanors to exposure in the public stocks and the loss of civic certification in one's resident Section.[107]

In the remaining four months of the National Convention, the Republic closed off all channels of collective protest and began to refine administrative mechanisms that would secure peace within the revolutionary capital. Less than a month after Prairial, the government shut down the public workshops for women in Paris because of their inefficiency and expense; women had the option of doing piece work at home with materials furnished by private entrepreneurs. Market conditions did not improve, but reliable National Guard patrols scrutinized marketplace behavior with daily bulletins of the gossip in the markets, brothels, and theaters. The sectional and *arrondissement* authorities retained the records of marked Prairial women and *sansculottes* militants, and the government reorganized the police administration to facilitate crossreferencing data on criminals and political suspects.

The Constitution of 1795 which the Thermidorians adopted in the final weeks of the National Convention assigned the *femmes du peuple* to much the same place they had occupied in the constitutional monarchy. With the memory of the anarchy of Germinal and Prairial still fresh, the constitution-makers identified wealth with political wisdom and sought to insure that men of property and education would govern the Republic. Whatever expectations the *femmes* had had at the outset of the Revolution died in the era of the Directory (1795–1799), when the government became increasingly bourgeois and accelerated Thermidorian measures to efface democratic institutions and the memory of 1793.[108]

Protest by women had ceased to be a problem for political stability and military security when Napoleon succeeded the Directory in 1799. However, General Bonaparte had witnessed the upheavals of 1789, 1793, and 1795, and had detested the aggressive manner exhibited by the Parisian market-women. He had a low regard for the intellectual capabilities and moral demeanor of women, and the *femmes du peuple* epitomized in his mind the innate evil and absence of reason of the second sex.[109]

The prerevolutionary schemes for improving public lighting, sanitation, water fountains, and the registration of prostitutes and roominghouse keepers had been suspended. Poorly phrased codes for the licensing of stallkeepers and vendors had led to thousands of ambulatory merchants crowding the bridges and obstructing entrances to the shops of more established merchants. Profiteers, who had benefited from the liberal economic policies of the Directory, played havoc with the distribution of supplies and the prices of commodities.

Napoleon intended Paris to be the administrative and cultural capital of his state, a model city of order and beauty. Orderly and respectful behavior by the *femmes du peuple* was a prerequisite for the fulfillment of his goal. Hence, Napoleon's Civil Code restated the patriarchal values of French society with more precision on the inequality of male-female relations than any previous national legislation and established more proficient centralized means for keeping women in their place than the absolutist state. A few comparisons between the conditions of the *femmes* in prerevolutionary and Napoleonic Paris highlight this point.

Throughout the Bourbon dynasty, the police had failed to formulate a viable policy for controlling prostitution. Nobles, and occasionally the clergy, had sheltered wayward women from the royal authority, and toward the end of the *Ancien Régime* procedures varied from one royal commissioner to another. No such irregularities marred the policing of prostitutes in Napoleonic Paris. Accepting prostitution as a necessary evil which protected "respectable women" from rowdy soldiers and young workers, the Napoleonic prefects aimed at perfecting registration procedures for prostitutes and brothel-owners. Since there were no longer the overlapping jurisdictions of privileged orders in the Napoleonic era, prostitutes were directly exposed to the police, who coordinated the disciplining of prostitution with hospital and judicial administrations. A similar pattern of control evolved in the licensing of merchants in the Parisian markets, in the policing of mendicants and vagrants, and in the supervision of patients in hospitals.[110]

The net result of all these regulations did not amount to a better standard of living for the *femmes du peuple*. Although there was some improvement in the variety and quantity of the Parisian diet during the Napoleonic years, there were periods of bread scarcity and a severe famine in 1811–12 which made the poor rely on "Rumford Soups" (Napoleon's version of the free soups formerly distributed by the Church). The number of prostitutes steadily progressed in the Napoleonic era, the great majority claiming they had no others means of earning their livelihood. The nascent cotton industry employed several thousand Parisiennes, but by the 1820s much of the industry was moving outside the capital. Napoleon's renovation of the markets, which began late in his rule, prompted the police to amplify their efforts to eliminate petty vendors who interfered with the completion of these projects. And the regimentation of hospital life so frightened women that expectant mothers preferred to use local midwives rather than risk incarceration in the city hospitals.[111]

The women of the people paid a bitter price for their attempt to participate in the revolutionary events. By asserting their interests in the markets and public galleries they became more visible to local and national authorities. From 1793 onward the government devised increasingly sophisticated mechanisms for controlling marketplace behavior and for returning women to their "place." Throughout the changing administrations of the revolutionary decade the leaders maintained the patriarchal values of the *Ancien Régime*, and women's aggressive manner in revolutionary protest only seemed to confirm men's stereotypes about the second sex as unreasoning creatures driven by "furies." The 1793 promise of egalitarian rights for women disappeared with the Constitution of 1795, and Napoleon's Civil Code clarified the inequality of male-female relations with more rigor than any previous French government. Even the loopholes in the absolutist structure that had given the *femmes* some latitude for maneuvering within the system closed up in the Napoleonic state.

Notes

Abbreviations used throughout:
B.N.   Bibliothéque nationale
A.N.   Archives nationales
A.P.P.   Archives de la Préfecture de Police

1.   Nicolas Edmé Restif de la Bretonne, "La Pétite paysanne trompée, " in *Les Nuits de Paris* (Paris: Aux Troix Compagnons, 1947), pp. 212–13.

2.   Jeffrey Kaplow, "Sur la population flottante de Paris, à la fin de l'Ancien Régime," *Annales historiques de la Révolution française,* 187 (January–March 1967): 12–14; Claude Delasselle, "Les Enfants abandonnés à Paris au XVIIIè siècle," *Annales: Economies, Sociétés, Civilisations,* 30 (January–February 1975): 212–14.

3.   Paul Lacroix, *The XVIIIth Century: Its Institutions, Customs, and Costumes; France, 1700–1789* (London: Chapman and Hall, 1876), pp. 88–92, 325–35; Albert Soboul, *La Civilisation et la Révolution française* (Paris: Arthaud, 1970), plates 166, 168.

4.   Léon Abensour, *La Femme et le féminisme avant la Révolution* (Paris: Ernest Leroux, 1923), p. 186. Prior to the sixteenth century, women had had more access to the corporations. See Henri Hauser, *Ouvriers du temps passé* (Paris: F. Alcan, 1927), pp. 142–44, and Gustave Fagniez, *Etudes sur l'industrie et la classe industrielle à Paris au XIIIe et au XIVe siècles* (Paris: Bibliothèque de l'Ecole des Hautes Etudes, 1877). By the eighteenth century the corporations we.e losing their monopoly over spinning and weaving to home industries. See Madeleine Guilbert and Viviane Isambert-Jamati, *Travail féminin et travail à domicile: Enquête sur le travail à domicile de la confection féminine dans la région parisienne* (Paris: C.N.R.S., 1956), pp. 9–11.

5.   Emile Coornaert, *Les Corporations en France avant 1789* (Paris: Gallimard, 1941), pp. 152–84, and his more recent *Les Compagnonnages en France du moyen âge à nos jours* (Paris: Editions ouvrières, 1966,)) pp. 178–79.

6.   Alfred Franklin, *Dictionnaire historique des arts, métiers et professions exercés dans Paris depuis le treizième siècle* (Paris: Universitaire française et étrangère, 1906), pp. xv, 489–90; René de Lespinasse and François Bonnardot, eds., *Histoire générale de Paris: Les métiers et corporations de la ville de Paris,* vol. 3 (Paris: Imprimerie nationale, 1879), pp. 1–34.

7.   Denis Diderot, *Encyclopédie, ou dictionnaire raisonné des sciences, des arts, et des métiers,* s.v. "Filature," "Verrerie en bois," "Relieure," "Agriculture," "Brodure," "Pape-terie." Approximately 10 percent of the working population of ambulatory merchants and textile workers were women. See George Rudé, "La Population ouvrière parisienne de 1789 à 1791," *Annales historiques de la Révolution française* 187 (January–March 1967): 25–27.

8.   E. Charles Roux et al., *Les Femmes et le travail du moyen âge à nos jours* (Paris: La Courtille, 1975), p. 84. Wages were somewhat higher in Paris than in the provinces and this contributed to the migration of women to Paris beginning in the mid-eighteenth century. See Abel Chatelain, "Migrations et domesticité féminine urbaine en France, XVIIIe siècle–XXe siècle," *Revue d'histoire économique et sociale* 67 (1969): 507–11.

9.   Sebastien Mercier, *Tableau de Paris,* 8 vols. (Amsterdam, 1783), vol. 4: pp. 53–58, 144–48, 245–47; Alfred Franklin, *La Vie privée d'autrefois,* ed. Arlette Farge (Paris: Librairie académique Perrin, 1971), p. 279. The culture of the marketplace is discussed in A. P. Moore, *The Genre Poissard and the French Stage in the Eighteenth Century* (New York: The Institute of French Studies, Columbia University, 1935).

10.   J.-B. Charles Le Maire, *La Police de Paris en 1770. Mémoire inédit composé par ordre de G. De Sartine sur la demande de Marie Thérèse,* ed. Gazier, in *Mémoires de la Société d'histoire de Paris et de l'Ile de France* 5 (1879): 89–90.

11.   The successful actresses were always a difficulty for the police because of their influential connections. See *Journal des inspecteurs de M. de Sartine, 1761–1764,* ed. L. Larchey (Paris, 1863), pp. 7–9, 27–28, in B.N., Lb 38 1347. The contemporary memoirists refer to Mlle. Bertin as the most successful *marchande des modes* of the 1780s. See, for example, Henriette Louise, baronne d'Oberkirch, *Mémoires de la Baronne d'Oberkirch sur la cour de Louis XVI et la société française avant 1789,* ed. Suzanne Burkard (Paris: Mercure de France, 1970), pp. 179, 191–92, 312–36.

12.   C.-L. Chassin, *Les Élections et les cahiers de Paris en 1789,* 4 vols. (Paris, 1888–1889), vol. 3, pp. 354–57.

13.   Jean Vidalenc, "Une Industrie alimentaire à Paris au XVIIIe siècle: La Préparation et la vente des tripes et abats," *Mémoires de la fédération des sociétés historiques et archéologiques de Paris et de l'île de France* 11 (1960): 373–75. A full discussion of the numbers of street hawkers and the items peddled is found in Jeffrey Kaplow, *The Names of Kings: The Parisian Laboring Poor in the Eighteenth Century* (New York: Basic Books, 1972), pp. 44–47.

14.   Charles Tilly, "Food Supply and Public Order in Modern Europe," in *The Formation of National States in Western Europe,* ed. Charles Tilly (Princeton: Princeton University Press, 1975), pp. 137, 144–47.

15.   M.-F. Hoffbauer, *Paris à travers les âges,* 3 vols. (Paris: Firmin-Didot, 1882–1885), vol. 2, p. 47.

16.   Marcel Fosseyeux, "Le Budget de la charité à Paris au XVIIIe siècle," *Revue des études historiques,* 85 (July–October 1918): 253–64; S. Mercier, *Tableau de Paris,* vol. 4, pp. 126–27.

17.   The French police system has more comprehensive administrative and judicial functions than systems in the Anglo-American tradition. See Philip John Stead, *The Police of Paris* (London: Staples Press, 1957), pp. 14–15.

18.   Marc Chassaigne, *La Lieutenance-Générale de police de Paris* (Geneva: Slatkine-Megariotis Reprints, 1975; 1st ed., 1906), p. 95.

19.   Leon Cahen, "L'Approvisionnement en pain de Paris au XVIIIe siècle et la question de la boulangerie," *Revue d'histoire économique et sociale* 14 (1926): 458–72; Kaplow, *The Names of Kings,* pp. 72–74.

20.   Jean Martineau, *Les Halles de Paris des origines à 1789. Evolution matérielle juridique et économique* (Paris: Editions Montchrestien, 1960), pp. 246–48.

21. Le Maire, *La Police en 1770*, pp. 129–31.

22. Shelby T. McCloy, *The Humanitarian Movement in Eighteenth-Century France* (Lexington, Ky.: University of Kentucky Press, 1957), pp. 239, 245. Lieutenant-general Le Noir (1776–85) made a great many of these regulations due to his interest in the public health movement. See Jean Lucien Gay, "L'Administration de la capitale entre 1770 et 1789: La Tutelle de la royauté et ses limites," *Mémoires de la fédération des sociétés historiques et archéologiques de Paris et de l'île de France*, 11 (1960): 373–75.

23. André Vaquier, "Un philanthrope méconnu, Cadet de Vaux," *Mémoires de la fédération des sociétés historiques et archéologiques de Paris et de l'île de France* 9 (1957–8): 388–92.

24. Eugène Dufrance, *Histoire de l'éclairage des rues de Paris* (Paris: Imprimerie nationale, 1904), pp. 75–76.

25. Although the police commissioners of the mid-eighteenth century had begun to register prostitutes, no concrete pattern of registration evolved until the Napoleonic era. See A.-J.-P. Parent-Duchâtelet, *De la prostitution dans la ville de Paris* (Brussels, 1836), pp. 20, 26. Contemporary methods are described in Le Maire, *La Police en 1770*, pp. 89–90, and Anne-Henri-Cabot, vicomte de Dampmartin, *Un Provincial à Paris pendant une partie de l'année 1789* (Strasbourg, n.p.: 1789), pp. 97–101, 154.

26. Torture was officially abolished from criminal procedure in 1780, but judges reserved the right to prescribe torture of convicted persons in order to extract information on accomplices. Moreover, the judges did not always observe the 1780 prohibition on the use of torture in inquisitorial proceedings. See the extensive discussion on the rules and execution of criminal ocedure in A. Esmien, *Histoire de la procédure criminelle en France, et spécialement de la procédure inquisitoire depuis le xiiie siècle jusqu'à nos jours* (Paris: L. Larose et Forcel, 1882), pp. 260–78.

27. In the mid-eighteenth century one commissioner revived the old custom of branding prostitutes in his quarter with a "P." However, most female criminals seem to have been branded with the "V" for *voleuse* (thief). See R. Anchel, *Crimes et châtiments au XVIIIe siècle* (Paris: Librairie académique Perrin, 1933), p. 9.

28. Prophyre Petrovitch, "Recherches sur la criminalité à Paris dans la seconde moitié du xviiie siècle," in *Crimes et criminalité sous l'Ancien Régime*, eds. A. Abbiateci et. al. (Paris: A. Colin, 1971, Cahiers des Annales, 33), p. 238; and empirical tables in G. Aubry, *La Jurisprudence criminelle du Châtelet de Paris sous le règne de Louis XVI* (Paris: Pichon et R. Durand-Auzias, 1971), pp. 108–10.

29. Des Essarts, *Dictionnaire universel de Police,* 7 vols. (Paris: Chez Moutard, 1788), vol. 1, pp. 40–43, s. v. "Accouchement."

30. Aubry, *La Jurisprudence criminelle*, p. 232.

31. A misbehaving servant was considered to be a threat to the patterns of deference and during the eighteenth century there was growing concern over the insolence displayed by servants. See Kaplow, *The Names of Kings*, pp. 49–51.

32. For examples, see Aubry, *La Jurisprudence criminelle*, p. 93, and Anchel, *Crimes et châtiments*, pp. 67–68.

33. Yvonne Bongert. "Délinquance juvenile au xviiie siècle," in *Crimes et criminalité sous l'Ancien Régime*, p. 61; cf. Aubry, *La Jurisprudence criminelle*, p. 114.

34. Anchel, *Crimes et châtiments*, p. 118.

35. The listing of all the local hospitals and charities is found in H. Monin, *L'État de Paris en 1789. Etudes et documents sur l'Ancien Régime à Paris* (Paris: Maison Quantin, 1889, Collection de documents rélatifs à l'histoire de Paris pendant la Révolution française), pp. 247–50. An excellent description of the dynamics of one of these local institutions is in Marcel Fosseyeux, "La Maison des Cent-Filles ou de la Miséricorde au Faubourg Saint-Marceau," *Bulletin de la Société d'histoire de Paris et de l'Ile de France* 50 (1923): 61–73.

36.   C. Bloch and A. Tuetey, eds., *Procès-verbaux et rapports du Comité de mendicité* (Paris: Imprimerie nationale, 1911), pp. 119–20.

37.   "Reglements de la Société de la Charité maternelle," in *La France en deuil ou le vingt-un janvier* (Paris: Mélanges littéraires, 1815).

38.   Jacques-René Tenon, *Mémoire sur les hôpitaux de Paris* (Paris: Royez, 1788). For additional details on the rates of infant and maternal mortality in Paris before the Revolution see J. Gelis, "Sages-femmes et accoucheurs: L'Obstétrique populaire au XVIIe et XVIIIe siècles," *Annales: Economies, Sociétés, Civilisations* 31 (July–August 1977): 928, 933; and Paul Galliano, "La mortalité infantile (indigènes et nourrissons) dans la banlieu sud de Paris à la fin du XVIIIe siècle (1774–1794)," *Annales de démographie historique*, 1966, 139–77.

39.   Doublet, *Mémoire sur la necessité d'établir un réforme dans les prisons* (1791), quoted in Henri Desgranges, "Les massacres de septembre à la Salpêtrière," *Mémoires de la fédération des sociétés historiques et archéologiques de Paris et de l'île de France* 2 (1950): 297.

40.   George Rudé, *The Crowd in the French Revolution* (Oxford: Oxford University Press, 1959), p. 25. In the riots of May 1775 the police were not entirely adequate due to the excessive numbers of rural rioters entering in the city disturbances. See Rudé, *Paris and London in the Eighteenth Century: Studies in Popular Protest* (New York: Viking Press, 1969), p. 56.

41.   Jean Lucien Gay, "L'Administration de la capitale entre 1770 et 1789," Part 5, *Mémoires de la fédération des sociétés historiques et archéologiques de Paris et de l'île de France* 12 (1961): 163–69, 210–11.

42.   Anchel, *Crimes et châtiments*, pp. 81–82. The longstanding history of this problem is discussed in David Hunt, *Parents and Children in History: The Psychology of Family Life in Early Modern France* (New York: Harper Torchbooks, 1970), pp. 60–67.

43.   Aubry, *La Jurisprudence criminelle*, pp. 95–97.

44.   Petrovitch, "Recherches sur la criminalité à Paris," p. 237.

45.   Anchel, *Crimes et châtiments*, pp. 69–71. Soldiers in the French Guards were also susceptible to taking bribes from women. See Victor Fournel, *Les Hommes du 14 juillet, Gardes françaises et vainqueurs de la Bastille* (Paris: Levy, 1890), pp. 23–24; and de La Bretonne, "Le Secret des blanchisseuses," in *Nuits de Paris*, pp. 48–49.

46.   Desbois de Rochefort, *Mémoire sur les calamités de l'hiver 1788–1789*, in C.-L. Chassin, *Les élections et les cahiers de Paris*, vol. 2, pp. 547–50; L.-P. Dufourny de Villiers, *Cahier du quatrième ordre, celui des pauvres journaliers, des infirmes, des indigènes* (n.p.: 1789), in B.N., Lb 39 1538. For the escalating bread prices see George Rudé, "The Outbreak of the French Revolution," *Past and Present* 8 (1955): 34.

47.   Femme Cheret, *Evénement de Paris et de Versailles, par une des dames qui a eu l'honneur d'être de la députation à l'Assemblée générale* (Paris, 1789), in B.N., Lb 39 7941; and a song commemorating the occasion entitled "le Voyage du Roi de Versailles à Paris, ou il fait sa résidence," in B.N., YE 35087.

48.   The best examinations of the interaction of the radical guards with the women before and during the insurrection are Dom H. Leclercq, *Les Journées d'Octobre et la fin de l'année 1789* (Paris: Letouzey et Ané, 1924), pp. 7–155, and Julia C. Stoddard, "The Causes of the Insurrection of the 5th and 6th of October 1789," in *University of Nebraska Studies* 4 (October 1904): 269–327. Specific examples of tracts in the era include *Premier dialogue entre une Poissarde et un Fort de la Halle sur les affaires présentes* (Paris, 1789), in B.N., Lb 39 7577; *Motion curieuse des Dames de la Place Maubert* (Paris, 1789), in B.N., Lb 39 2421. The impact of this progaganda in the markets is discussed in Cornwell Rogers, *The Spirit of the Revolution in 1789: A Study of Public Opinion as Revealed in Political Songs and Other Popular Literature at the Beginning of the French Revolution* (Princeton: Princeton University Press, 1949), pp. 160–75.

49.   Esmien, *Histoire de la procédure criminelle en France*, pp. 410–16.

50.   A.N., C 31 d. 261 A, p. 10.

51.   Ernest Mellié, *Les Sections de Paris pendant la Révolution française, 21 mai 1790–19 vendémiaire IV* (Paris: Société de la Révolution française, 1898), pp. 7–22.

52.   See, for example, J.-S. Bailly, *Mémoires de,* eds. Berville and Barriere, 3 vols. (Paris: Baudouin Frères, 1822), vols. 1–2. Bailly was the mayor of Paris between 1789 and 1791.

53.   Such protocol was unnecessary for visiting notorious brothels. See Stead, *The Police of Paris,* p. 65.

54.   James M. Thompson, *The French Revolution* (New York: Galaxy paper, 1966), pp. 127–28.

55.   Albert Mathiez, *Le Club des Cordeliers pendant la crise de Varennes et le massacre du Champ de Mars* (Paris: Champion, 1910); and an analysis of the participants in George Rudé, "La Composition sociale des insurrections parisiennes de 1789 à 1791," *Annales historiques de la Révolution française* 127 (July–Aug. 1952): 277–79. For a patriotic account stressing the suffering of women with children during the episode see Prud'homme's *Révolutions de Paris,* no. 106, July 1791.

56.   Albert Mathiez, *La Vie chère et le mouvement social sous la terreur* (Paris: Payot, 1927), pp. 29–49; Rudé, *The Crowd in the French Revolution,* pp. 97–98. These riots were called *taxation populaire* riots, and they harked back to traditional modes of protest. See Rudé, "La taxation populaire de mai 1775 à Paris et dans la région parisienne," *Annales historiques de la Révolution française* 143 (April–June 1956): 239–79.

57.   Ferdinand-Dreyfus, *Un Philanthrope d'autrefois, La Rochefoucauld-Liancourt, 1747–1827* (Paris: Plon, 1903), pp. 172–88.

58.   Jean Imbert, *Le Droit hospitalier de la Révolution et de l'Empire* (Paris: Sirey, 1954), p. 38.

59.   Beatrice Gibon-Larquet, "Les hôpitaux de Paris sous la Révolution," *Etudes d'histoire du droit parisien* (Paris: Presses universitaires de France, 1970), p. 436. A sympathetic treatment of the *religieuses* persecuted in this period is found in Jean Boussoulade, *Moniales et hospitalières dans la tourmente révolutionnaire: les communautés de religieuses de l'ancien diocèse de Paris de 1789 à 1801* (Paris: Letouzey et Ané, 1962), pp. 75–82.

60.   Alexandre Tuetey, ed., *L'Assistance publique pendant la Révolution,* 4 vols., (Paris: Imprimerie nationale, 1895–97), vol. 1, pp. 89, 95, 104–06, 142–43; vol. 2, p. 520.

61.   A.N., F 15 3581, fols. 83–84, 87, 105–06.

62.   Tuetey, *L'Assistance publique,* vol. 2, p. 466.

63.   The fraternal societies universally admitted membership from both sexes although men dominated the positions of leadership. These societies began to adopt more restrictive admission policies in 1792 just after the outbreak of the war and the more exclusive policies demanded more political commitment of members than the earlier societies. The organization and activities of these societies are described in Isabelle Bourdin, *Les Sociétés populaires à Paris pendant la Révolution française, 1789 jusqu'au la chute de la royauté* (Paris: Librairie du Receuil, 1937).

64.   For example, *Invitation de la Société fraternelle séante aux Jacobins St.-Honoré, aux Bons Citoyens, relativement aux barrières* (1791) in B.N., Lb 40 3300.

65.   Tuetey, *L'Assistance publique,* vol. 2, pp. 200–01.

66.   Leclercq, *Les Journées d'Octobre,* pp. 247, 504, 530–32; Rudé, *The Crowd in the French Revolution,* pp. 93–94.

67.   *Discours . . . 30 janvier 1792,* in A.N., AD XVI 73.

68.   Mathiez, *La Vie chère,* pp. 41–49.

69.   Edme Champion, "La Réforme de l'état civil," *La Révolution française* 2 (1887): 1061–66. The continued work of the *religieuses* in the impoverished faubourgs is discussed in

Jean Boussoulade, "Soeurs de charité et comités de bienfaisance des faubourgs Saint-Marcel et Saint-Antoine," *Annales historiques de la Révolution française,* 200 (April–June 1970): 350–74. The sisters were not required to leave their communities until August 18, 1792.

70. Desgranges, "Les Massacres de septembre à la Salpêtrière," p. 298; Ferdinand-Dreyfus, *Un Philanthrope d'autrefois,* p. 159.

71. A.N., D III 256 (4).

72. Charles-A. Alexandre, "Fragments des mémoires de," ed. Jacques Godechot, in *Annales historiques de la Révolution française,* 126 (April–June 1952), 155.

73. Crane Brinton, *The History of Illegitimacy during the French Revolution* (Cambridge, Mass.: Harvard University Press, 1936).

74. Jacques Godechot, *Les Institutions de la France sous la Révolution et l'Empire,* 2nd ed. (Paris: Presses universitaires de France, 1968), p. 444.

75. Albert Soboul, *Les Sans-Culottes parisiens en l'An II. Mouvement populaire et gouvernement révolutionnaire (1793–1794)* (Paris: Librairie Clavreuil, 1959), chaps. 1–2.

76. Mellié, *Les Sections de Paris,* pp. 288–90.

77. Gibon-Larquet, "Les Hôpitaux de Paris sous la Révolution," p. 438.

78. There were several early female recruits in 1792 who provided potent propaganda for the government. See Jeanne Bouvier, *Les Femmes pendant la Révolution* (Paris: Editions Eugène Figuière, 1931), pp. 198–207. Decrees against Amazons are in *Moniteur,* 16: 270; 18: 655. The government showed little favorable response to the women's petition for the recruitment of needy women. See *Départ de Neuf-cent citoyennes de Paris . . . Pétition à la Convention Nationale* (n.d.), in B.N., Lb 41 2791.

79. A.N., AF IV 1470, nos. 3, 16; A.N., DXL III 30 A–B.

80. *Archives parlementaires,* 58: p. 153. The entire episode is summarized in the *Décrets de la Commune de Paris. Extrait du Conseil Général* de Paris, février 23–26 1793, in B.N., Lb 40 1154g. The participants are discussed in Rudé, "Les émeutes des 25, 26, février 1793 à Paris d'après les procès-verbaux des commissaires de police des sections parisiennes," *Annales historiques de la Révolution française,* 130 (January–March 1953), 32–57.

81. Adophe Schmidt, *Tableaux de la Révolution (1789–1800),* 3 vols. (Leipzig: Veit, 1869), vol. 2, pp. 6–7, 16–17, 71.

82. Records of the sectional assemblies and watch committees as well as the National Guard proliferate in examples of feminine violence in public squares and markets and the public galleries of local and national assemblies. For some examples, see A.N., F7 4775 2 d. Roussel; F7 4746 d. Huet; F7* 2481, entry for April 8, 1793; F7* 2520, entry for April 15, 1793, W 1 d. 22; AF IV, nos. 5, 9.

83. Marie Cerati, *Le Club des citoyennes républicaines révolutionnaires* (Paris: Editions Sociales, 1966), p. 23. The Girondins firmly believed that the Revolutionary Republicans were bribed by the Jacobins to foment popular discontent about the Girondin administration. See *Rapport très précis de la commission des Douze,* in A.N., C 355 C$_{11}$ 1867, p. 1; J.-J. Gorsas, *Précis rapides des évènements qui ont eus lieu à Paris dans les journées des 30-1 mai premier et 2 juin à Paris,* in A.N., AD I 107; Bergoeing, *La Longue conspiration des Jacobins pour dissoudre la Convention nationale,* pp. 13, 38, in A.N., AD I 107.

84. Scattered reports in the papers for the Department of Paris in A.N., BB 3 81-1, BB 3 81-2, and BB 3 74, liasse 33. Also, see some of the early reports submitted by sectional watch committees to the Committee of General Security in A.N., F7 4775 14 d. Saunier, F7 4775 24 d. Taillandiers.

85. A.N., F7 4774 87 d. Rancon; F7 4633 d. Capmas; F7 4704 d. Feline; F7 4774 86d. Rada; F7 4775 16 d. Seglein; and a more serious case brought before the revolutionary tribunal in W 6 d. 272 (Femmes George and Burette).

86. A.N., BB 3 74, liasse 35, report of August 8, 1793; BB 3 81-1, pp. 232–38, 252.

87.   *Pétition des Citoyennes républicaines révolutionnaires lue à la barre de la Convention nationale,* August 26, 1793, in A.N., C 267 C11 638, p. 22; and for details on the society's relations with the radical *enragé* movement see R. B. Rose, *The* Enragés: *Socialists of the French Revolution?* (Melbourne: Melbourne University Press, 1965), pp. 53–54.

88.   Scott Lytle, "The Second Sex (September, 1793)," *Journal of Modern History,* 26, no. 1 (1955): 14–26. Abundant descriptions of these squabbles are in the papers of the Committee of General Security. See, for instance, A.N., F7 4775 26 d. Tellier; F7 4774 86 d. Raimond; F7 4627 d. Bulte; F7 4774 12 d. Lefevre; F7 4737 d. Guyard; F7 4774 90 d. Rentez; F7 4774 19 d. Leroux, F7 4682 d. Aubertin.

89.   Report of Latour-de-la-Montagne, September 20, 1793, in A.N., F7 3688 3, liasse 1. Many of these observers' reports have been reprinted in Pierre Caron, *Paris pendant la terreur. Rapports des agents secrets du Ministre de l'Intérieur,* vol. 1 (Paris: Picard, 1914). Also for reports on the infractions of the economic controls in the first months see Henri Calvet, *L'Accaparement à Paris sous la terreur. Essai sur l'application de la loi du 26 juillet 1793* (Paris: C.N.R.S., 1933).

90.   Many of the autumnal festivals were in honor of republican martyrs in order to promote the anticlerical campaign of Parisian radicals. See Soboul, *Les Sans-Culottes parisiens,* pp. 299–320.

91.   *Moniteur,* 17: 694–96; and Claire Lacombe, *Rapport fait par la Citoyenne Lacombe à la séance des Républicaines Révolutionnaires de ce que s'est passé le 16 Septembre à la Société des Jacobins,* in B.N., FM 35160.

92.   A.N., C 280 C11 761; and *Moniteur,* 18: 300. Specific examples of police vigilance are found in A.N., F7 4756 d. Lacombe; F7 4682 d. Dubois; F7 4683 d. Dubreuil; F7 4775 52 d. Warnier; F7 4774 9 d. Leclerc (including Pauline Leon papers).

93.   For some examples of the foreign working women apprehended during the marketplace purge, see A.N., F7 4741 d. Henderson; F7 4741 d. Herse; F7 4774 14 d. Leismeyer; F7 4774 28 d. Maddock; F7 4775 50 d. Whiteside. A more serious episode involving foreigners pertained to several workers found distributing royalist pamphlets; see A.N. F7 4774 89 d. Roque; and F7 4753 d. Keller. For a more systematic analysis of the arrests by the watch committees based on several hundred dossiers between 1793 and 1795, see Mary Johnson, "The Unruly Parisiennes in the First French Republic: Patterns of Law Enforcement on the Parisian Marketplace, 1793–5," unpublished paper, available on request, Temple University, Department of History.

94.   A.N., W 298 d. 282 (Marie Lacroix); F7 4633 d. Carlle.

95.   See the police observer's reports in A.N., W 180 1 A. Also see female testimonies during the Hébertist trial in A.N., W 77, Plaque 1, pp. 1, 54, 62–63, 69, 76; Plaque 2, p. 1; Plaque 5, pp. 291–92, 304, 311–13, 319–21, 328, 381; W 78, Plaque 1, p. 49; Plaque 2, p. 20; Plaque 3, p. 170.

96.   A.N., W 381, no. 877 *(Veuve* Padel, Angelique Jacquemont*);* cf. W 395, no. 895 *(Femme* Jannisson, Benoît Tribel*).*

97.   A.N., W 180 (Madeline Lacroix; W 389, no. 904 *(Les Rouges Chemises);* F7 4667 d. Delaroche; F7 4632 d. Camus; F7 4747 d. Imberty.

98.   A.P.P., Aa 240, fols. 119, 122, 128, 149, 152, 156, 193–94, 201–02; Aa 70, fol. 478; Aa 94, fols. 88, 167, 187–88, 240–41, 246, 261. Also see the report on abuse of prostitutes by the representative Bouin in A.N., F7 4611.

99.   A.N., F7 4774 23 d. Stalin; cf. F7 4731 d. Goyon.

100.   Kare Tønnesson, *La Défaite des sans culottes: Mouvement populaire et réaction bourgeoise en l'an III* (Oslo and Paris: Librairie Clavreuil, 1959), pp. 31–51. The civil committees had always had more moderate members because positions in these committees were unsalaried; see details on the bourgeois composition of the civil commissars in Mellié, *Les Sections de Paris,* pp. 169–72.

101.   Albert Mathiez, *After Robespierre, The Thermidorian Reaction,* trans. Catherine Alison Phillips (New York: Grosset, 1965), p. 34; cf. *Moniteur,* 21: 438–39.

102.   Georges Duval, *Souvenirs de la Réaction thermidorienne,* 2 vols. (Paris, 1844), vol. 2, pp. 132–33. The Sections focused almost exclusively on prosecuting male participants in the Germinal disturbances. See Tønnesson, *La Défaite des sans culottes,* pp. 227–30.

103.   For examples of contemporary accounts with specific allusions to the *femmes,* see Louis Costaz, *Histoire du batallion des jeunes citoyens à l'attaque du faubourg St. Antoine 4 Prairial III* (Paris, n.d.), in B.N., Lb 41 1827; and General Kilmaine, *Détails circonstanciès de ce qui s'est passé le 4 Prairial au Faubourg St. Antoine* (Paris, n.d.), in B.N., Lb 41 1826. The government account of 1 Prairial alludes to the prominence of *femmes* in the galleries; see the reprint of proceedings in *Moniteur,* 24: 496–515.

104.   For examples, see A.N., F7 4649 d. Claudel; F7 4712 d. Francis; and for more detail on the breakdown of women arrested in Prairial, see Johnson, "The Unruly Parisiennes in the First French Republic," pp. 20–25.

105.   A.N. F7 4585, Plaque 9, d. Barbant; F7 4775 53 d. Klispis; F7 4665 d. Deffau; F7 4665 d. Desclouse; F7 4774 31 d. Timbal.

106.   The papers of the military tribunal (A.N., W 546–48) contain valuable information on the most active men and women in the Sections because each of the defendants had to prepare a detailed account of his or her political career since 1789. The dossiers pertaining to the female defendants are W 546, nos. 12, 32, 26, 29, 33; W 547, nos. 46, 52, 66; W 548, nos. 71, 72, 74. Reclamations are included in the dossiers. The decisions rendered by the military commission of 4 Prairial were as follows:

Decision	Men	Women
Executed	36	0
Deported	12	1
Detention	18	7
Chains	7	3
Hold for more information	3	1
Acquittal	73	6
	149	18

107.   Examples are scattered throughout the F7 series of papers of the Committee of General Security, transcriptions of sectional deliberations in Prairial, and the police investigations. Among the more vivid descriptions of women's aggression are A.N., F7 4586 d. Barbot; F7 4595 d. Berjot; F7 4577 d. Albaque; F7 4702 d. Fabien; F7 4774 29 d. Monthot; F7 4581 d. Augien.

108.   Richard Cobb, "Note sur la répression contre le personnel sans culotte de 1795 à 1801," *Annales historiques de la Révolution française,* 134 (January–March 1954): 30–35. The organization of the police during the Directory became the basis for Napoleon's Prefecture of Police. See Brian Chapman, "The Prefecture of Police," *Journal of Criminal Law, Criminology and Political Science,* 44: 505–11.

109.   General Baron Gourgaud, *Talks of Napoleon at St. Helena,* trans. Elizabeth Wormeley Latimer (Chicago: A. C. McClurg, 1904), p. 86; cf. Maurice Guerrini, *Napoleon and Paris,* trans. Margery Weiner (Paris: Cassell, 1970), p. 15.

110.   On the registration procedures for prostitution see the *Memoirs of Chancellor Etienne Denis Pasquier,* trans. Douglas Garman (London: Elek, 1967), p. 107; and on the marketplace rules, see Jean Tulard, "Louis-Nicolas Dubois, Premier Préfet de Police (1758–1847)," *Revue de l'institut napoléon,* 1956, p. 14; and E. Levasseur, *Histoire des classes ouvrières et de l'industrie en France* (Paris: A. Rousseau, 1903), vol. 1, p. 337.

111.   L. de Lanzac de Laborie, *Paris sous Napoleon* (Paris: Plon, 1908–1913), vol. 5, p. 65.

Suggestions for Further Reading

Prerevolutionary Conditions for the Women of the People

An excellent survey of the material conditions and the mentality among the men and the women of the lower orders is Jeffrey Kaplow's *The Names of Kings: The Life of the Laboring Poor in Eighteenth-Century Paris* (New York: Basic Books, 1972). A. P. Moore's *The Genre Poissard and the French Stage in the Eighteenth Century* (New York: Columbia University, The Institute of French Studies, 1935) examines the contemporary literature in the popular argot with comments on the social organization among marketwomen and the physical conditions of the markets. Greater detail on the specific professions of marketwomen can be gleaned from Alfred Franklin, *Dictionnaire historique des arts, métiers et professions exercés dans Paris depuis le treizième siècle* (Paris: Editions Montchrestien, 1906). Emile Coornaert's *Les Corporations en France avant 1789* (Paris: Gallimard, 1941) summarizes the place of women in the *corps des métiers* during the eighteenth century. The dynamics between the police and the marketwomen are elaborated in the contemporary account of J.-B. Charles Le Maire, *La Police de Paris en 1770. Mémoire inédit composé par ordre de G. De Sartine sur la demande de Marie Thérèse*, ed. A. Gazier, in the *Mémoires de la Société d'histoire de Paris et de l'Ile de France,* 5 (1879). Two recent studies on the procedures and verdicts of the Châtelet, with specific comment on the criminality of women, are G. Aubry's *La Jurisprudence criminelle du Châtelet de Paris sous le règne de Louis XVI* (Paris: Pichon et Durand-Auzias, 1971), and Prophyre Petrovitch's "Recherches sur la criminalité à Paris dans la seconde moitié du xviiie siècle," in *Crimes et criminalité à Paris sous l'Ancien Régime,* eds. A. Abbiateci et al. (Paris: A. Colin, 1971, Cahiers des Annales, 33). More anecdotal but rich in detail on the treatment of adultery are sections in Robert Anchel's *Crimes et châtiments au XVIIIe siècle* (Paris: Librairie academique Perrin, 1933). Camille Bloch's *L'Assistance et l'état en France à la veille de la Révolution: Généralités de Paris, Rouen, Alençons, Orléans, Soissons, Amiens, 1764–1789* (Paris: Picard, 1908) outlines the organization and administration of prerevolutionary hospital services and includes an extensive bibliography of primary and secondary literature in the field.

The Expectations and Modes of Protest of the Women of the People During the Revolutionary Decade

George Rudé's *The Crowd in the French Revolution* (Oxford: Oxford University Press, 1959) analyzes the participants in the popular protest between 1789 and 1795 with observations on the preponderance of women in the crowds during the periods of acute economic hardship. Scattered in P.-J.-B. Buchez and P.-C. Roux's *Histoire parlementaire de la Révolution française,* 40 vols. (Paris: Paulin, 1834–1838) are numerous examples of contemporary reactions to the marketplace disruptions throughout the revolutionary period; Buchez and Roux made a point of documenting those times when women were most active in the public affairs. A thorough analysis of the women's march in 1789, based on the available primary sources, is Dom Henri Leclercq's *Les Journées d'Octobre et la fin de l'année 1789* (Paris: Letouzey et Ané, 1924). In English, two valuable works that discuss the convergence of political radicalism and economic protest in the fall of 1789 are Cornwell Rogers's *The Spirit of the Revolution in 1789: A Study in Public Opinion as Revealed in Political Songs and Other Popular Literature at the Beginning of the French Revolution* (Princeton: Princeton University Press, 1949), and Julia C. Stoddard's "The Causes of the Insurrection of the 5th and 6th of October in 1789," in *University of Nebraska Studies* 4 (October 1904): 269–327. Women's efforts to exert pressure on the national legislatures and the Parisian clubs in the constitutional monarchy are treated in Albert Mathiez's *La Vie chère et le mouvement social sous la Terreur* (Paris: Payot, 1927) and his *Le Club des Cordeliers pendant la crise de Varennes et le massacre du Champ de Mars* (Paris: Champion, 1910). Isabelle Bourdin's *Les Sociétés populaires à Paris pendant la Révolution française, 1789 jusqu'au la chute de la royauté* (Paris: Librairie du Receuil, 1937) has the fullest discussion of women's role in the early societies along with useful bibliographical information on the speeches and the careers of the most outspoken clubwomen. The *Souvenirs d'une femme du peuple,* ed. O. Boutanquoi (Senlis: Imprimerie Réunis, 1928) includes an interesting eyewitness account of women in the spectator gallery of the early Jacobin Society. For the period between 1793 and 1795, Albert Soboul's *Les Sans-Culottes parisiens en l'an II: Mouvement populaire et gouvernement révolutionnaire, 2 juin 1793–9 thermidor an II* (Paris: Librairie Clavreuil, 1958), and Kare Tønnesson's *La Défaite des sans-culottes: Mouvement populaire et réaction bourgeoise en l'an III* (Oslo and Paris: Librairie Clavreuil, 1959) are indispensable studies that cover the spontaneous and collective expressions of feminine protest. Marie Cerati's *Le Club des Citoyennes républicaines révolutionnaires* (Paris: Editions Sociales, 1966) concentrates on the political activity and the leadership of the Society of Revolutionary Republican Women; R. B. Rose's *The* Enragés: *Socialists of the French Revolution?* (Melbourne: Melbourne University Press, 1965) contains useful vignettes on the leaders Claire Lacombe and Pauline Leon. The more spontaneous behavior of women in the markets can be traced in Adolphe Schmidt, *Tableaux de la Révolution (1789–1800),* vol. 2 (Leipzig: Veit, 1869), and Pierre Caron, *Paris pendant la terreur. Rapports des agents secrets du Ministre de l'Intérieur,* vols. 1–4 (Paris: Picard, 1914). A useful summary of the contemporary reactions to the marketplace upheavals in the fall of 1793 is

Scott Lytle's "The Second Sex (September 1793)," *Journal of Modern History,* 26, no. 1 (1955): 14–26.

Institutional Changes for the Women of the People During the Revolutionary Decade

Jacques Godechot's *Les institutions de la France sous la Révolution et l'Empire,* 2nd ed. (Paris: Presses universitaires de France, 1968) traces the institutional developments and provides extensive bibliographies on each of the revolutionary institutions. The organization and enforcement of the police during the Revolution is outlined in Philip John Stead, *The Police of Paris* (London: Staples Press, 1957). Richard C. Cobb's "Note sur la répression contre le personnel sans culotte de 1795 à 1801," *Annales historiques de la Révolution française,* 134 (January–March 1954): 30–35, and Brian Chapman's "The Prefecture of Police," *Journal of Criminal Law, Criminology and Political Science,* 44 (1962): 505–11 discuss the refined policing methods developed after the spring uprisings of 1795. For details on the revolutionary attempts to create a national system of public assistance see Jean Imbert's *Le Droit hospitalier de la Révolution et l'Empire* (Paris: Librairie de Receuil Sirey, 1954), and Jean Boussoulade's sympathetic but comprehensive account of the secularization of the hospital personnel in his *Moniales et hospitalières dans la tourmente révolutionnaire: Les Communautes de religieuses de l'ancien diocèse de Paris de 1789–1801* (Paris: Letouzey et Ané, 1962). The workshops for women have attracted considerable attention since they anticipated later efforts in 1848 and 1870. Shelby T. McCloy's "Charity Workshops for Women, Paris, 1790–1795," *Social Science Review* 11 (June 1937): 274–84 summarizes the organizational problems in these shops, and Yvonne Forado-Cunéo, "Les Ateliers de charité de Paris pendant la Révolution française, 1789–1791," in *La Révolution française* 86 (1933): 317–42; 87 (1934): 29–123 gives a comprehensive account of the formation and the financing of the shops. The secular legislation of the Jacobin administration that pertained to the status of women is treated in the monograph by G. Thibault-Laurent, *La Première introduction de divorce pendant la Révolution et l'Empire* (Clermont-Ferrand: Imprimerie moderne, 1938), and in the study of Crane Brinton, *French Revolutionary Legislation on Illegitimacy* (Cambridge, Mass.: Harvard University Press, 1936). Albert Soboul's "Sentiments religieux et cultes populaires sous la Révolution: saints, patriots et martyrs de la liberté," in *Annales historiques de la Révolution française* 148 (July–September 1957): 195–213 is an excellent account of the ways in which the popular societies attempted to supplant religious allegiances with loyalty to the Republic.

Conditions for the Women of the People During the Napoleonic Era

L. de Lanzac de Laborie, *Paris sous Napoléon,* vols. 3 and 5 (Paris: Plon, 1908–13), and Alphonse Aulard, *Paris sous le Premier Empire,* 3 vols. (Paris: Plon, 1912–1923) are rich in description of the social control of the Napoleonic marketplace. A brief discussion of the policing of prostitutes introduces A.-J.-B. Parent-Duchâtelet's *De la prostitution dans la ville de Paris,* 1st ed. (Brussels, 1936). The essays in Bernard Schwartz's *The Code Napoleon and the Common Law World* (New York: New York University Press, 1956) consider the status of women in the Napoleonic Code. A more analytic treatment is found in André-Jean Arnaud's *Essai d'analyse structurale du Code civil français: la règle du jeu dans la paix bourgeoise* (Paris: L.G.J.D., 1972), and statistics on the Parisian divorce rates between 1793 and 1795 are included in Maxine Leroy's "Le Centennaire du Code civil," *La Revue de Paris*, 5 (1903): 511–33, 753–80. Jean Tulard's *Nouvelle histoire de Paris: Le Consulat et l'Empire, 1800–1815* (Paris: Hachette, 1970) provides an excellent survey of the conditions of the Parisian poor in the Napoleonic era with detailed bibliographical suggestions on primary and secondary literature.

6/Communist Feminism: Its Synthesis and Demise

Beatrice Brodsky Farnsworth

This study focuses on the effect of the Bolshevik Revolution on the lives of women within the orbit of the Communist party. It explores the immediate impact of revolution on women already politically conscious. Did the experience of war and revolution heighten their sense of themselves as a group? That is, did the women organize as women? Did they create women's institutions? If so, did a sense of a female collectivity endure beyond the first few years of revolutionary excitement? Were the women able to challenge successfully the basic values of the dominant male culture? Did women find themselves in fundamentally new roles? Relative to where the masses of women had been before the Revolution and where the communist women optimistically expected the Revolution to lead them, how far were their goals achieved?

A look first at the communist women active in the party at the time of the Revolution. Who were they and how did they, at the beginning of the new era, see their own roles? The women communists who entered the Bolshevik party before the Revolution and became prominent were for the most part from the privileged classes. Among them were N. Krupskaia, A. Kollontai, Inessa Armand, Z. Lilina, K. Samoilova, E. Bosh, E. Rozmirovich, E. Stasova, V. Iakovleva, S. Smidovich, and K. Nikolaeva. Generally middle-aged by the time of the Revolution (with the exception of Nikolaeva, who was also unusual for her working-class background), and with years of experience working for the party in exile or underground in Russia, they were strong women who had achieved their own education and liberation in the late nineteenth century. But that they were exceptional people may not have been the primary reason for their stature within the Bolshevik movement. A French socialist, criticizing her own party, noted that while in theory women were accepted as equals in socialist parties, in practice only the woman who joined with her husband, father, or brother was received without objection. The Bolsheviks were no exception. Bolshevik women usually had a male mentor.[1]

Some of the material in this study appears in slightly different form in my book, *Aleksandra Kollontai: Communists, Feminists, and the Bolshevik Revolution* (Stanford: Stanford University Press, 1979). Brief portions have appeared in D. Atkinson, A. Dallin, and G. Lapidus, *Women in Russia* (Stanford: Stanford University Press, 1977).

Whether because they avoided theoretical analysis, the area which conferred status within the party, or because they sensed that they would not be welcome in what was almost exclusively a male domain, communist women seemed inclined (Aleksandra Kollontai was a notable exception) to carry out practical tasks rather than to engage in political theorizing. The status of female revolutionaries tended to diminish still further after the Revolution. Not one of the women ever sat on the Politburo. Only Kollontai, Stasova, and Iakovleva ever served, and then briefly, on the Central Committee during the initial Soviet period.[2]

Communist women perceived themselves largely as agitators and organizers committed to bringing the communist work to masses of backward Russian working-class and peasant women. In this sense, the Bolshevik women of the 1920s resembled the *narodnitsa* of the 1870s, the radical young women who "went to the people." Nor would it be far-fetched to suggest that the communist women of the 1920s, seeking to enlighten their less fortunate sisters, were not altogether unlike the bourgeois feminists of nineteenth- and early twentieth-century Russia, whose assumption that society was split fundamentally by a sexual rather than a class division they scorned as politically misguided. The communists took a feminist position in that they, too, believed in a woman's right to decide her own destiny free from sex-determined stereotypic roles and from society's oppressive restrictions. But the bourgeois feminists worked for political and legal change within the capitalist system, and were concerned mostly with the female intelligentsia, while the communist-feminists sought a broader social and economic liberation and focused on the working class. The bourgeois feminist reformers gave priority to women's issues, but the communists subordinated women's special interests to larger political goals, for they believed that the Revolution was the essential first step toward the liberation of women.

After the Revolution, the concerns of women communists focused more specifically on women's needs. They saw the cycle of world war, revolution, and civil war much as Lenin did, as a catalyst for revolutionary change. War and revolution had hastened women's development, forced them to be independent and to take on the responsibilities of the absent men.[3] But within the first revolutionary years, party women became convinced that special measures were needed in order not to lose these women. With hunger and deprivation intensifying their customary resistance to change, the masses of Russian women after the Revolution were becoming dangerously alienated from the communist regime and therefore potential fodder for counterrevolutionary forces. Quite simply, the women of Russia, the workers, the peasants, the urban and village poor, did not trust the communists in the autumn of 1918. There was no reason why they should, for the Revolution had not lightened the burden of life for them. Their breadwinner was back at the front, away from the family, fighting in a civil war for the Revolution. Women's lives had become not easier, but more difficult.[4]

A group of women communists—veterans of the revolutionary move-ment—believed at the outset in the need for an educational campaign which would enable politically unconscious women to understand the larger, long-range impact of the Revolution on their lives. A dramatic first step was taken in November 1918 with the organization of a huge all-Russian working-women's conference aimed at providing Russian women with a new self-image. Party leaders addressed the women as serious revolutionary fighters upon whom the regime depended. The organizers hoped that the conference might tap and reinforce what faith in their abilities the women had developed by living alone and working in the last few years of war.

It is important to understand that the communist image of the new woman assumed that she would be a mother, as Russian women invariably were. It never occurred to the communists to speak in terms of women who might choose not to fulfill that role. One reason lay in the collective need for children to build the new society. But perhaps the Bolsheviks pictured socialist women in maternal roles for reasons that went beyond the society's need for children. Their impulse reached deep into the Russian symbolism of "Ma-tushka-Rus," the enduring and capable mother. The communists' unexamined assumption that the Russian working woman would, of course, bear children supports Vera Dunham's argument that the Russian ethos of the strong woman simply did not include the spinster.[5]

The view of the socialist woman as worker-mother, implicit in the ideology of the women in the Communist party, was incorporated in the program of the First All-Russian Congress of Worker and Peasant Women that met in Petrograd in November 1919. It was their duty to win the support of all working-class and peasant women for Soviet power, to combat domestic slavery and the double standard of morality, to develop collective child-rearing institutions, and to establish centralized and collective living arrange-ments in order to release women from household drudgery. This last point was summed up in the slogan "the separation of the kitchen from marriage is as vital as the separation of the church from the state." To these goals they added a commitment to bring women into the economy, to protect women's labor in shops and factories, to provide maternity legislation, and to end prostitution.

The "bureau" of communist women which existed in November 1918 was loosely organized around the editorial board of the women's newspaper, *Rabotnitsa* ("The Working Woman"). But the dynamics of revolution caused the "bureau" to seek a more structured women's organization that embodied the goals of the 1918 working women's conference. A Women's Commission was then established which in the autumn of 1919 became the Zhenotdel ("Women's Section") of the Central Committee. The Women's Section did not grow out of a consensus within the party, for many communists con-sidered work among women to have a low priority. Rather, it resulted from the persistent and rather unpopular efforts of a small group of women communists committed to the liberation of their own sex. Inspired by the organization for women established by Clara Zetkin within the German Social Democratic party, they argued that special measures were needed to protect backward women from counterrevolutionary propaganda and to draw them into revolutionary construction. Although the Zhenotdel resulted from female agitation, and although nearly all the women prominent within the communist movement eventually became members, not all communist women agreed initially on the wisdom of a separate organization. Nor did all Zhenotdel members accept with enthusiasm their own assignment to the Women's Section. Some feared that a separate Women's Section might be construed by their male comrades as feminist—and therefore divisive of working-class unity—an apprehension not altogether unrealistic. They wondered if the newspaper *Rabotnitsa* was not a sufficient rallying point for women. They had also internalized the male view that a Women's Section committed to drawing unenlightened women into the Revolution was, by definition, a lesser group. "That kind of work [did] not interest her," objected the Bokshevik Elena Stasova. And a younger communist, Polina Vinogradskaia, tried to refuse her assignment, arguing that she was not experienced in working among backward women. Similarly, a journalist, sister of a Women's Section leader, argued that she preferred to do important work at the front where she was needed rather than to work among women. Yet another woman who became a valued leader of the Women's Section, Vera Alexeyevna, recalled the hoots of laughter at the announcement that she would be working among women—she who had been in jail for revolutionary activity more times than she could remember and had built up a record of bravery![6] But the initial dismay gave way rather quickly to an esprit de corps. Even reluctant recruits served with distinction and ultimately endorsed the concept of a special section within the Central Committee devoted to making communists out of Soviet women.

The Zhenotdel planned to move from practice to theory, to demonstrate by concrete means to politically unsophisticated women, primarily to mothers, the potential benefits of socialism. For example, women organizers first built a nursery, then slowly tried to win over the local women.[7] In the beginning, Zhenotdel organizers sometimes met physical opposition from working women who feared that their children would be taken from them and put in public shelters. Dread and enthusiasm coexisted, but confidence grew with exposure. Many women, in fact, were reportedly disappointed by party promises of child-care facilities which failed to materialize.[8] But a positive outlook toward the Zhenotdel was uncommon. However much working women could be won over by a woman-to-woman approach, the majority of proletarian and peasant women did not immediately believe that the Zhenotdel represented their own interests. Conversely, the communist women's perception of what was in the working women's best interest was not necessarily the view of the working women themselves.

On the whole, what success there was during the 1920s in organizing women was greater among the proletariat and less impressive among the peasants, who were more difficult to reach and whose consciousness as a group the Zhenotdel scarcely penetrated. Proletarian women who only recently had been workers were seeing their own lives change. In the immediate postrevolutionary years they directed political sections in the army, organized public food distribution, and struggled with starvation and epidemics. Some even fought illiteracy, built reading huts, or took part in political campaigns.[9] But impressive changes sometimes also occurred in the few villages where the Zhenotdel was active during the 1920s. Zhenotdel leaders were convinced that the negative orientation of the peasants changed whenever they were given special attention. When the party held meetings, when party workers showed peasant women ways by which they could ease their lives, a broad circle of women began to favor the Revolution.[10] Soviet memoirs are filled with personal recollections of the process. For instance, a former peasant remembered her pride upon being elected a *delegatka*, a representative from her village to the network of informational meetings held weekly under the guidance of the local Zhenotdel. Suddenly she felt different about herself.[11] *Kommunistka*, the journal of the Women's Section, carried reports of peasant women who as early as 1920, despite male ridicule, had bravely organized their own work *artels*, had sought to build children's nurseries, and had requested further contact with advisers from the Women's Section.[12] Zhenotdel workers were surprised that not only young women attended their conferences. Here and there they saw the gray heads and the wrinkled faces of older women who believed that life still held new possibilities.[13]

If we go looking for change, chances are that we will find it. Distortion is inherent in generalization. Yet we cannot completely discount the testimonies of visitors to rural Russia in the 1920s. Many reported their astonishment at the progress made by peasant women in those few villages with active Zhenotdel organizers. Jessica Smith, a socialist who went to Russia with the American Friends Service Committee in the early 1920s, wrote a sympathetic but objective account. She especially recalled the performance of peasant women at a village meeting sponsored by the Zhenotdel. "Some of the women spoke well in clear, ringing voices," she wrote. Others "spoke stumblingly, and had to be prompted, and one broke down before she finished, and rushed weeping from the platform." But it was a miracle to see this sort of thing happening, she pointed out, to see the shining eyes of these hundreds of women in the dimly lighted hall; for the first time they realized that life held something for them beyond the dull routine of the past.[14]

Early Soviet fiction provides examples of these few rural women whose lives were radically and almost immediately changed by the Revolution. "Marya the Bolshevik" was one of the first "new women." An obedient and fearful wife before the Revolution, she awakened during the civil war. Elected as a joke to head the village council, she ruled with determination, became active in organizing a local Zhenotdel, read the newspaper, renounced religion, and divorced her husband. Marya became a Bolshevik *aktivistka*.

Another fictional heroine, Dasha Chumalova, was the most famous of the communist "new women." Left with the responsibility of a small child when her husband Gleb went to fight in the civil war, Dasha was transformed in response to the necessity of war. Once a clinging wife, she became a revolutionary fighter; hardened by her experiences, she was unable to resume the subordinate role her husband expected of her upon his return.[15]

The women within the Zhenotdel agreed on the need to draw working-class and peasant women into the party and to replace private domesticity with communal kitchens and dining halls. They also agreed on the need for children's homes—if not on the question of actual physical separation of child from parent. But other implications of the program which had been presented at the All-Russian Worker and Peasant Women's Conference in November 1918 and which affected the quality of personal life were more controversial.

Radical communist women like A. Kollontai, the director of the Zhenotdel in the early 1920s, spoke of an end to the double standard of morality and hailed a new kind of marriage. Kollontai predicted that the future would see new forms of sexual relationships, that it would be immaterial to the communist regime if marriages were short-term or lasting unions, for either type would provide the collective with healthy children whom Soviet society would care for. Debates over the ramifications of such predictions were common in the 1920s, both within the ranks of the Zhenotdel and among troubled young communist women uncertain as to what changes the Revolution would bring into their lives. One such debate in the Soviet press illustrates quite well the kind of anxieties engendered by the Revolution. Communist women might agree over an end to pots and pans, but they disagreed about the nature of marriage and motherhood, about sexual morality, birth control and abortion. Conservative thinking was surprisingly strong among them. No one expressed the conservative point of view more forcefully than the Bolshevik Sof'ia Smidovich, who in 1922 replaced Kollontai as director of the Zhenotdel. A strong woman who had risen to be a member of the powerful Central Control Commission in the mid-1920s, Smidovich believed in real political equality for women, in combatting male chauvinism, and in children's homes where children would spend their days and only visit their parents—much like the Israeli kibbutz. But she also had a conservative side.

She considered herself an orthodox militant who defended the proletarian vanguard against the ideas of the intelligentsia, in this case the idea of freer sex. In her widely published criticism of Kollontai's proposals, Smidovich took the line that the Soviet Union was still in a transitional era, moving painfully from capitalism to socialism; consequently Kollontai's theories were premature and would lead only to increased promiscuity. When a visitor inquired about sexual mores in the revolutionary society, Smidovich distinguished between generations. "Of course, we older communists believe that it is best to love one person and stick to him."[16] But the gap was ideological more than generational. Both Kollantai and Smidovich were middle-aged women and both had adherents among Russian youth.

Some young women clung to the familiar past and resisted a radical orientation of personal life. The communist woman who signed herself "Lida" wrote to Smidovich seeking guidance on sex and love, wanting to know whether she should succumb to male desires and engage in transient love affairs that meant the risk of crippling abortions or of raising a child alone. Lida did not seek material comforts. She just wanted to live openly in a lasting union with the man she loved.[17] Smidovich's answers were more conservative than avant-garde. She advised Lida to trust her cautious woman-ly instincts, and she explained that for a woman love was not transient passion but an extended process which included birth and nursing. In fact, a woman's relationship to love was determined to a large degree by her role as a mother. Significantly, Smidovich stated that she would not even discuss with Lida marriages without children: such marriages, she argued, were so rare as not to merit consideration.[18] Any discussion of childless marriages would have involved mention of birth control, an awkward subject for Smidovich. Overpopulation did not trouble the Russians: with their vast potential re-sources they could provide sustenance for many more people. And to many Marxists, who saw no lack of food and of material resources but only their unequal distribution, birth control seemed a measure of bourgeois defeatism.

But other young women, bolder than Lida, eagerly expected the Revolution to transform their lives. One such "new woman," named Nina Vel't, launched an angry attack on Smidovich, challenging her professed concern with the problem of women and marriage. Did Smidovich really care about women, or was she interested more in Soviet society's need for children? Nina considered Smidovich's advice to Lida "cheap moralizing" that neither she nor Lida needed. Rejecting Smidovich's admonition, in effect, to be continent or to be willing to assume the care of a family, Nina reminded Smidovich that a socialist did not bow to the laws of nature but sought instead to alter them. Nina ridiculed the party's ambivalence about birth control as an attitude that led not to the application of ointment to a hurt finger, as she put it, but rather to the amputation of the entire hand. Nina did not like abortions either. But did Smidovich think that four sickly children were better for society than two healthy ones? And what of the mother's life? With two children there was still some chance for employment, but four children excluded that possibility. Did Smidovich know the "new woman"? Surely she was not the married woman cut off from society and dependent for her livelihood on a man because she had abandoned work and studies for motherhood. Nor could she be the pathetic person whom Smidovich urged Lida to emulate, a woman who defined herself in terms of her relationship to a man. A fear for the kind of future the party had in mind caused Nina to press her attack, to question Smidovich's larger image of Soviet society. Why did Smidovich write approv-ingly of Lida's assertion that she did not seek a comfortable existence?

Sensing that Smidovich was using asceticism as a defense against sensuality, Nina demanded: Why should a communist woman not want life's comforts? Did socialism have to be drab? Was a silk blouse a sign that one must be driven from the party?[19] And so went the argument among communist women, young and middle-aged, uncertain as to how the Revolution would impinge upon their own lives.

Did Smidovich know the "new woman"? Let us pause briefly to ponder Nina Vel't's challenge to the older communist, to consider whether the experiences of revolutionary women born in the nineteenth century enabled them to understand the conflicts of postrevolutionary Soviet women. Could the revolutionary veterans relate to the problems of combining study, love, motherhood, and career? Did they, too, cope with conflicting roles as revolutionaries and as women? Was motherhood a part of their lives?

Sof'ia Smidovich insisted that for a woman love was inextricably bound to motherhood. But another revolutionary veteran, Olga Liubatovich, had warned: "It's a sin for revolutionaries to start a family. Men and women both must stand alone, like soldiers under a hail of bullets. But in your youth, you somehow forget that revolutionaries' lives are measured not in years, but in days and hours."[20] A look at the circumstances which motivated Liubatovich's sad conclusion will illuminate the conflicts faced by the older generation of women revolutionaries. During the 1870s Liubatovich had lived with another young revolutionary, N. Morozov, with whom she had fled from Russia to Geneva in 1880. Sometime later that year she had given birth to a daughter. Subsequently, Morozov had been arrested during a political mission in Russia. Liubatovich had left her infant daughter with a good friend in order to return to Russia and try to obtain her lover's release.

Although the woman revolutionary did not usually dwell on her emotions, Liubatovich's memoirs reveal her feelings upon leaving her child: "For a long time I stood like a statue in the middle of the room, the tired baby sleeping in my arms. . . . When I finally decided to lower her into the bed, she opened her eyes—large, serious, peaceful, still enveloped in sleep. I couldn't bear her gaze. Not daring to kiss her lest I wake her up, I quietly walked out of the room. I thought I'd be back: I didn't know, didn't want to believe that I was seeing my little girl for the last time."[21]

The baby died during her mother's absence, the victim of a meningitis epidemic. Liubatovich thus received the news: "I sat over Kravchinskii's telegram for hours on end before it fully registered on me that my daughter was dead. I didn't cry; I was numb with grief. For some time thereafter I suffered torments whenever I walked down the street or rode in a tram: the sweet, happy faces of small children tore at my heart, reminding me of my own child."[22]

Here and there, other revolutionary women recorded the pain of separation from beloved children. Aleksandra Kollontai, leaving her small son with her parents in the 1890s as she journeyed to Zurich to study, wept on the train the first night, tormenting herself with memories of his sweet little hands.[23] Similarly, Sof'ia Smidovich, arrested for revolutionary activity in 1910, recalled how painful it was to think of her fifteen-year-old daughter Tania weeping, worried about her mother in prison.[24]

It was no easier after the Revolution. The revolutionary woman continued to suffer from competing desires. Famous for her condemnation of the nuclear family, Aleksandra Kollontai claimed that motherhood was never the kernel of her existence.[25] Yet she filled diaries and letters with yearning to be with her son, even after he was grown. She wrote of her conflict between the desire to see him and the pressure of party work. While in Moscow in 1919, she described the torment of knowing that her son, a student in Petrograd, must be hungry, but that she could do nothing for him. She feared for him in the desolation of Petrograd during the civil war, yet the wonder of Revolution sustained her and enabled her to fulfill party responsibilities in Moscow. Sof'ia Smidovich was not without guilt and ambivalence after the Revolution. She delighted in family warmth, living with her husband and her three children in their Kremlin apartment. But as director of the Women's Section and later a member of the Central Control Commission, she advocated children's homes where children would live apart from their parents. Uneasy about the limited attention she could provide her own family, she fantasized that in a children's home her children would receive more stimulation and consistent care.[26] Dasha Chumalova, the fictional Zhenotdel leader of the early 1920s, put her small daughter in a children's home. Significantly, this stalwart leader of the local Women's Section succumbed to her emotions only in connection with guilt toward her child. In a moving scene, Dasha, saying goodnight to Nurka, asked her: "What do you want? Tell me." And Nurka replied, "I want to stay with you . . . so that you'd never go away and always be near." Dasha put Nurka to bed and left the children's home. She did not return as usual to the Women's Section, but rather she walked into a thicket where she flung herself down on the grass. And there she lay crying for a long time, digging with her fingers into the mold.[27]

Communist women leaders were not in agreement concerning sexuality or the nature of marriage. But as mothers, they were uniquely situated to empathize with the conflicts of the masses of women to whom they directed their message. The debate over sexual morality and motherhood in the Soviet press of the mid-twenties suggests several conclusions important for the future of Soviet women. Communist leaders agreed that women would be mothers and workers both. No one in command, whether male or female, seriously argued for alternatives. What has come to be called Soviet pronatalism was, in fact, implicit in communist thinking from the outset. Women were expected to provide the socialist collective with its future workers. The collective, in turn, owed it to the women workers to provide for their children. Abortion, although made legal in 1920, was regarded as an evil necessity, a response to the emergency of the civil war, rather than a permanent social institution.[28] Nowhere in communist revolutionary thinking does one find the current feminist concept that a woman has a right to control her own body. Finally, it is worth noticing that the forces of social conservatism which predominated in the Stalinist era were not new to Communist Russia. Conservative strains of thought existed and were debated with the Zhenotdel during the relatively freer and radical 1920s.

Talk about fundamental social change in Soviet society exceeded change itself in the 1920s. This became apparent with the inauguration of the "New Economic Policy" (NEP) in 1921, which meant the partial return of private ownership. The revolutionary regime—and with it the Zhenotdel—despite its new conception of female roles and its proclamation of women's absolute equality with men, was unable or unwilling in fact to protect women from traditional discrimination during periods of unemployment.[29] Consider, for instance, the case of a woman employed in a factory during the civil war, who then lost her position in 1921 as a result of the end of the war, of the demobilization of men, and of the partial return to a market economy. For such a woman, unemployed and caring for children in a tiny flat, economically dependent on a man, the Revolution made little difference, despite the formal legal and political equality she enjoyed under the revolutionary legislation of 1918.

Change came to the lives of the masses of Soviet women only at the end of the decade, after the enforced political demise of the Zhenotdel and with the frantic drive to industrialization of the first Five-Year Plan. The dismantling of the Zhenotdel in 1930 resulted from the reorganization of the Central Committee, and was a step toward a more authoritarian centralized regime. The elimination of secondary associations and allegiances throughout Soviet life abolished the institutional center for discussions about the liberated woman. Open debate receded from the Soviet press while, ironically, female employment became the rule. By 1936 women were 40 percent of the work force. Their employment opportunities were determined, however, neither by the Zhenotdel's conception of women's equality nor by their own needs. The reason for their growing employment was put bluntly by the government's Supreme Council of National Economy in an article headlined, "Women into Production! Fundamental Change of Woman Labor." The article stated: "The struggle for utilization of female labor according to the needs of the national economy is the most urgent current problem. Industry and collectivized agriculture are now greatly in need of woman labor."[30]

The members of the former Women's Section of the Central Committee witnessed the enormous growth of the female labor force. The conditions of women's employment, however, were not what the communists had imagined they would be. In fact, the situation was fundamentally in conflict with the original expectations of the Zhenotdel. Women with children were entering the labor force without the benefit of communal facilities and frequently without adequate child care. If women were to be in the labor force but also retain the framework of traditional domesticity, Kollontai had written, women with children would not be liberated at all. Rather, they would be doubly burdened.[31] Precisely this situation had come about.

We should not underestimate the decade of organized efforts by Bolshevik women to transform women's lives. It may be true, as Kollontai wrote, that without the few dedicated communist women who launched the Women's Section, little would have been done in the immediate revolutionary era to bring women out of the home and into the party and public life.[32] But Kollontai's boast may also have been premature. She did not anticipate the Five-Year Plan, which began in 1928, or the enormous needs of industrialization and modernization. These forces would have brought women into the labor force even without the ideological groundbreaking efforts of the Zhenotdel in earlier years. The enormous population losses—one historian calls 1914–21 a "demographic earthquake"—resulted in a population at the end of the decade about 30 million less than might have been expected. These figures are relevant to understand the stressful haste of the 1930s, for they reflect serious gaps in the labor force.[33] If Russia was to industrialize, women had to be brought fully into the economy. Indeed, industrialization was launched on such an enormous scale that the new demand for labor flooded the planners and the government offices.[34] The sudden drive to industrialize and the resulting employment of women was in itself a result of revolution. But it had little to do with the ideology of the Bolshevik women who had been active in the revolutionary movement before 1917 and who had founded the Zhenotdel in 1920. These women of the intelligentsia, whom Stalin scorned, became largely irrelevant after 1930.[35]

One of the questions asked at the outset was whether women found themselves in new roles as a result of the Revolution. There are indications that women's roles have been remarkably resistant to change. Of the drive to collectivization and industrialization which tore Soviet society apart during the 1930s, Moshe Lewin has written that in a matter of a few years the bulk of the population changed social position and roles, switched into a new class, or a new job, or a new way of doing it. Workers went to offices, peasants became workers or officials, many Russians found themselves in schools and universities, and millions of peasants suddenly experienced the shock of collectivization, the *kolkhoz* system.[36] If many Russian men found themselves in strange new roles by the end of the 1930s, the same cannot really be said of Russian women. Even if they were in the professions and in the labor force, their primary roles remained unaltered. They were mothers, wives, child-raisers, and housekeepers. The family had not withered away, communal living had not developed, and after 1936 not only was birth control still inadequate, but in order to increase the population abortions again became illegal.[37]

If the full equality which the organizers of the Zhenotdel anticipated in 1920 has not occurred, it is largely because the Soviet effort to emancipate women has, in fact, lacked centrality and deliberateness.[38] Modernization rather than equality has been the communist goal. The pursuit of modernization in the Soviet Union, through a system of unintended but powerful constraints, has shaped and limited the scope of equality. Moreover, the twin socialist goals of increased population and women's participation in society on a fully equal basis may have grown to be wholly at odds and therefore unattainable. For example, current proposals on how to reverse the decline in birth rate range from paying mothers to remain at home to allowing more part-time employment. Consideration of women's professional advancement and of genuine equality—the issues which engaged the Zhenotdel—are generally overlooked.[39]

To be sure, as Norton Dodge has pointed out, the changes in education and professional opportunities for masses of Russian women, largely illiterate before the Revolution, have been enormous. The numbers and proportions of Soviet women in interesting and challenging semiprofessional and professional occupations exceed by far the numbers and proportions of women in such occupations in any nonsocialist society.[40] But it is also true, as Gail Lapidus has shown, that women are integrated into the labor force in segregated and subordinate roles, clustered at the lower ranks of the professions. Men are thereby shielded from competition with women, and the situations in which women exercise authority over men are limited.[41]

On the other hand, if Russian men have readily accepted women in public life and in new occupations, it is also, ironically, because of the endurance of familiar attitudes and priorities. The traditional values of the dominant male culture remain the same sixty years after the Revolution. In whatever situations they are employed, Soviet wives maintain domestic roles and outward deference to male superiority.[42]

Why does the married woman in Russia, despite the Revolution and its invitation to women to participate fully, still feel that her primary responsibility is to her home and family? Why do social scientists conclude that many Soviet women "seem relieved that housework provides an acceptable excuse for avoiding political activity"?[43] The question brings us back to the first decade of the revolutionary era, to the role of the Women's Section within Soviet society.

The Zhenotdel, despite its commitment, was unable to protect women from the effects of unemployment; although a section of the Central Committee, it was powerless to influence political and economic planning. If, in retrospect, the Zhenotdel was nonetheless making a contribution toward transforming women's lives, its impact must be evaluated on another level. Pushing aside models of revolutionary change dictated from above and looking at the pervasiveness of deeply rooted cultural values, the remarkable old leaders of the Zhenotdel found it necessary to combat vigorously entrenched assumptions about female roles.[44] Indeed, if the contemporary Soviet woman still considers it prestigious to be a good housewife, if her career objectives are usually more limited than a man's, it is due in part to the demise of the Zhenotdel. The abolition in 1930 of the coherent center which furnished the radical female model made a break with customary values unlikely. If women's consciousness is to change, there must be a critical mass of protesters such as existed during the first decade of Soviet power, when women were organized in an interest group. In a number of instances, in fact, the activities of the Zhenotdel have been explicitly recalled by Soviet writers, even held up as a model of what can be done to inculcate in women a true dignity and awareness of their equal rights with men.[45]

Of course, the Zhenotdel was marginal to Soviet society. It would be wrong to exaggerate its effectiveness. One might even question the wisdom, in general, of separate organizations for women within larger political movements. By providing a convenient, out-of-the-way place to which the party could assign its women members during the 1920s, communist women may paradoxically have done themselves a disservice. The majority of women in the Women's Section appear to have worked within circumscribed roles, in the less militant, weaker groups, more easily put off with empty promises.[46]

Nor can it be said that the Zhenotdel during its brief life possessed the answers to the complexities of the woman question. In retrospect, it would appear that the position of the Zhenotdel was flawed in at least one respect. By seeking (and achieving) special privileges for working mothers in order to ease the burden of their presumed dual roles, rather than proposing to extend those benefits to working fathers as well, the Zhenotdel may in fact have hurt the cause of female equality.[47] Evidence suggests that the extension of special protective arrangements for women has tended simply to reinforce occupational and professional segregation and to inhibit rather than to promote genuine sexual equality.[48] A Soviet writer explained, for example, why it is more difficult for women than for men to be admitted to medical school and to rise in the profession: "Girls occupy a more complex position in medicine than do boys: marriage, immobility for purposes of assignment, departures from work—temporary or permanent—when family interests outweigh professional considerations. . . . Boys may not always have deeper knowledge nor do they know how to apply it any better, but given time they become dependable workers."[49] Women's reluctance to move to new posts and their temporary departures from work for daily priorities that outweigh professional obligations make men seem more reliable and entitled to preference. Clearly, an unintended consequence of socialist privileges for working mothers in the Soviet Union (as in Eastern Europe) has been to hinder them professionally.[50]

The political scientist Gregory Massell may also be correct in arguing that it is inherent to authoritarian revolutionary movements that women be kept from leadership roles. According to this theory, the successful achievement of power increases the masculine sense of dominance; having gained power in a revolutionary struggle, men are unlikely to share that power willingly with women, even with women whom they regarded as comrades during the early, less successful stages of the Revolution.[51] Massell suggests that it is difficult for women to wrest an equal share of power from triumphant men. But if his theory is correct, then an institution like the Women's Section, evolved by women themselves in response to the challenge of revolution, becomes indispensable. Despite the drawback of providing a "secondary" arena in which women could be assigned, the Women's Section had a vital revolutionary role to play. In the area of attitudinal change the Zhenotdel contributed to increasing women's self-confidence and transforming their feelings about their place in society. Had political conditions allowed it, such an institution could also have perpetuated a female collectivity to represent women's changing interests.

During its short life, the Zhenotdel demonstrated both its limitations and its potential, isolating and describing the problems that Russian women faced as workers and as mothers, but offering only partial solutions. This is not to say that if the innovative Zhenotdel had been permitted to continue, it could not have evolved creative options to deal with the difficulties of the woman question. The Zhenotdel was no more monolithic than other Soviet institutions in the 1920s. The pages of *Pravda* reflect lively disputes within its ranks over the ways in which the Zhenotdel might counteract government neglect of women's interests.[52] Kollontai, for example, suggested as early as 1923 that *after* the Revolution it was entirely appropriate for the socialist women's movement to adopt the policies of feminism rejected previously as divisive and as a threat to working-class solidarity. Her amalgam of socialist-feminism envisioned an expansion of Zhenotdel activities to include "special societies," clubs where women could work to raise their own political consciousness and, as feminists, to demand the fulfillment of their newly won revolutionary rights.[53] In *Pravda*, the former director of the Zhenotdel offered ideas which her successors might have pursued had the fluid conditions of NEP society continued. History is rich in contradictions: the relationship of the woman question to NEP society is a case in point. On the one hand, NEP dealt a heavy blow to Soviet women. For many, the partial restoration of a free economy in 1921 meant the immediate curtailment of government social welfare programs and the loss of employment. On the other hand, the years of the NEP, the only time in which Soviet society was relatively pluralistic, were peculiarly appropriate to the development of special interest groups.[54]

What, then, was the impact of the Revolution on the lives of Russian women? An immediate effect was to cause politically conscious communist women, bent on transforming the lives of their backward sisters, to organize a Women's Section within the party, an institution that was short-lived due to political forces beyond the control of its founders. In the years since the demise of the Zhenotdel the Soviet Union has not solved the fundamental problems peculiar to women any more effectively than any other society. To be sure, the lives of women are vastly improved. Relative to the condition of the masses of Russian women before 1917, Soviet success has been phenomenal. Soviet women now have legal equality, day-care centers, improved working conditions, social welfare legislation, and professional opportunities

Nancy Hart, heroine of the American Revolution, 1779

All photos courtesy of the Prints and Photographs Division, the Library of Congress

Parisian women of the people go to Versailles to fetch the King, 1789

Nurses in the American Civil War: the women of the United States Sanitary Commission, 1865

Mobilization of Japanese women for the war against Russia, 1905

The *soldaderas* of the Mexican Revolution, 1911

Seamstresses in a flag shop, Brooklyn Navy Yard, 1917

Peasant women supplying military trains, Russia, 1917

Signalwoman at training camp of the Women's Defense League,
Washington, D.C., 1917

Young munitions workers in Connecticut, 1942

British war propaganda describes this English munitions worker as a housewife, mother of five, good cook, and an active participant in community affairs, England, 1943

Members of the Royal Navy Women's Service, on surveillance duty
aboard British warship, 1942

Men who drop bombs meet women who make them, England, 1943

unparalleled in Russian history. It is an achievement not to be underestimated. But neither should it be attributed solely to the Communist Revolution. The Soviet experience cannot be separated qualitatively from the results of modernization without revolution in other countries, such as Sweden. For the women who are mothers, the sixty years since the Revolution have resulted not only in new opportunities but also in ambivalence, professional limitations, and in dual responsibilities rather than altered roles. Like women everywhere, Soviet women cope with pregnancies, families, housework, and outside jobs. Indeed, the strain of combining family and career, to which Soviet women seem oddly resigned, may even be greater in the Soviet Union than in other industrial societies.[55] Women in the Soviet Union appreciate their professional advancement, grumble about their heavy responsibilities, and do not expect dramatic changes.[56]

Alexander Dallin has pointed to a curious paradox, that Marxists "were most optimistic about the prospects of revolution when they were least successful, and least optimistic when at the peak of their power." He adds: "What was a welcome challenge to the hopeful and young revolutionaries of yesteryear—there were no mountains too high to climb... becomes an inordinately demanding task to the bureaucrats and managers ... a generation or two later.... it is no longer true that we have nothing to lose but our chains."[57]

Dallin's observation is particularly relevant to the experience of Communist women. When the Revolution was youngest and weakest, Soviet assurances to women were the most uniquely communist and utopian.[58] There is nothing women will not be able to do, A. Kollontai promised in 1918 at the Conference of Worker and Peasant Women, after outlining to her audience the advantages to socialist society of collective living and praising the projected upbringing of children.[59] But if for Soviet women an unexpected consequence of modernization and industrialization has been a retreat from optimism, it is not only because, as Dallin aptly put it, "the humanist ethos yields to production plans."[60] The retreat from optimism in regard to the woman question is also to be explained by the removal from the Central Committee in 1930 of a primary source of revolutionary enthusiasm, the Women's Section of the Communist party.

Notes

1. For remark of French socialist, see "Socialism Faces Feminism: The Failure of Synthesis in France, 1879–1914," in M. Boxer and J. Quataert, eds., *Socialist Women* (New York: Elsevier, 1978), p. 102. As for Bolshevik women: Krupskaia was married to Lenin; Armand followed Lenin, as Stasova looked to Iakov Sverdlov. Lilina was the wife of G.

Zinoviev. Bosh was married to Piatakov. Iakovleva was the sister of the revolutionary, N. Iakovlev. Vera and Liudmila Menzhinskaya were the sisters of V. Menzhinskii, successor to Felix Dzerzhinskii as head of the OGPU. Sof'ia Smidovich was married to Petr Smidovich, an old Bolshevik who was president of the Moscow Soviet in 1918. Kollontai and A. Balabanoff were the exceptions in that neither had an obvious male mentor.

2. Iakovleva was a candidate member. Krupskaia served on the Central Committee in her old age. Nikolaeva was elected in 1924 and demoted to candidate member in 1925. She was reelected to full membership in 1934. See R. V. Daniels, *The Conscience of the Revolution: Communist Opposition in Soviet Russia* (Cambridge, Mass.: Harvard University Press, 1960), pp. 422–433. For status of women, see Robert H. McNeal, "Women in the Russian Radical Movement," *Journal of Social History* 2 (Winter 1971–72): 143–163. And see chap. 8 in B. Farnsworth, *Aleksandra Kollontai* (Stanford: Stanford University Press, 1979).

3. For expression of this view, see A. Kollontai, *Rabotnitsa za god'revoliutsii* (Moscow, 1918), p. 4.

4. A. Kollontai, "Kak my sozvali pervyi Vserossiiskii S"ezd Rabotnits i Krest'ianok," *Kommunistka* 11 (November 1923): 4.

5. See Vera Dunham, "The Strong-Woman Motif," in Cyril E. Black, ed., *The Transformation of Russian Society* (Cambridge, Mass.: Harvard University Press, 1960), pp. 459–483.

6. For Stasova, see E. Stasova, *Stranitsy Zhizni: i Bor'by* (Moscow, 1960), p. 110; for Vinogradskaia, see P. Vinogradskaia, *Sobytiia i Pamiatnye Vstrechi* (Moscow, 1968), p. 199; and for Vera Alexeyevna, see Jessica Smith, *Women in Soviet Russia* (New York: Vanguard, 1928), p. 53.

7. A. M. Kollontai, *Rabotnitsa i Krest'ianka v Sovetskoi Rossii* (Petrograd, 1921), p. 33.

8. For reports of disappointment, see L. Trotsky, "Protiv prosveshchennogo b urokratizma (a takzhe i neproseshchennogo)" in L. Trotsky, *Sochineniia* (Moscow, 1927), vol. 21, p. 73.

9. Kollontai, *Rabotnitsa i Krest'ianka*, p. 19. For difficulty in organizing peasant women, see E. D. Emel'ianova, *Revoliutsiia, Partiia, Zhenshchina* (Smolensk, 1971).

10. For indication that three-fourths of the villages in the 1920s had no Zhenotdel organizers, see G. W. Lapidus, "Sexual Equality in Soviet Policy: A Developmental Perspective," in D. Atkinson, A. Dallin, and G. W. Lapidus, eds., *Women in Russia* (Stanford: Stanford University Press, 1977), p. 121. For views of Zhenotdel leaders concerning peasant women, see A. Kollotai, *Polozhenie Zhenschiny v Evoliutsii Khoziaistva* (Moscow-Petrograd, 1923), p. 197.

11. E. Bochkareva and S. Liubimova, *Svetlyi put'* (Moscow, 1967), p. 89.

12. Tov. Lilia, "Kak organizovali krest'ianki trudovuiu artel'," *Kommunistka* 3–4 (1920), pp. 30–31.

13. P. Vinogradskaia, "Odna iz ocherednykh zadach," *Kommunistka* 3–4 (1920), p. 31.

14. J. Smith, *Women in Soviet Russia*, p. 37.

15. See "Maria-Bol'shevichka," in A. Neverov, *Izbrannye Proizvedeniia* (Moscow, 1958), pp. 195–200. There are many women like her, the author concluded ruefully. For discussion of this story, see X. Gasiorowska, *Women in Soviet Fiction, 1917–1964* (Madison: University of Wisconsin Press, 1968), p. 35. For Dasha Chumalova, see F. Gladkov, *Tsement* (Moscow, 1928).

16. J. Smith, *Women in Soviet Russia*, p. 102. For Smidovich's views, see S. Smidovich, "O liubvi," in I. Razin, ed., *Komsomol'skii byt* (Moscow-Leningrad, 1927), pp. 268–273.

17. "Pis'mo komsomolki k tov. Smidovich," in Razin, ed., *Komsomol'skii byt*, pp. 172–173.

18. Smidovich, "Otvet na pis'mo komsomolki," in ibid., pp. 174–175.

19. Nina Vel't, "Otkrytoe pis'mo tovarishchu Smidovich," in Razin, ed., *Komsomol'skii byt*, pp. 181–183.

20. B. Engel and C. Rosenthal, eds., *Five Sisters: Women Against the Tsar* (New York: Knopf, 1975), p. 196.

21. Ibid., p. 183.

22. Ibid., p. 196.

23. A. Kollontai, *Iz Moei Zhizni i Raboty* (Moscow, 1974), p. 91.

24. L. P. Zhak and A. M. Itkina, *Zhenshchiny Russkoi Revoliutsii* (Moscow, 1968), pp. 427–428.

25. A. M. Kollontai, *The Autobiography of a Sexually Emancipated Communist Woman*, ed. Irving Fetscher, trans. S. Attanasio (New York: Herder and Herder, 1971), p. 11.

26. For Kollontai and her son, see Farnsworth, *Aleksandra Kollontai*. For Smidovich, see J. Smith, *Women in Soviet Russia*, p. 103.

27. F. Gladkov, *Tsement*, pp. 294–295

28. For Soviet agonizing over legalizing abortion, see N. Semashko, "Eshche o bol'nom voprose," *Kommunistka*, 3–4 (1920), 19–21. Em. Iaroslavskii referred to abortion figures in Moscow and in Leningrad as "horrifying." See quotation in E. H. Carr, *A History of Soviet Russia, Socialism in One Country, 1924–26*, vol. 1 (Baltimore: Pelican, 1970), p. 43. For Krupskaia and Kollontai's negative views of abortion as bourgeois selfishness, see N. Krupskaia, "Voina i detorozhdenie," *Kommunistka*, 1–2 (1920), 19–20, and A. Kollontai, *Polozhenie zhenshchiny v evoliutsii khoziaistva* (Petrograd, 1923), p. 178.

29. Under NEP cutbacks, women were the first to be discharged. For cutbacks, see G. N. Serebrennikov, *Zhenskii trud v SSSR* (Moscow, 1934), p. 52.

30. J. Grunfeld, "Women's Work in Russia's Planned Economy," *Social Research* 9, (February 1942), 1: 26–34.

31. Kollontai, *Polozhenie Zhenshchiny*, p. 150.

32. Kollontai, "Proizvodstvo i byt," *Kommunistka*, 10–11 (1921), 8.

33. The figures are 16 million dead in war, civil war, famine, and epidemics and the remaining loss due to calamities to potential parents. See M. Lewin, "Society, State, and Ideology During the First Five-Year Plan," in S. Fitzpatrick, ed., *Cultural Revolution in Russia, 1928–1931* (Bloomington, Ind.: Indiana University Press, 1978), p. 42.

34. Ibid., p. 53.

35. For Stalin's scorn, see Svetlana Alliluyeva, *Only One Year* (New York: Harper and Row, 1969), p. 381.

36. M. Lewin, "The Social Background of Stalinism," in R. C. Tucker, *Stalinism: Essays in Historical Interpretation* (New York: Norton, 1977), p. 118.

37. Abortions were legalized once again in the mid-1950s. Birth control remains inadequate.

38. G. W. Lapidus, *Women in Soviet Society* (Berkeley: University of California Press, 1978), p. 5.

39. Ibid., p. 309.

40. See Norton Dodge, "Women in the Professions," in Atkinson, Dallin, and Lapidus, *Women in Russia*, p. 224.

41. Lapidus, *Women in Soviet Society*, p. 280.

42. See Vera Dunham, "Surtax on Equality: Women in Soviet Postwar Fiction," paper prepared for Conference on Women in Russia, Stanford University, May 29–June 1, 1975.

43. See J. F. Hough, "Women and Women's Issues in Soviet Policy Debates," in Atkinson, Dallin, and Lapidus, *Women in Russia*, p. 372.

44. See G. W. Lapidus, "Sexual Equality in Soviet Policy," in *Women in Russia*, p. 117.

45. Lapidus, *Women in Soviet Society*, p. 332.

46. The experience of the Russian Zhenotdel may be instructive to women in current

politics who debate the value of separate organizations for women within larger political movements. For indication of such debates, see P. C. Sexton, "Ms./ Comrade," *Dissent* 24 (Spring 1977) 2: 206–209.

47. Privileges for working women to safeguard their position as mother-worker were incorporated in the Social-Democratic Party Program in 1903. See program in *Kommunisticheskaia partiia Sovetskogo Soiuza v rezoliutsiiakh i resheniiakh s"ezdov, Konferentsii i plenumov Tsk* 1 (Moscow, 1953), pp. 40–42.

48. Lapidus, *Women in Soviet Society*, p. 128.

49. Ibid., p. 150.

50. For women in Eastern Europe, see Hilda Scott, *Does Socialism Liberate Women: Experiences from Eastern Europe* (Boston: Beacon, 1974).

51. G. J. Massell, "The Limits of Sexual Equality in the Soviet System," paper presented at Conference on Women in Russia, Stanford University, May 29–June 1, 1975.

52. See article by V. Golubeva, "Rabote zhenotdelov v novykh usloviakh," *Pravda*, February 1, 1923.

53. Such clubs for women were utilized in the Soviet East where women did not assemble publicly with men. For Zhenotdel work in the East, see G. J. Massell, *The Surrogate Proletariat: Moslem Women and Revolutionary Strategies in Soviet Central Asia, 1919–1929* (Princeton: Princeton University Press, 1974). For Kollontai on special societies, see her "Ne 'printsip,' a 'metod' " *Pravda*, March 20, 1923.

54. For suggestions as to how interest groups do make themselves felt in the Soviet Union, see H. Gordon Skilling and F. Griffiths, eds., *Interest Groups in Soviet Politics* (Princeton: Princeton University Press, 1971), and Jerry F. Hough, "Women and Women's Issues in Soviet Policy Debates," in Atkinson, Dallin, and Lapidus, *Women in Russia*, pp. 355–374.

55. See Dallin, "Conclusions," in Atkinson, Dallin, and Lapidus, *Women in Russia*, pp. 385–398.

56. See novella by Natal'ia Baranskaia, "Nedelia kak Nedelia," ("A Week Like Any Other"), in *Novyi Mir* 11 (November 1969), 23–55.

57. See Dallin, "Retreat from Optimism: On Marxian Models of Revolution," in S. Bialer, ed., *Radicalism in the Contemporary Age*, vol. 3 (Boulder, Colo.: Westview Press, 1977), pp. 153–155.

58. See A. M. Kollontai, *Sem'ia i Kommunisticheskoe Gosudarstvo* (Moscow, 1918).

59. A. M. Itkina, *Revoliutsioner, Tribun, Diplomat* (Moscow, 1970), p. 197.

60. Dallin, "Retreat from Optimism," p. 155.

Suggestions for Further Reading

Insight into the activities of the socialist women's movement and its institutional home, the *Zhenotdel*, is best gained by reading the theoretical journal of the Women's Section, *Kommunistka*, published in Moscow from 1920 to 1930 under the general editorship of N. Krupskaia. To understand Zhenotdel activities in the Soviet East, see Gregory Massell, *The Surrogate Proletariat:*

Moslem Women and Revolutionary Strategies in Soviet Central Asia, 1919–1929 (Princeton: Princeton University Press, 1974). For insight into the situation of women in Russia from earliest times to the present day, see the fine collection of scholarly essays in Dorothy Atkinson, Alexander Dallin, and Gail W. Lapidus, *Women in Russia* (Stanford: Stanford University Press, 1977). See also Richard Stites, *The Women's Liberation Movement in Russia: Feminism, Nihilism, and Bolshevism, 1860–1930* (Princeton: Princeton University Press, 1978), an excellent narrative, based on archival and memoir material, and the only such study available in English. Stites discusses the emergence of the "woman question" and the responses to it: the feminist, the nihilist, and the radical. He analyzes the alternate paths to liberation taken by feminists and by socialist women in the years up to 1917. The final part of the book deals with women's liberation within the Soviet system. The most thorough analysis of the economic and political situation of women in the Soviet Union today appears in G. W. Lapidus, *Women in Soviet Society: Equality, Development and Social Change* (Berkeley: University of California Press, 1978). Her thesis, based on meticulous research, is that Soviet policy was shaped less by the concerns of socialist-feminists or Marxists than by a strategy of modernization in which the transformation of women's roles was perceived by the regime as the means of tapping a major economic resource.

For an intimate picture of women of various backgrounds who were involved in the revolutionary movement of the nineteenth century, see the translated memoirs of five revolutionaries: Vera Figner, Vera Zasulich, Praskovia Ivanovskaia, Olga Liubatovich, and Elizaveta Kovalskaia, in B. Engel and C. Rosenthal, *Five Sisters: Women Against the Tsar* (New York: Knopf, 1975). For a useful social history and for new approaches to understanding the emergence of the "woman question," see David Ransel, ed., *The Family in Imperial Russia* (Urbana: University of Illinois Press, 1978), which includes thirteen papers, some based on archival research, which explore the relationship of parents and children in prerevolutionary Russia.

7/Women in the Chinese Communist Revolution: The Question of Political Equality

Joan M. Maloney

As Mao Tse-tung proudly testified in 1949, "the Chinese found the universal truth of Marxism-Leninism . . . and the face of China was changed."[1] Women have been both important agents and prime beneficiaries of this transformation. However attracted—whether for reasons of patriotism or socialism—the first generation of women to join the communist cause included many feminists. In a largely male-defined revolutionary ideology, they accepted the Marxist premise that goals of sexual equality must be subordinated to the class struggle. When national conditions dictated that the women's movement be separated from the revolutionary mainstream, these women turned to organizing one of the largest mass groups in history—and with much success. This essay seeks to analyze the reasons for that separatism and the effects it has had on the achievement of genuine political equality for women in China.

The Revolutionary Struggle

The Chinese communist revolution was born of the precepts of Marxism-Leninism. Marxism requires the subordination of all other social causes to the class struggle. With the seizure of the means of production will come full equality for all people. Thus, the end to female bondage becomes contingent upon the victory of the proletariat. Implicitly, this reasoning should require equal participation of women in the revolutionary struggle and within the socialist apparatus. However, the political events in Russia in 1917 placed the Marxist cart of the superstructure before the horse of the economic base. Lenin used state power to transform the economic system and social relations by a series of decrees. Several of these focused on improving, if not fully equalizing, the status of women. Soviet legislation of 1918–19 was impressive for its speed and scope, but the new regulations did not solve the basic problem of the utilization of women. Their backwardness and the urgency of their cooperation encouraged the reasoning that separate organizations would be required. Bolsheviks and Mensheviks alike had generally resisted earlier demands by women for their own organization on the grounds that it would fragment the class struggle. But Lenin was beginning to perceive that separation was a tactical necessity. And he later summarized the issue:

> Our ideological conceptions give rise to principles of organization. *No separate organizations for women.* A woman communist is a member of the party just as a man communist, with equal rights and duties. . . . Nevertheless, we must not close our eyes to the fact that the party must have bodies, working groups, commissions, committees, bureaus or whatever you like, whose particular duty is to arouse the masses of women workers, to bring them into contact with the party, and to keep them under its influence.[2]

The first Soviet Woman's Bureau was formed in 1917. A year later the party authorized the formation of commissions and propaganda teams to carry out women's work, and in 1919 the various bodies were reorganized into the Zhenotdel, under the jurisdiction of the party Central Committee. With rare exceptions, only women were assigned to these agencies, since few male cadres were supportive. As Lenin was to admit, the men lacked correct understanding, considered women's work "an incidental matter" and believed it should "only concern women."[3] Given this bias and the dearth of trained women cadres, the approach was destined to fail—and the failure would be placed on the women cadres.

The Chinese Communist Party (CCP) was formed under Soviet tutelage in July 1921, and continued to be directed by Moscow through its early years.[4] The second CCP Congress (May and July 1922) explicitly acknowledged the direction of the International and included among its most immediate aims "equality of the rights of men and women."[5] Following Soviet advocacy, in 1923 the CCP appointed Hsiang Ching-yü as its first director of women's work. Hsiang, who enjoyed the distinction of being the first woman named to the CCP Central Committee (CC) by the second congress, was a respected feminist who had independently arrived at the Marxist view that women must become coparticipants in the general revolutionary struggle. She may well have been dismayed at being selected to head a separate women's department, although, like Lenin, she was acutely aware that the political illiteracy of the vast mass of women dictated such an approach.[6]

Chinese women were even more oppressed than their Russian sisters. The traditional ethic had not only deprived them of legal, educational, and vocational rights, but had also encased them in a system of peer isolation and familial servitude. The bound feet of northern women symbolized the bound minds and spirits of almost all women. As evidenced by the mother-in-law/daughter-in-law relationship, females were often pitted one against the other, rather than united against common forms of male oppression. As Mao Tse-tung remarked with perspicuity, suicide became a wish for life—not death—by women being destroyed by their society.[7]

Late nineteenth-century endeavors by the Chinese Self-Strengtheners and foreign missionaries helped to alleviate some of the worst forms of oppression. The educational reforms that followed in the wake of the Revolution of 1911 were another step forward. But for decades to come, over 90 percent of all women remained illiterate. The ratio of male to female—107.5: 100 as late as 1953—indicated that, even if female infanticide had been drastically curtailed, preference for boys over girls had not. Thus, from the first the Chinese communists had to deal with the same dilemma that had troubled Lenin. How could women become active participants in the revolutionary process when their social conditioning made this a formidable, if not impossible, goal?

The answer to the utilization of women lay in the Leninist tactic of assigning the few available female cadres to organizing women's groups at the grassroots level. Under CCP tutelage new recruits could then be trained to further extend this work. In the cities the drive would be concentrated in those industries that employed a high percentage of women for, although all workers were exploited, females were the worst victimized. In the rural areas, where traditional bias was the strongest, the organizers could anticipate great resistance. As in the Soviet experience, male cadres shunned assignments, arguing that "there is little chance for contact between men and women."[8] But the first generation of women cadres was mostly from urban backgrounds, comparatively well educated and for the times quite liberated. These cadres found it difficult to relate to women of the peasant class.

Hsiang Ching-yü recognized the problem. Not a few of the women volunteers were more romantic than realistic. Their advocacy of personal freedom was intermingled with their endorsement of a free-love society, and their message often seem irrelevant to their countrywomen.[9] Other cadres had problems identifying with their constituents. Fan Chin, who was later to become a deputy mayor of Peking, recalled those days: "We women of middle-class background and from the big cities had very different ways from those of the peasant women. . . . [Our job] was to explain to these semislaves that they could be emancipated and to enroll them in the struggle. . . . We organized them into self-defense groups and mutual-aid groups so they could stand up to the men."[10] A secretary of a rural women's committee confirmed: "We educated women find women's work very difficult [since] our lives, habits and standards of culture are so different."[11]

The September 28, 1928, Resolution on the Peasants' Movement of the sixth CCP Congress warned that failure to win over the women in the villages would "definitely result in the failure of the agrarian revolution."[12] Yet the villagers continued to be wary of the bobbed-hair "liberated strangers." As one remembered, "it isn't easy being a woman . . . life is a lot of hard work [so] I don't take part in any kind of women's activities, political or otherwise."[13] Older women were especially apt to be critical of the cadres. Younger women were often motivated by material prospects of better food and clothing or by the hope of alleviating a bad family arrangement. If their personal situation improved, they were prone to drop out of the organization. Furthermore, if the cadres concentrated upon primarily feminist interests in order to attract members, they risked censure from the party center for isolating their work from the class struggle.[14] The combination of criticism from above and suspicion from below was enough to cause frustrated organizers to yearn for less hazardous assignments.

The responsibilities for women's work shifted in 1923. Under the Moscow-inspired United Front between Sun Yat-sen's Kuomintang (KMT) and the Chinese communists, the CCP merged its women's department into the KMT's Central Women's Department. Hsiang Ching-yü, who had apparently failed to be reelected to the CCP CC at the third and fourth congresses (1923 and 1925), was sent to Moscow; KMT activist Ho Hsiang-ning took over direction of the Central Women's Department. Born in 1878 and educated in Japan, Ho had joined forces with Sun Yat-sen in 1905 and was already well known for her efforts to draw women to his cause. Now, in the KMT base area in Kwangtung, she named several CCP women leaders to her staff, including Ts'ai Ch'ang and Teng Ying-ch'ao. Teng was to become Ho's executive secretary.

Sun Yat-sen's ideological concepts barely touched on the woman question. In his extended commentaries on the Three People's Principles he made only passing reference to the role and rights of women, by concluding that Western history proved that sexual equality first required that women become a vital part of the labor force[15]—a development most unlikely in the China of the 1920s. After Sun's death, in 1925, the intense power struggle within the KMT threatened that party's structure. Despite her husband's assassination and attempts on her own life, Ho Hsiang-ning persevered. By incorporating the various women's associations born of the Revolution of 1911, which were concerned with equality in marriage, inheritance, and suffrage, with the some 300,000 women in the communist-directed associations, the KMT Women's Department claimed to have organized over 1.5 million women by 1927.[16]

By the end of 1927, Chiang Kai-shek had wrested leadership of the KMT from his rivals, established control over the warlords, and gained the support of Chinese businessmen and the Western powers. The new Nationalist government in Nanking appeared to have finally effected unity and in 1928 the Organic Law confirmed Chiang's authority over it. These developments posed a threat to the survival of the women's movement. If Sun's commitment had been deficient, Chiang was hostile. His attempted restoration of Confucian social precepts—ironically termed the New Life Movement—canonized the women who quietly engaged in matters such as sponsorship of orphanages and subjected women concerned with public life to outright harassment. Later, during the anti-Japanese war, Chiang was to rate the "need to awaken our countrywomen" even below his concern to improve animal husbandry.[17]

Although the KMT retained its Women's Department, it carefully controlled the elections of women delegates to party conferences. The program of the 1941 conference for women's work perfectly mirrored the generalissimo's dictate by affirming "it is harmful for women to take part in politics."[18] Not surprisingly, many of the most dedicated women organizers, including Ho herself and Sung Ch'ing-ling, the widow of Sun Yat-sen, eventually defected from the KMT. Whether because of the poverty of KMT policy or their own developing commitments, many of these women eventually gravitated to the communist-sponsored associations.

Despite Chiang Kai-shek's clear intention to eliminate all communists, Soviet policy continued to urge nonresistance in the interests of preserving the United Front. In a few areas, however, the communists determined to fight back. The most significant of these revolts, led by Mao Tse-tung, occurred in September 1927 in Hunan. After a bitter defeat, Mao and his remnant forces retreated to Chingkangshan in southern Kiangsi province, where he established a rural soviet that was to become the base for the communist revolution. Chiang pursued relentlessly.

Nationalist propaganda of the time made great capital of popular mistrust of the communists' efforts to organize women. Rumors circulated of "naked women's parades" in the red areas. Scanty bathing suits were said to be the standard uniform of the female communist cadres, and stories were told of these cadres on rampages to bob the hair of frightened countrywomen. Since the female cadres did usually wear men's clothing and sometimes shared their living facilities with male cadres, credence was given to the rumors and emotions ran high. There were reports of women in the areas regained by the Nationalists being forced to stand naked to the waist in public for days as punishment for their flirtation with the communists. Ts'ai Ch'ang recalled the situation vividly:

> More than 1,000 women leaders were killed . . . not all were communists, some were bourgeois and there were many students, but all were revolutionary leaders. . . . I think the brutality of the killing has no parallel in all the world. . . . When girls were arrested in Hunan they were stripped naked, nailed on crosses and their noses and breasts cut off before they were killed. . . . After girl students were beheaded, their heads were put into men's coffins and the gendarmes said "you have your free love now." . . . The girls' bodies were always horribly mutilated. . . . It is actually true that if a girl had bobbed hair she was subject to execution as a communist in Hunan and Canton.[19]

The communists interpreted these attacks as proof that interests of class always transcend those of sex, since women of the upper class were sometimes in the forefront of the persecutors. Once again, the work to organize women's associations began. At the sixth CCP Congress, which had to be held in Moscow, in the summer of 1928, Teng Ying-ch'ao was chosen as director of the Central Committee's Women's Department to replace Hsiang Ching-yü, who had been executed by the Nationalists. Despite the fact that the chief concern in the soviets was survival, Mao Tse-tung also oversaw legislation designed to promote women's rights. New laws governing marriage, divorce, and equality in land distribution and in pay doubtlessly attracted more supporters.[20] The Constitution of the Soviet Republic, adopted November 7, 1931, further specified: "It is the purpose of the soviet government of China to guarantee the thorough emancipation of women," and promised to create the conditions necessary for their full participation in the "social, economic, political and cultural life of the entire society."[21]

The communists were not so quick, however, to move women into positions of political equality. In the Central Executive Council of the Soviet Republic, where membership conferred prestige, if not power, the few women members probably owed their inclusion more to the stature of their husbands than to their own reputations.[22] Nor was the situation different within the ranks of the CCP itself. From the establishment of the party in 1921 until the end of World War II, only two women served as full members of the Central Committee.[23]

In 1934, when the Nationalist military encirclement of the central soviet area was accelerated, the communists were forced to begin the legendary Long March. A year and some 6,000 miles later they regrouped in northern Shensi, near the border of the USSR and its satellite, Outer Mongolia. In 1936, they moved their center to Yenan. Early in 1935, Mao Tse-tung had been elected CCP chairman by an enlarged meeting of the Politburo. He now prepared for an eventual attack by the Nationalists and, after 1937, by the Japanese.

The problems that had troubled the women's movement resurfaced in Yenan, where men outnumbered women by about 18:1 and very few women were literate. The leadership, increasingly sensitive to Nationalist propaganda depicting Yenan society as one of "communal wives" as well as communal property, promoted puritanical attitudes.[24] But, as political necessity and social caution inhibited liberalizing policies, some of the women organizers were becoming restive. The best-known example is that of the famed writer, Ting Ling. Born of a wealthy landlord family, Ting early flouted contemporary mores by living openly with lovers and toying with anarchist philosophy. When she felt hemmed in by the strict conventions of Yenan, Ting used her acid pen to accuse the CCP leadership of fostering a double standard. Single women were ridiculed and married women chastised if they tried to engage in political activities, but they were also slandered as backward if they traded political for family responsibilities.[25]

Despite their geographical isolation and the effects of the anti-Japanese war, the communists were able to expand membership in the women's associations from some 130,000 in 1937 to over 1.5 million by 1943. In 1949, membership was over 22 million. Through their participation, women were able to overcome some of the most blatant forms of discrimination and enter the labor force in substantial numbers. Group endeavor also raised political consciousness and many women were able to win party membership. Estimates of the ratio of women in the CCP go as high as a third, although it was probably closer to a tenth.[26] The party leadership showed its approval of the direction of women's work at the seventh CCP Congress in 1945 by re-electing Ts'ai Ch'ang to the Central Committee and naming veteran organizers Teng Ying-ch'ao and Ch'en Shao-min as alternates. Yet the CCP had not been able to eliminate discrimination within its own ranks and women cadres were still assigned almost exclusively to women's work.

The Construction of Socialism

The Women's Federation of China (WF)[27] was founded on April 3, 1949, several months before the communist victory. By consolidating the various communist and noncommunist women's groups, the WF started with a membership of over 22 million and a potential membership of hundreds of millions—making it one of the largest mass organizations in the world. Its goals were to work in various fields of national construction, to protect women's rights and interests and promote child welfare, to ensure equality for women, and to raise the level of their political understanding and vocational ability.[28]

Organizationally, the WF would oversee units at the various geopolitical levels: province, county, village, and neighborhood. Each body would have its own congress, which would elect a representative committee to carry out programs such as the formation of literacy classes, vocational training, and the delivery of health and child care. These services would permit women to become the essential back-up force for national construction. Tactically, the WF would depend upon seasoned organizers to train candidates. Ideologically, the cadres were cautioned not to let their enthusiasm for women's interests detract from the national task and were urged to "overcome old intellectual concepts of looking down on labor" and to eradicate "any thought or method tending to one-sidedness and isolation."[29]

By the early 1950s the CCP ranks had swelled to over six million, but since the recruitment of women still held low priority, probably only about 600,000 members were female.[30] Party literature classified the cadres into three groups: those seriously concerned with women's work, the indifferent, and the obstructionists.[31] Although the female cadres usually fell within the first category, they had problems in work style. The more zealous risked overshooting their authority and antagonizing their constituencies. The indifferent needed training to overcome attitudes that women's work was "tedious and troublesome" and to see their assignments as "an indispensable part of the work of socialist revolution."[32] The antagonistic would have to be subject to strict discipline from above.

The eighth CCP Congress, meeting in 1956, heard a report by Teng Ying-ch'ao on the problems involved in women's work and then took two supportive actions. First, the number of women in the Central Committee was increased to four. Four additional women were named as alternates. Despite this real gain, females still constituted only 4.2 percent of the full member-ship and 5.4 percent of the alternates. The other decision was perhaps more significant. Although Ts'ai Ch'ang, Teng Ying-ch'ao, and Chang Yün—the first, second, and third secretary of the CC Women's Department—con-tinued to concentrate almost exclusively on the Women's Department, the other women in the CC began to receive positions in the regular party structure commensurate with their new status. Thus women moved into positions that did not relate directly to women's issues, but rather to such areas as the trade union movement, the Control and Organization Depart-ments, and the provincial control commissions.

By the eve of the Great Proletarian Cultural Revolution, women were fairly well established at the lower rungs of party and state organizations and beginning to move into the middle echelons. For example, 17.8 percent of the deputies to the third National People's Congress, in December 1964, were women, and seventeen were named to the ninety-four-member Standing Committee. In the various ministries and commissions of the State Council, seven women held posts as vice minister or deputy director. Although the higher jobs were still usually closed to women, indications were that with time and experience women in this middle echelon would be promoted.

In the larger society, women continued to make steady, sometimes dra-matic gains in the decade from the mid-1950s to the mid-1960s. In 1957, the third WF Congress had stressed nondiscriminatory integration of women into the regular labor force, as well as improvements in supportive services and more assertive roles in the family. The introduction of the Great Leap Forward in 1958, to work toward the goal of national economic self-sufficiency, greatly expanded educational and especially vocational oppor-tunities for women.

The Cultural Revolution, which began in 1966, had a profound effect on the entire women's movement. From a positive standpoint, many more women, especially younger ones, were encouraged to become politically active. After the 1969 CCP Congress, where quotas were adopted to increase female membership in the party, the results were impressive.[33] During the period 1966–73 about a fourth of all party recruits were female.[34] As the CC journal thundered, "it is their [women's] right and obligation to engage in politics and class struggle."[35] The constitution adopted by the tenth CCP Congress, in August 1973, added the criterion that leading bodies at all levels should "combine the old, middle-aged and young" (Article 5). Consequently, in 1977, when party membership reached 35 million, the party included many more women, the majority of whom were under forty. Paradoxically, these numerical gains did not necessarily advance the women's movement. Veteran organizers were too often bypassed in favor of young activists who had little zeal for women's work.[36]

The WF was not a principal target of the Cultural Revolution, but it shared the fate of the other mass organizations: seeing its leadership collapse. After some WF officials were charged with antirevolutionary activities, the constituency tended to drift off to the new revolutionary committees. In 1966, Tung Pien, a secretary and editor-in-chief of the WF journal, *Women of China,* was accused of being anti-Maoist. Ts'ai Ch'ang apparently had to rely on her lifelong friendship with Mao to avert a blanket indictment of the WF.[37] Even so, the journal was suspended. Some insight into the conflicts raging at the time may be gained from the fact that Tung Pien was criticized in its last issue for being "intoxicated" with feminists' issues when politics should be dominant.[38]

The ninth CCP Congress met in April 1969 to end the radical phase of the Cultural Revolution and confirm Lin Piao as Mao's designated successor. Women accounted for 7.6 percent of the full and 10 percent of the alternate members of the new Central Committee.[39] However, the appointments renewed assumptions that nepotism was a key factor in the woman's promotion—especially when Chiang Ch'ing (Mme. Mao Tse-tung) and Yeh Ch'ün (Mme. Lin Piao) became the first women to sit in the powerful CCP Politburo. Similarly, Ts'ao Yi-ou, formerly identified only as a "responsible person," clearly owed her election to her husband, K'ang Sheng, who was himself elected to the ninth Politburo. The same was true for several of the other women members.[40]

There were important exceptions. These members were drawn from local CCP committees or owed their position to their reputation as model workers or peasants. These women had at least two characteristics in common: they had become political activists during the Cultural Revolution, and they had only peripheral interest in or responsibility for women's work. Unlike the eighth CC, the party leadership of the ninth Congress did not generally confer posts appropriate to the new status of these women.

The principal task of the tenth CCP Congress, meeting in August 1973, was to rectify the work of its predecessor. With the reported deaths of Lin Piao and his wife following his abortive coup, Chiang Ch'ing and her associates were able to improve their position at the party center. The percentage of women in the new CC showed an increase to 10 percent of the full and 16 percent of the alternate members and another woman, Wu Kuei-hsien, was named as alternate to the Politburo. Eleven of the women who were full members of the CC were reappointments. Of the nine new female members, several held office in top-level revolutionary committees or came from the ranks of model workers.

Mao Tse-tung died on September 9, 1976. Weeks later, his successor, Hua Kuo-feng, arrested Chiang Ch'ing and her closest associates,[41] the so-called Gang of Four. By July 1977, Teng Hsiao-p'ing had become a co-leader and Peking's key ideologue, and China moved toward the new national goal of the Four Modernizations.[42] The CCP launched a major effort to purge the radicals and rehabilitate their victims and also ordered the restoration of the mass organizations. Each of these events had an effect on the direction of the women's movement.

Failures to achieve set goals of the women's movement have been laid squarely on the Gang of Four. Chiang Ch'ing is accused of having attempted to take over the WF as part of her power base. Despite the vehement protestations of some women leaders that Chiang Ch'ing "never had anything to do with China's women's liberation movement,"[43] the Gang was able to place "female henchmen" and "black generals" in some of the regional offices of the WF,[44] and to prevent the national officers from meeting.[45] In 1973, when women's congresses were held in the provinces, autonomous regions, and special municipalities, the principal addresses were given by male party secretaries. Ch'ing is said to have advanced a pseudo-feminist line that women, since they alone are childbearers, are "the most productive force," in the hopes of creating her own matriarchy. But there can be no doubt that her attacks against male chauvinism alienated and antagonized many people—male and female.[46]

Because the most impressive influx of women into the CCP occurred after the start of the Cultural Revolution, it was to be expected that many of these women would become suspect. The eleventh CCP Congress was convened in August 1977 to solidify the leadership and to cleanse the CCP ranks of the influence of the Gang of Four. Women accounted for 6 percent of the full and 10.6 percent of the alternate members of the new CC. While percentages did not differ much from the previous CC, the personnel did: 44 percent of the CC members were new appointees. The only woman to be named to the Politburo was Chen Mu-hua, who was an alternate. Her principal activities had been in the area of state administration. Among the fourteen women elected to full membership in the CC, the majority were reappointments.[47] The only two new members were Hao Chien-hsiu and K'ang K'e-ch'ing. Hao, then aged forty-two, was a model worker promoted up through the ranks to become vice minister of textiles. K'ang, widow of the venerated revolutionary general Chu Teh, was then sixty-five. She joined the CCP in 1931, is a survivor of the Long March, and has held a series of assignments in the field of women's work. She alone, among all the women promoted to the ninth, tenth, and eleventh CCs, could be considered to owe her position primarily to her experience in women's work. Ambitious female cadres might conclude that women's work is not the surest route to promotion.

The mass organizations have been reconstituted since the eleventh CCP Congress. There have been few more poignant moments in the history of the women's movement than the scene in Peking's Great Hall of the People on September 8, 1978, when veteran feminist Ts'ai Ch'ang called the fourth National Women's Congress to order before an assembly including most of the CCP's leaders and virtually all of her most respected women cadres. After a hiatus of twenty-one years since its last congress, the WF appeared to have survived its enemies, to be blessed by the party center, and to be ready to move its struggle for equality into a new epoch.

The various calls to action preceding and during the fourth National Women's Congress justify strengthening the WF. Female illiteracy still persists in rural areas, particularly those of the national minorities.[48] "Feudalistic ideas are on the rampage and women are continuously subjected to persecution."[49] Parents still coerce offspring into marriages based on material gain,[50] wives are subordinate to husbands, and female workers do not always receive equal pay. In fact, in her Work Report to the fourth Women's Congress, K'ang K'e-ch'ing claimed that the Gang of Four had "totally negated the achievements of women's work [made] prior to the Cultural Revolution."[51]

The first of the "five lofty tasks" set for the women's movement in the post-Mao era mirrors the goals of the party center by calling upon women to perform meritorious service in the three great revolutionary movements: class struggle, increased production, and the Four Modernizations. The other tasks pertain more exclusively to women and call upon them to serve as the main logistical force, take care in the upbringing of the next generation, develop socialist modes for marriage and family relations, and strengthen the national and international united front of all women.[52]

Will these logistical functions satisfy the female cadres? Here, a survey of the women holding upper echelon posts in the state and CCP organizations and the degree of interlocking with WF offices can be instructive. The majority of women holding high posts in the national government have no meaningful role per se in the field of women's work. The fifth National People's Congress, meeting in March 1978, named Sung Ch'ing-ling, Ts'ai Ch'ang, and Teng Ying-ch'ao as three of the twenty vice chairmen. The three were named honorary chairmen of the fourth Women's Federation. But among the fourteen women on the 175-member NPC Standing Committee, only six were elected to office in the fourth WF. Chen Mu-hua, who is the only female vice premier, has no more than fringe connections with the women's movement.

Of the fourteen women who were elected to full membership in the eleventh CCP Central Committee, four are also upper echelon state administrators, but only six hold WF offices. Assuming that two of the fourteen have been purged, this means that half of the women now in the Central Committee have apparently opted to curtail their responsibilities for women's work.

The 1978 selection of WF officers reflects emphasis on rewarding and restoring veteran organizers. Several of these appointments vindicate the work of women who suffered disgrace during the Cultural Revolution. The most notable cases are those of Tung Pien, who was vilified in 1966 but is now a WF secretary, and Lo Ch'iung, who was a founding member of the WF, was accused in 1967 of propagating the "black line," and is now restored as first secretary. Similarly, the election of Li Po-chao to the standing committee marked a reversal of Cultural Revolution attacks on her husband, Yang Shang-k'un, an important party leader accused of spying for a foreign power, as well as a reversal of the attack on Li herself for advancing an anti-Maoist line.[53]

The WF was careful to avoid speculation that nepotism is still a criterion for selection of women. The wives of China's leaders Hua Kuo-feng and Teng Hsiao-p'ing have no major role, although Hua's spouse, Han Chih-chuan, was elected to the 250-member executive committee.[54] The omission of the wives of CCP leaders from the inner circle of the WF probably reflects the determination of their husbands to avoid any parallels to the political rise of Chiang Ch'ing, but may also indicate a subconscious downgrading of the women's movement.

The appointment of K'ang K'e-ch'ing as chairman of the fourth WF, as well as the selection of other major officers, signals the development of a situation that will be troublesome to the women's movement. The advanced age of some women leaders will soon mandate their replacement. And the high retention rate of officers—however advantageous to morale—means that the majority of officers are now in their sixties and seventies.

Ultimately, the future of the Federation and of the women's movement will require the training and placement of large numbers of young cadres. The fourth WF Congress recognized this point by calling for the reestablishment of women's cadre schools and, in his keynote speech, a Politburo spokesman affirmed the urgency of actively training and boldly using and placing female cadres. In fact, he alluded to the need to retain a quota system in his suggestion that "when we train skilled personnel in various fields, we should consider women and train a certain percentage of them."[55] In contrast, in its article marking the end of the congress, the national paper, *People's Daily,* admitted that Chinese women "still have much less cultural and scientific training than men" and that "there are still some leading comrades who pay no attention to women's work, regarding it as trivial."[56]

The present leaders of China have indicated their desire for the women's movement to serve principally as a support to modernization. Hua Kuo-feng, who has been described in party journals as one who "always valued women's role and is always concerned about women's work,"[57] contributed an inscription in his own calligraphy to the fourth WF. "Chinese women of all nationalities," it says, "unite and work to build China into a great, powerful, socialist country."[58] As the local women's congresses began convening, late in 1978, they were reminded that "the class struggle must now revolve around the central task—the struggle for production and scientific experiment."[59]

With the stress on modernization, Chinese women may anticipate that their contributions to the labor force will be more highly prized and that their professional opportunities will be increased. Now fully half of the rural work force is female and many women are gaining employment in the industrial sector. For example, in 1957, on the eve of the Great Leap Forward, there were about 3 million women workers. Now there are over 30 million.[60] Women now comprise almost a third of the corps of 4 million scientists, engineers, and technicians.[61] In the words of a WF vice chairman, the modernization drive ultimately "will mean further emancipation for women, freeing working women from heavy manual labor and from household chores."[62] Similarly, relaxation of stringent social regulations should give women more personal freedom and promote the breakdown of traditional patterns of familial subordination. However, patterns of discrimination are likely to persist in the socioeconomic sphere. Women workers in rural areas are still rarely able to earn the maximum workpoints, and feminist leaders consider the right to equal pay to be the most pressing priority. Although girls constitute fully half of all elementary school enrollment, less than a third of all college and university students are female.[63] Consequently, women will continue to be underrepresented in the professions.

More significantly, political advancement has not kept pace with socioeconomic gains. Press statements celebrating the 1979 observance of International Women's Day stressed that already "a fair number of women" hold party and state offices. Special pride was taken in the fact that seventeen of China's top twenty-six revolutionary committees now have a woman vice-chairman, although no woman has been chosen as a chairman and the incumbents actually are low-ranking assistants.

If women are to achieve the political equality that Marxism-Leninism-Maoism has professed to be the indispensable condition of the accomplishment of socialism, then the leadership must strengthen the twin pillars of political consciousness-raising and cadre training for women. The CCP has returned to the principle that women cadres should be assigned to organize women "since they understand their sufferings."[64] Thus, while the secretary of the Yunan provincial CCP committee told a women's forum that more attention must be paid to "cultivating and promoting female cadres," he also made plain that these cadres "should be assigned to women's work."[65] Yet many younger women activists may be coming to the conclusion that such assignment is a career deadend. Should they come to settle for more secure and less troublesome assignments while the ranks of the veteran cadres are being depleted by advancing years, the progress of the women's movement will be slowed, if not stalled.

To the extent that the national goals of modernization are achieved, women will share in the increasing prosperity. But the concomitant de-emphasis of strictly feminist goals could easily result in a continuation of their politically inferior status. Not unlike the situation in Western countries, then, the women of China will have little voice in the decision-making process that alone can guarantee full equality.

Notes

1.   Mao Tse-tung, "On People's Democratic Dictatorship," *Selected Works of Mao Tse-tung*, vol. 4 (Peking: Foreign Language Press, 1961), p. 413.

2. Clara Zetkin, "Lenin on the Woman Question" (1920), in *The Woman Question* (New York: International Publishers, 1951), p. 90. Emphasis added.

3. Ibid.

4. Peter S. H. Tang and Joan M. Maloney, *Communist China: The Domestic Scene, 1949–1967* (South Orange, N.J.: Seton Hall University Press, 1967), p. 35 and *passim.*

5. Conrad Brandt, Benjamin Schwartz, and John K. Fairbank, *A Documentary History of Chinese Communism* (Cambridge, Mass.: Harvard University Press, 1959), pp. 63–64.

6. Helen Foster Snow, *Women in Modern China* (The Hague: Mouton, 1967), p. 247.

7. Mao Tse-tung, "Women and Suicide," *Ta Kung Pao*, Nov. 30, 1919, in Rozanne Witke, "Mao Tse-tung, Women and Suicide," *China Quarterly,* no. 31 (July–Sept. 1967), pp. 128–147.

8. Ch'en Yun, *How to Be a Good Communist* (1939), in Brandt et al., *Chinese Communism*, p. 326.

9. Suzette Leith, "Chinese Women in the Early Communist Movement," in *Women in China,* ed. Marilyn B. Young (Ann Arbor: Center for Chinese Studies, University of Michigan, 1973), p. 50.

10. K. S. Karol, *China: The Other Communism* (New York: Hill and Wang, 1967), pp. 110–113.

11. Agnes Smedley, *Battle Hymn of China* (New York: Alfred Knopf, 1943), p. 354.

12. Brandt et al., *Chinese Communism,* p. 159.

13. Jan Myrdal, *Report From a Chinese Village* (New York: Pantheon, 1965), p. 238.

14. "Resolutions of the Conference of Secretaries of Women's Committees," March 1931, in M. J. Meijer, *Marriage Law and Policy in the Chinese People's Republic* (Hong Kong: Hong Kong University Press, 1971), p. 41.

15. Sun Yat-sen, *San Min Chu I: The Three Principles of the People,* ed. L. T. Chen (New York: Capo Press, 1975), p. 260.

16. Helen F. Snow, *Women in China,* p. 107.

17. Chiang Kai-shek, *Collected Wartime Messages of Chiang Kai-shek* (New York: John Day, 1943), p. 381.

18. Maude Russell, *Chinese Women Liberated* (New York: Far East Reporter, n.d.), p. 7.

19. Helen F. Snow, *Women in China,* pp. 241–42.

20. Delia Davin, *Women-Work: Women and the Party in Revolutionary China* (New York: Oxford University Press, 1976), pp. 24–49.

21. Brandt et al., *Chinese Communism,* p. 203.

22. Derek J. Waller, "The Evolution of the Chinese Communist Political Elite, 1931–56," in Robert A. Scalapino, ed., *Elites in the People's Republic of China* (Seattle: University of Washington Press, 1972), p. 48.

23. Li Fu-ch'uan is now regarded as one of the founders of the CCP. Hsiang Ching-yu, who died on the eve of the sixth Congress, was replaced by Ts'ai Ch'ang. Ts'ai was active in the women's movement in the Kiangsi soviet by 1932 and in 1936 was placed in charge of women's work in Yenan. But at the time she was elected to the CC she probably owed the honor more to the importance of her husband, Li Fu-ch'uan, a lifelong friend of Mao's, than to her own efforts.

24. Edgar Snow, *Red Star Over China* (New York: Grove Press, 1968), pp. 241–42; Helen Foster Snow, *The Chinese Communists: Sketches and Autobiographies of the Old Guard* (Westport, Conn.: Greenwood Publishing Co., 1972).

25. Merle Goldman, *Literary Dissent in Communist China* (Cambridge, Mass.: Harvard University Press, 1967), p. 23; Davin, *Women-Work,* p. 36. Ting Ling was subjected to intensive self-criticism sessions, stripped of her assignments, and eventually purged as a "rightist."

26. Helen F. Snow, *Women in China*, p. 16.

27. The official title until 1957 was the All-China Democratic Women's Federation. Then the adjective "democratic" was deleted to signal the new stage of socialism. The term Women's Federation is used throughout for consistency.

28. "Introducing the All-China Democratic Women's Federaiton," in Elisabeth Croll, *The Women's Movement in China: A Selection of Readings 1949–1973* (London: Anglo-Chinese Educational Institute, 1974), p. 4.

29. Ibid.

30. John W. Lewis, *Leadership in Communist China* (Ithaca, N.Y.: Cornell University Press, 1963), p. 109.

31. "Report of the Hunan Provincial Government," July 1950, in Meijer, *Marriage Law*, p. 120.

32. Editorial, *Women of China*, no. 2 (Feb. 1962).

33. Joan Maloney, "Women Cadres and Junior-Level Leadership in China," *Current Scene*, nos. 3–4 (March–April, 1975): 16.

34. "Guided By Chairman Mao's Red Line," *People's Daily*, July 1, 1973.

35. "Bring the Role of Women Into Full Play," *Red Flag*, no. 10 (Sept. 1971): p. 60.

36. Joan M. Maloney, "Problems in China's Party Rebuilding," *Current Scene*, no. 3 (March 1977): 6.

37. "Mao Writes Inscription," *Peking Review*, no. 36 (Sept. 2, 1966): 5.

38. Editorial, *Women of China*, no. 8 (August 1966).

39. Among the women members of the eighth CC, Ou Meng-chüeh, Ch'ien Ying, Chang Yün, Li Chien-chen and Shuai Meng-ch'i became purge victims of the Cultural Revolution. See Peter R. Moody, Jr., *The Politics of the Communist Party of China* (Hamden, Conn.: Shoe String Press, 1973), p. 58, *passim*.

40. Donald W. Klein and Anne B. Clark, *Biographic Dictionary of Chinese Communism 1921–1965*, vol. I (Cambridge, Mass.: Harvard University Press, 1971), p. 127.

41. Wang Hung-wen, Chang Ch'un-ch'iao, and Yao Wen-yuan.

42. The modernization of agriculture, industry, science and technology.

43. New China News Agency (NCNA), Peking, March 6, 1977.

44. Anhwei Radio, Dec. 9, 1977, in Foreign Broadcast Information Service, *Daily Report: People's Republic of China*, 78–39, G-1; "A Wicked Person," *Liaoning Daily*, Nov. 13, 1978.

45. NCNA, Peking, March 4, 1978.

46. "Pipe Dream of an 'Empress,' " *Peking Review*, no. 12 (March 18, 1977), 21.

47. They were Ts'ai Ch'ang, Teng Ying-ch'ao, Lu Yu-lan, Ts'ao Yi'ou, Wang Hsiu-hsiu, Wu Kuei-hsien, Chen Mu-hua, Chien Cheng-ying, Hsing Yen-tzu, Lin Li-yün, Paojih-le-tai, and Pasang.

48. Kunming/Yunnan Radio, July 10, 1978, in FBIS 78–135, J-1.

49. Kang K'e-ch'ing, "Lofty Tasks," NCNA, Peking, Sept. 13, 1978.

50. "It Is Essential to Smash the Shackles of Venal Marriage," *China Youth News*, Dec. 16, 1978.

51. NCNA, Peking, Sept. 9, 1978.

52. Ibid.

53. Li was born in 1911, joined the communist movement while a student in normal school, worked in the soviets in various CCP assignments, and was named to the WF executive committee in 1953.

54. Han was born in 1931 and has apparently held minor posts in the public sector. See "The Family of Hua Kuo-feng," Hong Kong *Cheng Ming*, no. 2, Oct. 1978, and "Hua's Real Name," Taipei *Free China Weekly*, Oct. 8, 1978, p. 3.

55. NCNA, Peking, Sept. 9, 1978.

56. "Women of All China's Nationalities, Mobilize for the New March," *People's Daily*, Sept. 17, 1978.

57. "Give the Reins. . ." *Red Flag*, no. 3, March 1978.

58. NCNA, Peking, Sept. 12, 1978.

59. Hunan Radio, Nov. 27, 1978, FBIS 78–232, H-1.

60. "China's Women Discuss Life and Work," *People's Daily*, March 9, 1979.

61. NCNA, Peking, March 5, 1979.

62. NCNA, Peking, March 6, 1979.

63. Ibid.

64. "Actively Train and Boldly Use Women Cadres," *People's Daily*, Feb. 1, 1973.

65. Yunnan Radio, March 4, 1978, in FBIS 78–50, J-7.

Suggestions for Further Reading

John King Fairbank's *The United States and China* (Cambridge, Mass.: Harvard University Press, 1971) is a highly readable and authoritative introduction to the complex modern history of China (available in paperback). The two-volume *Biographic Dictionary of Chinese Communism 1921–65* (Cambridge: Harvard University Press, 1971) by Donald W. Klein and Anne B. Clark is a useful source of information on the leadership.

Several accounts of the revolutionary struggle by Western partisans and participants are invaluable for local color. These include Anna L. Strong's *China's Millions* (New York: Coward-McCann, 1928); Agnes Smedley's *Battle Hymn of China* (New York: Knopf, 1943); Helen F. Snow's *Women in Modern China* (The Hague: Mouton, 1967); and Jack Belden's *China Shakes the World* (New York: Harper, 1949).

Among the major secondary sources on the women's movement in China, three important works are *The Women's Movement in China* by Elisabeth Croll (London: Anglo-Chinese Educational Institute, 1974), an anthology of Chinese documents and commentaries; *Women in China*, Marilyn B. Young, ed. (Ann Arbor: Center for Chinese Studies, University of Michigan, 1973), which contains articles by Chinese and Western women dealing with various facets of the movement; and Delia Davin's *Woman-Work: Women and the Party in Revolutionary China* (New York: Oxford University Press, 1976). Although Davin's book concentrates primarily on the 1950s, it is still the most comprehensive and analytical single source and contains a useful bibliography.

Chinese Communist sources are still fragmentary and more propagandistic than factual, but they give important insight into how the Chinese perceive their own progress. Peking's Foreign Language Press has published several pamphlet-sized accounts, including *New Women in New China* (1972), with articles by "achievers." The weekly magazine *Peking Review* also has relevant documents and occasional articles. The U.S. Department of Commerce until 1978 published daily translations from the Chinese press in the series *Survey of the Chinese Mainland Press* and *Survey of People's Republic of China Press.* At present, the best translation service is that of *Daily Report: People's Republic of China,* distributed by the same agency, which monitors daily radio broadcasts from the mainland.

8/Revolution and *Conciencia:* Women in Cuba

Lourdes Casal

Revolutionary change in Cuba is only in its first stages, dealing with questions of institutional or structural change. Ultimately, the transition to socialism necessitates the building of a new man and a new woman, the transformation of human consciousness, a radical alteration in our conception of what it means to be a person.

It is a fundamental component of a Marxist view that "human nature," in the sense of an invariable, permanent set of psychosocial characteristics, does not exist at all. Instead, man is seen as the product of specific historical circumstances, as the variable resultant of the particular set of production relations obtaining in a society at a given moment, and specifically of the class-bound ideologies associated with them.

The structural changes involved in the transition to socialism, such as the elimination of private ownership of the means of production, the development of forms of workers' participation in the decisions concerning the productive process, economic planning, and the allocation of surplus lead to transformations of consciousness, to the development of a "new man" and a "new woman."

However, it is clear that the relationship between the material base and the superstructure, between production relations and ideology, cannot be interpreted in mechanical ways. Transformations of consciousness do not automatically or instantaneously follow changes in the economic base. There is a *décalage,* a time lapse between transformations at the structural level and the corresponding changes in the superstructure.

But even beyond this *décalage,* the superstructure must be analyzed and described as having a relative autonomy, because superstructural elements can be independently transmitted by various socializing agencies like the family, the schools, and the mass media. Thus, they have mechanisms to reproduce themselves in spite of changes at the structural level which make them obsolete or dysfunctional. Hence, the need for specific strategies directed toward the transformation of consciousness, for the development of a new political culture and the expansion of new values, egalitarian and collectivistic: in sum, a cultural revolution.

The Spanish word *conciencia* means both consciousness and conscience; it therefore refers to the mental apparatus and to moral sense. Revolutionary change involves changes in *conciencia,* in the human view of the world and of humanness itself, and also in the set and hierarchy of prevailing values. In the Cuban case, prerevolutionary society had four basic dimensions of inequality which the revolutionary process has sought to redress: social class cleavages; rural-urban differentials; black-white differentials; and male-female inequality.[1] It is the purpose of this study to examine the status of women in prerevolutionary Cuban society and to assess the scope and nature of the changes which the Revolution has provoked.

As Jancar suggests, equality is a *process* by which diverse social groups become integrated into the body politic via two fundamental political steps: first, the ability to make demands upon the government, and second, actual participation in policy making.[2] However, the multilayered nature of this process is emphasized here. From structural barriers which limit access of women to the job market, to ideological factors which determine the preservation of sexual roles, there are a wide range of issues and indicators by which this process of equality can be measured in a society. The process perspective also implies a look not only at a cross-sectional view, at a frozen picture of the status of Cuban women at any given moment, but also at the vectors of change, at the direction of movement.

A Marxist theory of women's liberation within "the context of class struggle" has been a highly controversial issue since the beginning of the struggle for socialism itself.[3] A discussion of the theoretical and practical debate about feminist socialism is beyond the scope of this study. However, it is hoped that the perspective and findings presented here will contribute positively to the debate.

The most important element to keep in mind, particularly in Cuba (although this is also true of most of the countries which have attempted the transition to socialism, including the Soviet Union in 1917) is that the Revolution took place in an underdeveloped country. Therefore, the transition to socialism has to be conceptualized as a lengthy and complex process in which the first priorities are related to traversing a noncapitalist road to development and modernization. To further complicate things, these revolutionary societies have had to attempt the transition in the context of a capitalist world system which establishes constraints even upon countries attempting to escape it. These constraints impose concrete limitations, distortions, and constant struggles upon this process of transition.

This unavoidable primacy of economic development tasks, essential as a precondition for the construction of socialism, is at the root of many of today's controversies about socialist societies as they exist in the real world. The revolutionary regimes' approach to the woman question has, therefore, developed within this perspective and it has emphasized integration of women into the labor force, development of female resources by means of education, and the mobilizaiton of women to struggle for the general goals of socialist construction and not necessarily for feminist goals.

However, although these priorities are understandable, the promise of Marxism-Leninism with respect to full equality and the final liberation of women must also be realized.[4] And this implies a struggle in the ideological realm, the abolition of the ideology of male supremacy embodied in the sexual division of labor within the family.

If it is true that because of the primacy of the tasks of consolidating revolutionary power and achieving economic development, these cultural changes cannot be expected during the first years of the revolutionary transformation, it is also true that these cultural transformations must begin at the earliest stages of the Revolution, lest they become permanently postponed.

Women in Prerevolutionary Cuba

A perusal of a recent bibliography on Cuban women in the twentieth century by Nelson P. Valdes supports few generalizations about the status of women. Most of the existing literature pertains to women in postrevolutionary Cuba; and there is a serious scarcity of research materials on the role and status of women, whether in pre- or postrevolutionary times. No systematic comprehensive discussion of the role of women in prerevolutionary society has been published.[5]

Martinez Alier's monumental investigations of the status of blacks, women, and in particular, black women, in nineteenth-century Cuba throws significant light on some issues, such as the role of virginity and its relationship to *machismo*.[6] These issues are still useful in looking at women in twentieth-century Cuba insofar as certain cultural patterns and definitions managed to survive with slight modifications for many years. Basically, she argues that female honor was an index of family prestige in the highly stratified nineteenth-century Cuban society; that the value of virginity is inversely proportional to the degree of social mobility in a society; and that strict control over female sexuality was fundamental for the preservation of the class system in Cuban colonial society.

Fox interviewed recently-arrived émigré working-class men to attempt to see the impact of revolutionary transformations of sex roles upon their decision to leave, but also to determine their conceptions of sexual roles.[7] He describes the distinction between *la casa* ("the house") and *la calle* ("the street") as fundamental to an understanding of sexual roles in prerevolutionary society. *La casa,* he writes, is "generally considered the province of women" while "*la calle* is seen as the proper testing ground for masculinity, but is dangerous and inappropriate for women. Because *la calle* embraces everything outside the home, the role of the woman is narrowly restricted indeed."[8] Fox's respondents found it tolerable that a woman work outside the home if this were necessary for the family to maintain a certain life style, but no respondent entertained the idea that a man should work inside the home. Men were admired for being hard-working, good providers and caretakers. Women were admired for submissiveness to their husbands and for the avoidance of unwomanly activities.[9]

Purcell[10] precedes her analysis of revolutionary policies concerning women with a brief survey of information about women in prerevolutionary society. She presents a view of a complex situation: Cuban women's legal status was advanced when compared to that of women in other Latin American countries. Social indicators such as education also suggested considerable progress. However, female participation in the labor force was low, women were underrepresented at the highest educational levels (and hence in high-status professions), and the overwhelming majority of professional women taught in the primary schools. Their job was considered acceptable for females, and therefore it conferred low status and was poorly paid compared to other professions. The double standard prevailed, as did the view that a woman's place was in the home, although obvious class differences existed in the possibility of approaching such a cultural ideal.[11]

A survey of legal and social indicators of the status of Cuban women would indeed suggest a complex picture. It has been stated that "perhaps in no other Latin American country, with the exception of Argentina and Uruguay, had women achieved such a high level of equality as they had in Cuba."[12] The historical roots of this situation are briefly outlined here.

During colonial times and in the early years of the republic, women's position was one of total subordination to parents or husbands under the 1902 Constitution and Civil Code, tailored with respect to women's rights after the colonial Napoleonic Civil Code of 1886. A significant number of legal advances were achieved between 1917 and 1950. A law passed on July 18, 1917 represented the first breakthrough, abolishing those articles in the Civil Code which prescribed that a woman upon remarriage lost her *patria potestas* rights over her children by the former marriage. The new law also guaranteed women certain rights, including administration of their own property and appearing in court without their husbands' permission.[13]

On July 30, 1918, another landmark law was passed, despite great controversy and Catholic opposition. This was the Divorce Law, which included a simple agreement of the partners among other possible grounds for dissolving the marriage contract.[14]

The first Cuban Women's Congress met in Havana in 1925, with the participation of at least two dozen women's organizations. Advances in labor legislation were first obtained in 1925, insuring such rights for female workers as time off to feed nursing children, separate toilets, and the right to an appropriate locker room. There were basic provisions aimed at giving women employment in businesses which primarily sold women's apparel (100 percent female employment required in the sales force) and other products ranging from sports equipment to stationery (50 percent female employment required). This far-reaching law was a triumph for Cuban feminists at the time.[15]

Cuban women obtained the right to vote in 1934, in the aftermath of the anti-Machado revolution which saw significant levels of female participation.[16] Cuba was the fourth country in Latin America to grant the vote to women—after Ecuador, Brazil, and Uruguay.[17]

In 1934, a Maternity Law was also passed, regulating the working mother's maternity insurance fund; it covered delivery-related expenses with employer-employee contributions, the right of the mother to paid leave for six weeks before delivery and six weeks after delivery, the right to keep a job regardless of pregnancy, and the right to medical services.[18]

The advances obtained by women in the 1917–1940 period were elevated to constitutional rank by the 1940 Constitution. It prohibited discrimination on the basis of sex (Art. 20); reaffirmed the right of the woman to maintain her Cuban citizenship regardless of marriage (Art. 16); gave women the full right to control their private property and salary (Art. 43); introduced the principle of equal pay for equal work (Art. 62), and universal suffrage (Art. 97); assured the equality of single and married women with respect to work (Art. 68); and reasserted the working woman's right to paid maternity leave and to other privileges.[19]

These provisions represented the legal norm; the extent of their enforcement in practice is another matter. As was frequently the case with the more advanced social provisions of the 1940 Constitution, they represented the aspirations of the 1933 revolutionaries, but the needed complementary legislation and enforcement were slow in materializing, if they materialized at all. Not until December 1950 did a law on women's civil rights establish the detailed regulations needed to implement women's full legal equality.[20]

These achievements can be attributed only partially to the existence of a powerful feminist movement. The Cuban Republic, particularly in the period 1934–1944, was ruled by Colonel Batista, who attempted to develop coalition politics to guarantee peace and order after imposing them by force in the aftermath of the 1933 revolution. In the changed international context of the late thirties, with the emergence of fascism and the development of alliances between the Western powers and the Soviet Union, Batista fostered highly progressive legislation, particularly on labor matters but also in areas appealing to other special groups, such as women.

Thus, much of the advanced social legislation passed by the short-lived revolutionary government of Grau and Guiteras was eventually consolidated under Batista's rule. The 1940 Constitutional Convention, in which the Cuban Communists played a very significant role, incorporated into the Constitution very progressive thought. Particularly with respect to women, the 1940 Constitution was influenced by international currents, such as the 1932 Lima Declaration on Rights for Women.

Much of the advanced legislation concerning women passed in the pre-1959 period can be traced to the action of the Cuban labor movement and to the important female component within the unions. Economic conditions and sexual role differentiation, which forced men into the labor force at an early age and maintained a high level of unemployment, had the dual effect of preventing faster incorporation of women into the world of work and of allowing women to enter the educational system in significant numbers, except at the higher educational level.

Information on literacy rates reveals that in 1953, a higher percentage of females (78.8 percent) than males (74.1 percent) of the population aged 10 and over were literate. More men (27.6 percent) than women (23.0 percent) received no schooling. More females (72 percent) than males (67 percent) attended grade school. However, the female advantage evaporated as one moved up the educational ladder. The figures on higher education show that roughly twice as many males (35,900) as females (17,500) received some university education.

In 1953, 22.5 percent of the total urban female population, compared to 84.1 percent of the urban male population, and 12.5 percent of the total rural female population, compared to 90.8 percent of the rural male population, were classified as economically active.[21]

The percentage of economically active females has been gradually increasing since the beginning of the century, although the progress has been very slow. However, female workers have been heavily concentrated in certain categories and almost totally absent from others. In the teaching profession 81.1 percent of all workers were women. Other occupations with a high female representation were social work and the clergy (45.2 percent); typing (52.5 percent), and clothing manufacturing (45.1 percent). But the occupational category in which female dominance was greatest was that of domestic service (89.2 percent). Actually more than one out of every four women working was employed in domestic service; one out of every five was employed in the manufacturing industries (with heavy concentration in clothing, food, and tobacco industries); one out of every six was a professional (but of these roughly 84 percent were teachers); and one out of every seven was an office worker.

In summary, the picture of the status of women in prerevolutionary Cuba is one of marked progress in terms of achievement of legal equality; but of significant discrimination in practically all other indicators: very limited incorporation in the labor force, overrepresentation in the low-income, low-status jobs, and underrepresentation in the best-paid, high-status occupational categories. Data concerning sex role stereotypes and attitudes are scanty because of a lack of systematic research, but some ideas can be gathered from historical studies, fiction works, travel diaries, newspaper articles, and other anecdotal records. The ideal cultural norm placed the woman in the house, although marked social class differences existed, with lower-class women incorporated into the labor force mostly as domestics and industrial workers, and some members of the middle sectors working in traditional female occupations such as teaching and social work. The variety of female occupations was limited; "unwomanly" occupations included not only those involving hard physical labor but also those high-prestige, high-pay occupations which would have brought women into positions of authority vis-à-vis men. With respect to the family, strict division of labor was enforced, especially at the upper and middle social levels, but even at the lower levels when it was financially feasible. Males had provider roles, and were basically unconcerned with management of household affairs and with performance of any household chores. The double standard of sexual morality was, by and large, enforced; males had predatory rights while women were supposed to remain monogamous and faithful. Virginity had a high social value, and its preservation led to elaborate rituals of chaperonage and formal courtship among the middle and upper classes.

Revolutionary Changes in the Position of Cuban Women

The participation of Cuban women in the paid work force has increased significantly since the Revolution, from 17.2 percent women in the labor force at the time of the last prerevolutionary census (1953) to 30.1 percent in 1979.[22] The increase, although significant, fails to be impressive in strictly numerical terms if it is not analyzed within the context of a society under tremendous political and economic pressures, attempting to break from its position as a United States client state and from the world capitalist system.

It is true, for example, that participation of Cuban women living in the United States in the American labor force has reached much higher levels (54 percent) than has the participation of Cuban women in Cuba.[23] Thus, Dominguez has argued that "the experience of personal change through international migration and the generally higher levels of education among exiles were far more powerful than the revolutionary experience in Cuba in bringing women into the work force."[24] However, this analysis is incomplete and insufficient on many grounds.

With respect to Cuban women in the United States, it could be argued that the economic pressure for this incorporation into the labor force was the paramount variable. As émigrés attempted to reconstitute a middle-class style of living in the United States and to enter the consumer society in full force, female employment became the necessary route toward the desired family income levels, given the usual loss of occupational status and income by males. But the most important set of factors pertain again to the differences in the developmental level of the two societies in question. It is one thing to foster integration of women into the labor force in a developed, industrialized society and another to incorporate women into the labor force of an underdeveloped country, particularly one facing squarely the tasks of a noncapitalist developmental strategy.

There have been several structural factors affecting the rate of female incorporation into the Cuban labor force. Among these have been the levels of prerevolutionary unemployment; the investment levels necessary to create new jobs, particularly in the industrial sector; the general economic difficulties associated with the United States blockade of Cuba; the general economic difficulties associated with systematic changes from dependent capitalism to construction of socialism; the emigration of a significant percentage of the best-educated prerevolutionary labor force, both male and female; the difficulties in the availability of consumer goods, the lack of convenience foods, the limited availability of time-saving household appliances; and the economic problems that have also limited the expansion of collectivized services such as day-care centers and public laundries. Furthermore, by its redistributive policies and its guarantee of basic needs, such as health, education, food, housing, and recreation, the Revolution may have been a disincentive for the incorporation of women into the labor force. During the late sixties and even in the early seventies there was a relatively high degree of "socialist inflation," expressed not in a rise in prices, because prices are controlled, but rather in an excess of circulating money with respect to the goods available for purchase. This also discouraged the incorporation of women into the labor force. Finally, the expansion of educational opportunities also may have contributed to slowing down the rate of female participation in the labor force. It provided an alternative occupation and the possibility of a better job in the future. To these structural factors, we must add, of course, the still pervasive ideology of male domination and sex stereotyping, discussed below.

At the beginning of the Revolution, as a consequence of accelerated developmental programs, particularly the expansion of services, and of emigration, there was a labor shortage, which facilitated the incorporation of women into the labor force. However, since the reintroduction of economic controls and efficiency criteria during the seventies, labor shortages in the secondary and tertiary sectors have disappeared. Under these conditions, in spite of minor setbacks at the beginning of the decade, female participation in the labor force has continued to grow, and this must be considered a significant achievement.

It is obvious that Cuba occupies an intermediate position in comparison to other countries. It stands above other "underdeveloped" countries, but below industrialized capitalist countries and much below Eastern European socialist countries. For example, Cuba had 18.5 percent women in the economically active population in 1970, compared to 37.2 percent in the United States, 46.2 percent in Poland, and 49.8 percent in the Soviet Union for the same year.[25]

The gradual increase in female labor force participation has led some writers, such as Dominguez, to state that "a modernization hypothesis is sufficient to explain the trends" and that "it is difficult to perceive any effects of the advent of the revolution on women's employment, since the rate of incorporation [has been] fairly steady" before and after the Revolution.[26] Yet such an interpretation is profoundly misleading. After the triumph of the Revolution in 1959, two major categories of prerevolutionary female employment (household service and prostitution) were almost immediately eliminated. This, together with the significant percentage of émigrés in teaching, the main "middle-class" category of female employment, should have provoked a catastrophic temporary decrease in the female labor force participation rate. The fact that it was possible to mobilize new recruits to the labor force and to provide replacement jobs in new categories must be termed a definite effect of the Revolution, not reducible to "modernization" terms.[27]

The revolutionary impact is thus particularly visible in terms of the occupational distribution of female workers. "Domestic servants" constituted the largest single category of employment for women before the Revolution (30 percent of all women employed in 1953). This category had virtually disappeared by 1975. The greatest relative increases are in the areas of health and education.[28] This must be seen in the context of the great expansion of the sector of social services within the economically active population. During the early years in power the Cuban Revolution followed a course in which "social justice and social welfare took precedence over immediate economic concerns."[29] Thus there was an extraordinary expansion of health and educational services. Women moved quickly into these sectors, partially because these services fitted the traditional ideology about proper female roles and their extension into the world of work but also because they were the sectors in which there was a significant expansion of jobs. Also, during the early years of the Revolution, special training schools were organized for prostitutes, domestic servants, and peasant women to help them achieve basic skills and to provide specific training for clerical, commercial, and administrative jobs.[30]

In spite of the above explanations, the occupational distribution of women in the labor force still leaves much to be desired. Jancar has discussed the feminization of job categories in socialist countries as a factor affecting the advance of women to high-status, decision-making jobs. She points out the concentration of women in agricultural work in Eastern Europe and in the Soviet Union and also the feminization of sectors within industry which are associated with traditional female occupations, such as textiles and other branches of light industry.[31] In Cuba, it is possible to observe a similar trend in terms of the high proportion of women engaged in the textile industries (77 percent of the total work force); in plastics (37 percent); in tobacco (57.5 percent), and in light industry generally (47 percent).[32] However, Cuban women do not generally work in agriculture; only 14 percent of all agricultural workers are female.

Finally, one of the most significant effects of the Revolution has been the massive incorporation of women into community volunteer work, through the Federation of Cuban Women. Over a million women participate in the Movimiento de Madres Combatientes (Fighting Mothers Movement) which provides support womanpower in the schools, where they substitute for absent teachers and work in the school lunchrooms and in school maintenance. Over 130,000 other women participate in other volunteer community, health, and economic development activities.[33]

The importance of the mobilization of women into these organized, massive community service activities is great, not only in terms of the general revolutionary goals which these activities serve, but also in terms of the impact they have on the traditional ideology of the sexes. These activities bring women into *la calle,* out of the confines of *la casa.* They also represent an intermediate step toward female incorporation into the paid labor force.

Women and Educational Opportunity

It has been pointed out above that before the Revolution Cuban women had a relative advantage over men in terms of their educational attainment—at least, at the preuniversity levels. However, this was in the context of a society in which a quarter of the population aged ten years and older "had never attended school at all, and less than a quarter had completed primary school."[34]

In the 1978–79 school year, women, who constitute 49 percent of the Cuban population, were 41.2 percent of all students. The percentage of women in the grade schools was 47.5; in the secondary schools it was 50.8; and in the teacher training schools it was 55.5.[35] In higher education the percentage of women was 40.6. Furthermore, "in advanced and technological studies, statistics show a distribution of sex unheard of anywhere else in Latin America, or in the capitalist world in general. Science—50 percent women; Biochemistry and Biology—60 percent; Technology—22.7 percent; Agricultural Studies—35 percent; Medicine—50 percent."[36]

Thus, through educational attainment, Cuban women are being incorporated into the highest levels of the educational system, and particularly into the high-status, technical careers that are now emphasized by the revolutionary regime. This suggests that the educational preconditions for massive incorporation of women into the world of professions are being effectively met in Cuba. It also suggests that the preconditions for female participation in the highest levels of decision-making are also being laid down.

It has been pointed out that "political elite recruitment patterns in the Soviet Union and Eastern Europe indicate that doctors and teachers are not expected to become political leaders in Communist countries . . . but that a political future is more likely for engineers."[37] This generalization is not applicable to Cuba at this time. There is not enough information on patterns of political elite recruitment in Cuba, but if membership in the Cuban Communist Party is taken as a gross indicator, still at this point any professional career is a definite disadvantage. Party members with higher education in Cuba have never been more than 5 percent.[38]

If the pattern of engineer-administrator-government official were to hold in Cuba in the future, Cuban women seem to be in a better position than their counterparts in most other socialist countries. Nearly 23 percent of technology students are women in the Cuban higher education system, compared to 43.2 percent female engineering students in Romania, 39.0 percent in the Soviet Union, 27.1 percent in Bulgaria, 19.7 in Yugoslavia, 19.6 percent in Hungary, 16.0 percent in Poland, and 15.0 percent in Czechoslovakia.[39] But perhaps much more significant is the fact that among students enrolled in economics, the career which most directly seems to prepare administrators in Cuba at the present stage, women represent 42 percent of the enrollment.[40]

Material Resources Required for Female Labor Force Participation

In Cuba as well as in other socialist countries, certain specific lacks or limitations of resources, associated with economic underdevelopment, hinder female labor force participation: scarcity of housing; lack of communal services, such as day-care centers and laundries; and a scarcity of labor-saving appliances. In this section. the various strategies followed in Cuba to alleviate these problems are discussed.

The development of day-care centers has had high priority. In 1973, Cuba had about 50,000 children ranging in age from forty-five days to five years, placed in roughly 600 *circulos* (day-care centers); this is approximately three times the number of children enrolled at the time in the five boroughs of New York City which have the same population as Cuba.[41]

The day-care centers are administered by the Federation of Cuban Women; so are all the supportive training activities, from courses for *asistentes* (paraprofessional child-care workers) to the *Escuelas de Educadoras* (training schools for professional child-care workers). Cuban *circulos* are open to children of working mothers, and until 1978 they were free. Now fees are charged on a sliding scale according to family income.

In spite of the great effort in opening, maintaining, and staffing *circulos,* there are huge waiting lists. The government has estimated that for each 1,000 women with small children who join the work force, it is necessary to invest $280,000 in Cuban *pesos* in day-care centers, $16,000 in equipment, 125 *asistentes,* three nurses, and a physician. The 1976–1980 five-year plan projected the construction of 400 day-care centers, bringing the total capacity of the Cuban day-care center system to 150,000 children.[42]

Besides the Federation of Cuban Women, in 1969 the Cuban Federation of Workers organized the Feminine Front, a part of the labor union organization to deal specifically with the problems affecting working women. They advise the Federation of job openings, they check on absenteeism and tardiness and try to resolve its causes; they coordinate services, from access to day care to laundry.[43]

Special provisions have been made to ease the burden of working women, such as the Plan Jaba, whereby working women can leave their shopping bags at the grocery store to have their quotas of rationed food filled by the grocer without having to stand in line; the introduction of special shopping days and hours for women workers so that they can purchase clothing and household items; and the distribution of labor-saving appliances, such as washing machines, to working women through their work centers.[44]

By the midseventies the availability of consumer goods improved and many formerly rationed items became available in the "free" market. Special stores were opened to serve, for example, newlyweds and new parents. In general, a distribution system parallel to the rationing system developed, which eased somewhat the difficulties of access to most goods.[45] These changes had a positive impact on women.

Legal Change

The revolutionary government did not find it necessary to legislate extensively to develop a framework for female equality because basic legislation existed from prerevolutionary times. However, there have been significant developments since 1959.

The 1976 Cuban Constitution deals with women's rights in a much more comprehensive manner than either the 1940 Constitution or the 1959 Fundamental Law. In its Article 45, the 1976 Constitution establishes that "Women have the same rights as men in the economic, political and social fields, as well as in the family." Thus, female equality is explicitly extended to the realm of the family, and the Constitution establishes a broad framework to change the internal politics of the household.

This attempt to change the normative system with respect to power relations within the family is even clearer in the Family Code of February 14, 1975. Articles 24 through 28 of the Family Code spell out equality of rights and duties of men and women within the matrimonial bond, including the duties of supporting the family, caring for it, and sharing in household duties so that both partners can pursue their professions or careers. These provisions of the Family Code are obviously difficult to enforce, but the code does provide and articulate a new set of norms for family life and for equality within the family, although within a pretty conservative view of the role of the family in general and particularly during the transition to socialism.[46]

Even in areas where preexisting legislation was relatively advanced in comparison to other countries under capitalism, the Revolution has meant significant changes. For example, since 1934, Cuban women have enjoyed maternity health legislation under social security. However, peasant women, domestic servants, and other women in marginal occupations have not had access to the benefits of this legislation.

In 1963, the benefits of social security legislation were generalized to guarantee maternity benefits to all women workers, expand paid maternity leave to twelve weeks, and establish a daily one-hour leave for working women so that they could tend to their children. In 1974, maternity benefits were further expanded. Medical attention for mother and child are now guaranteed through the pre- and post-natal periods, paid materity leave is extended to eighteen weeks, and to twenty weeks in cases of twin births or miscalculation in estimated delivery date.

Female Participation in the Political Structures

Jancar has pointed out that-there seems to be a "woman's place" in Communist politics. At the national level such place is "either as a deputy chairman or deputy president of the legislative body, or as head of a ministry whose sphere of interest is close to women's traditional role: health, education or light industry."[47] The Cuban pattern seems to fit this generalization but with some significant differences.

Within the Cuban Communist Party, women are seriously underrepresented. At the time of 1975 party congress, women represented roughly 15 percent of the membership, but only 2 percent of the municipal, 4 percent of the provincial, and 6 percent of the national leadership.[48] The thesis on internal party life established, as a goal for 1980, representation of women in the party itself at least equal to the level of female participation in the paid labor force.[49] This meant increasing female membership 100 percent in a five-year period. The 15 percent figure for female party members places Cuba behind other communist countries. Data for 1972 quoted by Jancar places female party representation between 16.1 percent in Yugoslavia and 27.4 percent in Czechoslovakia.[50] However, the Cuban pattern of female representation in the party leadership does not fit the common generalization that "women are more visible at the local levels, and less visible in the highest echelons of government."[51] The Cuban pattern is more complex; in the party leadership, as well as in the elected state organs, there is an actual reversal of this generalization, suggesting the commitment of the leadership to fostering female participation at the higher levels.

Figures quoted above indicate 6 percent women in the party national leadership, and only 2 percent at the local level. Data about the elected Organs of Popular Power follow the same pattern. In the 1976 elections, women were only approximately 8 percent of the local, municipal delegates and 14 percent of the provincial delegates, but 22.2 percent of the 481 deputies elected to the National Assembly.[52] The latter figure represents an unprecedented level of female participation in a legislative body in Cuban history. Prerevolutionary female participation in the House of Representatives never reached 5 percent, and there were even lower figures in the Senate.[53]

The reverse pattern observed in female percentages at the different levels of the Cuban Organs of Popular Power reflect leadership commitment to female participation because at the highest levels the possibility of influencing the results of the election are greater than at the base. In the Cuban electoral system, local candidates are nominated in open assemblies and elected by direct, secret vote. At the provincial and national levels, however, elections are indirect. Provincial delegates and national deputies are elected by the municipal delegates from states in which the party and the mass organizations have decisive input.

Female representation remains low at the top organs of the political system. Thus, 13 percent of the members of the Council of State, the supreme organ of the National Assembly, are women.[54] In 1975, among the 112 members of the Central Committee, 5.4 percent were women. There was virtually no change from the 5 percent female representation in the 1965 Central Committee. However, of the 12 alternate members elected in 1975, 5 were women, bringing the total female representation in the Central Committee to 9 percent.[55] In the highest party organs, such as the Political Bureau and the Secretariat, there is still a total lack of female representation. As for the top governmental structures, the Council of Ministers and the ministerial Institutes, there is very low female representation and it follows the pattern described for other Communist countries: a woman is minister of education and another is minister of light industry.

But female participation in mass organizations at the various levels is very encouraging. In the Committees for the Defense of the Revolution, women constituted 49 percent of the 1979 membership, 41 percent of the local leadership, 36 percent of the zone leadership, 30.8 percent of the municipal committee leadership, 31 percent of the provincial committee leadership, and 30 percent of the national committee leadership.[56] In the unions, women are well represented in the local organizations, where 39.4 percent of the leadership is female. In the municipal committees, women constitute 43.7 percent of the leadership, but only 17.9 percent of the provincial councils and 17.1 percent of the secretariats of the national unions.[57]

Many factors affect female political participation, including, of course, ideological and cultural variables. But in the Cuban case, the existence of a "triple shift" seems to be a determining factor. In a survey of voters conducted at the time of the 1974 Matanzas Popular Power elections, 54 percent of the women said that they were not willing to serve if elected. Typically the reasons they gave were the burdens of home duties, their job responsibilities, and the lack of child-care facilities.[58] Writers about female status have coined the phrase "double shift" to refer to the condition of working women in the West, who must perform their duties as workers and then a second shift at home. In the Cuban case, studying to acquire elementary or advanced skills constitutes a third activity in which a significant number of women are involved. In 1979, 35 percent of Cuban working women were also enrolled in an educational program.[59]

Most women belong at least to the Federation of Cuban Women and to the Committees for the Defense of the Revolution. If they are working, they also belong to a union. Thus they also have duties associated with membership in these mass organizations. Under these conditions, participation in additional activities, such as those associated with becoming a party member or being elected a Popular Power delegate, requires an additional time commitment that women perceive as an inordinate burden.

Continuity and Changes in the Realm of Ideology

United States feminists observing changes in the role of Cuban women have been somewhat disappointed by the "limitations" they perceive in progress toward equality. In 1971 Purcell pointed out that "the Castro regime had made little or no effort to refute many traditional notions regarding the particular suitability of certain roles for females."[60]

This is definitely too harsh a judgment, but we should also consider the time element: the campaign against sexism in the Cuban mass media did not reach its peak until the midseventies. Cartoons and jokes in the popular humorous tabloids *Palante* and *Dedete*, feature articles in *Granma* and *Bohemia,* the treatment of female heroines in movies such as Humberto Solas' masterpiece *Lucia* and black female director Sara Gomez's *One Way or Another*, and even special antiprejudice documentaries, such as *Con las Mujeres Cubanas,* have been used to attempt to change the traditional image of women. The media have also attempted to change the attitudes of Cuban males toward female work and the conventional ideas about the intrinsically feminine (and feminizing) character of household work.

Some significant changes are taking place in the younger generations; for example, both male and female adolescents in rural junior and senior high schools are required to participate in cleaning and maintaining their living quarters and to work part-time in agricultural or industrial jobs. However, old conceptions die very hard. Women are still thought to have primary, if not sole, responsibility for household and child-care activities. The Family Code has established new norms of equality in this respect, something which no other capitalist or communist country has done so far. But the practical impact of the Family Code, which must be seen as an educative instrument, will depend on the long-range development of a new consciousness among Cuban women and men. An indicator of the changes in women's status and of the strains associated with the redefinition of sexual roles is the divorce rate, which multiplied fivefold in the 1958–1968 period.[61] Women are almost exclusively in charge of young children's care and it will probably take much longer before it becomes conceivable to have Cuban men on the staff of day-care centers.[62]

Typical statements from the leadership, even the female leadership, reflect a strong mixture of the new, egalitarian values and of the old ideology about sexual roles. For example, Electra Fernandez, alternate Central Committee member and president of the Childhood Institute, when asked about men staffing day-care centers and elementary school classrooms, asserted the new norm: "The educative function . . . pertains to men as well as to women." But she also stated, without criticizing it or expressing concern for changing it, the view that "social practice has determined the predominant participation of women in children's education." Thus, she reasserted the traditional ideology that the need of preschool children for tender loving care can be met only or predominantly by women.[63]

Yet the situation remains dynamic. Traditional sex role stereotypes and the ideology of machismo are fast losing ground. Fidel Castro himself reported that "some were frightened when the discussion of the Family Code was launched."[64] But he added: "We don't see why anyone should be so frightened, because what should really frighten us as revolutionaries is that we have to admit the reality that women still do not have absolute equality in Cuban society."[65]

In an analysis of Cuban women's roles based on the stories published in *Granma*'s weekly English edition, Olesen confirms many of the changes outlined so far: the increased rate of female participation in the labor force, the altered opportunities at all levels in the job market, and changes in legislation concerning marriage and divorce and in access to contraceptive devices.[66] But these changes, she finds, are coupled with residual cultural themes such as the importance of the family and of family ties and a relative persistence of sex role differentiation. Certain aspects of the traditional sexual ideology remain almost unchallenged, for example, the image of woman as mother and the primacy of her biological function. Associated with this conception are a number of beliefs about women's health requirements, and therefore about jobs which are suitable or unsuitable for women. Thus, Article 43 of the 1976 Cuban Constitution states that women should be "given jobs in keeping with their physical makeup." Even in the aftermath of the enactment of the Family Code and with the new emphasis on combatting sexual discrimination through the mass media, the late 1970s have seen a reaffirmation of Resolution 48, which prohibited women from taking certain jobs. A decree of June 1976 listed nearly 300 occupations from which women were excluded.[67] The list is rather odd; it includes a wide variety of occupations such as those involving underwater work, standing on scaffolds five meters above the ground, and working with toxic chemicals. But it also includes cemetery work and other jobs whose relationship to health issues is hard to see.

The persistence in the late 1970s of forbidden occupations for women may be related to the pressures created by the new policies of economic efficiency and by the need to secure certain lines for male employment.[68] However, informal interviews with Cuban officials as well as the text of the decree itself emphasize health reasons. Discussing the decree, Cubans frequently refer to the need to protect "female reproductive organs." Yet no similar concern has ever been expressed for protecting the more exposed male reproductive organs. Obviously, concern for female reproductive organs is associated with the basic definition of woman as mother. The possibility that a woman may choose not to become a mother remains alien to Cubans.

In other countries undergoing the transition to socialism, this concern for the maternal aspect of the feminine role has been historically associated with and enhanced by preoccupation with negative demographic trends. But in Cuba this is not a factor, at least at this time. The country experienced a mild population explosion right after the Revolution, and although the birth rate has been decreasing since the late sixties, there has been a healthy population growth. In spite of sizable emigration, Cuba now has close to ten million inhabitants. If the policy toward population growth is an indicator (and abortions and contraceptives are readily available in Cuba), there does not seem to be anxiety about demographic trends, one way or the other.

Postrevolutionary changes in female status and sex roles can be summarized as follows: the economic basis for female oppression has been basically destroyed; significant although not radical changes in the level and nature of female employment have been achieved. There have also been significant changes in the level of women's participation in collective activities (other than paid labor) and in mass organizations generally. Changes in the legal system must be seen within the context of the substantial legal equality already achieved by Cuban women before the Revolution. Post-1959 legislation has further emphasized women's rights and it has established the equality of males and females within marriage in every respect: from responsibility for the support of the home to responsibility for the care of the children and for household duties. Participation of women in the political system has improved markedly with respect to prerevolutionary levels, but membership in the party and in the key party, state, and government structures remains rather low, although it is improving.

The most encouraging signs are the obvious commitment of the leadership to promoting women to high elected and appointed offices and the data on the educational level of Cuban women, particularly in higher education and in scientific and technical careers. Also significant is the Cuban willingness to experiment with plans to help working women, plans which have not as yet been tried by any other society attempting the transition to socialism.

Changes in the attitudes of men and women, and in the cultural definitions of male and female roles, especially with respect to intersex etiquette, sexual mores, and the politics of the household, have been slower in coming, and the present picture can best be described as mixed and transitional. New egalitarian norms coexist with strong residues of the old sexual ideology and with a generally conservative view of the role of the family.[69]

But this picture of women's position in contemporary Cuba would not be complete without a discussion, however brief, of the Federation of Cuban Women, the mass organization especially concerned with utilizing and channeling female participation in the overall political system.

The Federation of Cuban Women

The Federation of Cuban Women (FMC) was founded in 1960, and originally it had a modest membership of about 17,000. By 1978, its membership had reached 2,248,000; it now includes the majority of Cuban women fourteen years and older. But a number of basic points must be understood about the conceptualization of the FMC, the views of its leadership about the struggle for female rights, and the general revolutionary position on the woman question.

The FMC sees itself as a feminine, not a feminist organization.[70] Vilma Espin, president of the FMC since its foundation, has stated that men "had a chance to develop more than women. And that's why the Federation was needed. Otherwise there wouldn't have been any point in having an organization just for women."[71] The FMC is basically seen as an instrument for the mobilization of Cuban women and for their integration into the revolutionary process.[72] Like all other mass organizations in Cuban society, it functions as a two-way communication system: it transmits directives from above, interpreting political decisions and mobilizing people for their implementation; and it transmits concerns, opinion, and reactions from below, so that these can be incorporated into the decision-making process.[73]

During the 1960s, the mass organizations were primarily responsible for the institutionalization of change. Participation then occurred mostly at the level of implementation. However, with organizational development and maturing, and particularly after the process of institutionalization of the Revolution began in the early 1970s, the role of the mass organizations as representatives of special interests began to be emphasized.[74] They also have developed an increasing role in decision-making about their ares of interest and a relative sphere of semiautonomous control. But they are only semiautonomous because all mass organizations, as well as all other institutions in the political system and the society in general, operate under the guidance and the control of the Cuban Communist Party.

But the FMC does control, for example, the development of the day-care centers and of the Childhood Institute as well as the management of the social centers, of vacations, and of the Plan CTC, a special distribution system of consumer durables through the unions. The FMC has also continued to play its traditional role as a service organization. It has organized training courses, such as the Ana Betancourt Schools for Peasant Women and social rehabilitation programs for prostitutes. It has played a significant role in the recruitment of women into the labor force, and it continues to be a major instrument for organizing women for volunteer work, through the Madres Combatientes por la Educacion and other groups.

In recent years, the FMC has developed an important role in mobilizing women for political participation and has cooperated in the establishment of Popular Power structures at various levels. The federation, as well as other mass organizations, also plays a "lobbying" role within the political system; that is, it articulates group interests before party leaders and structures; and it performs a brokerage role with respect to the various bureaucracies involved in the formulation and implementation of policy.

Finally, the FMC plays a significant role in publicizing the Cuban view of the struggle for female equality within the context of socialist transition. This view distinguishes sharply between bourgeois feminism and a struggle for female equality aimed primarily at integrating women into the general goals of the Revolution (economic development and the construction of socialism), at maintaining the priority of the class struggle, and at subordinating the struggle for women's rights to general societal needs. Any student of the role of bourgeois and petty bourgeois women in the Chilean Revolution would have to concur that the FMC and the general strategy of the Cuban Revolution concerning women have successfully prevented the mobilization of women against the Revolution.

General participation in revolutionary survival, economic development, and the tasks of socialist construction are obviously the priorities in the beginning stages of a socialist revolution. The question is whether transformations are to remain at this level. Are the cultural revolution, the radical alteration of values, of culture, and even of human nature to be permanently postponed or will the struggle for cultural change continue, instead of being frozen out? In the Cuban case transformations at the cultural and ideological level with regard to the status of women have experienced limited success. What is important is that these transformations have begun and that they seem to continue twenty years after the triumph of the Revolution. Actually, emphasis on the ideological struggle has been particularly obvious in the last five years. Will this process continue or will it level out before equality and the final demise of traditional sexual ideology are achieved? In the case of the Cuban Revolution, this is still an open question. And the fact that the question remains open is no small achievement.

Notes

1. See Jose A. Moreno, "From Tradition to Modern Values," in Carmelo Mesa-Lago, ed., *Revolutionary Change in Cuba* (Pittsburgh: University of Pittsburgh Press, 1971), pp. 471–497.

2. Barbara Wolfe Jancar, *Women Under Communism* (Baltimore and London: The Johns Hopkins Press, 1978), p. 4.

3. Norman Soltz Chincilla, "Mobilizing Women: Revolution in the Revolution," *Latin American Perspectives* 4 (Fall 1977): 83–102.

4. For the viewpoint of a radical socialist feminist, see Alexandra Kollontai's *The Autobiography of a Sexually Emancipated Communist Woman* (New York: Herder and Herder, 1971).

5. Nelson P. Valdes, "A Bibliography of Cuban Women in the Twentieth Century," *Cuban Studies Newsletter* 4 (June 1974): 1–31.

6. Verena Martinez Alier, *Marriage, Class and Color in Nineteenth Century Cuba* (London: Cambridge University Press, 1974).

7. Geoffrey E. Fox, "Honor, Shame and Women's Liberation in Cuba: Views of Working Class Emigré Men," in Anne Pescatello, ed., *Female and Male in Latin America* (Pittsburgh: University of Pittsburgh Press, 1975).

8. Ibid., pp. 280–281.

9. Ibid., pp. 283–285.

10. Susan K. Purcell, "Modernizing Women for a Modern Society: The Cuban Case," in Ann Pescatello, ed., *Female and Male in Latin America* (Pittsburgh: University of Pittsburgh Press, 1973).

11. Ibid., pp. 259–261.

12. Moreno, *From Tradition to Modern Values,* p. 478.

13. Ricardo Hortensia, *Documentos para la historia de Cuba* (Havana: Instituto del Libro, 1973), vol. 2, pp. 411–412.

14. Ibid., pp. 413–416.

15. Ibid., vol. 3, pp. 314–319.

16. Gerardo Machado was Cuban dictator from 1925 to 1933. A populist revolution, carried forth by an alliance of workers, students, soldiers, and members of the petty bourgeoisie and the intelligentsia, led to his downfall in 1933. The revolutionary government of Grau San Martin, with Antonio Guiteras as its leading force, passed highly advanced social legislation, but it was short-lived: the U.S. never recognized it. The Grau administration was followed, after January 17, 1934, by a series of caretaker governments under the control of Colonel Batista.

17. Purcell, "Modernizing Women," p. 260.

18. Grupo Cubano de Investigaciones Economicas, *Un Éstudio sobre Cuba* (Miami: University of Miami Press, 1963), pp. 747–8.

19. L. de la Cuesta, *Constituciones Cubanas desde 1912 hasta nuestros dias* (New York: Ediciones Exilio, 1974).

20. L. Rodriguez Esguivel, *Capacidad civil de la mujer* (Havana: Editorial Lex, 1955).

21. Grupo Cubano de Investigaciones Economicas, *Un estudio sobre Cuba,* p. 806.

22. Jorge Dominguez, *Cuba: Order and Revolution* (Cambridge, Mass.: The Belknap Press of Harvard University Press, 1978), p. 499; also "Una pregunta a Vilma Espin," *Granma Resumen Semanal,* March 18, 1979, p. 7.

23. Rafael J. Prohias, and Lourdes Casal, *The Cuban Minority in the United States* (Washington, D.C.: Cuban National Planning Council, 1974), p. 63.

24. Dominguez, *Cuba: Order and Revolution,* pp. 499–500.

25. JUCEPLAN, *Aspectos demograficos de la fuerza laboral femenina en Cuba* (Havana: Dept. de Demografia, Direccion de Estadistica de Poplacion y Censos, 1975), p. 39.

26. Dominguez, *Cuba,* pp. 498–99.

27. Lourdes Casal, "Toward a Conceptual Framework for Women and Development Studies," paper presented at the Institute of Cuban Studies Conference on Women and Change, Boston University, May 6–7, 1977. Available from the author.

28. Jancar, *Women Under Communism,* p. 249.

29. Nita Manitzas, "Cuba and the Contemporary International Order," paper presented at the seminar "Democracy and Development in the Caribbean" sponsored by the Center for Inter-American Relations, May 6–8, 1979, p. 14. Available from the author.

30. Dudley Sears, et al., *Cuba: The Economic and Social Revolution* (Chapel Hill: The University of North Carolina Press, 1964), pp. 209–210. See also Carol Benglesdorf and Alice Hageman, "Emerging from Underdevelopment: Women and Work," *Cuba Review* 4 (1974): pp. 3–12.

31. Jancar, *Women Under Communism,* pp. 19–28.

32. Figures taken from data on female membership by unions published in *Granma Weekly Review,* March 18, 1979, p. 6, and also from breakdowns of female labor force in the Ministry of Light Industry in *Memoria II Congreso Nacional de la Federacion de Mujeres Cubanas* (Havana: Editorial Orbe, 1975), p. 19.

33. "Una pregunta a Vilma Espin," *Granma Weekly Review,* March 18, 1979, p. 7.

34. Sears et al., *Cuba,* p. 164.

35. "Una pregunta a Asela de los Santos," *Granma Resumen Semanal,* March 18, 1979, p. 7.

36. Margaret Randall, *Cuban Women Now: Interviews with Cuban Women* (Toronto: The Woman's Press, 1974), p. 16.

37. Jancar, *Women Under Communism,* p. 18.

38. Dominguez, *Cuba,* p. 317.

39. Jancar, *Women Under Communism,* p. 20.

40. Ramiro Pavon, "El emples femenino en Cuba," *Santiago,* 20 (December 1975): 14.

41. Marvin Leiner, *Children Are the Revolution* (New York: Viking Press, 1974), p. 5.

42. *Granma Resumen Semanal* (March 18, 1979), p. 6.

43. Benglesdorf, "The Fronte Femenino," *Cuba Review* 4 (1974): 27–28.

44. For a description of the Plan CTC (distribution of consumer durables through the work centers), see *Granma,* October 30, 1972, 2.

45. Mesa-Lago, ed., *Cuba in the 1970s: Pragmatism and Institutionalization* (Albuquerque: University of New Mexico Press, 1978), pp. 40–44.

46. The issue is too complex to be discussed here. Radical socialist feminist thought has had to grapple with the paradox of the strengthening of the family during the transition. For example, Perez-Stable states: "At least in theory . . . the abolition of the family emerges from within Marxism as the ultimate condition for the emancipation of women, just as, again in theory, the withering away of the state under communism is the logical outcome of a classless society. In practice, both the family and the state have been central to the transition to socialism." Marifeli Perez-Stable, "The Emancipation of Cuban Women," paper presented at conference "Woman and Change" held at Boston University, May 6–7, 1977, p. 5. Available from the author.

47. Jancar, *Women Under Communism,* p. 99.

48. Departmento de Orientacion Revolucionaria, *Sobre el pleno ejercicio de la igualdad de la mujer* (Havana: Departmento de Orientacion Revolucionaria del Comite Central del Partido Comunista de Cuba, 1976).

49. Lourdes Casal, "Cuba: On Socialist Democracy," paper presented at the Annual Meeting of the Latin American Studies Association, Pittsburgh, April 5–7, 1979. Available from the author.

50. Jancar, *Women Under Communism,* p. 93.

51. Ibid., p. 88.

52. See *Granma Resumen Semanal,* December 5, 1976, p. 1, and December 12, 1976, p. 5.

53. Dominguez, *Cuba,* pp. 502–503.

54. See *Granma Resumen Semanal,* December 12, 1976.

55. Ibid., January 4, 1976, p. 9.

56. "Una pregunta a Vilma Espin," *Granma Resumen Semanal,* March 18, 1979, p. 7.

57. Ibid.

58. Departmento de Orientacion Revolucionaria, *Sobre el pleno ejercicio,* pp. 28–30.

59. "Una pregunta a Vilma Esin," *Granma Resumen Semanal,* March 18, 1979, p. 7.

60. Purcell, "Modernizing Women," p. 267.

61. J. Hernandez, et al., *Estudio sobre el divorcio* (Havana: Centro de Informacion Cientifica y Tecnica Humanidades Seve Ciencias Sociales, 1973).

62. Elizabeth Sutherland, *The Youngest Revolution* (New York: The Dial Press, 1969), p. 184.

63. "Una pregunta a Electra Fernandez," *Granma Resumen Semanal,* March 18, 1979, p. 7.

64. Important Cuban laws and codes undergo an extensive process of public discussion that begins in the party and is followed by massive discussion at the assemblies of the Committees for the Defense of the Revolution, the unions, and other mass organizations. Draft laws are modified by means of this process. The Family Code had been discussed by 2,195,537 persons in 66,513 assemblies by November 1974, four months before the discussions ended. See Dominguez, *Cuba,* p. 301. As a result of this process, of the 167 articles in the published draft, 79 were changed and seven were substantially altered. Ibid., p. 531.

65. Fidel Castro, Speech at the Closing Session of the II Congress of the Federation of Cuban Women, *Granma Resumen Semanal,* December 8, 1974, p. 2.

66. Olesen, "Context and Posture: Notes on Socio-Cultural Aspects of Women's Roles and Family Policy in Contemporary Cuba," *Journal of Marriage and the Family* 33 (August 1971): 548–60.

67. *Granma Resumen Semanal,* June 1, 1976, p. 2.

68. Perez-Stable, "The Emancipation of Cuban Women."

69. Nancy Robinson Calbet, "The Role of Women in Cuba's History," *Granma Resumen Semanal,* January 15, 1978.

70. Steffens, "FMC: Feminine, Not Feminist," *Cuba Review,* 4 (1974): 22.

71. Randall, *Cuban Women Now,* p. 301.

72. Azicri, "Political Participation and Social Equality in Cuba: The Role of the Federation of Cuban Women," *Secolas Annals,* 10 (March 1979): 66.

73. The other mass organizations are the CDRs (Committees for the Defense of the Revolution); the CTC (Confederation of Cuban Workers); the ANAP (the National Association of Small Farmers); the Pioneers (young children's organization); the FEEN (Federation of Students of Intermediate Education); and the FEC (Federation of University Students).

74. This role has developed within an ideological framework that stresses the possibility of nonantagonistic contradictions during the transition period. Thus, the role of the mass organizations is to articulate and promote special interests, although within the framework of a proletarian state under Communist Party leadership.

Suggestions for Further Reading

Any study of Cuban women should begin with Nelson P. Valdes's bibliography, "A Bibliography of Cuban Women in the Twentieth Century," *Cuban Studies Newsletter,* 4 (June 1974): 1–31. There is a fundamental source for the status of women—particularly black women—in nineteenth-century Cuba: Verena Martinez Alier, *Marriage, Class and Color in Nineteenth*

Century Cuba (London: Cambridge University Press, 1974). A few books and a variety of articles, some journalistic, others more scholarly, have explored aspects of the woman question in revolutionary Cuba.

Margaret Randall's *Cuban Women Now* (Toronto: The Woman's Press, 1972) and Oscar Lewis et al., *Four Women Living the Revolution* (Urbana: University of Illinois Press, 1977), provide us with testimonies and experiences, very much in need of systematic analysis. Although not dealing specifically with Cuba, the works of Isabel Larguia, an Argentinian feminist theoretician living in Cuba, must definitely be consulted. See Isabel Larguia and John Dumoulin, *Hacia una ciencia de la liberacion de la mujer* (Caracas: Universidad Central de Venezuela, 1975), and Isabel Larguia, "The Economic Basis of the Status of Women," in Ruby Rohrlich-Leavitt, ed., *Women Cross-Culturally: Change and Challenge* (The Hague: Mouton Publications, 1975).

Mirta Mulhare's *Sexual Ideology in Pre-Castro Cuba: A Cultural Analysis* (Ph.D. diss., University of Pittsburgh, 1969); Polly F. Harrison's *Changes in Feminine Role: An Exploratory Study in the Cuban Context* (M. A. thesis, The Catholic University of America, Washington, 1974) and Lourdes Casal's *Images of Cuban Society Among Pre- and Post-Revolutionary Novelists* (Ph.D. diss., Graduate Faculty of Political and Social Science, The New School for Social Research, 1975) remain unpublished, although accessible through University Microfilms and interlibrary loans.

Max Azicri has written "Cuba: The Women's Revolution Within the Revolution" in Patricia A. Kyle, ed., *Integrating the Neglected Majority* (Brunswick, Ohio: King's Court Communications, 1976), a very general, introductory presentation; and also an important study of the Federation of Cuban Women: "Women's Development Through Revolutionary Mobilization: A Study of the Federation of Cuban Women," *International Journal of Women's Studies,* 2 (Jan.–Feb. 1979): 27–50.

Also to be consulted are Susan Kaufman Purcell's "Modernizing Women for a Modern Society: The Cuban Case" in Ann Pescatello, ed., *Female and Male in Latin America,* pp. 257–271; Carol Benglesdorf and Alice Wageman's "Emerging from Underdevelopment: Women and Work," *Cuba Review,* 4 (1974): 3–12; Geoffrey Fox's "Honor, Shame and Women's Liberation in Cuba: Views of Working Class Emigré Men," in Pescatello, ed., *Female and Male*; Virginia Olesen's "Context and Posture: Notes on Socio-Cultural Aspects of Women's Roles and Family Policy in Contemporary Cuba," *Journal of Marriage and the Family* 33 (August 1971): 548–560; C. Camarano's "On Cuban Women," *Science and Society* 25 (1971): 48–57; L. Gordon's "Speculations on Women's Liberation in Cuba," *Women: A Journal of Liberation* 1 (1970), and Heidi Steffens's "FMC: Feminine, Not Feminist," *Cuba Review* 4 (1974): 22–24.

Sheila Rowbotham's *Women, Resistance and Revolution* (New York: Random House, 1972); Elizabeth Sutherland's *The Youngest Revolution* (New York: The Dial Press, 1969); Jorge Dominguez's *Cuba: Order and*

Revolution (Cambridge, Mass.: The Belknap Press of Harvard University Press, 1978) and Barbara Wolfe Jancar, *Women Under Communism* (Baltimore and London: The Johns Hopkins Press, 1978) contain sections on Cuban women worth consulting. For information regarding the Cuban female labor force, see JUCEPLAN, *Aspectos demograficos de la fuerza laboral femenina en Cuba* (Havana: Dept. de Demografia Direccion de Estadistica de Poblacion y Censos, 1975).

PART THREE

THE RETREAT TO PATRIOTIC MOTHERHOOD

Part Three: Introduction

In the years following the American Revolution, during that period self-consciously defined by participants and historians as the "nation-building years," a new role was formulated and articulated for the white American woman. Neither Constitution nor explicit legislation declared that role, yet historians such as Linda Kerber and Mary Beth Norton have astutely located its sources and reconstructed its functions and ideology. This Republican Motherhood was a remarkable amalgam of tradition and innovation, restricting women to the domestic sphere yet attributing to that sphere a political meaning. The American woman found herself occupying a separate *civic* sphere; she was not citizen, but civic backbone of the new nation, the moral educator of its citizens-to-be and the model for American virtue. Domesticity was idealized as consciously—and conscientiously—patriotic. The notion of separate spheres for the sexes was not new, but the politization of mothering was.

What had compelled this redefinition of women's role? The answer appears to lie in part in the transition following the Revolution from traditional authority to constitutional nationalism. Once the legitimation of government rested, or was said to rest, on a broadened base of sovereignty and a consensus among a plurality of interests, the inculcation of loyalty to government became a vital concern. Nurturing national pride and obedience to the new authority became primarily a duty of the family. Within the family, it fell to women to socialize the new generation. And it fell to elite women to serve as models of the new American mother.

Diverse as the histories of the Western nations are, Republican or, more appropriately, Patriotic Motherhood appears frequently as a postrevolutionary role for women. The essays in this final section give evidence of its universality and of its endurance as a modern identity for women. The scholars represented here are each concerned with the ideology buttressing that role and with the degree to which women themselves have internalized an image of themselves as Patriotic Mothers.

It has been argued that Republican Motherhood was indeed a progressive development for the white American woman. It fell far short of any egalitarian goals, yet it was the first recognition of women as civic figures, and it brought a dignity and a sense of purpose to domestic duties previously without significance outside the narrow circle of the home. But in Napoleonic France the establishment of the "mother-teacher" identity for elite women marked not progress but a decline in actual political influence and participation. In her essay on the new domesticity of postrevolutionary France,

Barbara Corrado Pope shows us a role remarkably similar to Republican Motherhood, a role that reduced the prestige and power of the women who accepted it.

In part, as Pope explains, the decline of political power once enjoyed by elite women in royal France was an accidental by-product of the postrevolutionary program for modernization. In the days when patronage was the route to office and sinecure, the women of Versailles or of the salon were often in a position to place the necessary hint or win the vital favor. The rewards went to the men they championed, yet their influence was a form of political power. As such, it was respected. The Revolution and the Napoleonic reforms ushered in a new bureaucratic structure that made hint and friendship less significant. The entrée to office was no longer the informal network but the formal acquisition of credentials in academy and university. As the progression of men's careers was thus rationalized and institutionalized, women's isolation from politics increased

But the narrowing of women's sphere of activity and direct political involvement was not solely unintentional. In the 1780s and 1790s, male revolutionaries had sought an end to the political power of court women; after Napoleon's rise to power, male elites sought its end as well. The former acted in the hopes of destroying the privileged classes; the latter, in the hopes of preserving them. Napoleon formed his coalition with the French elites by offering stability and order after years of uncertainty. He promised a time of consolidation and a new bureaucratic structure in which elite males were, once again, assured of an advantage. To these men, restoration of a stable society meant the reestablishment of a stable family, a family in which the hierarchy of roles served as a model for a hierarchy of social classes. Thus in Napoleon's France the laws of property and of marriage were revised to meet the needs of class, not the egalitarian spirit of the Revolution.

In this manner elite women were sacrificed to the needs of their class. Yet here, as in the American republic, the new domesticity was defined not as mere confinement and segregation but as a vital civic role. Women were proclaimed the moral and civic educators of their nation. Superior and sober duties elevated an inferior role. Pope offers an important and controversial interpretation of women's part in molding, if not creating, the "mother-teacher" identity. For she observes a psychic resiliency in these women, who were suddenly forced into retreat and isolation. It was they, she argues, who elevated the role, idealized it, and insisted that its mothering and teaching aspects were central to national well-being. In their histories and their memoirs, they transformed the criticisms of their prerevolutionary frivolity and political "meddling" into self-criticism; they mastered their fate by declaring it freely chosen. One might dismiss this process of recreating the self as mere rationalization. But Pope does not argue that these women *chose* the "mother-teacher" role from among many options, nor does she share their conviction of its absolute advantage. She shows us how they understood their own history—a vital task of any historian—and she suggests that, even in circumstances not of their own choosing, women, like men, have played an active part in shaping their fate.

Only a few decades after Mmes. de Rémusat, Guizot, and Necker labored to perfect the "mother-teacher" ideology, a similar female identity was taking shape in a newly unified Italy. Here, in Judith Howard's essay, we can most clearly see the patriotic mother as an alternative to equality. Unlike American women, Italian women of the upper and middle classes had been politically mobilized during the long struggle for unification. Their involvement blurred, and often dissolved, the traditional boundaries between the private and the public arenas. Their expectations for egalitarian reforms in the new nation were based on their participation in the revolution and on a faith in that revolution's liberal ideology. After nationhood, however, there were no serious efforts to provide full citizenship to women of any class. Instead, women found themselves, as in France, at a distinct competitive disadvantage within a new nation that established both sex-discriminatory legal codes and formal institutions that debarred women from social mobility. Howard, like Pope, sees the "patriot mother" as a casualty of male progress in a liberal state. But, like Pope, Howard argues that this new female identity was as much the creation of the postunification women as of their men. Sex discrimination forced supporters of egalitarianism into retreat, yet these Italian activist women regrouped, and expanded and manipulated a vaguely defined role to every possible advantage. If, for example, they were to be "angels of the hearth," then many insisted that they must be allowed the rights, the education, the respect, and the independence necessary to make that role truly worthy of its idealization. If they were to be civic and moral educators, they must be allowed to press for social reform. Wrapped in the domestic mantle, many feminists and liberal reformers challenged each facet and institution of male supremacy without openly challenging the whole cloth of patriarchy. It was, as Howard shows, a sexual revolution by finesse.

Yet, in the brave and patient efforts of these women educators, writers, and social reformers, we can see the dilemma of minorities in every republic: denied equality, they struggle to prove themselves worthy of it; hoping for acceptance, they must make their demands palatable to those in power. In the posture of delicate dissembling, in the insistence that radical changes will not really upset the status quo, the danger is that the members of the minority may come to believe in the posture itself.

Like the women of the Risorgimento, American women soon transformed the Republican Mother ideology into an argument for activism and social reform. As Barbara Steinson shows, what began as a rationalization for the isolation of women from politics became the raison d'être for political participation in the era of feminism and suffrage reform. In her account of the pacifist and war-preparedness movements of World War I, Steinson raises several important, if paradoxical, points about the vicissitudes of an ideology. First, her essay is a testimony to the endurance of Republican Motherhood, which is still vital a century after its formulation as "nurturant motherhood."

Elaborated and redefined by nineteenth-century theories of biology and psychology, flexible enough to adapt to new social realities, Republican Motherhood is the organizing identity for women of the most diverse movements and opinions. The ideology has grown to encompass a full definition of gender; woman's special nature is no longer the excuse for her position in society, it is an explanation for a distinct feminine perspective on and critique of all human interaction. Many American activists, both declared feminists and antifeminists, may have so internalized the notion of a separate identity that its origins are no longer seen in the political compromise of two-tiered citizenship but in nature itself. Yet this very conviction of a special, and superior, identity appears to have led such women to dismantle the compromise of separate spheres.

In the activism of the women Steinson studies, we see the strength and the limitations of a reliance on this identity as a means to an egalitarian society. There can be no doubt that a belief in women's duty to nurture a citizenry and guard its morals would eventually impel efforts to end their isolation from the public sector. By World War I, American women of the privileged and middle classes had a half-century-long history of public participation by "social housekeeping." Under that rubric they had introduced consumer, educational, and political reforms. When world war became a possibility, such women mobilized rapidly. What separated the women of the Peace Party from the members of the Women's Section of the Navy League was not just their divergent interpretation of what nurturant motherhood ought to endorse. What separated them was the degree to which they were conscious of the repercussions and implications of their activism. In so far as the former were feminists, they linked their service to American society to an increased formalization of their rights within that society. But the latter continued to believe in an organic, informal influence upon public and political policy.

In the end, the women's war-preparedness mobilization provided more psychic rewards to its members than tangible evidence of influence over policy. They enjoyed a sense of purposefulness, of novelty, of excitement in their campaigns and programs. They experienced sisterhood, and felt the pleasure of managing their own affairs. In these experiences of self-discovery, they were drawn closer to the women who had been their opponents on the war issue. Belief in nurturant motherhood had given both groups the strength to enter the fray.

Yet, as Steinson points out in her conclusion, nurturant motherhood was ultimately as crippling as it was supportive. The posture was too fully internalized and thus too identical with the self; only rarely, even among the declared feminists, did a truly egalitarian critique of American society emerge from those who saw themselves as "nurturers."

The essays in this section explore the complex relationship between ideology and reality. Thorny problems arise in such an endeavor: To what extent was Patriotic Motherhood in all its forms a social rationalization? To what extent was it a genuine personal identity? These essays suggest that its origins lay in the determination of political leadership to preserve patriarchy and to design legal and institutional structures that would make equality, by class or sex, an impossibility. Thus, historians must always examine the material basis for women's inequality within a society. The ideology of Patriotic Motherhood appears to be a construct of traditional beliefs that fortuitously justified a role policymakers created. Yet, as scholars in this final section remind us, ideology has no static reality; its internalization often means its metamorphosis. The women discussed in these essays are proof of human versatility and the healthy drive to a mastery of circumstances. If, ultimately, historians judge that an ideology is not in itself a sufficient vehicle for social change, or that it is not a satisfying explanation for historical realities, still no humanistic model of the past can be constructed without considering the impact of ideology.

9/Revolution and Retreat: Upper-Class French Women After 1789

Barbara Corrado Pope

The Great French Revolution of 1789 gave political emancipation and authority to adult upper-class males. During the Revolution itself, much was done to give more liberty to sons, daughters, and wives of all classes. But nothing was done for women outside of their familial roles. And so, after the dust had settled, with the passing of the Napoleonic Code and the coming of the Restoration, adult women did not gain political emancipation. Indeed, according to most observers, their roles in the public sphere of life had been reduced. Much more than in the final years of the *Ancien Régime*, the women of the upper classes came to see themselves, and to be seen, as private persons whose concerns should be confined to home and family. How this happened, how women as actors and subjects found themselves in more restricted roles as a result of revolutionary experiences and Napoleonic institutions, is the subject of this essay.[1]

Any investigation of a seeming restriction in roles should start with an assessment of the possibilities for liberation. These possibilities stemmed from two very different sources: the specific role that some upper-class women played in society during the *Ancien Régime* and the feminist issues raised during the Revolution itself.

Eighteenth-Century Sociability and the Possibilities for Liberation

During the eighteenth century two distinct ideals for upper-class women emerged.[2] Both seemed justified by the Enlightenment belief that happiness was a human possibility and a valid goal for men and women. The first, the *domestic* ideal, is much closer to contemporary experience, which holds that happiness can be derived from family life. Domesticity rested upon the tradition of household economy, whereby every member contributed to the productive capacity of the family, and upon the ethics of Christianity, which stressed female chastity and conjugal duty. Among the new dicta of eighteenth-century domesticity were: daughters should have some say in the choice of their future spouses; husbands and wives should act with respect and affection toward one another; and mothers and fathers should give their children tender care. The most famous exposition of this point of view was Rousseau's *Emile* (1762). After its publication some women, even at the Versailles court and in Parisian society, began to breastfeed their own children.

That maternal breastfeeding should be cause for surprise—even satire— shows the strength of the other feminine ideal, that of *sociability*. The habitués of the world of sociability moved in the highest circles of society and referred to themselves quite simply as *le monde* or the world. What mattered in this world were not the private and domestic virtues of fidelity, thrift, and order but the more public virtues of wit, generosity, magnanimity, grace, and taste. These were virtues which came easily to the very wealthy and espe- cially to the high-born.

From the point of view of female emancipation, the salons of Paris were much more promising than the court life at Versailles. A salon might best be defined as a regular gathering of a select group of people for discussion, readings, and performances. The most important activity was discussion. In the drawing rooms of famous eighteenth-century hostesses, the international leaders of the Enlightenment first tried out their ideas. The salons also offered many men and some women a means of social mobility, for they provided a setting in which commoners could learn the manners and conversational skills proper to the elite.

The role of hostess afforded women many advantages they could not find elsewhere. It gave them a public or at least a semipublic role free of domestic constraints. In these circles, too, it would have been considered bad form to rail against or use a husband's legal right to punish an unfaithful wife. Long- term relationships between lovers were accepted in polite society as a reasonable solution to the problem of early, arranged, and often loveless marriages.

Ideas about equality were not limited to attitudes toward sexual matters. Since the salons offered a place where men of all ranks could meet as intellectual peers, it seemed natural that the notion of women as peers should also arise. Many of the eighteenth-century *philosophes* argued against the old stereotype of women's natural perversity, blaming female faults upon educa- tion and an unsympathetic, corrupting environment instead.

Above all, this was an environment where women's ideas were taken seriously. The hostesses set the tone for the discussions. Their influence went beyond their own drawing rooms, for they lobbied for appointments, awards, and pensions for male friends. If they were wealthy, they became patrons in their own right by awarding gifts and pensions. Such powers were not inconsiderable. In the days before the secular university and mass newspapers and book publications, many up-and-coming men depended upon the salons not only as a means to attain a certain de rigeur education but also for their livelihood.[3]

Later on, the development of such institutions as the popular press and the prestigious national Université reduced the salons' ability to assure patronage.

The Université especially granted men the certification necessary to pursue certain kinds of professional and bureaucratic careers. This formal reform of education and the civil service worked against the kind of informal power wielded by the salon women.

Similarly, the advent of constitutional government, with elected officials and representatives, cut off court ladies from their ability to manipulate patronage. The power of the women of Versailles was traditional, although certainly never institutionalized. It depended upon the personality of the monarch. When people referred to the "sway of women" in the eighteenth century, they usually were talking about the influence of a few highly placed ladies—Mme. de Pompadour, mistress to Louis XV, and Queen Marie Antoinette. Both of these women acted as patrons of the arts and of the luxury trades; they pressed for certain policies and promoted or blocked the careers of functionaries.

In the nineteenth century this kind of power was defeated not only institutionally but ideologically as well. Under a constitutional government, both male and female republicans and liberals consistently denounced "intrigue" and the "illegitimate sway of women." They used the history of the Versailles court to assert that women did not deserve public roles. Even the salons underwent an ideological critique in the nineteenth century. After the disruptive experiences of the Revolution, many men and women of the upper classes perceived the Church and the family as important pillars of society. In their view, the eighteenth-century salon carried the taint of Enlightenment skepticism.

Diane Alstad has written that both the eighteenth-century ideals of domesticity and of sociability had something to offer women. Because of its stress upon marriage as an emotional rather than an authoritarian relationship, domesticity gave them freedom *within* the family; sociability gave them freedom *from* the family. Alstad also argues that the ideal of sociability represented an aristocratic way of life, domesticity a bourgeois one. This second statement is only true in the broadest sense, for two other factors were as important as birth to the career of an aspiring salon woman: wealth and location. Certainly the wife of the richest shopkeeper could not aspire to polite society. But the Parisian wives of wealthy financiers and functionaries, recently ennobled or not, became as famous and respected as their blue-blooded counterparts.

For a brief time during the Revolution more possibilities inherent in the notion of women's emancipation *within* the family were realized than possibilities for women's freedom *from* the family. This had much to do with the social origins and ideas of male revolutionaries who made the laws. The general drift of the Revolution from informal power and privilege to formal male rights was part of a pattern of changes which, in the end, would prove inimical to women's participation in public life. An examination of the Revolution itself should make this clear.

The Revolution and the Possibilities for Emancipation

Revolutions raise unprecedented hopes for human liberation. In France these hopes began to arise even before the overthrow of absolutism. Yet, at least initially, the responses to possibilities for new freedom, for equality, and for community arose from experiences of a class and sex. Insofar as their lives were more enclosed, women may have been less likely than men to overcome sexual and class barriers. As it turned out, there was little in the revolutionary experience to bring women together in common pursuit of their rights.

When the government called for a list of grievances, women's demands for reforms came directly from their working and family lives. Middle-class women wanted a better education so that they could become better wives and mothers; both men and women of the class asked for more equity in marriage and for divorce. Laboring women wanted better elementary and professional training; they also wanted an end to male encroachment on female occupations. The women of the provinces called for better training for midwives.

The most radical demands for women's full entry into the public sphere came from an aristocratic male, the Marquis de Condorcet, who knew freedom and privilege firsthand. Condorcet was not only a habitué of the salons, but also a partner in a marriage founded upon mutual affection and respect. His *Sur l'admission des femmes au droit de cité* (1789) and *Cinq mémoires sur l'instruction publique* (1790) declared that women should have the full rights of citizenship and that they should receive the same education as men—even in the same classrooms.

The various revolutionary assemblies were most responsive to the pleas for family reform.[4] They made marriage a civil contract that could be abrogated by divorce, and they gave wives the right to share family property. Under the Legislative Assembly, twenty-one became the age of majority for both men and women, which meant, among other things, that they could then marry without their parents' consent. But the most important and far-reaching reforms dealt with inheritance. The revolutionaries abrogated the aristocratic custom of primogeniture and made equal inheritance, for sons and daughters, the law. One of the most controversial measures was a law which gave children born out of wedlock equal rights, under certain circumstances, with children born into legitimate families. This law benefited not only bastards but their mothers as well. Under the previous legal system unwed mothers could lay no claims to financial support for their children—nor would they be able to do so in the future.

Some upper-class women such as the Jacobin Louise Keralio took up the feminist cause in their writings, but by and large women of her class did not directly participate in revolutionary activities. Although they attended the sessions of the assemblies, many of them initiated or continued careers as salon hostesses, actively trying to influence political decisions. Yet the increasing violence of the Revolution and the growing suspicion of wealth and aristocracy dimmed the brilliance of polite society. Many "political" women of these circles were forced into exile, put under house arrest, or even executed.

Women of the revolutionary clubs were often behind these persecutions. Most of them belonged to the lower classes, although some middle-class women were involved.[5] These women were militant feminists in their actions but did not have a feminist ideology. They took to the streets with their men to make economic demands and to stop those who would forestall or betray the Revolution. Except for their devotion to their own clubs, they made few demands for themselves as women.

Only a few demanded political rights, sexual equality, and even military participation on the same basis as men. These exceptions were women who on the whole had no clear class affiliation or family obligations.[6] The most famous were the actress, playwright, and illegitimate daughter of a Montauban butcher, Olympe de Gouges, and the sometime singer and demimondaine, the self-styled Amazon, Théroigne de Méricourt. The actress Claire Lacombe and the chocolate-maker Pauline Roland led a revolutionary women's club and allied with the radical male *Enragés*. Perhaps these women had such keen perceptions about women's place in society because they themselves had no place. But if these women were the most likely to understand the contradictions of women's roles, they were also the most likely to be dismissed and mocked.

Thus, when the Jacobin leadership cracked down on all extreme dissidents such political women were easy targets. In fact, male revolutionaries moved to eradicate the very notion of women entering politics. This is clear from a November 1793 article in the *Moniteur* which reported the execution of three very different women. Although Marie Antoinette was a counterrevolutionary aristocrat, Mme. Roland a bourgeois liberal, and Olympe de Gouges a radical feminist, the anonymous reporter painted all three with the same brush, describing them as meddling and unnatural women.[7] Within the same month the Jacobin Chaumette also condemned the "haughty" Roland and the "impudent" de Gouges for forgetting that women were "the divinity of the domestic sanctuary."[8]

Increasingly, politics had little to recommend itself to the women who had inhabited the circles of sociability. They certainly did not identify with the self-proclaimed Amazons or market women who fought in the streets. The language of the counterrevolution only reinforced the class divisions among women. The lower-class banshee became as much a part of reactionary portraits of the revolutionary past as the upper-class female intriguer or martyr.

The bloodiest stage of revolutionary violence—and the most threatening to upper-class women—passed with the dismantling of the Terror in the summer of 1794. This did not mean that lives returned to normal. Many families did not return to France or from the provinces to Paris until well into the Napoleonic era; those most loyal to the Bourbon monarchy waited until the

Restoration. Social life under the Thermidorians (1794–95) and the Directory (1795–99) had a frenetic quality. "New women" like Josephine de Beauharnais became prominent because of their connections with men who owed their wealth and position to the Revolution. Dandies and *merveilleuses* paraded around in showy clothes and held macabre balls for the victims in celebration of their own narrow escape from execution.

By the time Napoleon came to power in 1799 the ruling circles were ready for a period of consolidation, order, and authority. The financial system was a shambles; public education virtually nonexistent; the law an overlay of various revolutionary legislative acts. That the establishment of permanent institutions fell not to revolutionaries concerned with democracy and equality (at least for males and *within* the family) but to Napoleon and his notables meant the end of any feminist hopes and of most feminist gains. Napoleon did carry through some of the revolutionary program, especially that which tended towards the creation of the modern state.[9] The ensuing rationalization, bureaucratization, and centralization increasingly closed the kind of informal channels that some highly placed women had once used. Of course these closures were slow and uneven. But there was no counterpart for women to the new formal rights and political authority of upper-class males, whose dominance the Napoleonic, Bourbon, and Orleanist regimes actively fostered in the first half of the nineteenth century.

The Civil Code and the Université are two of the most important and permanent legacies of the Napoleonic era. They affected upper-class women at every stage of their lives. They conferred authority, learning, and participation in professional and political life on males and set up clear structural barriers against female emancipation—both *within* and *from* the family.

The Civil Code and Women's Place

The Napoleonic Codes were an amalgam of the laws and theories of the *Ancien Régime* and the legislation of the Revolution. Among the revolutionary principles written into the codes were equality before the law, freedom of conscience, the secularity of the state, trial by jury, the ownership of private property as a simple and absolute right, and the sanctity of free contracts between individuals. In almost all the measures that dealt with the matter of equality, however, the code-makers blunted the revolutionary intent by restricting rights according to class, sex, and age. The reaction against equality of rights reflected the mood of the times, the high-handed manner in which Napoleon pushed through the passage of his codes, and the personalities of those who wrote the laws.

Because Napoleon took a special interest in the formulation of the family law, his own attitudes are significant to understanding why the code was so hostile to women. Like many antifeminist men, he was ambivalent about women. He admired feminine charms as long as he did not feel victimized by them. During the freewheeling days of the Directory, he had even expressed a certain delight in the sway that women held over Parisian social life.[10] But his attitudes hardened as his personal power increased. In 1802, after six years of marriage to Josephine, he spoke of the need to "contain women." During the deliberations on the Civil Code he continually depicted women as frivolous, weak, and treacherous. "A man," he told the Council of State, "should be able to say to his wife, 'Madame, you shall not go out, you shall not go to the theater, you shall not receive such and such a person; the children you bear shall be mine!' "[11]

In their private and public dealings with prominent women Napoleon and his ministers demonstrated this attitude of containment. Although Napoleon's court grew more complex and similar to that of the *Ancien Régime*, corresponding informal power was not given to women. Josephine was able to grant some favors, pick her courtiers, and take many families off the exile list. But her actions conformed to the desires of Napoleon himself, who longed to be surrounded by the trappings of legitimacy.

The women of the salons were by no means allowed to use their drawing rooms as forums for discussing politics. Napoleon exiled and ruthlessly pursued the liberal Mme. de Staël for trying to continue the political role she had played during the *Ancien Régime* and the early years of the Revolution. He even exiled the very popular and apolitical Mme. Récamier, merely because she had visited Mme. de Staël at Coppet. Furthermore, the militarism which characterized Napoleon's regime left women ipso facto far away from the most vital decision-making.[12]

The lawyers who wrote the code were no more likely to support the notions of female freedom or of polite society than was Napoleon himself. These "artisans of the new laws" came from the *noblesse de la robe*—families whose titles of nobility had been earned by judicial service to the crown—of the eighteenth century and carried within them the "fundamental traits" of that milieu: moderation, austerity, even a bit of Jansenism.[13] The inherent moderation of the lawmakers made it possible for them to compromise between traditional and revolutionary claims, between the southern and the northern legal systems. It directed them to emphasize institutions that assured the stability of the state. The family was one of these institutions. Their concern for family life, coupled with their moral austerity, led them to restrict severely the rights of women and to try to shape laws that assured women's loyalty and devotion to home life. Apparently their attitudes were in tune with those of the male ruling class, for at no time during the proceedings was there a concerted effort to defend women's rights or the revolutionary conception of equality within the family.[14] Under the new code divorce was once again severely restricted and married women were reduced to the legal status of minors. Fathers' control over children was strengthened and women's dependence insured by the broad discretion given to husbands over their dowry.[15]

Clearly, the laws governing marriage were written for the benefit and in support of a stable, property-owning society. Most of the provisions pertained only to certain segments of the population: prosperous peasants, the land-owning bourgeoisie and urban property owners. The family laws were irrele-vant to the experiences of the laboring class, particularly the increasingly large migratory part of it. The complications and expenses involved merely in getting married discouraged many working-class people from complying with the laws and the rites of the secular state. Since no one could be married in church unless first wed in a civil ceremony, many working-class people did not marry at all.[16]

The notion of womanhood that emerged from the code fit the semirural, property-owning French society for which it was written. The emphasis on property provisions mirrored the traditional view that marriage was a rational business transaction between families as well as a sexual union. The code tended and was intended to see women only in their domestic capacities. The provisions covering the *femme commerçante* were the exception, and they recognized the still predominant role that women played within the shop-keeping class.

Education for Separate Spheres

Like the legal codes, the educational system fostered strict class and sex divisions. The imperial government gave full attention only to the needs of upper and middle-class boys. The Université was conceived as a way of integrating young men into the modern state as patriots, soldiers, profes-sionals, and bureaucrats. This system directly influenced only a small mi-nority of the population in the nineteenth century. But because of the dis-tinctive training and certification it gave, the Université indirectly also helped to shape the relationship between classes and sexes.

During the Restoration the education of middle- and upper-class males was the subject of intense ideological debate and the focus of much political strife. Catholic schools competed with the secular state-controlled Napole-onic system for the privilege of shaping and training the future leaders of France. Although the two competing educational systems aimed at producing men of very different political beliefs, the schools shared assumptions that were very important to French society.

In the best schools, boys were expected to read Greek and to read and write Latin. This seemingly impractical classicism defined the educated elite and was the sine qua non of access to influential positions. A sound grounding in classical languages, for example, was absolutely necessary for admission to higher educational and professional schools.

Classicism, then, divided the rich from the illiterate and barely literate poor. It also divided upper and middle-class men from women. Cultivated men thought that the ideal world of the classics was too rarified a territory for the minds of the poor and of women, for it might give them ideas about bettering the world or themselves. The poor, they argued, needed a very practical education geared to the needs of a developing country.[17] Nonworking women needed only a domestic education. Class distinctions among women were important, too. A girl was to learn only those homemaking skills compatible with her class. Thus, there were two reasons that education in the home was preferred for upper- and middle-class women: it provided the proper ambience of domesticity, and it tended to limit contacts with people from other social classes. This policy of domestic, or even better, maternal education, conformed to and supported the new ideal of domesticity.

Given the advanced Enlightenment ideas about women's character and the real, albeit temporary, reforms that had occurred during the Revolution, there were protests against this legal and educational retreat on women's rights. With regard to the law, the most popular cause among bourgeois men and women was the reinstitution of liberal divorce. By the 1840s the presentation of petitions asking for divorce became an annual event in the Chamber of Deputies. Frédéric Herbinot de Mauchamps' *Gazette des femmes* demanded civil and political equality for bourgeois women. Mauchamps argued that women who paid taxes had a right to representation, a liberal stance that did not include class equality. The Saint-Simonians and Fourierists, who attracted a few bourgeoises and many working-class people, advocated sexual and economic as well as political equality. A number of articulate working-class women who joined these movements became leaders of feminist efforts during the revolutions of 1848.[18]

The second very popular demand was for better education, but this had two very different thrusts. Relatively few people endorsed Condorcet's radical notion of coeducation, or even similar education, for the two sexes. Some, like the schoolmistress Josephine Bachellery, took the more moderate position that there should be serious vocational training for poor and lower-middle-class girls. In 1848 Bachellery asked the revolutionary government to found a female Université. Nothing came of her plea.[19] Not until the late 1860s was there any concerted action on the government's part to provide schooling for upper-class girls. By then liberal politicians, including Victor Duruy and Jules Simon, had become alarmed by the way in which separate educations had come to divide pious wives from their secular husbands.

The Maternal Educators and Revolutionary Experiences

By and large, serious education for women during the Restoration and the July Monarchy meant improved training for marriage and motherhood. The dominant movement in the first half of the century was not toward a recovery of feminist gains but toward the ennoblement of domesticity for upper-class women. Women took the ideological initiative in this movement. They did not merely react against the structure of male ideas and institutions. Rather they formed an ideal for women that gave them moral dignity and psychological power. The ideal role they set out for themselves and for others was that of the "mother-teacher" (*mère-institutrice* or *mère-éducatrice*). According to their formulation, a mother-teacher had three possible functions: the moral education of her children; the instruction of boys and girls in elementary subjects; and the total supervision of a daughter's education until her marriage. Although the perfect mother-teacher performed all three tasks, her most important duty was moral education.

Why did women feel the need to stress the maternal and wifely roles as much as they did? They stressed these roles, it appears, because of personal experience. The lessons women had learned led them to a compromise between the world of sociability and that of domesticity. This can be demonstrated in two ways: first, through brief accounts of how the Revolution affected the lives of the five women who wrote the most important works on maternal education, and second, through an analysis of what might be called the nineteenth-century version of French women's history.

The following biographies are not in any strict sense representative of *the* revolutionary experience. Rather they reveal the variety of experiences that upper-class women had when they emerged from the old world into the new. Yet a common thread runs through them that helps to explain the moralizing that was so much a part of the interpretation of the past. All these women emerged from the tradition of sociability, broadly defined, yet they would reject in their writings all or part of that tradition. All of them concluded that the modern woman must be serious, dutiful, and rational. *As women,* they lived up to their own dicta more or less well and in different ways. *As historians,* they and other writers gave to their own time very striking images of the contrast between prerevolutionary and postrevolutionary society which supported their case for a certain kind of domesticity. Indeed, many of these images they created of the seventeenth, eighteenth, and nineteenth centuries are still vital today.

Only a revolution could have made Mmes. Maisonneuve and Campan the mentors of middle-class housewives. Born in 1764, Françoise-Thérèse-Antoinette Le Groing Le Maisonneuve came from an old and powerful provincial family. She entered an exclusive contemplative order of nuns at the age of sixteen and spent her days before the Revolution studying and translating the classics and writing novels. During the Revolution, Maisonneuve emigrated and supported herself and her family, first by needlework, then by teaching. These unexpected hardships directly affected her pedagogical ideas, for she gave a high priority to economics and sewing. Despite her own teachings, she was well known for her interest in literature; and during Napoleon's time she frequented some of the most fashionable salons. After the Restoration, her attempts to refound her religious order failed.[20]

Jeanne-Louise-Henriette Genet Campan was born in Paris in 1752. Her father, a minor official at court, educated her. By the time she was fifteen she had acquired a reputation as a prodigy and was appointed reader to the daughters of Louis XV. Later she became a lady-in-waiting to Marie Antoinette. Campan claimed, in the famous memoirs she wrote of the court, that she remained loyal and devoted to the queen. During the September Days of 1792 she narrowly escaped capture at the palace and retired, with relatives, outside Paris. During the Directory, bankrupt and with a sick husband and small son to support, she returned to the capital. She wrote one hundred letters stating her intention to open a school. Her National Institute at St. Germain quickly gained a brilliant reputation. Nouveaux riches parents sent their daughters there, hoping they would benefit from Mme. Campan's close acquaintanceship with old-world courtly manners.

Intelligent, sprightly, adaptable, Mme. Campan was surely the female counterpart to the more famous male *perpetuels,* who managed to survive and even prosper throughout the revolutionary and Napoleonic periods. Napoleon found her charming (and perhaps for that alone, suspect). Yet he appointed her to "bring up mothers" for France in one of his Legion of Honor schools for girls. She claimed to have produced pious, dutiful, thrifty women worthy of becoming the wives and mothers of citizens. Like most post-revolutionary authors, she never referred to women as *citoyennes.* That revolutionary expression faded quickly at the turn of the century, for it implied, of course, the right to participate in public life.[21] Mme. Campan did not fare well during the Restoration because the returning royal family had become very suspicious of her loyalty.[22]

Since both of these women were teachers it may seem ironic that they were considered important advocates of the idea of maternal education. But both ostensibly had a double purpose for writing their books. They wrote not only to publicize their own work, but also to provide a handbook for mothers. Further, when Baudouin Frères published *De l'éducation* in 1824 and François Cattois bought out the third edition of Maisonneuve's book in 1844, the publishers, more than the authors themselves, stressed the moral superiority of education by mothers in the home.[23]

By that time a movement was in full swing. Scores of manuals, hundreds of books written for children, and several serious women's magazines devoted to the education of mothers and daughters appeared in France. The most important works of this movement were Claire de Rémusat's *Essai sur l'éducation des femmes* (1821), Pauline Guizot's *Lettres de famille sur l'éducation* (1824), and the three volumes of Albertine Necker de Saussure's *L'Education progressive* (1828–1838). Their works and names were so prominent that the critic Sainte-Beuve singled them out in 1842 as the three women of his century "vitally concerned with the destiny of their sex in a society that is still in the making and still rests on a shaky foundation."[24]

De Rémusat, born to an aristocratic Parisian family in 1780, fled into exile during the Terror. Her father and grandfather were imprisoned and subsequently executed. She married at sixteen and she lived a quiet, studious life in the countryside until her husband received a post at the Napoleonic court. She did not like the intrigue that she saw there, as her famous memoirs of the Empire reveal.[25] She attained a reputation for seriousness and maternal devotion. Throughout her life she remained the most trusted counsellor of her son Charles, the famous politician and memoirist. She also devoted herself to teaching her younger son Albert, who was severely retarded.

As a prefect's wife during the Restoration, de Rémusat took up charity work. In these years she grew more conservative and religious. Her *Essai,* in which she hoped to lead the "wives and mothers of citizens" (again, never *citoyennes*) to a proper understanding of their destiny, was left unfinished at the time of her death. Her son Charles published it.[26]

Unlike Claire de Rémusat and so many of her contemporaries, Pauline Guizot never abandoned the liberal beliefs of the Enlightenment. Nor did she undergo a religious conversion after the Revolution. This despite the fact that she trembled during any discussion of those years. Sainte-Beuve, who obviously admired her greatly, succinctly summarized her experiences and achievements in her transition from the eighteenth to the nineteenth century: "Here is a woman wholesomely penetrated with the ideas of work and duty, such as regenerated society imperatively demands; and such Mme. Guizot always remained. *Issuing from the idle and polished salons of the eighteenth century, she becomes a shining example of vigorous, intellectual, efficient womanhood in the first rank of the middle class [classe moyenne]."*[27] (Italics mine.)

Born Elisabeth-Charlotte-Pauline de Meulan in Paris in 1775, Guizot did indeed move in the most elegant social circles of Paris until the Revolution. Then she moved to the suburb of Passy, taking over the management of her family's finances after her father's death in 1790. In order to support herself, she became a writer for *Le Publiciste,* a magazine which, according to Charles de Rémusat, was "informed by an eighteenth-century philosophy that had been enlightened and chastened by the Revolution."[28] In the editor's salon she met François Guizot. This was, according to her male biographers, a very felicitious event because it made her more "serious" and "useful."[29] What they meant was that as a result of her relationship with Guizot, she turned away from writing literary criticism and defenses of eighteenth-century Deism; and she took up the fulfillment of wifely and maternal duty and the production of educational works and of children's stories.

More than the other women writers, Guizot was able to accept the new world with eagerness rather than resignation. This positive view pervades her justly famous *Lettres de famille.* She agreed that women should become useful and rational, but she extended this vision to include the utilitarian values of technological advancement. If she rejected eighteenth-century sociability, it was not because it was skeptical or irreligious, but because the *philosophes* had only "played with ideas." The new bourgeoisie used ideas to change the material world.[30] She believed thoroughly in the new emphasis on work, although she carefully groomed her fictional daughters to be wives and mothers only.

Albertine Necker de Saussure was less positive about what she perceived as the new materialism. But she accepted willingly the fact that women would no longer be involved in political decisions. The daughter of a famous

Genevan scientist and patrician, she, like Guizot, had early been accustomed to the life of sociability. In 1785 she married the handsome French soldier Jacques Necker. At that time it was the custom of young couples in her social class to take a grand tour of Europe in order to learn about international polite society. And so, even after the birth of their first two children, Jacques and Albertine visited the famous salons of prerevolutionary Paris. She left her children with her parents, something that she, in her later role as educator, would never have condoned.

Although the repercussions of social revolution were not as terrifying to the Genevan upper classes as to the Parisian, they were still felt. Mme. Necker's family was once besieged in its home and also underwent several financial reverses. During much of the Revolution she was away from the city. On her country estate she devoted herself to teaching her four children. Later, during the Restoration, she continued these pedagogical labors by writing the most respected work of domestic education, the *Education progressive*. She also continued to host a salon and kept up with her cousin de Staël. However, growing deafness and personal tragedy combined with political experience to make her increasingly severe and religious. The *Etude de la vie des femmes*, the third volume of her work, reflects this severity.[31]

An Interpretation of Women's History

Upper-class women publicized and received an interpretation of their own history in many forms: in memoirs and magazine stories, in educational manuals and analyses of the "condition of women," even in fashion. For example, the Comtesse de Flesselles' *La Jeune Mère institutrice*, written sometime during the Restoration, tells the story of the passage from the old world to the new as a parable. The Comtesse de Flesselles was the pseudonym of an author of over thirty children's books. *La Jeune Mère institutrice* was ostensibly a vehicle for the stories that the fictional Mme. de Melville told her five children. But the most significant morality tale of this book was about Mme. de Melville herself: that is, about adults and the lessons of experience.

The setting for the Melville stories was the emigration. Flesselles described Mme. de Melville as a typically leisured eighteenth-century upper-class woman, leading a life of sociability. She had spent her time dressing, visiting, and reading novels. Only hardship changed her. Her husband died fighting for the Duke of Condé against revolutionary forces. She escaped to Geneva without her fortune and had to take on the task of educating her children. But since she had read only "frivolous" books during her youth, it took the counsel and encouragement of a wise old man to convince her that she could gain the knowledge necessary for this all-important duty.

To her surprise, Mme. de Melville discovered she liked good solid books which served as "a precious resource against *ennui*." She also came to know the value of work.

Instructed by the lessons of misfortune, [Mme. de Melville] got rid of many of
the prejudices with which her youth had been imbued. She did not think that it
was humiliating to serve herself. She did not abandon to a class less elevated
than her own the beautiful privilege of acquiring useful knowledge which could
shelter her from events and allow her to be independent of the vicissitudes of
fortune. She owed the conviction that work never degrades man, that on the
contrary it honors him, to her own experiences.[32]

Of course Mme. de Melville's greatest joy lay in raising her children and
teaching them the new morality of discipline, hard work, moderation, and
love of home life. Here art (or morality tale) imitates life. Mme. de Melville's
lessons bear close resemblance to Sainte-Beuve's portrayal of Mme. Guizot's
experiences. Even the attitude toward the salons is similar: they are remembered for their "frivolity" and not for the place they had in the development of
important Enlightenment ideas.

The resilient and resourceful Henriette-Lucy de La Tour du Pin struck the
same themes in her memoirs. They tell of her escape from France, her life in
exile, her love of family and her return to the homeland. She wrote her
memoirs for her children, and she told them about how she had been raised
"among the scandalous examples of Parisian society" without the aid of a
religious or moral education. In the 1830s she wrote: "The older I grow, the
more sure I become that the Revolution of 1789 was only the inevitable
consequence and, I might also say, the just punishment of the vices of the
upper classes. Vices carried to such excess that if people had not been
stricken with a mortal blindness they must have seen that they would
inevitably be consumed by the very fire they themselves were lighting."[33]

For de La Tour du Pin, as for many of her class, one of the consequences
of her experiences had been religious conversion and a return to the teachings
of the Catholic Church.

It is not surprising that both de La Tour du Pin and de Flesselles took a
moralizing posture toward the past. History after all had long been taught,
and would continue to be taught to nineteenth-century girls, as a course in
morals and psychology. Traditionally one looked to the past for examples of
noble and ignoble actions and for clues to human behavior. A revolution that
had seemed for a while to turn the world upside down presented unlimited
possibilities for psychological analysis and for moral lessons.

But the Revolution itself was seldom analyzed in these writings. Except for
Mme. de Staël, the upper-class female historians, moralists, and journalists
looked upon the Revolution as a hiatus, an interruption between their past
and present, rather than as a monumental series of events worthy of detailed
analysis. They did not look to the daily happenings of the Revolution, to the
flurry of ideas, to the actions in the streets, or to the revolutionary legislation
that affected their sex. Rather, like de Melville and de La Tour du Pin, they
looked to the periphery, to the misjudgments and weaknesses of their own
class before the Revolution, and to the sacrifices and martyrdoms played out
on the guillotine or in exile. This introspection was determined both by their

class and by their sex. Because of it many upper-class women criticized the old world of sociability. Not as consciously, by turning away from the acts of women during the Revolution, they rejected something else as well: the exciting possibility of female equality.

If upper-class women had any concept of their own history, it went something like this: Starting in the seventeenth century the women of the Parisian aristocracy and *grande bourgeoisie* had gained a cultural ascendency through the salons. Most of these chroniclers felt that the new influence that women exerted had been to good effect, for the great ladies were learned and cultured and at least ostensibly held strict moral and religious views. They had added charm and grace to a society which was harshly authoritarian and hierarchical. Yet even this good female influence could be turned to bad, if overextended. The concentration of women's talents outside their proper sphere of home and the family was in itself dangerous.[34] The overrefinement of the salons had led directly to some of the faults of the eighteenth century.[35]

Almost everyone agreed that the Regency and the reign of Louis XV had ushered in a period of immorality during which famous mistresses to the king had come to power. "Under absolute monarchies," wrote Mme. Campan in 1822, "women used their charms to extend their influence until they helped to decide the fate of empires. Too often the boudoir of the favorite became the king's privy council."[36] In the salons, wrote Mme. de Rémusat, the ideas of the *philosophes* made it easy for the nobility to take a superficial attitude toward serious subjects like private morality. "This witty elegance which is known as French lightness and which we have long claimed as the first of our merits," she commented, "had become the worst of our faults."[37] As for the family, Louis Aimé Martin wrote simply in *De l'éducation des mères de famille* (1834), "the depravity of society had killed [it]."[38]

In the 1770s two events had signalled an improvement in morals. The first had been the appearance and popularity of such works as Rousseau's *Emile* and his *La Nouvelle Heloïse*. The second was the coming to power of Louis XVI and his wife, Marie Antoinette, who had not been afraid to show conjugal and familial affections.[39] But before such improvements could have their effect throughout society, the Revolution broke out. It was during this upheaval that women had demonstrated an unexpected strength, courage, and devotion, in exile, in poverty, and even on the scaffold. They had also led the movement toward the renewal of family affections. "Manners became more natural, intimate relations more affectionate," wrote Mme. de Rémusat. "Mothers and daughters appeared everywhere together. Family members no longer found it embarrassing to show that they knew each other, even loved each other. At the center of family life the heart felt more at ease." This was so true, she continued, "that sometimes one could almost be happy about the reverses which had brought about the liberation of feelings."[40]

The Restoration brought with it the return of the exiled nobility and the appearance of the "romantic woman." As Mme. de Rémusat described her, the virtues of this woman were those of warmth, feeling, and seriousness.

Women were no longer the *françaises* of yesterday, but "misfortunes or at least the spectacle of misfortune had awakened their sensibility and heightened their imagination. They became, if not reasonable, at least much more serious. The experiences of privations had led them to search for all their joys and consolations in their feelings. The need for emotion had replaced the need for amusement. Seriousness, imagination, sensibility—these were the qualities of the romantic type."[41]

The goal that the maternal educators and the editors of serious women's magazines like Josephine Sirey, Fanny Richomme, and Henriette Simon-Viennot set for themselves was to convince women to be both serious and rational.[42] They hoped to show women how to control their "natural" tendencies toward imagination and sensibility by developing their reason. The favorite words of these writers were "rational," "serious," and "dutiful," and they used them to describe the true new woman of the postrevolutionary era. This mentality fit in very well with the French concept of marriage as a reasonable enterprise and with the many provisions of the Civil Code covering the rights and duties of spouses.

Upper-class women could grasp this interpretation of their past in a visual, almost sensuous way through changing fashions and the paintings, engravings, books, and magazines which recorded them. The extremely formal attire and rather stilted poses of seventeenth-century paintings had given way in the eighteenth century to a softer, more indulgent depiction of upper-class life. The gilded and complicated costumes of the aristocracy seemed designed for an existence devoted to leisure and beauty. After 1789 revolutionary women had dressed in the modest and simple clothes appropriate to the *citoyennes* of the Republic of Virtue. Plain white muslin dresses marked only by ribbons of revolutionary colors had been very popular. The postrevolutionary relaxation of dress—and of morality—is clear from the great portraits by Ingres and David.

With the Restoration, necklines went up, waistlines went down, and skirts became fuller. But a certain fanciful quality remained and was expressed in elaborate hair styles, mutton sleeves, and the crisscrossed sandals which could be seen below the ankle-length dresses. Clothes steadily became plainer, heavier, and more modest, until skirts fell from the waist in a full line directly to the shoe; the styles of the thirties and forties matched the image of the serious and rational new women.

An illustration from the *Journal des demoiselles* of 1835 demonstrates how easily accessible this interpretation of history was to women and girls. The frontispiece is composed of two pictures captioned simply as eighteenth and nineteenth century. Neither a story nor a moral was attached to these pictures. Yet the frontispiece reveals a wealth of contrasts between the new society and the old.

The eighteenth-century couple is sitting on a couch conversing pleasantly, almost gallantly, while the woman rolls up yarn and the man does needlepoint.

The latter, at least, was surely an activity of leisure time. In the contrasting picture an older man is reading a newspaper while a young man is consulting several heavy tomes; that is, both are engaged in serious work. They are seated at a table and behind them a woman is opening a box, which probably contains tobacco. Perhaps she is going to stuff a pipe for her husband (or brother) and father. In any case, one assumes that she will do something to ease the burdens of male labors. The clothes of these nineteenth-century figures are much plainer and so is the furniture. While the aura of the eighteenth century is light (the sun is beaming through the window), that of the contrasting picture is somber. The room needs a lamp, a candle, and a fireplace to provide enough light for the readers. Finally, a clock sits on the nineteenth-century mantle and seems to express a new sense of time, of work, of discipline.[43]

An understanding of the past served not only to explain why things had changed but also to reconcile women to the new roles that they were called upon to play. Charles de Rémusat said that his mother wrote her *Essai* to answer women's complaints about the present that seemed inhospitable to them, and to judge whether the times were indeed disadvantageous to her sex.[44] She, and almost every other moralist who addressed this question, concluded that the change had been very good for women because it was bringing out their true virtues and the talents appropriate to their sex. They conceded, however, that there were obvious losses. Society, in Mme. Necker de Saussure's words, was less "piquant" than it had been before the Revolution.[45] Men paid less attention to women and spent less time with them. By 1830 these women assumed that their sex had less "social influence" than before.[46] Thus the decline in sociability was perceived.

Yet decline did not mean complete rejection. There were many salons in nineteenth-century France, perhaps more than before, because there were more wealthy bourgeois women. Yet their influence declined, not only because of the change in the political system and the growth of mass institutions but because the concept of the leisured man gave way to the work ethic. And even in the world of the salons, mothering had come to be considered a completely normal and highly valued task. In her book on the nineteenth-century salon, the playwright Virginie Ancelot inadvertently showed how domesticity and sociability could be reconciled. Commenting about evening entertainment at her home, she mentioned that she sat near the door so that she could both greet guests and be available in case the baby started crying.[47]

Educated mothering, the key to the new dominant ideology of women, represented a good compromise between sociability and domesticity. To its advocates the role of mother-teacher was a distinguished one. So many famous upper-class women advocated it, after all. The ideal mother was to be educated, cultured, and confident enough to transmit religion, *politesse*, and learning to her children. These essential qualities had once been attained in the world of sociability. At the same time, she was also to take up the practical tasks of house management and childcare as a necessary and sacred trust.

The role of the mother-teacher fit the mood of the nineteenth century, too, for it was both moral and useful. Given the gaps in the educational system—no primary schools for upper-class children and little regulation of girls' institutions—maternal education filled a real need. It also made possible a middle ground in the political and religious socialization of children. The *intent* of maternal educators, at least, had not been to re-Catholicize the country, but to moralize it. Given the choice between Catholic schools and *lycées*, putting the moral education in the hands of mothers seemed to give families more control over what children learned and offered a chance to convey a sense of ethics and religion that was neither too secular nor too sectarian. Maternal education did not give women any legal authority, for the code had seen to that. But it did confer a certain moral or psychological power within the home and—according to its proponents—over society as well.

That there was a real attraction to the important role of mother and wife is evident, but of course there is another side. In eschewing revolution and equality, upper-class women also gave up a chance to play a role of authority in the public, professional, and political world. Catherine Bodard Silver, a sociologist familiar with French life, has contended that upper-class French women still have a relatively low level of participation in professional careers because of the importance they place upon their highly valued cultural and moral role in the home.[48] Relative to other modern countries, French women received the right to vote late, in 1945. Some of the most oppressive features of the Civil Code's family law were only abrogated in the 1960s and seventies. Obviously it has taken upper-class Frenchwomen a long time to recapture many of the possibilities inherent in the Enlightenment and later revolutionary movements.

Notes

1. There are other explanations for the "retreat of women," for example, the effects of such major "impersonal forces" as industrialization and urbanization. The first of these asserts that when production moved out of the home, women were ipso facto taken out of public economic life. This explanation does not really pertain to the time period described above. Family businesses were very persistent in France; so were women's roles in them. The fears which affected the middle and upper classes experiencing the growth of cities offer a more relevant partial explanation. Particularly in France, the experience of a social revolution may have made urban life more threatening and caused people to make the home "a haven."

Demography, another great "impersonal" force, is less often considered. Suffice it to say that France experienced two demographic revolutions almost simultaneously: declining death rate and declining birth rate. This affected family life. Because of the decline in the infant mortality rate, parents could make more of an emotional investment in their children. The upper and middle classes in France were also the first to limit their families. This made an educational and emotional investment in each individual child a realistic possibility and facilitated the movement for maternal education.

2.   Much of the discussion of sociability that follows relies upon the accounts of Diane Alstad, "The Ideology of the Family in Eighteenth-Century France" (Ph.D. diss, Yale University, 1971); Peter Brooks, *The Novel of Worldliness* (Princeton: Princeton University Press, 1969); and John Lough, *An Introduction to Eighteenth-Century France* (London: Longman's, 1960).

3.   Robert Darnton, "The High Enlightenment and the Low-Life Literature in Pre-Revolutionary France," *Past and Present* (1971), no. 51, 79–115, discusses the connection between sociability and patronage.

4.   What follows is not meant to be a full account of revolutionary legislation or female activity, but an attempt to show how the women of certain social strata experienced the Revolution and why they later came to reject or ignore most of the aspirations expressed by active feminists. For a fuller explanation of women's roles in the Revolution, see the studies by Mary Durham Johnson and Darline Gay Levy and Harriet Branson Applewhite in this volume.

5.   Ruth Graham, "Women in the French Revolution," in Renate Bridenthal and Claudia Koonz, eds., *Becoming Visible: Women in European History* (Boston: Houghton Mifflin, 1977), p. 252.

6.   Paule-Marie Duhet, *Les Femmes et la révolution, 1789–1794* (Paris: Julliard, 1971), pp. 75–77 speaks about the role of "marginal women."

7.   This article is reprinted in ibid., pp. 205–206.

8.   Quoted in Winifred Stephens, *Women in the French Revolution* (London: Chapman and Hall, 1922), pp. 267–268.

9.   Georges Lefebvre, *Napoleon* (New York: Columbia University Press, 1969, 2 vols.), vol. 1, p. x.

10.   In 1795 Bonaparte wrote to his brother Joseph: "The women are everywhere—plays, public walks, libraries. You can see very pretty women in the scholar's study room. Only here, of all places on earth, do women deserve to wield such influence, and indeed the men are mad about them, think of nothing else, and live only through and for them. A woman, in order to know what is due her and what power she has, must live in Paris for six months." Quoted in *The Mind of Napoleon*, J. Christopher Herold, ed. and trans. (New York: Columbia University Press, 1955), p. 13.

11.   R. Savatier, *L'Art de faire les lois: Bonaparte et le Code civil* (Paris: Librairie Dalloz, 1927), pp. 27–29. In these pages Savatier clearly puts the blame for Napoleon's intransigent attitudes about women on Josephine's behavior.

12.   Lefebvre, *Napoleon*, vol. 1, pp. 85–86; Jean Robiquet, *La Vie quotidienne au temps de Napoléon* (Paris: Hachette, 1942), p. 69.

13.   André-Jean Arnaud, *Les Origines doctrinales du Code civil français* (Paris: R. Pichon et R. Durand-Anzias, 1969), pp. 29–39.

14.   James F. Traer, "Marriage and the Family in French Law and Social Criticism from the End of the Ancien Regime to the Civil Code" (Ph.D. diss University of Michigan, 1971), pp. 271–272, 291.

15.   Ibid., pp. 271–291; H. A. L. Fisher, "The Codes," *Cambridge Modern History*, 13 vols., New York: Macmillan, 1920–1912, vol. 9, pp. 115–161; and Maïte Albistur and Daniel Armogathe, *Histoire de féminisme français*, 2 vols. (Paris: Editions des femmes, 1977), vol. 2, pp. 359–364.

16.   Edith Thomas, *The Women Incendiaries* (New York: George Braziller, 1966), p. 8, and Theodore Zeldin, *France, 1848–1945*, 2 vols. (Oxford: Clarendon Press, 1973–1977), vol. 1, p. 287.

17.   In response to the "needs and tastes of a more complex, rich and demanding civilization" Guizot instituted the "higher primary schools" which gave commercial training; R. D. Anderson, *Education in France, 1848–1870* (Oxford: Clarendon Press, 1975), p. 35.

18.   Albistur and Armogathe, *Histoire*, vol. 2, pp. 405–426, 449–464; Marguerite Thibert, *Le Féminisme dans le socialisme français de 1830 à 1850* (Paris: Marcel Giard, 1926).

19.   Josephine Bachellery, "Lettre au Citoyen Carnot, Ministre de l'instruction publique," in *Lettres sur l'éducation des femmes* (Paris: Lemoine et Mansert, 1848), pp. 211–237.

20.   For biographical information on Maisonneuve, see the "Notice biographique" which prefaces the third edition of the *Essai* and M. Michaud, ed., *Biographie universelle ancienne et moderne* . . . (Paris: A. Thoisnier Desplace, 1843), 23, pp. 646–647.

21.   Albistur and Armogathe, *Histoire*, vol. 2, p. 368.

22.   On Henriette Campan see F. Barrière's introduction to her *De l'éducation* (Paris: Baudoin Frères, 1824) and his "Notice sur la vie de Mme. Campan" in her *Mémoires sur la vie de Marie-Antoinette* (Paris: Firmin-Didot, n.d.), reprinted in several editions and translations of this work. See also Mary Fitton, *The Faithful Servant: Jeanne-Louise-Henriette Campan* (London: Oldbourne, 1965).

23.   F. Barrière's introduction to *De l'éducation*, pp iii–vii, and Cattois' preface to *Essai sur l'instruction*, pp. xxx–xxxvi.

24.   Charles-Auguste Sainte-Beuve, "Madame de Rémusat," in *Portraits des femmes* (Paris: Garnier Frères, 1845), p. 488.

25.   *Memoires de Madame de Rémusat, 1802–1808* (New York: D. Appleton and Co., 1880).

26.   For a concise sympathetic biography see Gilbert Stenger, "Mme. de Rémusat: Epouse et mère," *Grandes dames du XIXe siècle. Chronique du temps de la Restauration* (Paris: Perrin et Cie, 1911), pp. 180–243.

27.   Sainte-Beuve, "Madame Guizot," *Portraits des femmes*, p. 235.

28.   Quoted in ibid., p. 225.

29.   Among these male biographers are Sainte-Beuve and Charles de Rémusat, who was asked by François Guizot to write his "Notice sur la vie et les ouvrages de Mme. Guizot" immediately after her death. Originally printed in the *Revue encyclopédique*, it was reprinted as the introduction to her *Conseils de morale ou essais sur l'homme, les moeurs, les caractères, le monde, les femmes, l'éducation* (Paris: Pichon et Didier, 1828). A later historian, Edouard Dolléans, seems to agree with their assessments, although he describes the relationship as mutually advantageous: "Lettres de Guizot à Pauline de Meulan," *Revue des deux mondes* (Sept.–Oct. 1954), 140–147.

30.   *Lettres de famille sur l'éducation*, 3rd ed. (Paris: Didier, 1841), vol. 1, pp. 174–180.

31.   The best and most complete biography of Necker de Saussure is Etienne Causse, *Madame Necker de Saussure et l'éducation progressive*, 2 vols. (Paris: Editions "Je Sers," 1930), which is based on several family archives and contains many beautiful illustrations.

32.   Limoges: Barbou Frères, n.d., pp. 8–10.

33.   *Memoirs of Madame de La Tour du Pin* (New York: McCall, 1971), p. 27.

34.   Fanny Mongellaz, *De l'influence des femmes sur les moeurs et les destinées des nations, sur leurs familles et la société et de l'influence des moeurs sur le bonheur de la vie* (Paris: L. -G. Michaud, 1828, 2 vols.), vol. 1, p. 336.

35.   Claire de Rémusat, *Essai sur l'éducation des femmes* (Paris: l'Advocat, 1824), p. 50.

36.   Campan, *De l'éducation*, p. 3.

37.   de Rémusat, *Essai*, p. 67.

38. Paris: Charles Gosselin, p. 24.

39. Mongellaz, *De l'influence*, p. 193.

40. de Rémusat, *Essai*, p. 77; Josephine Sirey expresses much the same opinion in her *Conseils d'une grandmère aux jeunes femmes* (Paris: Schwartz et Gognot, 1838), p. 21.

41. de Rémusat, *Essai*, pp. 77–78.

42. Richomme edited *Journal des femmes* from 1832 to 1835, when it was a very serious magazine with a determined educational purpose; Simon-Viennot edited *Journal des mères et des jeunes filles* (1844–1847) and Sirey, *La Mère de famille* (1832–1835).

43. E. P. Thompson wrote about the connection between clocks and the work ethic in "Time, Work-Discipline and Industrial Capitalism," *Past and Present* (1967), no. 38, 56–97; Erna Hellerstein develops the theme that the orderly household was a response by the bourgeoisie to their growing fears of the city in "French Women and the Orderly Household, 1830–1870," *Proceedings of the Western Society for French History* (1976), vol. 3, pp. 378–389.

44. "Preface de l'éditeur," to Claire de Rémusat's *Essai*, pp. i–iii.

45. Albertine Necker de Saussure, *L'éducation progressive* (Paris: Pauline Frères, 1844), vol. 2, p. 533.

46. Ibid., pp. 239–241; Nathalie de Lajolais, *Le Livre des Mères de famille et des institutrices, sur l'éducation pratique des femmes* (Paris: Didier, 1842).

47. Virginie Ancelot, *Un Salon de Paris, 1824–1864* (Paris: Dentu, 1866), pp. 28–29.

48. Catherine Bondard Silver, "Salon, foyer, bureau: Women and the Professions in France," *American Journal of Sociology*, 78, no. 4, 836–851, and "France: Contrasts in Familial and Societal Roles" in Janet Z. Giele and Audrey C. Smock, eds., *Women: Roles and Status in Eight Countries* (New York: Wiley, 1977), pp. 259–299.

Suggestions for Further Reading

Given the number of works on the English and American Victorian woman, the upper and middle-class nineteenth-century French woman has received surprisingly little attention. The best comprehensive treatments are the chapters "Familles et règles de vie," "Femmes," and "Les relations sociales" in Adeline Daumard's *La bourgeoisie parisienne 1815 à 1848* (Paris: S.E.V. P.E.N., 1963); "Marriage and Morals," "Children," and "Women" from the first volume of Theodore Zeldin's *France, 1848–1945: Ambition, Love and Politics* (Oxford: Clarendon Press, 1973); and the two articles by Catherine Bodard Silver, "Salon, foyer, bureau: Women and the Professions in France," *American Journal of Sociology*, 78, No. 4, pp. 836–851 and "France: Contrasts in Familial and Societal Roles" in Janet Z. Giele and Audrey C. Smock, eds., *Women: Roles and Status in Eight Countries* (New York: Wiley, 1977), pp. 259–299. Bonnie Smith's *A World Apart: Women of the Nord, 1789–1914* will soon appear. This is a revised and expanded version of her recent dissertation, "The Women of the Lille Bourgeoisie, 1850–1914," unpublished Ph.D. diss. (University of Rochester, 1976). Undoubtedly there are many other historians working to fill this gap. Balzac, Flaubert, and Stendhal all tried in their own way to present the reality of women's lives and remain an invaluable source of information and individual insight. Evelyn Sullerot's study of women's magazines and newspapers, *Histoire de la presse féminine en France des origines à 1848* (Paris: Armand Colin, 1966) is also very useful.

Even with regard to specific subjects, many of the works on French women are old and outdated. On education, the three major sources all date from the early 1880s. Octave Gréard's *L'Enseignement secondaire des filles* (Paris: Delalain Frères, 1883) still remains the best source on schooling. Paul Rousselot's two-volume *Histoire de l'éducation des femmes en France* (New York: Burt Franklin reprint, 1971; 1st ed., 1883) is the most comprehensive treatment of women's ideas on education. From a Republican standpoint the second volume of Gabriel Compayré's *Histoire critique des doctrines de l'éducation* (Paris: Hachette, 1883) is more critical of domestic education and its effect on French children. His concern, however, seems to be mostly for boys. There is a short illustrated article in English, "Mme. Campan," which discusses the Legion of Honor schools; see Barbara Scott, *History Today* (Oct. 1973).

On the law, all of the works cited in the text are useful, but none of them gives a full historical account of the effects of the Civil Code on women. French feminism has been better served. Maïte Albistur and Daniel Armogathe's two-volume *Histoire du feminisme français* (Paris: Editions des femmes, 1977) is a good summary and analysis of existing sources and brings the story down to the present. Although the concept of the mother-teacher is alluded to in many works, there is as yet no study of it. But see B. Corrado Pope's essay on this subject in the 1976 *Proceedings of the Western Society for French History*.

10/Patriot Mothers
in the Post-Risorgimento:
Women After the Italian Revolution

Judith Jeffrey Howard

Italy was unified in 1861 after a century of rising national consciousness, armed conflict, social disruptions, and political maneuvering.[1] The Risorgimento, as the Italian revolution was called, was not a mass movement. The politicized classes included liberal aristocrats and some of the upper, middle, and artisan classes; the armies of the popular general Giuseppe Garibaldi enlisted more students than peasants. And, not surprisingly, the revolution was not in any sense feminist in intent; with unification achieved, state policies attempted to establish social and political stability, not a new social order. However, during the revolution, women as well as men were raised in politicized families, read revolutionary literature, took up arms, hid fugitives, went to prison, and fled into exile in Italy and abroad. The boundaries between political activity and private life blurred, and traditional roles often assumed political significance. After unification, many women participants turned the political networks they had developed and the political experiences they had gained toward raising Italian women's status in both public and private life. Unification provided national institutions, new targets for women's reform initiatives, a national market for ideas, and, with the introduction of a unified educational system, a means to reach out to the masses of Italian women.

This study explores the political roots of the activists' sex consciousness, outlines their movement into the national educational system in order to turn it to women's needs, and examines the "patriot mother" ideals they often used as rubrics for basic social changes. To illustrate the range of women's experiences and their thought, four women who created distinct patriot mother images are discussed in some detail. Erminia Fuà Fusinato represented the liberal establishment and the "right wing" of the woman's movement, focusing on women's "true emancipation . . . from ignorance." Aurelia Cimino Folliero de Luna sought more basic changes in women's status, particularly new work roles, but accepted the framework of the constitutional monarchy. Sara Nathan exemplified the republican revolutionary who urged women as mothers to fight for the republic, but neglected feminism as a separate issue. And finally, Gualberta Alaide Beccari maintained one of the most effective post-Risorgimento women's networks, through her journal, *La donna*, which developed and spread feminist ideas. In the course of their activity, these women themselves became role models, representatives of the range of reformist and feminist views on women's status and on social change.

The large group of women here identified as activists represented the classes politicized in the revolution, but believed that their interests constituted the interests of all women. They expressed a variety of opinions on women's roles, but all agreed that women needed better education, greater earning capacity, more authority in the home, and some sense of political identification or involvement as Italians. "Patriot mother" is a useful rubric for this basic reform consensus.[2] Reformers portrayed the patriot mother type as an educated, religious bastion of the liberal state and of the constitutional monarchy, and they used the image to extend women's traditional roles into the public sphere. Feminists also emphasized extending traditional roles, but they were quicker to identify the sex oppression connected with those roles. Feminists carried on a more clearly focused attack against patriarchy in the state, the Church, and the family, and they gradually redefined "women's sphere" to include all aspects of public and private life. Their ideal patriot mothers were anticlerical, republican women organized in opposition to the existing state. While patriot motherhood assumed myriad forms between these extremes, and had weaknesses as well as strengths as a basis for emancipation, it was a logical beginning for efforts to make fundamental social change in a conservative society.

Indeed, one finds that women had both conservative or traditional and nontraditional objectives in the 1870s. For even as women's literacy rate increased in absolute terms after unification, it declined slightly relative to men's literacy. Even as jobs in schools and telegraph offices opened to women of the middle and artisan classes, the same jobs, at higher pay rates with better working conditions, opened to men. In addition, some women actually lost status as Italian citizens. Women of Lombardy, Venetia, and Tuscany lost political rights and in some instances private authority previously exercised. In view of the hopes unification had spawned, and their stark contrast with post-Risorgimento reality, the patriot mother ideal, in all its forms, took on a double meaning. It became not only useful to convince men in power to support needed reforms, but also provided a program of action for women with goals that were both public and domestic. Extended roles in the public sphere were now seen to be essential for the achievement of women's proper position in the home; the dignity the "angel of the hearth" supposedly enjoyed in the private sphere too often eluded these women. In Italy, the citizen mother image not only provided a perception of motherhood as a basis for sisterhood and women's activism, and a convenient rubric to advance women into the public sphere, but also a realization that private goals could only be achieved by public means, that the personal was political.[3]

An understanding of these goals begins with women's experience during the revolution. During Italy's century of political upheaval, women's roles expanded in both theory and practice. Theory developed in the context of Giuseppe Mazzini's revolutionary republicanism that placed women at the center of a most radical vision for a new society. Essentially, Mazzini contributed to the feminist version of the patriot mother ideal by politicizing the "angel of the hearth," transforming the passive, domestic paragon of traditional religion and morality into a maternal anticlerical revolutionary in her own right, companion and mother to men and women who shared her ideals. Such women carried forward a new morality of social commitment and social justice. Indeed, Mazzini portrayed nationalist revolution as a moral crusade; women were welcome and many took part. Both Mazzini and Garibaldi idealized women as the mothers of patriots, but neither hesitated to acknowledge women's independent contributions as fundraisers, nurses, couriers, confidants, soldiers, and martyrs.

Women often experienced a continuity of revolutionary and domestic roles as daughters, wives, and mothers of patriots. Some women were more influenced by their fathers, others by their mothers. Beccari and Folliero, for example, were raised in politicized families. Other women, like the Mazzinians Sara Nathan and Carlotta Benettini, entered the nationalist movement on their own initiatives, becoming themselves parents who saw their political ideals mold the thought and action of their children. Mazzini traced his own political socialization to his mother's republicanism.

New duties as well as new ideas were introduced into Italian family life during these decades of turmoil. Women managed family affairs while husbands were in battle or in prison. They assumed economic responsibilities in exile. The aristocratic Folliero, for example, turned her musical "accomplishments" into needed family income during more than a decade of exile from her native Naples. Even as a woman like Carlotta Benettini "mothered" Mazzini and Garibaldi, sending them sweets, or linens, or socks, she also hid fugitives, including Mazzini, and went to prison for her political activities. Undeterred, Benettini and others like her continued to raise money for arms and propaganda. Women transformed traditional roles like nursing the sick into political acts like caring for the wounded in rebel cities; 6,000 women reputedly contributed their energies to the short-lived Roman republic of 1848–49. In short, a large number of women became politicized in the wars of the Risorgimento, and in many instances such experiences influenced their concept of woman and her roles. Women's own experience proved their capacity for political participation and public initiatives, as well as for household management, patience, and suffering.[4]

As their revolutionary activities extended beyond the family circle, women formed national and international political networks. While before unification ties of friendship and consanguinity existed among aristocratic women from various provinces, support of the national cause, disruption of family life, and often exile created public and expressly political contacts among women of different social backgrounds. In some instances, women who had joined together for traditional wartime activities like nursing the wounded continued this connection during postwar years.

Two women at the center of one such network were Laura Solera Mantegazza (1815–1873) and Ismene Sormani Castelli (1811–1903), both active in Milan. Mantegazza married at seventeen and devoted a great deal of energy to educating her own children. But during the Revolution of 1848, she organized a committee and raised money to help the wounded. Her financial efforts proved successful, and with surplus funds she established the first day-care center for infants in Milan. The center enabled working women to leave babies in a healthy environment with wetnurses and medical help available. The center also disseminated general health information to working mothers. Mantegazza was joined in this work by Sormani, another woman who had collected funds for the national revolution in the past, and who used her Risorgimento political connections to further her activism on women's behalf for decades. In 1852 the day-care center was followed by a school for illiterate adult women, where Mantegazza taught. With the outbreak of war in 1859, both women again nursed the wounded. After Italian unification in 1860, they returned to women's issues, and in the early 1860s they joined with working women to form the Women's Mutual Aid Association for Working Women.[5]

Women's political activities cut across the political differences among those working for unification. Most women activists were influenced by Mazzini to some degree, and during the decade 1860–1870, Mazzinian women significantly contributed to the revolutionary movement for the liberation of Venetia and of Rome.[6] But by 1870 a number of them had altered their political ideas, in some cases moving to the right, in others to the left. Sormani, for example, abandoned democratic republicanism for constitutional monarchism as early as 1853, after the failure of a Mazzinian uprising. Other women activists supported unification under the Savoyard monarchy in the women's committees of the Italian National Society. These committees ultimately overshadowed the society itself. They raised large sums for wounded veterans, and they remained active until Rome was taken in 1870. Not only did they exemplify ideals of "sacrifice and unanimity" important to patriots, but they also embodied the fundamental ideal of the patriot mother who extended her domestic role into the public sphere.[7]

In addition to these national contacts, women in the Italian revolution built an international network of political allies involved first in unification and later in women's issues. For instance, the Ashurst family, Mazzini's "second family" in England, developed lasting ties with the Italian movement. In the 1870s, Caroline Ashurst Biggs edited *The Englishwoman's Review*, which occasionally excerpted articles from Italian women's periodicals or published items on the status of Italian women. The Ashurst family worked with the Nathans to help Mazzini and to support Josephine Butler's International Federation for the Abolition of State Regulation of Vice.[8] Here as elsewhere men joined women in their struggle for national liberation and women's rights.[9]

Thus, it is clear that the political revolution in Italy extended women's traditional roles into the public sphere and exposed women to a variety of radical political activities. The revolution affected more than the power relationships between Austria and Sardinia or between religious and secular authorities. Power relationships within the family were also challenged; class relationships were scrutinized in some circles; the power of the Church, which opposed unification, was openly defied; and for some, to submit to oppression of any kind became intolerable. Many women looked forward to wider roles as citizens and mothers working with men to forge a new Italy.

With unification achieved, women's networks acquired a new dimension as women confronted national institutions that would shape their lives. Gross inequalities under the Civil Code led to concerted protests and contributed to the development of the Italian feminist movement.[10] But an equally important obstacle to women's progress was the educational system. Like the law, the educational system potentially affected all women, and educational reform was an area where women's efforts could change women's status. In a society in which coeducational schools were generally regarded with suspicion, and in which the absence of girls' schools marked the gravest lacuna in a broadly inadequate educational system, women had to exert themselves on behalf of women's education or leave the majority of their sex illiterate. Thousands of women chose to move into the state educational system as teachers, administrators, or as critics with alternative proposals to meet women's educational needs. From daughters of Garibaldini to widowed ladies of the liberal establishment, women took with them the various concepts of women's roles which would shape the immediate post-Risorgimento generation.

United Italy's response to the illiteracy problem was the Sardinian Casati Law of 1859, which mandated two years of elementary education for both boys and girls and required local communities to provide free public schools for both sexes. But the law was not strictly enforced and thousands of villages built no schools. In communes able to support any free elementary school at all, boys' schools took precedence. Thus women, who suffered a higher illiteracy rate than men in 1861, were not able to keep pace with men's growing literacy in the period to 1881. In these decades, male illiteracy nationwide dropped from 68 percent to 55 percent, while female illiteracy fell from 81 percent to 69 percent.[11]

Women's literacy improved as teacher-training programs for the elementary schools spread in the 1880s. Women's other opportunities for secondary education, severely limited in the 1860s and 1870s, increased dramatically in the 1880s. In 1883 boys' technical and college preparatory schools (*ginnasi* and *licei*) were legally opened to women, partly because so many girls were already attending.[12]

Universities were opened to women in 1874, though four young women from Mazzinian families had enrolled even earlier. There were no formal restrictions on women's course work, but individual professors all over Italy sometimes excluded women from their classes. Yet the freedom to study did not constitute free entry into all professions. For instance, women were allowed to practice medicine, but were excluded from the legal profession until 1919. As an alternative to university study there were two istituti superiori di magistero (teachers' colleges), which prepared women to teach in normal schools; but they did not provide the equivalent of a university education.[13]

In short, in the area of education the political unification of Italy brought no sudden change. Rather, it created possibilities that were realized slowly in some cases, while potential for change was thwarted in others. Nonetheless, it is important to consider what education could mean to some Italian girls and how women tried to use education to change women's status. First, public schools taught the Italian language, as distinct from local dialects. Even imperfectly learned, Italian was a necessary passport out of provincialism, a first step toward exploring the ideas and the literature of a wider society. Italian opened doors to employment as a teacher, telegraphist, or government clerk. Despite generally exploitive wages and working conditions, such jobs offered artisan and middle-class women some opportunities for economic independence and social mobility. Italian was the language of emerging women's literature, of radical newspapers, of feminist journals, and of political debate. It was the common language in which activist women reached out beyond the elite and attempted to communicate with all women. Secondly, a secular and more rigorous public education provided an alternative to Catholic schools and the possibility of creating new concepts of women's roles. In addition to the Italian language, students learned Italian history and geography, arithmetic, reading, writing, and some science and penmanship. Needlework was stressed as a useful skill for girls, since it was sometimes crucial to the family economy.

It was commonly charged that a Catholic education enabled girls to read the lives of the saints and nothing else. While in this period the Jesuits dropped their opposition to literacy for peasant women, in the late 1880s they still inveighed against exposing girls to politics or philosophy, fields that would corrupt women's morals. Ignorance was equated with innocence and considered essential to women's salvation; knowledge was dangerous and any knowledge imparted by an Italian state created despite bitter Church opposition smacked of the Antichrist. Catholic women educators took a more enlightened position, but by the 1880s their conflicts with feminists over religion and divorce intensified. Increasingly, they became advocates of self-abnegation, prayer, and suffering as the foremost female virtues.[14]

Post-Risorgimento Italy rang with debates over public education. Should it be more vocational or more theoretical? Should it be the same for both sexes, or sharply differentiated, reinforcing traditional sex roles? Women educators could be found on all sides of these arguments, but basically the citizen mother ideal necessitated three basic changes in women's status:

literacy; improved earning capacity, whether in the sweatshop needle trades or in the professions; and some political awareness, whether simple patriotism or an understanding of the republican political critique. No potential for such an education existed in Catholic schools. For all the myriad shortcomings of the public school system, from poorly trained and overworked teachers to continuing Catholic religious influence, the public schools were essential to any major improvement in women's status. They also became one source of alternative concepts of women's roles.

To provide this basic education, the government relied on the Casati Law and the often heroic efforts of young women teachers. The Casati Law extended opportunities for women by commanding localities to build girls' elementary schools, by mandating free education, by providing for normal schools to train women teachers, and by regulating teacher certification requirements. It established virtually the same curriculum for men and women in normal schools, but provided an important precedent of wage inequality; even as women and men worked together to improve conditions in their profession, women had to carry on a separate struggle for parity with men.[15]

Laws and statistics, however, only frame the picture of women's education. Education became available because young women became teachers, and literary sources reveal what a teaching career cost many of them. By the 1880s their working conditions were a public scandal. Conditions were worst in poor rural areas. A young graduate might find herself in an area suspicious of "foreigners" (graduates were sent to distant parts of Italy in government attempts at regional integration), overtly hostile to independent young women, and indifferent to the benefits of education. Teachers were sometimes cheated of promised salaries; young women might arrive at their post to find their wages lower, their living conditions harsher, than promised. With few or no reserves of their own, they were often forced to remain once they had arrived. Under Article 320 of the Casati Law, two tiny villages might share a teacher, who was forced to commute on foot from one to the other. Teachers often lacked basic supplies, sometimes even a classroom. Sometimes they turned to manual labor to earn enough to eat; skilled workers reportedly made a better living. In many areas, they were exposed to attempts at sexual exploitation by local officials who controlled their livelihood. Suicides were not uncommon, causes ranging from seduction to starvation. In urban areas and in the north, salaries were generally higher, but in every case wages were only a fraction of a man's for the same work. On her meager salary, a teacher had to maintain a proper dress, decent shoes, a suitable hat, and gloves. Although cities provided better conditions, often including the protection of one's family, candidates far outnumbered positions and many women could work only as substitutes, eking out a living by collecting half the salary of the already underpaid teacher she replaced. Until the turn of the century, women teachers had to resign if they married.[16]

It is under these conditions that women acted to take control of their lives and to increase their influence on women's condition. Women teachers trained women students, and education represented a women's victory. Women joined teachers' associations to work for better wages and conditions, and to be heard in the debate on the nature of girls' education. Teaching opened avenues of social mobility to artisan women and became women's most important profession (in Italy, as in France, nursing remained dominated by nuns). In the north, especially, teaching became a viable career, providing a living wage. Women used their financial independence as a basis for activism. Visible women, including the magazine publisher Olimpia Saccati, supported themselves through teaching and school administration. Leading feminists of the 1890s, for instance Linda Malnatti, were often self-supporting teachers, and teachers moved into the ranks of the feminist movement. In women's associations, in radical organizations where they joined with men, in women's publications and the political press, in state schools and alternative schools, women reached out to each other to change their status by acting independently among themselves and within the framework of the new state.

The public and private dimensions of women's Risorgimento experience, their activism, and their impact on women's status can be further examined through a closer look at Fuà, Folliero, Nathan, and Beccari, all of whom used the patriot mother image in attempts to improve women's status.

Fuà was a widely respected patriot whose concept of woman in many ways represented that of the group of women from well-to-do but not aristocratic Italian families who took positions in the unified educational system. She was born in 1834 into a Jewish liberal family in Venetia, then under Austrian control. Educated at home, she began to compose poetry as a child and as she grew older references to tyranny and freedom in her poems took on clearly political overtones. In the 1850s she defied her parents and converted to Catholicism to marry Arnaldo Fusinato, a famous poet and patriot. But even this breach with her childhood was healed when her parents were reconciled to her marriage. In 1864 Fuà and her young family fled Austrian territory for refuge in Florence, where she associated with some of the most prominent intellectual and political figures of the period, including Niccolò Tommaseo, Gino Capponi, Atto Vannucci, and Cesare Correnti. With unification achieved, she began her administrative career in 1871 when Correnti, minister of public instruction, appointed her to the post of school inspector for Rome and Naples, a newly created position intended to standardize girls' educational programs. Later, Fuà worked successively as a professor of literature at the women's normal school in Rome, as director of the women's college (Scuola Superiore) there, and as founder of the Society for Women's Higher Education, which presented lecture series, given by men, for Roman ladies and elementary school teachers. Fuà died in 1876, but she had used her official positions and, no doubt, her personal friendships with men in government, to promote an educational ideal that long defined liberal orthodoxy.[17]

Fuà's Risorgimento experience was reflected in her concept of woman and of the continuity of women's traditional roles with social progress. Above all else, women remained wives and mothers. Better education would make them better wives and mothers, as well as more moral individuals. Against Jesuits who equated knowledge with corruption, against positivists who warned that developing the mind would wither the womb, Fuà argued that education was good because it helped women fulfill their traditional roles. Indeed, if it did not, she proclaimed, *she* would close all the schools. And Fuà apparently exemplified her own ideal: she was described as one who knitted baby clothes while engaged in salon conversation.[18]

Nevertheless, Fuà extended women's traditional role into the public sphere. In her pedagogical writings, patriotic themes were often suggested for student essays, and her model woman was patriotic without being political. Further, Fuà's educated woman served as "mother in the school, teacher in the family." Fuà emphasized the nobility of teaching, its usefulness to other women and to society, and its desirability as a career. She looked forward to a time when women would take responsibility for all elementary education. Teaching constituted woman's "mission" in society. It was thus a civic responsibility, without becoming a political act.[19]

At the same time, teaching was a means to economic self-sufficiency. Like other activist women in this period, Fuà emphasized, even glorified, a work ethic for all women. She rejoiced that middle-class women were moving into the labor force, and that the old ideal of idleness was receding. Economic independence helped women of all classes, women who never married, women whose husbands fell ill, widows, and dutiful daughters. Ideally, women's work would complement family life: the teacher might ultimately leave the students she mothered for her own children whom she educated; the artisan woman received an education that made her a better worker, though not an independent thinker. In every case, work and education enabled women to extend traditional roles without fundamentally changing them.[20]

There were important elements of sisterhood in Fuà's teaching. Patriotism, charity, and motherhood bound all women together. And Fuà suggested themes for student essays which touched a range of women's experiences. For example, a topic for a friendly letter was to write to an aunt about winning a scholarship; a theme for a "family dialogue" involved two working-class girls discussing their finances: one kept a savings account while the other played the lottery. In Fuà's writing assignments all mothers taught charity: there is always someone poorer than you are; the best charity is giving of your time and talents. And Fuà warned her students, to whom she referred as "my sisters," against superstition, which too often isolated old women, branded as witches and ostracized rather than helped by their neighbors. While Fuà's message was meant for all women, she focused primarily on the middle and artisan classes. Women were to guard against delusions of social mobility. Education, work, and charity would improve their status without altering the existing social order. Fuà created a feminine universe based on dedication, charity, and patriotism, where women lived as richer and poorer sisters, with little reference to men, whose ultimate control was distant, benign, and susceptible of moral persuasion.[21]

Early in the 1870s, Fuà separated herself from feminists who took more radical stands on women's issues. She cautioned her students against the *scapigliate emancipatrici* (iconoclastic emancipationists), variously accused in contemporary literature of advocating an antifeminine "man-woman" ideal and of going to "excesses" like demanding political rights. Instead, Fuà declared: "For me, the true, the only possible emancipation is that from ignorance, the perennial source of all material and moral poverty." "True emancipation" became the watchwords for those who favored education and work that extended women's traditional roles, and some family law reform, but who rejected an all-out assault on patriarchy in all its forms, especially the monarchy or the Catholic Church. Olimpia Saccati's popular periodical, *La missione della donna* and Adele Woena's *L'aurora* adopted the "true emancipation" stance. While feminists began to encourage women to experiment with nontraditional roles, "true emancipationists" opposed such ventures. While feminists demanded a more thorough secularization of society, especially the public schools, Fuà and Saccati urged continued Catholic moral influence. And while feminists grew increasingly concerned with political rights and fundamental social change, Fuà's followers persisted in regarding education and employment as the only vehicles for enlarging women's traditional sphere.[22]

Thus Fuà drew the limits of her own protest. Hers was an exhortation to action over passivity, to community involvement over familial isolation, to a degree of sisterhood and charity over old regional and class prejudices. She wanted women to be educated, moral, patriotic, self-supporting, and integrated into a progressive, literate society. Her challenge to patriarchy was limited to that implicit in a woman's capacity to support herself. Yet, as one contemporary concluded, her cautious but sincere and nonthreatening reformism had a major impact. Sketched in the outlines of a patriot motherhood, it helped to draw Italian girls away from the nuns and into a more secular educational system.[23]

More radical than Fuà, yet still accepting the confines of the constitutional monarchy, was Aurelia Cimino Folliero, the only southerner in this sampling of activists, a descendant of Spanish-Neopolitan aristocrats on her mother's side and of Italian patriots on both sides. Folliero came from a more privileged sector of society than did Fuà. Her mother was known for her writings and received a prize from a Parisian intellectual society for an essay on girls' education. In the 1830s Folliero was taken to Paris for her education; her parents' home was a gathering place for notable Catholic intellectuals, for equally notable Italian rebels, and indeed for some men like Niccolò Tommaseo who were both.

Folliero had a good singing voice and longed for an operatic career, but her parents thwarted that ambition. At nineteen, having returned to Naples, she married the librettist and poet Giorgio Tommaso Cimino. Exiled after the 1848 uprising in Naples, the couple spent most of the next twelve years in England. For Folliero, dislocation definitely involved assuming new economic roles. Until her return to Italy in 1860, she gave language and singing lessons to help support a family that eventually included ten children.[24]

Folliero's experiences shaped the attitudes and goals she promoted in her journal, *La Cornelia*, founded in Florence in 1872. Folliero's message was directed chiefly toward women of the upper classes who enjoyed secure wealth and social position. From the position of their unassailable respectability, Folliero believed they could lead women's cause: demands for better education, for work or better work, for legal reform of the family law and more authority in the family, and for some role in civil life. Folliero's patriot mother figure was a citizen and a family manager. The ideal was not class-bound, despite Folliero's aristocratic orientation. For example, she based her claim for greater equality in the family law on the evidence that throughout history women in all social strata had proven their capacity for family governance. Wherever women had had authority, they had exercised it responsibly. Thus all women were to direct their abilities toward improving women's status and toward making Italy a more progressive society.[25]

One of the ways women would accomplish their goals was to recognize the dignity of work for women of all classes. Work was a source of dignity and virtue and emotional as well as financial well-being. Poor women needed training to improve their earning capacity and associations with other women for help in time of need. Wealthier women had to overcome prejudices against work and take advantage of all possible opportunities. Folliero urged her readers to read Samuel Smiles' *Self Help*, and then to read it to their children. She also recommended biographies of women by Plutarch and the poem "Excelsior!" by Longfellow. These models of successful individual initiative would help all women to recognize that Italy could become a progressive, prosperous society only through their combined efforts as mothers, as concerned citizens, and as activists attentive to women's needs. At the same time, everyone had to recognize women's right and responsibility to become all they were capable of being.[26]

Folliero's ideas on sisterhood, class, social change, and women's roles were exemplified in her work on agricultural education for women. When she went to France in 1878 to attend the International Congress on the Rights of Women, she carried with her a government commission to study girls' agricultural education. There were many agricultural and industrial colonies for women in France. After visiting the colony at Darnètal, Folliero wrote articles to influence Italian public opinion, and reports and letters urging the government to establish a comprehensive program of agricultural training for girls. She also wanted courses on an advanced, theoretical level to interest ladies in scientific agriculture, to enable them better to manage their estates, to develop a respect for and love of the countryside, and perhaps to raise a generation of modernizing landowners in the British tradition, instead of more young professionals further to crowd the ranks of the bureaucracy. In the 1880s she established her own school for orphan girls at Cesena. Though her work was praised, she received no commitment of government funds for the training of financially and intellectually independent women agriculturalists. The feminist content of Folliero's plan was winnowed out; facilities remained inadequate in number and they fell far short of being the sources of creativity and independence she had envisioned.[27]

While Fuà directed her energies toward the public elementary school system, and Folliero worked to expand that system in new directions, Sara Nathan and other women worked to establish alternatives both to the liberal educational system and to the government itself. Sara Nathan was born in Pesaro, soon orphaned, raised in Modena, and married at seventeen to a Frankfurt gentleman. She lived with her husband in England, and bore twelve children between 1839 and 1860. Her home became a gathering place for Mazzinians and she an indefatigable republican revolutionary. In turn, Mazzini considered her "the best Italian friend I have, one of the best women I know, pure, virtuous, sweet, devoted—and unconsciously so—to all that is Beautiful and Good."[28]

Nathan was the embodiment of both the maternal and the revolutionary ideal. Mazzinians continued to idealize "feminine" qualities, like woman's "infinite power of love and poetry," and their special roles in the family. But unlike the "Christian mother" who lived in subjection to the status quo, the Church and the king, the Mazzinian mother was an agent of historical change, dedicated to progress. Such mothers were the "initiators of the future," the focal point of the family organized as a revolutionary association moving humanity forward. Separate but equal social functions were to mean equal rights and duties, including the vote; disenfranchised women could not raise republican children.[29]

Mazzini's followers proselytized for this concept of woman in newspapers like *Il dovere*, published in Rome from 1877 to 1884. *Dovere* protested their oppression, supported women's emancipation, encouraged working women's organizations, attacked licensed prostitution, and reprinted some of Anna Maria Mozzoni's feminist speeches, almost always with enthusiasm. Nathan and other women encouraged workers to organize and to become politicized in associations formed to meet their material needs and to raise their activist consciousness. But women were to remain within the Mazzinian movement. In 1878 *Dovere* criticized the International Congress on Women's Rights convened in Paris for treating women's issues as separate issues. Only a coalition of women and workers could bring about the republican revolution that was the prerequisite of a just society for both sexes.[30]

Nathan translated this ideal of maternal radicalism into action in her Mazzinian school for girls, founded in a workers' quarter of Rome in 1872. Its purpose was to give working-class girls an elementary education, a trade, and a strong dose of Mazzinian ideals. All students spent at least one hour a day at handicrafts or sewing, and students training for a trade worked at it, with two hours of elementary education. There was no religious instruction, only an infusion of moral ideals. Nathan began with seven students and struggled against the fierce opposition of the Catholic Church; reportedly, priests barred her students from church. But the school survived. In 1877 *Dovere* reported that thirty students completed their elementary education, ready to become self-supporting workers, "good daughters, conscientious mothers, and virtuous citizens"—and Mazzinians. In a later sketch of the school an enrollment of 115 students was reported, and in 1890 the school, now under the direction of Sara's daughter, Ada Nathan Castiglione, included 120 students. With the school, Sara had started a Sala Mazziniana for lectures and a workers' Sunday school to spread Mazzini's ideas. Prominent Mazzinians lectured there on topics ranging from prostitution to the family, from suffrage to the social question. Thus Sara Nathan provided both an alternative education and an alternative concept of woman to that of the liberal state.[31]

In 1868, at the age of eighteen, Gualberta Beccari founded what was to become the most important women's journal in Italy, *Donna*. It became the center of a large women's network that lasted into the twentieth century and prepared a second generation of activists. Beccari grew up with the revolution. Her father lost his fortune and his position in the period after the failed Venetian revolution of 1848. Threatened with prison for anti-Austrian activities, he took his family into exile. He worked as he could after that, and at one point Beccari acted as his secretary, noting, "I had overstepped the bounds conceded to my sex." Indeed, feminist perceptions followed quickly after revolutionary politics in Beccari's intellectual development. Her family survived the economic and emotional hardships of exile, she recalled, because her parents shared political convictions, familial authority, respect, and companionship. She was their only daughter and the only child to survive past infancy. Her own health was very poor, leaving her periodically unable to walk or talk. Although she never married and had no children, Beccari was often seen as a maternal figure, gentle and dedicated, even by those who disliked her feminism or her republican politics. She identified with other women's suffering. "Above all," she wrote, "I felt myself stirred to rebellion when I learned of some brutal husband who had beaten his wife; and I felt myself . . . painfully humiliated if I heard what happened from the woman herself." Even as a child, she could not tolerate misogynist remarks: "In every way, since I was a small child, I aimed at an order of things very different from what we had, in favor of women." Thus *Donna* grew out of the sense of sisterhood Beccari felt with all women, and that sense grew out of the strong national and sex identification of her childhood.[32]

True to its Risorgimento roots, *Donna* aspired to be a journal for all Italian women. Begun in Venice, it later moved to Bologna, where it expanded in the 1880s before falling on hard times at the end of that decade. *Donna* gathered in all the voices of activism in its early years, giving expression to all women who were concerned with women's education and socialization and who believed that these could be shaped by women's efforts, both formally in the educational system, and informally through women's literature and associations. Once again a network of female working relationships emerges. The reformer Adele Woena published her first essay in *Donna* beside famous women writers like Fuà; materialists like Maria Serafini appeared with poets like Francesca Zambusi del Lago; northerners like Beccari and southerners like Folliero could be read beside radicals like Mozzoni. Woena began her own women's journal, *L'aurora*, in 1872, the same year in which Folliero founded *Cornelia*. Olimpia Saccati, a contributor to *L'aurora*, began her own moderate journal, *Missione della donna*, which published articles by the far-from-moderate Ernesta Napollon Margarita, helping Napollon support herself and her children. Here anticlericals like Napollon engaged in debate with Catholic women educators. Thus the women's journals provided for a lively exchange of ideas, enabled activist women to keep in touch with each other, and kept readers informed on a wide variety of issues.

It is much more difficult to identify *Donna's* readers than its contributors. Begun as a four-page weekly, it became a sixteen-page bimonthly in 1871. Beccari tried to keep the cost down, but it may still have been more than working-class women could afford. One assumes that workers' associations subscribed, as they did to Mazzinian papers, while women and men of more comfortable means subscribed individually. The journal also reached legislators and teachers, and the Jesuits, who took pains to condemn its anticlerical feminism. Foreign subscriptions and those for "Italian provinces subject to Austria," or *Italia irredenta*, cost slightly more. *Donna* enjoyed an international reputation; articles were reprinted in *The Englishwoman's Review* in the 1870s and Julia Ward Howe encouraged subscriptions in America to bolster its finances.[33]

While *Donna's* contributors offered a wide range of ideas on women and their roles, Beccari clearly had an ideal of her own, that of "citizen mother." Her ideal intended to dignify women's traditional role, while emphasizing its political importance in the new state. Men in power were to be forced to recognize women's rights. Beccari's ideal was exemplified by her friend Adelaide Bono Cairoli. Cairoli had married at seventeen and had borne two daughters and five sons; all survived infancy, but only one of her sons survived the revolution. Her politics was, to a large extent, the politics of martyrdom. Announcing Cairoli's death in a black-bordered issue of *Donna* in 1871, Beccari chose terms like "self-abnegation," "sacrifice," "outstanding wife, heroic mother," to praise her friend.[34] These terms conformed to the most traditional description of women's role as the long-suffering "angel of the hearth." But there was much more to Beccari's eulogy. First of all, Cairoli's sacrifice had been an explicitly political act. Like Cornelia, the mother of the Gracchi who had sacrificed her children to the cause of social justice in ancient Rome, Cairoli had sacrificed her children to a political ideal. Beccari concluded that the ideal of the citizen mother was no "utopian dream," but a reality, exemplified in Cairoli and women like her. Women were a political example and a political force.

Thus Beccari's patriot mother image carried a sometimes veiled and sometimes naked threat to men in power. Women politicized children; ostracized, oppressed women would raise generations of politically alienated men and women, not true Italians. Women of the revolution would abandon the men of their party if the revolution continued to neglect women's needs. Even as she dignified women's role at home, Beccari and others insisted that women could not fulfill this role until they had better education, a reformed family law, and political rights. As political pariahs, women would undermine the nation they had helped to create. Men allied with women activists carried this message into Parliament.[35]

In 1874, Beccari's annual tribute to Cairoli stressed yet another aspect of citizen motherhood and revealed that women's goals in the revolution looked not only outward to political life, but inward to the family. Beccari wrote of the joys and humiliations women shared in their maternal roles. She observed that mothers of all classes would give their lives for their children, and for the dreams they had for them. But women received little return for these great outpourings of love. Children sent to elementary school soon scorned uneducated mothers; sons once doted upon soon emulated authoritarian husbands. Women bound themselves in a role that too often became their only identity.[36] But a citizen mother like Cairoli was recognized as a central force in her children's lives. The dignity and moral authority supposedly exercised by the "angel of the hearth" in fact belonged to the citizen mother who educated herself and who taught her children civic responsibility and principles of justice. Women like Cairoli or Laura Mantegazza provided the models for improving women's status in both private and public life.

In addition to her political commitments, the citizen mother was often a woman wage earner. In 1885 Beccari measured women's progress since unification by the jobs open to women in various classes, from opportunities in teaching to political journalism to skilled handicrafts that provided a living wage. But again she emphasized the connection between personal necessity and political gains for women as a group. As early as 1871, she promoted the idea of an exposition of women's work to prove the extent of women's economic contribution to Italy. To Beccari, the purpose of such an exposition was to "force man to acknowledge . . . and to concede [to woman] . . . [the rights that] he had usurped."[37]

Education constituted another essential element of women's status, and *Donna* consistently carried articles on all levels and aspects of women's instruction. But by 1878 it was clear to Beccari that no combination of new roles in education and work with traditional goals in the home could solve women's problems and they all fell within women's proper sphere of action. In its first issue of 1878, *Donna* focused openly on women's gravest problem, legalized prostitution, and the necessity of women's organized opposition to it. Women had to act as an organized political force to raise their status. Citizen motherhood thus merged into the other images of women running through *Donna's* pages; political organizers, teachers, university students, working women, women in associations. While never divorced from citizen motherhood, these models began to build toward the image of an independent woman.

Perhaps Beccari's citizen mother was a "utopian dream" after all, for she was a woman who had dignity, love, and a sense of fulfillment in her family life, who had education and work that gave her the capacity for economic independence, and who also had a sense of community with other women and all Italians. She was the fulfillment of the revolution, a free citizen in a progressive, unified state, a symbol of equality and social justice that has yet to be realized.

It is evident that the revolution affected attitudes toward women's roles, at least in the politicized classes. The women of the revolution combined traditional "women's work" with revolutionary political activity and in the process gained political skills that activist women turned to women's issues after unification. In addition to continuing political networks with men in their own factions, women joined with women in other political groups to promote needed reforms. They used the national educational system to educate other women, to support themselves, and to extend the ideal of womanhood: through their work, their example, and their teaching, they posited a citizen mother ideal in contrast to otherworldly images of "the angel of the hearth" and the Blessed Virgin Mary. For women to achieve their most traditional roles, those roles had to acquire a public dimension. The patriot mother image represented the unity of women's private and public lives and women's demand for more rights in both spheres.

The lives of Fuà, Folliero, Nathan, and Beccari illustrate how women acted to bend the results of the national revolution to meet their needs. They built on their own political experience, including female political networks. They fostered various ideals of the patriot mother to improve their position in public and private life. And they used the national educational system created by the revolution, along with their own alternative programs and institutions, to reach out to all Italian women and to alter the status of women in fundamental ways. While feminists extended the image of woman beyond Mazzini's ideal of the mobilized republican mother and toward an image of the independent woman, reformers like Fuà countered, at the very centers of liberal patriarchalism, the resignation, passivity, privatization, and other-worldliness of the Blessed Virgin Mary ideal. Both approaches, sometimes working in cooperation and sometimes in conflict with each other, were essential to creating possibilities for change in the status of Italian women.

Notes

1. The first Italian parliament met in 1861; Venetia became part of Italy in 1866, Rome in 1870. Thus women's action within the institutions of unified Italy started in 1861, even as their revolutionary activity continued in other areas for another decade.

2. Gualberta Alaide Beccari and the Mazzinians often used the phrase *"madre cittadina"*; others, like Erminia Fuà Fusinato, evoked the ideal of the patriotic woman and mother without the phrase. The image dominated women's literature in the 1870s.

3. As politicizing step, see Linda Kerber, "Daughters of Columbia: Educating Women for the Republic, 1787–1805," in *The Hofstadter Aegis: A Memorial*, ed. Stanley Elkins and Eric McKitrick (New York; Alfred A. Knopf, 1974), p. 58; as sisterhood, contrast Nancy Cott, *The Bonds of Womanhood: "Woman's Sphere" in New England, 1780–1835* (New Haven: Yale University Press, 1977) with Kathryn Kish Sklar, *Catharine Beecher: A Study in American Domesticity* (New Haven: Yale University Press, 1973).

4. On Carlotta Benettini see especially Evelina Rinaldi, "Una fida seguace di Mazzini: Lettere di lui a Carlotta Benettini," *Rassegna storica del Risorgimento* 10(1923): 535–600.

5. In 1870 a vocational school for Milanese girls with an elementary education but no job skills opened to prepare girls for trades where they could support themselves; tuition was waived for daughters of members of the mutual aid society. After Mantegazza died in 1873, Sormani continued. Reaching other activists through the pages of *Donna*, she solicited funds for the day-care center and received enthusiatic support for the vocational school, while contributing regular reports on feminist speeches in Milan.

On Mantegazza, see Giuseppe Mazzini to Laura Solera Mantegazza, December 9, 1850, in Mazzini, *Scritti editi ed inediti*, 100 vols. (Imola: Cooperativa Tipografico-Editrice, 1906–43) 45:51–52, hereafter cited as *Scritti*. For surplus funds, see Emilio Bruno, ed., *La donna nella beneficenza in Italia*, 4 vols. (Turin: Ditta Eredi Botta, 1910–13) 2:22–3, hereafter cited as *Beneficenza*. Biographical articles on Mantegazza are in Francesco Orestano, ed., *Eroine, ispiratrici, e donne di eccezione*, Series 7 of *Enciclopedia biografica bibliografica italiana* [EBBI] (Milan: Istituto editoriale italiano, 1940), p. 250; *Dizionario del Risorgimento nazionale: dalle origini a Roma capitale, fatti e persone* [DRN], 4 vols. (Milan: Vallardi, 1930–37) 3: 474–75; Gualberta Alaide Beccari, "Necrologia: Laura Solera Mantegazza," *Donna*, October 10, 1873, pp. 1556–57; Giovanni Urtoller, *"Laura Solera Mantegazza* di Paolo Mantegazza," *Cornelia*, Aug. 1, 1877, pp. 129–30.

On Sormani see DRN 2:596–97; *Eroine*, EBBI, p. 93. For works by Sormani, see "Appello alle giovani madri milanesi," *Donna*, Dec. 25, 1873, p. 1654; "Sul rendiconto dell'associazione di mutuo soccorso," *Donna*, Apr. 10, 1874, p. 1763.

On the school, see Ernesta Napollon Margarita, "La scuola professionale femminile di Milano," *Donna*, Feb. 19, 1971, p. 597; for an example of a report on Mozzoni, see I.S.C. [Sormani], "Corrispondenza da Milano," *Donna*, Jan. 15, 1871, p. 577.

6. For one Mazzinian women's group, see Rinaldi, "Una fida seguace," p. 546; Oscar Greco, *Bibliobiografia femminile italiana del XIX secolo* (Venice: Presso i principali librai d'Italia, 1875), p. 450, hereafter cited as *Bibliobiografia*; and Mazzini, *Scritti* 72: 121–22. Among a dozen members, two were shopkeepers, designated as "workers." On Mazzinians as revolutionaries and as feminists, the best source is *Donna*. See further, Franca Pieroni Bortolotti, *Alle origini del movimento femminile in Italia 1848–1892* (Turin: Einaudi, 1963), and Judith Jeffrey Howard, "The Woman Question in Italy, 1861–1880," (Ph.D. diss., University of Connecticut, 1977).

7. Raymond Grew, *A Sterner Plan for Italian Unity: The Italian National Society in the Risorgimento* (Princeton: Princeton University Press, 1963), pp. 449–50, 411–13.

8. E. F. Richards, ed., *Mazzini's Letters to an English Family*, 3 vols. (London: John Lane, 1920). See also Giuseppe Mazzini to Matilde Ashurst Biggs [January 16, 1865], *Scritti* 80: 17–20. Articles in *The Englishwoman's Review* include Ernesta Napollon's letter, "An Italian View of Women's Suffrage," September 15, 1880, pp. 395–96, trans. and reprinted from *Cornelia;* and original articles, "Salvatore Morelli," Nov. 15, 1880, pp. 495–98: "Women of the Working Classes in Italy," Aug. 14, 1886, pp. 337–44. See further Sara Nathan "L'incapacità delle donne," *Donna*, Dec. 5, 1883, pp. 2–4, trans. Luisa To-sko from *The Englishwoman's Review*; note obituary for Caroline Ashurst Stansfeld, *Donna*, May 2, 1885, pp. 299–300; and "La spigolatrice—onoranza a Giuseppe Nathan," [eulogy for Joseph and Sara Nathan by Emily Ashurst Venturi], *Donna*, Dec. 31, 1883, p. 23.

9. For example, Caroline Ashurst Stansfeld's husband, James Stansfeld, was a prominent early figure in Butler's movement, and Joseph Nathan was the early organizer for Butler's crusade in Italy.

10. See Judith Jeffrey Howard, "The Civil Code of 1865 and the Origins of the Feminist Movement in Italy," in *The Italian Immigrant Woman in North America: Proceedings of the 10th Annual Conference of the American Italian Historical Association and the Canadian Italian Historical Association*, ed. Betty Boyd Caroli, Robert F. Harney, and Lidio F. Tomasi (Toronto: Multicultural History Society of Ontario, 1978), pp. 14–23.

11. In the period 1881–1901 male illiteracy nationwide dropped to 42 percent and female illiteracy to 54 percent. Regional disparities must also be noted. In 1881, 32 percent of the population over five in Piedmont was illiterate, compared to 81 percent in the area around Naples and in Sicily. All illiteracy figures are from Maurice F. Neufeld, *Italy: School for Awakening Countries. The Italian Labor Movement in Its Political, Social, and Economic Setting from 1800 to 1960* (Ithaca: New York State School of Industrial and Labor Relations, Cornell University, 1961), p. 523.
    In 1862–63, 1,807 Italian comunes provided no girls' elementary schools, while only 253 areas of comparable size made no provision for boys. See Italy, Statistica del Regno d'Italia, *Istruzione pubblica e privata: anno scolastico 1862–63*, 2 vols. (Turin: Enrico Dalmazzo Tipografo, 1865), p. xx, hereafter cited as *Statistica, 1862–63;* Giovanni Scavia, *Dell'istruzione professionale e secondaria femminile in Francia, Germania, Svizzera e Italia: Memorie ed osservazioni presentate al Ministero della Pubblica Istruzione del Regno d'Italia* (Turin: Tommaso Vaccarino, 1866), p. 151, hereafter cited as *Istruzione.*

12. In 1862–63, there were 13,817 women elementary school teachers, outnumbered by 17,604 male counterparts. (*Statistica, 1862–63,* p. xx). In 1866, 26 teacher-training schools constituted the total number of secondary schools "accessible to girls of any rank or condition" (Scavia, *Istruzione,* p. 150). But in 1872–73, there were 79 women's teacher-training schools, and their enrollments far exceeded that of the 36 men's schools. By 1900, there were 5,513 girls in boys' secondary schools. See Italy, Ministero di Agricoltura, Industria e Commercio, Direzione Generale di Statistica, *Notizie statistiche sulla istruzione pubblica e privata nel regno* (Rome: Tipografia Eredi Botta, 1882), p. 36; and Dina Bertoni Jovine, "Funzione emancipatrice della scuola e contributo della donna all'attività educativa," in *L'emancipazione femminile in Italia: un secolo di discussione 1861–1961* (Florence: La Nuova Italia, 1963), p. 239, hereafter cited as "Funzione emancipatrice."

13. See Bertoni Jovine, "Funzione emancipatrice," p. 247.

14. See the Jesuit attack by Francesco Salis Seewis on Fanny Zampini Salazar's moderate journal, *La rassegna femminile,* "Rivista della stampa," *Civiltà cattolica,* 9 (Dec. 1887–Apr. 1888): 465–73; Salazar's answer was "Difendiamoci," *Rassegna femminile,* March 1888, pp. 141–47; for the debate between Catholic spokeswoman Marietta Bianchini and feminists Ernesta Napollon and Erminia Canevini see *Donna*, Nov. 30, 1878, pp. 49–54; July 15, 1879, pp. 163–65; in *Missione della donna,* see Bianchini, "La questione femminile," 6(1879): 129–35; "La donna emancipata," 10(1883): 52–56; and "Lettera aperta alla Signora Erminia Canevini," ibid., pp. 359–60, which show the progression of her thought.

15. On the significance of the normal schools and of the Casati Law, see Dina Bertoni

Jovine, *Storia dell'educazione popolare in Italia* (Bari: Laterza, 1965), p. 139, hereafter cited as *Storia dell'educazione*; "Funzione emancipatrice," p. 228, and her "La legge Casati," in *Problemi dell'unità d'Italia: Atti del II convegno di studi gramsciani* (Rome: Editori Riuniti, 1962), pp. 441–47.

16. This account based on exposé articles by Matilde Serao in her paper *Corriere di Roma*, "Per le signore; la maestra," June 8, 1886, p. 1; "Le vie dolorose; la maestra Donati," June 23, 1886, p. 1; "Le vie dolorose; la maestra rurale," June 24, 1886, p. 1; "Le vie dolorose; il rimedio," June 26, 1886; p. 1; "Per le signore; la maestra De Tranis," July 27, 1887, p. 1; "La condanna del seduttore," Oct. 2, 1887, p. 2.

17. Greco, *Bibliobiografia*, pp. 235–54; Maria Bandini Buti, ed., *Scrittrici e poetesse*, 2 vols. (Rome: Istituto editoriale italiano, 1941), 1: 279–80, hereafter cited as *Scrittrici*; P. G. Molmenti, ed., *Erminia Fuà-Fusinato e i suoi ricordi* (Milan: Treves, 1877); R[uggero] Bonghi, "Lettera alla Direttrice," [Fanny Zampini Salazar], *La Rassegna degli interessi femminili,* Jan. 15, 1887, pp. 3–5.

18. Erminia Fuà Fusinato, *Scritti educativi*, 2 vols. (Rome: Franco Campitelli, 1931). For her image, see Greco, *Bibliobiografia*, p. 253, and Aurelia Cimino Folliero, "Erminia Fuà Fusinato," *Cornelia*, Oct. 16, 1876, p. 171.

19. For patriotic themes see Fuà, *Scritti* 2: 192, 237, 313; "Madre nella scuola e maestra nella famiglia," *Donna*, August 25, 1871, pp. 753–55; on teaching, see Fuà, *Scritti* 2:134–37; 179–81. Translations from the Italian are mine.

20. Fuà, *Scritti* 2: 170, 311; on her limits see Bertoni Jovine, "Funzione emancipatrice," pp. 235–37 and *Scritti* 2: 168–72. On the work ethic for women in postrevolutionary periods see Kerber, "Daughters of Columbia," pp. 41–43.

21. Fuà, *Scritti* 2: 152, 189, 210, 238, 291–94; "Ciascuno al suo posto," *Cornelia*, May 16, 1873, pp. 89–90.

22. Fuà, Ibid., pp. 134–35. On split see Bortolotti, *Origini* pp. 125–26; Niccolò Tommaseo was also an influential advocate of "true emancipationist" ideas. For his influence on the tone of *Missione* see Olimpia Saccati to Niccolò Tommaseo, Feb. 28, 1874, Biblioteca Nazionale Centrale, Florence, Carteggio Tommaseo, 126/4.

23. Greco, *Bibliobiografia*, p. 248.

24. See Bortolotti, *Origini*, pp. 34–133–34; and Cecilia Folliero de Luna, *De l'éducation des femmes, ou moyens de les faire contribuer a la félicité publique, en assurant leur propre bien-être* (Paris: Ambroise DuPont et Cie, 1827); on Aurelia, see Greco, *Bibliobiografia*, pp. 205–6; DRN 2: 696; and especially Theodore Stanton's biographical editorial note to her "Italy: A General Review" in *The Woman Question in Europe: A Series of Original Essays* (New York: G. P. Putnam's Sons, 1884), p. 310. See also her disguised autobiographical sketch, "La poesia del lavoro, " *Cornelia*, October 16, 1874, pp. 169–71.

25. Aurelia Cimino Folliero de Luna, "Alle donne italiane," *Cornelia*, Dec. 1, 1872, pp. 1–3; "L'indolenza in Italia e le donne italiane," *Donna*, Jan. 1, 1871–Feb. 5, 1871, pp. 566–67; 571–72; 575–76; 579–80; 583–84; 587–88; "La moglie e la madre," *Cornelia*, Feb. 16, 1876, pp. 41–43; "Pei nostri figli," *Cornelia*, May 1, 1876, pp. 81–83.

26. See Folliero, "L'indolenza," *Donna*, January 1, 1871, p. 576 on Smiles; "Excelsior!" *Cornelia*, March 16, 1873, pp. 57–8. On the "self-help" literature in Italy, see Bertoni Jovine, *Storia dell'educazione*, pp. 84–89.

27. Folliero's correspondence, Ministero d'Agricultura, Industria, e Commercio, 1861–1890, Busta 50, f.6; report published as *Stabilimenti agrari femminili e lavori industriali delle donne all'esposizione di Parigi,* 2nd ed. (Florence: Tipografia cooperativa, 1879), and in *Cornelia* from Aug. 1, 1879 to Sept. 1, 1879, pp. 130–32; 139–41; 147–50. For international attention to Darnètal following Folliero's account, see *La Nazione* (Florence), Jan. 23, 1881, pp. 1–2; on Folliero's school, se *Rassegna femminile,* May 15, 1888, pp. 322–23, and Bortolotti, *Origini*, pp. 151–52.

28. A[ntonia] Fratti. *Sara Levi Nathan* (Pesaro: Nobili, 1888). See also Janet Nathan to

Jessie White Mario, Instituto per la Storia del Risorgimento italiano, Rome [ISR], Carteggi Jessie White Mario, Busta 435, n. 61; Mazzini to Mrs. P. A. Taylor, Aug. 23, [1870], *English Family* 3:241. Translation is mine.

29.   See "La donna e l'operaio," *Il Dovere*, Aug. 11, 1878, p. 1; and "Il clero e la scuola," ibid., June 5, 1877, p. 1. See also *Donna cattolica e donna mazziniana; Lettera critica d'un medico* (Rome: Associazione democratica Giuditta Tavani Arquati di Roma, 1891); and Mazzini, "The Duties of Man," in [Emily Ashurt Venturi], *Joseph Mazzini: A Memoir.* (London: Alexander and Shepheard, [1885]), pp. 53–54. On Nathan as role model see "Letter to Sarina Nathan," *Il Dovere*, March 11, 1877, p. 1, and her reply, ibid., April 6, 1877, p. 3.

30.   See "Il Comizio dei comizi," ibid., Feb. 16, 1881, pp. 1, 2; on Congress, "La donna e l'operaio," ibid., Aug. 11, 1878, p. 1; and Bortolotti, *Origini*, p. 145.

31.   See "Scuola Mazzini," *Il Dovere*, March 26, 1877, p. 2; Sara Nathan to Jessie White Mario, "Sottoscrizione per fondare una scuola chiamata Scuola Mazzini," ISR, Carteggi Jessie White Mario, Busta 430, n. 22 [5]; Jessie White Mario's manuscript on the school, ibid., Busta 405, n.6 [3], and "La premiazione delle fanciulle alla scuola Mazzini di Roma," *L'emancipazione* (Rome), February 23, 1890, p. 1.

32.   See Giulia Cavallari, ed., "Alcune lettere di Adelaide Cairoli," in *Miscellanea di studi storici in onore di Antonio Manno*, 2 vols. (Turin: Bocca, 1912) 2: 528n; DRN 2: 215; Bandini Buti, *Scrittrici* 1:74. Translations are mine.

33.   [Raffaele Ballerini], "Una moderna educatrice della donna italiana," *Civiltà cattolica*, 11 (June 11, 1870–Sept. 10, 1870): 659–663; 2 (March–June, 1871): 31–32; articles in *The Englishwoman's Review* included one by Georgina Saffi under "Foreign Notes and News," Aug. 15, 1876, p. 371; for the reference to Julia Ward Howe's letters in the Samuel Ward Collection, New York Public Library, I am indebted to Mary Grant of George Washington University.

34.   *Donna*, April 2, 1871, p. 621; see also issues of March 27, 1872, pp. 973–75, and March 7, 1873, pp. 1357–59.

35.   See Anna Maria Mozzoni, *Del voto politico delle donne: Lettura tenuta da A. M. Mozzoni. Estratto dal periodico La Donna A. IX—30 marzo 1877*, N. 290 (Venice: Tipografia del commercio di Marco Visentini, 1877), p. 18; on p. 34 Mozzoni pays tribute to Mazzini for his ideals and to Benedetto Cairoli, who presented a bill for women's suffrage in Parliament. Mozzoni circulated a suffrage petition after her speech.

36.   Gualberta Alaide Beccari, "Adelaide Cairoli-Bono. La scienza del cuore," *Donna*, March 27, 1874, pp. 1737–40; Olimpia Saccati, "La donna qual'è e quale dovrebbe essere, ovvero se l'istruzione della donna sia un bene od un'utopia," *L'Aurora*, June–July, 1873, pp. 268–76; Folliero, "L'indolenza," *Donna*, Feb. 5, 1871, pp. 587–88.

37.   Gualberta Alaide Beccari, "Il nostro quindicesimo anno di vita," *Donna*, Dec. 15, 1885, p. 2: Gualberta Alaide Beccari, "Esposizione de'lavori femminili in Firenze," ibid., April 16, 1871, p. 632. Translation is mine.

Suggestions for Further Reading

Works helpful to the general reader or beginning researcher for background in nineteenth-century Italian history include Maurice F. Neufeld, *Italy: School for Awakening Countries. The Italian Labor Movement in Its Political, Social, and Economic Setting from 1800 to 1960* (Ithaca, N.Y.: New York State School of Industrial and Labor Relations, Cornell University, 1961); Giuliano Procacci, *History of the Italian People*, trans. Anthony Paul (London: Weidenfeld and Nicolson, 1970); Christopher Seton-Watson, *Italy from Liberalism to Fascism, 1870–1925* (London: Methuen, 1967); and Edward R. Tannenbaum and Emiliana P. Noether, eds., *Modern Italy: A Topical History Since 1861* (New York: New York University Press, 1974). More specific information on revolutionary organizations is found in Alessandro Galante-Garrone, *I radicali in Italia (1849–1925)* (Milan: Garzanti, 1973), and in Raymond Grew, *A Sterner Plan for Italian Unity: The Italian National Society in the Risorgimento* (Princeton: Princeton University Press, 1963); Grew provides material on women's organizations while Galante-Garrone does not. Also see Priscilla Robertson, *Revolutions of 1848: A Social History* (Princeton: Princeton University Press, 1952) for material on women in the Risorgimento.

Few English-language sources deal with women's status in nineteenth-century Italy. Theodore Stanton, ed., *The Woman Question in Europe: A Series of Original Essays* (New York: Putnam, 1884), contains two still-useful essays and sometimes more useful notes by Stanton. The activist Fanny Zampini Salazar reported on women's status in "Condition of Women in Italy," *Report of the International Council of Women* (Washington, D.C.: Darly, 1888); other proceedings of international congresses are listed in Judith Jeffrey Howard, "The Woman Question in Italy, 1861–1880" (Ph.D. dissertation, University of Connecticut, 1977), p. 236, the only recent, book-length study on the topic. Other current scholarship includes Louise A. Tilly, "Urban Growth, Industrialization and Women's Employment in Milan, Italy, 1881–1911," *Journal of Urban History* 3 (August 1977): 67–84; and essays by Mary Gibson on prostitution, by Emiliana P. Noether on southern Italian peasant women, and by Judith Jeffrey Howard on legal oppression and feminist beginnings, all in Luciano J. Iorizzo and Robert F. Harney, eds., *The Italian Immigrant Woman in North America* (Toronto: Multicultural History Society of Ontario, 1979).

Any discussion of the Italian scholarship must begin with Franca Pieroni Bortolotti, *Alle origini del movimento femminile in Italia, 1848–1892* (Turin: Einaudi, 1963), the pioneering work in the field, which contains invaluable bibliographical material. Some excellent essays appear in Società Umanitaria (Fondazione P. M. Loria), *L'emancipazione femminile in Italia: un secolo di discussione 1861–1961* (Florence: La Nuova Italia, 1963). Dina Bertoni Jovine, *Enciclopedia moderna della donna*, 2 vols. (Rome: Riuniti, 1965–1969) is also useful. See further, Emiliana P. Noether, "The Status of Italian Women's History," *Conference Group in Women's History Newsletter* 3 (April 1978): 2–4.

Italian women's periodicals are indispensible for this research. One should begin with the Biblioteca Nazionale in Florence where the longest runs of *La donna* (Venice, then Bologna), *Cornelia* (Florence), *La missione della donna* (Alba), *L'aurora* (Modena), and other important titles are located. Compare and contrast on women's issues, *Civiltà cattolica*, widely available in the United States, and *Il dovere* (Rome), found at the Biblioteca di storia moderna e contemporanea in Rome.

For individual biographies, indispensable bio-bibliographies, and manuscript materials, see notes.

11/"The Mother Half of Humanity": American Women in the Peace and Preparedness Movements in World War I

Barbara J. Steinson

The outbreak of World War I in Europe in August 1914 spurred the formation of wartime relief, peace, and military preparedness organizations by American women. Their endeavors, which coincided with the increased momentum of the suffrage campaign, made the war years a time of unprecedented female activism in the United States. This essay delineates some key themes woven throughout the fabric of women activists' wartime experiences.

Although women channeled their energies into diverse and often conflicting efforts during the war, they frequently invoked the same ideology of nurturant motherhood to justify and to promote their efforts. An explanation of the meaning of this ideology in the early twentieth century is followed by a discussion of its application in two organizations with very different goals—the Woman's Peace Party and the Woman's Section of the Navy League. The essay then explores the personal and social implications of women's wartime activism. It will be argued that women experienced increased self-esteem and discovered unknown capabilities in their own sex. As they immersed themselves in these activities, they gained strength from supportive companionship of other women, which often evolved into a feeling of sisterhood. Although frequently covert, a current of feminism surfaced in many of their organizational activities.[1]

The Ideology of Nurturant Motherhood

The ideology of nurturant motherhood presupposed that women's maternal and reproductive roles made them sexually distinct from males not only physically but also temperamentally, psychologically, and intellectually. This credo, pervasive in early twentieth century American society, held that women instinctively gave their unselfish devotion to the nurture and protection of life. The female role was one of sacrifice and of service to others. Women with diametrically opposed views on contemporary issues and on the implications of this ideology in relation to their role outside the home accepted the basic premise that they were endowed with special sex-linked personality traits and responsibilities.

Early twentieth-century feminists combined the belief in the ideology of nurturant motherhood with the conviction that women should have equal political, legal, educational, and economic rights with men. Many contemporary feminists, "steeped in a tradition which saw women as civilizing and moralizing forces in society," charged that society's problems were the result of male domination.[2] Men, by nature aggressive and warlike, had created a society that denigrated the value of life itself. The expansion of woman's sphere beyond the narrow confines of the home would imbue the public sector with qualities that only women possessed. Full female participation in public life would create a more humane and peaceful world.[3]

But the ideology of nurturant motherhood also permeated the language of those opposed to an expansion of the female role. Antifeminists argued that women's physical and temperamental uniqueness made them unsuited for active roles in the public sector. Women should instead influence society through their husbands and children. They were to nurture, protect, and serve those within their homes; only men were responsible for conducting the business of the world outside the home. The nurturant mother thus depended on men for protection and support. Women's participation in the male sector would not purify it, as the feminists argued, but would only corrupt women as they abandoned their duties in the home.[4]

Since the ideology of nurturant motherhood was both pervasive and versatile, it is not surprising that it was often employed by women activists to explain and support their efforts during World War I. Similarly, women's belief in their temperamental and physical uniqueness frequently influenced the form of the organizational activities. Many women deliberately chose to form new organizations limited to their own sex or, at least, to work in groups in which they had some influence. They were not content to pour their energies into male-dominated groups that lacked appreciation for their special attributes and ignored their viewpoints.

The determination to form autonomous organizations was demonstrated as early as August 1914 by women planning a peace parade in New York City.[5] They spurned offers of cooperation from males who "expressed themselves heartily in accord with the movement." When the parade idea was proposed, the organizers explained, men were simply "overlooked" because it was to be a "woman's protest against all warfare amongst civilized nations." After further reflection, however, they consciously decided their demonstration should be exclusively a "feminine achievement." Males wishing to protest would have to "organize a parade of their own."[6] The *New York Times* accurately concluded that the parade of fifteen hundred women down Fifth Avenue in late August was evidence of a "definite determination on the part of a considerable number of women to exert a practical influence on a field of public action from which in the past they have been almost wholly withdrawn."[7]

Women's decision to form their own war-related organizations as well as the versatility of the ideology that helped to shape their attitudes can be seen in two new women's groups that opposed each other during the war. The Woman's Peace Party (WPP), an organization that rested on feminist and pacifist principles, combined the traditonal ideology of women as the nurturing and protective sex with feminist demands for new responsibilities in the public sector. Supporters of the Woman's Section of the Navy League (WSNL), the largest women's group promoting increased national defense, provide a more ambiguous case study. Elements of both the feminist and antifeminist interpretations of women's nurturant role are evident in Women's Section declarations.[8]

In both organizations nurturant motherhood gave members distinctive positions within their respective movements that insured some measure of recognition for their viewpoints. Certainly not all supporters of these groups utilized the stereotypical view of the female temperament or women's biological and nurturant role as mothers to promote their causes, and undoubtedly some made these appeals for reasons of expediency only. It is also clear, however, that nurturant motherhood, regardless of its usage, was not merely a rhetorical ploy. These early twentieth-century activists had internalized this ideology and seldom questioned its basic premises. References to women's nurturing and protective functions served as rallying points, especially in the early phases of organization or in challenging situations.

Without female participation, it is unlikely that there would have been a viable peace movement in the United States after 1914. Primarily newcomers to the movement, women infused a new spirit at a time when established, male-dominated organizations were rapidly becoming dormant. The new peace movement was more innovative, activist, and critical of the government than the prewar societies. Women supplied much of the initiative, leadership, and fervor, and performed much of the difficult, but unrecognized, behind-the-scenes organizational work that made the existence of the post-1914 peace movement possible.[9]

The formation of the Woman's Peace Party was an event of signal importance in the emergence of the new peace movement. Jane Addams issued a call for a woman's peace conference in January 1915 largely in response to popular pressure created by two European feminist pacifists, Rosika Schwimmer and Emmeline Pethick-Lawrence. They had succeeded in directing the vague horror and distress felt by many American women into a demand for a national woman's peace movement.[10] Critical of the ineffectual male-dominated peace societies and deploring the "man-made" war, the women who gathered in Washington, D.C., developed a platform that included planks calling for neutral mediation, limitation of armaments, democratic control of foreign policy, removal of the economic causes of war, and "the further humanizing of governments by the extension of the franchise to women."[11] The WPP platform placed the new organization in the vanguard of the American peace movement; this was the most comprehensive peace plan yet adopted by an American body.

The suffrage plank became the most controversial feature of the platform.

Although the constitution required only "substantial sympathy with the fundamental purpose of the organization" for membership, few antisuffragists joined the WPP. Jane Addams, among others, defended the suffrage plank as "absolutely fundamental to the undertaking" and essential to the goal of a "humanizing conception of government."[12] If women were to ease the international situation, they had to have a voice in their governments. The WPP, a feminist organization, visualized an expansion of the female role.

The dual components of early twentieth-century feminism—the ideology of nurturant motherhood and the demand for women's equal participation in the world outside the home—were evident in the preamble to the WPP constitution written by Anna Garlin Spencer. Spencer, a minister and social reformer with years of frustrating experience in the male-dominated peace movement, provided the rationale for a separate women's organization. Her preamble took as its credo the role of women as protectors and conservators of humanity. As "custodians of the life of the ages," women felt a "peculiar moral passion of revolt" against the cruelty and waste of war. They had responsibility for children and for the "helpless and unfortunate"; they would no longer "endure without protest the added burden of maimed and invalided men and poverty-stricken widows and orphans which war places on us." The responsibility for starting "each generation onward toward a better humanity" belonged to women, but war denied the rule of reason and justice and "rendered impotent the idealism of the race" which women had sought to instill in their children. For these reasons, Spencer explained, "as human beings and the mother half of humanity, we demand that our right to be consulted in the settlement of questions concerning not alone the life of individuals but of nations be recognized and respected." Women must share in decisions involving war and peace "in all the courts of high debate—within the home, the church, the industrial order, and the state."[13] Spencer's preamble elicited an enthusiastic response from women at the mass meeting of the Washington conference because it articulated a system of beliefs to which they subscribed intellectually and emotionally.

Other speeches delivered at the January mass meeting echoed the message in the preamble. For example, Rosika Schwimmer reminded her listeners that like the mothers of Europe they were "voiceless to prevent some incident" that might "bring for your children what has happened to our children."[14] Critical of the failure of men to prevent war, other speakers suggested that the initiative had passed to women. Although there were "thousands of men . . . convinced that this sacrifice of the human race is unnecessary," Jane Addams noted they were not speaking out to stop the war. "If women in Europe . . . hear a message from the women in America protesting against this sacrifice," she speculated, "they may take courage to protest too; then men may think it is time to call a halt."[15]

Undoubtedly the most eloquent address at the meeting was delivered by Anna Howard Shaw, then president of the National American Woman's Suffrage Association and one of the suffrage movement's most effective orators. Shaw subsequently took no part in WPP activities, but her speech was a moving declaration of the stake that women had in war. "And when the question comes—who is the most deeply interested in war," she asked, "shall the very sex which furnished more than mere implements of war, shall that sex sit dumb in the face of outrage against them and that which deeply concerns them?" Women had to be given a voice in these decisions because of their contributions as mothers: "And looking into the face of that one dead man we see two dead, the man and the life of the woman who gave him birth; the life she wrought into his life! And looking into his dead face someone asks a woman, what does a woman know about war? What, what, friends in the face of a crime like that, what does man know about war!"[16]

Many of these same arguments were repeated at the International Congress of Women held at The Hague in April 1915.[17] Over forty American women, most of them WPP members, participated in the congress convened to "protest against war and to discuss ways and means whereby war [would] become an impossibility in the future." Membership in the congress required agreement with the two principles that "international disputes shall be settled by pacific means" and that "parliamentary franchise should be extended to women."[18] Rosika Schwimmer pleaded emotionally and successfully for the congress to send delegations of women with their resolutions to foreign capitals. "When our sons are killed by millions," she exclaimed, "let us, mothers, only try to to do good by going to the kings and emperors, without any other danger than a refusal!"[19] With their diverse nationalities and their differences of opinion on the mediation question, the delegates were eager to affirm that as mothers or potential mothers they shared a sisterhood that transcended nationality and controversies pertaining to mediation. Reflecting on the bonds between women at the congress, Madeline Doty, a feminist lawyer, concluded that solidarity was achieved through a shared belief in the sacredness of life.[20] Poet Angela Morgan, another American delegate, thought the congress had manifested the "strongest cosmic force in the world"—motherhood.[21]

The pervasive belief among WPP members that women's maternal role gave them a special stake in opposing war did not mean that there was unanimity within the organization concerning policies and tactics. WPP branches were allowed considerable discretion in pursuing local activities, and were only asked for "substantial agreement" with the WPP platform. This flexibility enabled the WPP to encompass a wide range of opinions and permitted the branches to respond to current events as they saw fit.[22]

The efforts of the organization in 1915 and 1916 were primarily along educational lines: informing the public about the necessity for neutral mediation and about the dangers of military preparedness. Although agitation for mediation was, of course, directed mainly at President Woodrow Wilson, their antimilitarist propaganda was directed not only at Washington but also at state and local governments. In 1916, WPP efforts increasingly centered on opposition to universal military training in the schools, a program of action that enabled the party to capitalize on women's concerns as mothers.[23]

Diversity of opinion within the organization became more pronounced as the United States moved closer to war with Germany. Following the break in diplomatic relations in early February 1917, the WPP and other peace organizations faced a "testing time." Many branches ceased all their activities, some disbanded, and the national WPP avoided policy decisions by deferring matters to the branches. Although many WPP leaders supported agitation for a referendum on war, for example, the party took no official position on the matter. After the United States entered the war in April, national WPP leaders focused their attention on proposals for the international women's peace conference after the war and eschewed any active antiwar agitation.[24]

The only branch to continue challenging government policies after April was the one in New York City (NYC-WPP) led by Crystal Eastman, a feminist lawyer and social activist. In an attempt to persuade Addams, the national WPP president, that the party must continue to play an active role, Eastman invoked the ideology of nurturant motherhood to buttress her arguments. As mothers, women had a "more intimate sense of the value of human life" and thus, she contended, there was more "meaning and passion in a woman's organization to end war than in an organization of men and women with the same aim." Concerned the party had lost sight of this fundamental premise, she suggested WPP sponsorship of a series of mothers' mass meetings to organize the "instinctive feelings of the common woman" for peace. She warned Addams that unless the WPP took advantage of woman's "greater regard for life, both intellectually and emotionally," there was no reason to maintain a separate woman's peace organization.[25]

The national WPP rejected Eastman's recommendation, and the New York mothers' mass meeting did not serve as a model for other branches. The episode is important, however, in demonstrating the persistence of the motherhood ideology as a rationalization for action, in this case for action that many perceived as radical and provocative. It also reveals that the belief in the ideology of nurturant motherhood crossed generational lines within organizations. Eastman, later described by Freda Kirchwey, editor of *The Nation*, as a "symbol of what the free woman might be," was often at odds with older national WPP leaders. They regarded her as a radical not only politically but also because in her "passionate joy in the adventure of living her own life," she had rejected the precepts of Victorian morality which they held dear.[26] Nonetheless, Eastman and the older women subscribed to the same notion that women as mothers and nurturers had a unique relationship to war, even though they differed on when and how to make this known.

Nurturant motherhood was an ideological umbrella not only for women with diverse goals and opinions within the WPP but also for women in causes diametrically opposed to the feminist pacifists. The earliest and largest women's preparedness organization, the Woman's Section of the Navy League, indicated the adaptability of the notion.

Men like General Leonard Wood, founder of the Plattsburg training camps for civilians, and former President Theodore Roosevelt dominated the preparedness movement, and powerful industrialists, influential politicians, and most major Eastern newspapers backed the cause. Thus, it is not surprising that female participants in the military defense movement were overshadowed. Female preparedness advocates did not have as great an impact on the preparedness movement as feminist pacifists had on the peace movement, and they sought advice and approval from males more frequently than did their pacifist counterparts.[27]

Nonetheless, their efforts were important for the movement and for the women themselves. They added their voices in significant numbers to preparedness clamorings, countered the propaganda of feminist pacifists, and attracted valuable publicity. Furthermore, these women, as evident in the WSNL, had a special position in the movement, controlled their own activities, and, in some instances, adopted policies at variance with male organizations. Like women in the peace movement, they often justified their activities with appeals to the "maternal instinct."

War relief for Europe lead many women into preparedness activities. Horrified by tales of German atrocities in Belgium, American women initiated numerous relief schemes. Although their first concern was to aid Europeans, many women, believing that Belgium's fate contained valuable lessons for the United States, sought to secure an increase in the nation's defensive strength.[28]

The WSNL and other women's preparedness ventures were also spurred by the sinking of the *Lusitania* in May 1915. Public outrage following the submarine attack facilitated the work of preparedness propagandists. Navy League officials used the tragedy as a pretext for beginning a major campaign to gain public support for increasing the strength of the navy.[29] Wishing to reach all segments of society and aware of the immense propaganda value of attracting the support of American women, in July 1915 the Navy League responded affirmatively to the plans of a Washington, D.C., journalist, Elisabeth Ellicott Poe, to establish a woman's section.[30]

The main rationale for the Woman's Section of the Navy League was to guard the country "against the possibility of being invaded by a foreign foe" and to arouse patriotism among American women.[31] However, the desire to dispel the antimilitary image of women created by the feminist pacifists and to counter the publicity received by the International Congress of Women was a major impetus behind the new organization. Scorning female peace advocates as old-fashioned sentimentalists who "wept upon the mere mention of [a] cannon," WSNL supporters stressed that they were realists who had joined a "man's movement."[32] They charged that the feminist pacifists were "visionaries [and] emotionalists" who slandered the patriotism and insulted the intelligence of American women, and failed to understand that an adequate defense was the only way to maintain peace.[33] Woman's Section supporters wanted America to be "so strong that she will never lose a life on the battlefield or on a battleship because no power will venture to attack her."[34]

Despite these attacks on the WPP, WSNL supporters shared the belief of their pacifist opponents that because women were responsible for the nurture and protection of children, they had a special right to be heard on matters that might endanger those lives. Unlike the pacifists, however, they accepted war as inevitable and they contended that women's protective functions made it their duty to demand strong military defenses. "Woman has always been the conservator of home and life," Vylla Poe Wilson explained. "It is only just that her voice, raised in a cry for preparedness to protect the lives and homes she has been the chief factor in building up, should be harkened unto." For Wilson and other female proponents of preparedness, their demand was nothing less than a cry for "provision against the wholesale slaughter of the lives they [had] gone into the valley of the shadow of death to bring into the world."[35] There was a striking similarity between her language and that of Anna Garlin Spencer in the WPP preamble.

WSNL members directly challenged the WPP contention that mothers did not want their sons to go to war. In part this reflected their antithetical attitudes toward war itself. A high proportion of female preparedness supporters were active in women's patriotic societies. These societies glorified war; their members, proud descendants of veterans, viewed war as heroic and ennobling and romanticized military life. Mary Simmerson Logan, widow of a Civil War hero and mother of a son killed in the Spanish-American War, was appalled by the slogan, "I didn't raise my boy to be a soldier." She exclaimed that it was shameful for any woman to suggest that her son would not serve his country and she noted that "mothers of other wars" deserved "the satisfaction of knowing that their sacrifice was not in vain, that the freedom their men died for [was] permanent."[36]

Annie Cothren Graves, less concerned with redeeming previous sacrifices than with preventing new ones, directly linked the "instinct of motherhood" to support for increases in the nation's naval and military strength. Graves, with a son of military age, acknowledged that "every mother with sons feels her heart stand still with the horror of what war might bring to her" but she affirmed that whether they willed it or not their sons would "go out to fight at their country's call." She was confident that American mothers wanted their sons to fight behind "great ships and guns, equipped for service and victory" and did not want them to go "like sheep to the shambles to be slaughtered in unpreparedness by the disciplined and more numerous ships and soldiers of a prepared foe." Persuaded that it was "the very instinct of motherhood" that prompted her to work for a strong defense, Graves proclaimed that a " 'navy second to none' [was] the best hope for mothers, for the safety of their sons and for the safety of their country."[37]

WSNL supporters used the ideology of motherhood not only to justify formation of a separate woman's organization, but also to launch in the spring of 1916 the National Service Schools, a series of quasi-military training camps for young women. Camp promoters and planners took pains to reconcile nurturant motherhood with the training camps in order to erase the impression that the camps might undermine the conventional female role.

Spurning suggestions that the camps teach women how to use weapons, organizers Elisabeth Poe and Vylla Poe Wilson established a program that emphasized domestic over martial arts, even though the domestic training was placed within the routine of a military camp.[38] Poe received praise in the Navy League journal for formulating a plan that was "comprehensive, feasible, and free from dangerous innovations that might draw American women from their traditional and sacred duties of feeding the hungry, nursing the sick and caring for the sorrowing. . . ."[39]

Camp organizers obviously did not believe that women's protective functions extended to a direct role in the physical defense of their country or homes. Although the "soldier quality" was glorified, some important military virtues—bravery and aggression—were absent from the camps; while others—obedience and self-sacrifice—which were consonant with the traditional female role, were fully impressed upon the trainees and emphasized in camp propaganda.[40]

Lest the camps be viewed as subversive of that role, Honorary Commandant Mary Scott, speaking at the conclusion of the First National Service School, dismissed the military training and camp life as "merely incidental" and used only to achieve efficiency. She emphasized that women must continue to perform their traditional duties so well that no one would question their supremacy in this area, and that only women who cherished the traditional nurturant role would be able to stir others to their patriotic duties when they returned to their homes after attending the camps.[41]

Female advocates of military preparedness were not consistent in their use of the nurturant motherhood ideology. Some women viewed their efforts as an extension of women's traditional role, and they emphasized that it was natural for them to operate in the public sector on behalf of this cause.[42] But for others, it had antifeminist tones because it emphasized women's dependence on men. "When war comes it is the women and children that suffer most," one woman asserted, "hence [men] should do all in their power to see that we are properly protected."[43] Ironically, the nurturant mother had to organize in the public sector to ensure that men would accept their responsibility to protect her in her helpless state of dependency.

This inconsistency in the application of the motherhood ideology by WSNL supporters reflects the fact that, unlike the WPP, the WSNL carefully avoided a stand on the suffrage issue and attracted women on both sides of the suffrage question. Antisuffragists, in particular, tried to use the preparedness movement to further their own cause, but WSNL leaders remained neutral. The WSNL stressed that women influenced government not through votes, but because they were the "only active force 'behind the throne.' "[44] They hoped to exercise this "force" by inviting the spouse of every member of Congress and every senator to serve as a vice-president. Although a dispute over female suffrage at the WSNL National Defense Conference in November 1915 attracted much press attention, there was actually little conflict over this issue within the organization. Given the antagonism between antis and suffragists at this time, their joint efforts on behalf of the national defense is one of the most remarkable features of the woman's preparedness movement.[45]

By espousing the ideology of nurturant motherhood, female activists in World War I, like most female reformers in the late nineteenth and early twentieth centuries, contributed to a stereotypical view of their sex in order to justify activities in the public domain. However, the pervasive notion of women as the nurturant and protective sex provided only a general framework which women modified in accordance with their beliefs on specific contemporary issues. Supporters of the WPP, an explicitly feminist organization, broadened the scope of nurturance to include a demand for the "right to be consulted in the settlement of questions concerning not alone the life of individuals, but of nations."[46] In contrast, the message of the WSNL was in part much more restrictive in defining the role of nurturant motherhood. Women were dependent keepers of homes and children, and they required protection from men. The WSNL, however, also held that the protective and nurturant functions of women extended naturally beyond the home to include the demand for national defense.

Nurturant motherhood served very different ends for the female supporters of peace and of military preparedness. Yet women on both sides, even preparedness women who emphasized female dependence, operated with resolute determination in the public sector. Reflecting on the careers of reformers Jane Addams and Lillian Wald, Jill Conway concluded that the "failure to see women's activism for what it was, a real departure from women's traditional domesticity, indicates the controlling power of the stereotype of the female temperament which continued unaltered from the 1870s to the 1930s."[47] Female activism during World War I provides much evidence to support her view.

Personal and Social Implications of Activism

Women's wartime activism did little to undermine the ideology of nurturant motherhood, but it did have significant personal meaning for many participants. Although enhanced self-esteem defies quantification, the comments of many female activists suggest positive alterations in their self-conception and in the estimation of their own sex. Women's improved self-images were often closely linked to their need for recognition.

Organizational activities during World War I provided a release from the numbing sense of uselessness that many middle-class women experienced. The lack of demand for their talents outside the home troubled many women in the early twentieth century because they believed they could make real contributions to society if they could only find suitable outlets. "Nothing so deadens the sympathies and shrivels the power of enjoyment," Jane Addams explained in *Twenty Years at Hull House,* "as the persistent keeping away from the great opportunities for helpfulness and a continual ignoring of the starvation struggle which makes up the life of at least half the race."[48] Although eliciting conflicting forms of activism, the war furnished "great opportunities for helpfulness"—the outlet for which many women had been searching.

For some, of course, this activism took the form of opposition to war as a barbaric method of settling international conflicts. For those groping for a constructive way to protest, the formation of the WPP was an event of great personal significance. Elizabeth Glendower Evans, a Boston social reformer and active supporter of the Women's Trade Union League, described herself as "an imprisoned spirit set free!!!!!" Throwing herself into organizing the new peace party with her "whole soul" and losing "doubts and self-disparagement," Evans proclaimed, "I am so on fire that I can pass the flames along."[49] By the end of January 1915, she concluded that her two weeks of peace activity were already worth "half a lifetime." "I feel as if I were twenty persons," she confided to her friend Belle LaFollette, "and before this Peace Party was born, I did not feel big enough to fill my own skin."[50] Evans thought the WPP had "transformed and translated" her life by giving her a new message. "Last summer I was like a person who had died and whom others had forgotten to bury," she explained. "All the autumn I had been feeling like a corpse that was defiling those of the earth. It is into that dead body that a new life has come."[51] Evans's feelings of jubilant excitement and of heightened self-esteem probably were deeper than those of most early participants in the WPP. Nonetheless, at least initially, the party raised the hopes of female opponents of war that they had an immediate and vital role in educating the public and influencing political leaders with their promediation and antimilitary propaganda.

The WPP was hampered from the beginning, however, by the fact that women longing for worthwhile activity also wanted results. WPP goals seemed too abstract to many, and promoting the peace cause did not provide concrete accomplishments. For example, a supporter in Georgia complained that women were "unwilling to study causes and to work for a remote and really ideal condition."[52] Another WPP leader asked if the branch in her state might not affiliate with a war relief committee. She pointed out that it might strengthen the peace cause by "showing that we can be practical while working for a condition not yet attained."[53] National WPP secretaries Harriet Thomas and Eleanor Karsten were well aware of this problem and believed the only way to keep WPP members interested in the organization was to keep them busy. They encouraged WPP branch leaders to find local activities that would actively involve the members.[54]

Much to the dismay of the feminist pacifists, European war relief projects and preparedness ventures successfully met the personal needs of scores of women, who also found "new meaning" in their lives as a result of these activities. Women threw themselves into war relief with a zeal born of the conviction that they served a uniquely noble cause. They also believed that through their efforts they would gain recognition and respect for themselves.

Indeed, the quest for recognition was so pronounced in women's relief organizations that it prevented cooperation between them, both before and after the United States entered the war. Each independent relief group sought exclusive control over some phase of war relief and guarded its domain against encroachment by others. Women were guided by self-interest as much as by altruism; although sincerely moved by the plight of European war victims, they were determined to receive full credit for their help. This was a matter of self-esteem, not self-promotion. Many thought they were doing something vital in the public sector for the first time in their lives and their self-conception required public notice and approval.[55]

Enhanced self-respect was also a part of the experience of young women enrolled in the WSNL National Service Schools. The camps required women to perform daily military calisthenics, drills, and marches, attend lectures on preparedness and patriotism, and complete Red Cross training in the preparation of surgical dressings. Optional courses ranged from lessons in knitting socks and mufflers to code work and telegraphy. Campers took their training seriously. Dorothy Potter and Emily Wickett provided insight into the meaning of the camp experience for two "patriotic young spirits" in essays published in *Sea Power,* the Navy League journal. Both women became dedicated proponents of preparedness, but they differed from male advocates of preparedness in that they stressed the importance of trained women as part of the nation's defense effort. They were convinced that women had important functions to perform in serving their country as a second line of defense.[56] Implicit in the camp experience was an expansion of the female role and, for the leisured daughters of the middle and upper classes, a new sense of self-worth. "It is a long step from slavery to freedom," Potter exclaimed, "but neither so long nor so high as the leap from worthless inactivity to usefulness."[57]

Female activism during World War I had other personal meanings for participants. A feeling of sisterhood sometimes evolved among women within organizations as they worked closely with and developed new respect for members of their own sex. The National Service Schools provided a unique atmosphere in which the campers developed a special kind of soldierly sisterhood. Living together in tents, dressing identically, and going through the training produced a strong collective spirit among the campers. "I could perceive a feeling of pride growing among us—not pride in ourselves as individuals," Wickett remarked, "but in our particular squad when in line, or in our class work, then in our company as a whole."[58] Sharing the camp experience, being part of a unit, and knowing their individual actions affected the performance of the whole increased their feelings of personal responsibility, but more importantly, their sense of solidarity with their sister campers.

Sisterhood emerged among activists in far less exceptional circumstances than the women's camps. Supportive female friendships and a sense of sisterhood were crucial for women in the peace movement. Confusion, doubt, and fear plagued the peace supporters as their position became more unpopular. After the United States entered the war in April 1917, these feelings were heightened. The WPP held a convention in December 1917 that differed markedly from earlier ones. They had no mass meetings, shunned publicity, and barred admission to all but the delegates. This reflected the WPP's legitimate fear of attracting hostile attention and was also the only way of guaranteeing they would be able to express their views freely. These women felt increasingly isolated and the meeting furnished an opportunity to be with others who sympathized with their views or at least respected their right to differ from the prevailing temper of the country.[59] "Our business," Anna Garlin Spencer noted in a statement written for the WPP board in October 1917, "is to help mitigate all horrors of war by consistently refusing to make any sacrifice of human fellowship and good will."[60] A spirit of sisterhood transcended the differences within the WPP regarding the role of pacifists in wartime. The fact that the organization continued to exist during the war, however limited its activities, symbolized this sisterhood and was in itself solace for many women.

Shared beliefs created bonds of sisterhood without personal contact between women. Individuals who could not personally participate in an organization's activities expressed solidarity with members of groups that espoused their ideals. Women living in areas without WPP branches, for example, poignantly noted that no matter how isolated they were in their own communities, the existence of the WPP meant they were no longer alone.[61]

Not only sisterhood but also a nascent feminism appeared in women's organizational activities during World War I. This was true not just in the WPP, but also in the WSNL, an organization that did not espouse the major tenets of early twentieth-century feminism as part of its program. The concept of feminism, of course, encompasses far more than a specific set of principles at a certain time. There is evidence of a developing feminist self-consciousness among women activists who reached that point of recognition that Gerda Lerner has described as awareness of men as "the other."[62] The increased self-esteem, the evolving sisterhood based on the friendship of co-workers and on shared beliefs, and the confrontations with males who were often patronizing and at times obstructive caused some women to make at least the first steps toward a feminist awareness. Some even began to articulate their grievances against the male power structure.

Joining a "man's movement," WSNL members initially viewed themselves as following the lead of men even though they formed their own organization. Yet there is evidence of their desire to reach their own decisions independently of male leadership as early as the first months of the WSNL's existence. In November 1915, the WSNL held a National Defense Conference in Washington. A man presided over the meeting and many of the speakers were male, but their resolutions indicated that the women were not unduly influenced by the men. Although preparedness leaders were attacking the Wilson administration and the foreign-born with vehemence, the women defeated a resolution banning the use of foreign languages in the schools and passed resolutions affirming support for the president in his demands for strengthening the military forces.[63]

There was a budding feminist awareness evident in the comments of campers at the WSNL National Service Schools, but it was most apparent in the WSNL Comforts Committee, organized in March 1917 to provide knitted garments for American soldiers. The Comforts Committees, which were located throughout the nation, attracted many women who had not taken part in the preparedness activities. The popularity of these committees demonstrated the tremendous appeal of traditional forms of women's relief work.[64] Knitting relief, however, was not accompanied by attitudes of docile femininity, and the women surprised government officials and leaders of the Navy League with their firm resistance to male interference.

By the summer of 1917, it seemed that nothing could stop the women's knitting needles or dampen their enthusiasm. However, a feud between Josephus Daniels, secretary of the navy, and the male leadership of the Navy League resulted in Daniels banning persons with any association with the Navy League from entering national stations, reservations, or ships. The ban threatened the efforts of the Comforts Committees because Daniels allowed the women to contribute their knitted items only if it was clearly understood that they had no association of any kind with the Navy League. He strongly urged that they form a Red Cross group.[65] WSNL Comforts Committee leaders, desirous of maintaining their own organization, resisted his advice and offered to form a new committee independent of both the Navy and the Red Cross. They were adamant about not disbanding or being absorbed by the Red Cross. "It would seem unwise," Elizabeth Van Rensselaer Frazer, leader of the group, observed, "to stop the activities of an already organized society just now when the necessity that originated this work continues to exist."[66] Informing the officers and members that Daniels had refused arbitrarily to permit the navy to accept their "comforts," she warned that his suggestion to form a Red Cross auxiliary would "supplant us in a field which we have ploughed and with which we are familiar."[67] She urged the Comforts Committees to disregard Daniels' suggestion. The women circumvented his order by sending articles in the name of Mildred Dewey, the honorary leader of the committee and the widow of Commander George Dewey.[68]

The women believed Daniels' obstruction of their efforts was especially galling because they in fact had no connection with the Navy League leaders. These men, who had previously paid no attention to the women's activities, further annoyed them by publicizing the Comforts Committee's difficulties to stir public sympathy for the Navy League's own plight. Navy League leaders even tried to use the women to curry favor with Daniels. Comforts Committee leaders vehemently objected to a letter drawn up by the men proposing that the League and the Comforts Committee cooperate with the Red Cross in "carrying out the routine prescribed in the order of the Secretary of the Navy."[69] Spurning this attempt to appease Daniels and to sacrifice their principled opposition to his orders, the women forced the Navy League to abandon its ploy. The surprised men only then realized that the women considered themselves autonomous participants in the war effort who had set their own course.

Despite the ban, most of the Comforts Committees continued their knitting relief efforts through 1918, although some eventually cooperated with the Red Cross and the organization adopted additional forms of service activities. The fact that the group was still active in the fall of 1918 despite the difficulties encountered indicates the women's persistence in pursuing their own projects.[70] The shift from the innovative National Service Schools to the Comforts Committee knitting program revealed not a retreat but an even greater determination on the part of women to pursue their own activities free from male interference. These women, accustomed to defining themselves in terms of their relationships to men, had indeed become aware of men as "the other"—the first step in developing a feminist self-consciousness. Their behavior gave many males their first inkling that women were gaining a new self-awareness and were not operating in the public sector solely to serve male interests.

Although the sense of men as "the other" was already a part of the consciousness of many WPP members, their activities in the peace movement reinforced their feminism. The WPP supporters' sharp criticism of the male-dominated peace movement and their perception of war as "man-made" were immediate indications of the feminism in the organization. The International Congress of Women at The Hague was one event that particularly bolstered this feminism. Congress participants represented only a small minority of women in the Western world, but they had a symbolic importance greater than their numbers. They demonstrated that sisterhood and shared humanitarian concerns transcended narrow national chauvinism. As Crystal Eastman explained, the "fact that women of the warring nations met and discussed the war problem sanely and in friendship while all their male relatives were out shooting each other [was] significant in the history of human progress and significant in the history of women's progress."[71] The strong sense of female solidarity at the congress and the high level of feminist consciousness in evidence there cheered American feminist pacifists. Most of the women's efforts were, of course, far less dramatic than the congress, but similar currents of feminism and sisterhood ran through their efforts—important sources of strength in the face of hostility.

Much of the verbal abuse directed at pacifists from 1914 to early 1917 was not sex-specific; nor was the curtailment of their civil liberties after the United States entered the war. In some instances, however, feminist pacifists were singled out for ridicule by male opponents of the peace movement because they were women and feminists. Further, men within the peace movement were wary of cooperation with women, and they revealed sexist attitudes.

In a widely publicized letter of April 1915, Theodore Roosevelt described the WPP program as "hysterical . . . silly because it is futile . . . base [and] influenced by physical cowardice." His choice of derogatory terms was clearly designed to highlight negative stereotypical female character traits.[72] Roosevelt's comments elicited a debate in the *New York Times* between WPP members and supporters of his views. Feminist pacifists challenged his dismissal of women "because they can only bear children and not arms" and his categorization of them as "physical cowards" with arguments derived from the ideology of nurturant motherhood and with praise for the international feminist spirit of their organization.[73] National WPP Secretary Lucia Ames Mead asked, "Is it not time that, hearing the bitter cry of our outraged sisters, we turned our attention to the cause of war and the conditions necessary to obtain that justice which alone can insure world peace."[74]

Louis Cuvillier, chairman of the Committee on Military Affairs in the New York State Assembly, found it "amusing to think that the female sex should have the effrontery" to believe it could influence the war situation. But more significantly, he refused to recognize the women's own independent initiative and he also ridiculed their feminism: "It looks to me . . . as if the pacifists of the male sex have captured these women for the purpose of using them as shields; and women, being easily influenced, imagine that with chatter—which is their greatest asset—and by assembling at The Hague, together with a few 'scraps of paper' resolutions, they can cause the great belligerent nations to cease their struggle for national existence with the argument that war shall never again be declared, except with the advice and consent of all womankind."[75] These criticisms, although focusing on the women's antiwar activities, were tinged with antifeminism and typical of the response of many males to the WPP. These men realized the women challenged the social order through their feminism as much as their pacifism.

Even men who shared the feminist pacifists' views on war issues were sometimes unwilling to accept women as equal co-workers in the peace cause. The most striking example is the experience of two young feminist pacifists who were not members of the WPP—Rebecca Shelly and Lella Faye Secor. Among several other efforts, in 1916 they organized the American Neutral Conference Committee. Their group was to pressure Wilson to convene an official conference of neutral nations to mediate the conflict. They encountered resistance because of their age and inexperience, but also because of their sex.[76] Although Shelly believed that she was best qualified to do the actual "creative, pushing, executive *attaining* work," she recognized the need to attract a prestigious peace advocate to head the committee.[77] After several had refused, Hamilton Holt, who had participated in the prewar peace movement and had become leader of the conservative League to Enforce Peace, consented to serve as chairman as long as he did not have to raise funds. "There . . . is nothing else to do but work with the people who will even in a limited measure help the cause," Shelly remarked with resignation.[78] The partnership was an uneasy one. Although Shelly and Secor did all the organizing work, Holt took pains to assure supporters that they could not take any action without consulting him.[79] Shelly and Secor found this arrangement restrictive and their efforts discouraging. "I used to think that there was nothing so desirable in the world as to be young and to be a woman," Secor lamented, "but there have been moments in which I felt that both of these were a curse."[80] Their annoyance with Holt peaked when he objected that the Committee of One Hundred they had assembled did not include enough of the "more conservative type citizen." Apparently the "more conservative type" was supposed to be male because Holt "crossed off many good peace women on the grounds of keeping [the] committee 'non-pacifist.' "[81] Cooperating with men was proving to be more difficult than the women had expected.

The break in diplomatic relations terminated their organization. Shelly and Secor expressed some relief in severing connection with "reactionaries" like Holt. Their subsequent experiences in radical antiwar efforts were, however, more disillusioning as far as their treatment by males was concerned. Although they played pivotal roles in the organization of the People's Council in the summer of 1917, they were eased out of the organization in the fall.[82] Shelly was offered a paid secretarial position if she would relinquish all her prerogatives as a member of the board. When she declined the offer, Louis Lochner, the executive secretary of the group and an active participant in many previous phases of the post-1914 peace movement, dismissed her.[83] Shelly, who thought that the "last drop of blood" she and Secor had injected into the effort had led to the formation of the People's Council, regarded her ouster as a personal tragedy. She charged that Lochner had turned "out of the movement the woman who started it."[84] Although all feminist pacifists encountered countless obstacles in their efforts to promote peace, Shelly and Secor's difficulties were compounded by conflicts between men and women within their advocacy groups. Since so many women had abandoned their peace activities, those who continued to dissent were in special need of support and sympathy from women who shared their views. Shelly and Secor missed that supportive sisterhood and found themselves, too often, the unequal partners of men. The current of male resistance and resentment evident in their experience would continue to inhibit the "progress of women" in subsequent decades.

The war provided women with numerous opportunities for activism. They responded to the challenge in ways that were not only significant for the various causes but also valuable for the women themselves. The traditional ideology of nurturant motherhood spurred, justified, and facilitated much of women's wartime activism. Believing strongly in this ideology, many women organized in order to call attention to the stake of the "mother half of humanity" in war. The serviceable ideology rationalized a broad range of activities outside the traditional female sphere and was frequently invoked to meet challenges to women's right to such participation. It also served as a protective shield behind which women could venture into the public sector.

Many, perhaps most, of the women had previously engaged in women's club activities, charitable ventures, or reform efforts, but there was an urgency about their wartime activism that made it seem more vital. The chance to do something they believed would help their country and even the rest of the world, regardless of the nature of that activity, was a tremendous boost to the self-esteem of those who chafed at a society that had no place for them outside the home. As they made the leap from "worthless inactivity to usefulness" many women seemed to be saying, "I am a person."

The personal value an individual derives from experiences like those of female activists during World War I is difficult to measure. Assessing the worth of an experience on the basis of a person's subsequent activities is unsatisfactory because numerous variables influence one's life choices, and enhanced self-respect does not always manifest itself in ways that are historically visible.

This caveat seems particularly appropriate because the initiative taken by women in many different wartime activities, combined with the suffrage victory, raised expectations about the role of women in American society that were not realized in subsequent decades. Given the economic discrimination faced by women and the deeply rooted social inequalities, the high expectations were unwarranted and unrealistic. The war provided what were ultimately only temporary opportunities for women to perform vital activities in the public sector. Many women themselves viewed the war as a passing crisis summoning them to action and made no attempt to transfer their wartime activism into peacetime channels. More importantly, reactionary political and social currents at the end of the war created formidable obstacles for those who viewed their activism as a continuing proposition. This climate inhibited many women, but others, whose vision had been broadened by their wartime experiences, continued their voluntary activities in many different causes during the 1920s and 1930s.

Any attempt to assess the impact of women's wartime activism must finally come to terms with the pervasive ideology of nurturant motherhood. Since so many of their efforts were launched under the banner of nurturant motherhood, chances of defining new roles encompassing real sexual equality were mitigated, regardless of other social, economic, and political factors. So strongly entrenched was the ideology that the women activists could not envision a female role distinct from nurturance—whether in the home or in the larger society.

Notes

1. I am referring here to the beginning of a feminist self-consciousness, which Gerda Lerner has described as the recognition of a wrong, of seeing man as "the other." See Gerda Lerner, *The Female Experience: An American Documentary* (Indianapolis: Bobbs-Merrill, 1977), pp. xxiii–xxiv.

2. Jill Conway, "Women Reformers and American Culture, 1870–1930," in Jean E. Friedman and William G. Shade, eds., *Our American Sisters* (Boston: Allyn and Bacon, 1976), p. 309.

3. For other discussions of early twentieth-century feminism, see: Robin Jacoby, "Feminism and Class Consciousness in the British and American Women's Trade Union Leagues, 1890–1925," in Berenice Carroll, ed., *Liberating Women's History* (Urbana: University of Illinois Press, 1976), pp. 136–137; and Carol Ruth Berkin, "Private Woman, Public Woman: The Contradictions of Charlotte Perkins Gilman," in Carol Ruth Berkin and Mary Beth Norton, eds., *Women of America. A History* (Boston: Houghton Mifflin, 1979), pp. 165–168.

4. Aileen S. Kraditor, *The Ideas of the Woman Suffrage Movement, 1890–1920* (Garden City, N.Y.: Doubleday, Anchor Books edition, 1971), pp. 12–26, 82.

5. "Minutes of the Peace Parade Committee," August 12, 1914, Fanny Garrison Villard Papers, Folder 3993, Houghton Library, Harvard University, Cambridge, Mass.

6. Peace Parade Committee, press release, n.d., Villard Papers.

7. *New York Times,* August 30, 1914.

8. For a detailed discussion of the participation of women in antiwar and preparedness activities from 1914 to 1919 and full citations, see Barbara J. Steinson, "Female Activism in World War I: The American Women's Peace, Suffrage, Preparedness and Relief Movements, 1914–1919" (Ph.D. diss., University of Michigan, 1977).

9. Women held leadership positions in the American Union Against Militarism, sparked the Ford Peace venture and were the "moving spirits" behind the American Neutral Conference Committee, the Emergency Peace Federation, and the People's Council. See Steinson, "Female Activism," chaps. 2, 3, 5, 6.

10. Schwimmer was from Hungary and Pethick-Lawrence from Great Britain. For the background on the formation of the WPP, see Steinson, "Female Activism," chap. 1; C. Roland Marchand, *The American Peace Movement and Social Reform, 1898–1918* (Princeton: Princeton University Press, 1972), pp. 182–208; and Marie L. Degen, *The History of the Woman's Peace Party* (Baltimore: Johns Hopkins Press, 1939). Marchand, in particular, emphasizes the role of suffragists in the formation of the WPP.

11. "Woman's Peace Party, Preamble and Platform Adopted at Washington, January 10, 1915," WPP Papers, Box 1, Swarthmore College Peace Collection (SCPC), Swarthmore, Penn.

12. Addams to Mrs. Augustus Hemenway, January 30, 1915, WPP Corr., Reel 12.5, SCPC.

13. WPP, "Preamble and Platform, January 10, 1915," WPP Papers, Box 1.

14. "Speeches from the Mass Meeting, January 10, 1915," p. 12, WPP Papers, Box 1.

15. Ibid., p. 16.

16. Ibid., p. 27.

17. For more information on the International Congress, see *Report of the International Congress of Women, The Hague 28 April–1 May 1915* (Amsterdam: International Women's Committee of Permanent Peace, 1915); Degen, *History of the WPP*; Steinson, "Female

Activism," chap. 2; Jane Addams, Emily Balch, and Alice Hamilton, *Women at The Hague* (New York: Macmillan, 1915).

18.   Emily Balch, mss. of Hague trip, May 19, 1915, p. 12, Emily Balch Papers, Box 4A, SCPC.

19.   *Report of the International Congress of Women,* pp. 169–176. The delegates adopted the American proposal, written by Julia Grace Wales, for continuous mediation without armistice. The plan, like the plank in the WPP platform, called for neutral nations to convene a conference for the discussion of peace terms. This was the resolution the delegates were most eager to discuss with foreign leaders.

20.   Madeline Doty, *Short Rations: An American Woman in Germany, 1915–1916* (New York: Century, 1917), p. 16.

21.   Angela Morgan, ms. comments on Hague Conference, Angela Morgan Papers, Michigan Historical Collections (MHC), Ann Arbor, Mich.

22.   Steinson, "Female Activism," chap. 3. There were 165 group memberships in the WPP at the end of the year; thirty-three were local branches. Membership in the organization peaked at around twenty thousand in 1916.

23.   Wilson, although interested in mediation, never considered their plan seriously because he wanted to serve as the sole mediator rather than work with a group of neutral nations. For information on WPP propaganda efforts, see "Report of the Office Secretary," June 1, 1916, WPP papers, Box 2.

24.   Steinson, "Female Activism," chaps. 5 and 6. The war referendum question was a divisive issue in the WPP; it did not have the full support of the organization, as indicated in Ernest C. Bolt, *Ballots Before Bullets: The War Referendum Approach to Peace in America, 1914–1941* (Charlottesville: University Press of Virginia, 1977). Harriet Thomas, executive secretary of the WPP, favored the continuation of an activist role for the party and termed the break in relations "a testing time of pacifists." Thomas to Anna Garlin Spencer, March 7, 1917, Anna Garlin Spencer Papers, Box 1, SCPC.

25.   Eastman to Addams, June 28, 1917, WPP Corr., Reel 12.8. For attitudes of the NYC-WPP, see their publication, *Four Lights,* which was banned by the postmaster general.

26.   Freda Kirchwey, "Crystal Eastman," *Nation,* 127 (August 8, 128), pp. 123–4. The National WPP board, for example, did not want Eastman to assume leadership of the NYC-WPP because they considered her "too youthful." See WPP Ex. Bd., "Minutes," October 19, 1915, WPP papers, Box 2. For more information on Eastman, see Blanche Cook, *Crystal Eastman on Women and Revolution* (New York: Oxford University Press, 1978).

27.   Women's role in the preparedness movement receives very little attention in recent histories of the movement. For background information on the preparedness movement, see Armin Rappaport, *The Navy League of the United States* (Detroit: Wayne State University Press, 1962); John P. Finnegan, *Against the Specter of a Dragon: The Campaign for American Military Preparedness* (Westport, Conn.: Greenwood Press, 1974); Walter Millis, *Arms and Men: A Study of American Military History* (New York: New American Library, Mentor Book edition, 1956); and John G. Clifford, *The Citizen Soldiers: The Plattsburg Training Camp Movement, 1913–1920* (Lexington: University Press of Kentucky, 1972). For the role of women in these activities, see Steinson, "Female Activism," chaps. 4 and 7.

28.   For examples of these concerns, see *New York Times,* November 16, 20, 27, 1914; Josephine Bates to Carrie Chapman Catt, February 6, 1915, WPP Corr., Reel 12.6; I. Bagley to Mary Logan, November 21, 1914, John Logan Family Papers, Box 23, Library of Congress (LC), Washington, D.C.

29.   Rappaport, *The Navy League,* pp. 5, 48–50.

30.   "Successful Work of Women," *Seven Seas,* 1 (September 1915), p. 30.

31.   Woman's Section of the Navy League, *Manual of Voluntary Aid* (Washington, D.C., 1916), p. 5.

32. Sarah Addington, *New York Tribune,* August 22, 1915.

33. Mary Colvorcoresses, "The Woman's Peace Party," *Seven Seas,* 1 (November 1915), p. 31.

34. "Women to the Front," *Seven Seas,* 1 (October 1915), p. 36.

35. Ibid., p. 37. The WSNL claimed to have over 25,000 members within three months. Later membership totals were between 50,000 and 100,000. There is no way to verify these claims.

36. Ibid., p. 36. The WSNL was endorsed by nine women's patriotic groups including the DAR, United Daughters of the Confederacy, and Ladies of the Grand Army of the Republic.

37. Ibid. Graves' son would have challenged her statement on the willingness of young men to serve their country. He was secretary of the Colleagiate Anti-Militarism League. Karl Karsten to Eleanor Karsten, July 2, 1916, WPP Corr., Reel 12.6.

38. The First National Service School opened at Chevy Chase, Maryland, on May 1, 1916, and served as the model for three other camps in California, Wisconsin, and Rhode Island. William S. Dupuy, "When Woman Prepares," *Sea Power,* 1 (June 1916), pp. 5–9.

39. *Sea Power,* 1 (August 1916), 30.

40. "When Woman Prepares," p. 7.

41. Mrs. Hugh [Mary] Scott, "The National Service School," *Sea Power* 1 (July 1916), p. 38.

42. "Women to the Front," *Seven Seas,* 1 (October 1915), p. 37.

43. Ibid.

44. Ibid.

45. The conflict at the conference was between Alva Belmont, a wealthy supporter of the militant suffragists, and Josephine Dodge, president of the National Association Opposed to Woman Suffrage. *New York Times,* November 16, 1915. For examples of antisuffrage attacks on the WPP, see "Peace or Politics," *Woman's Protest,* 6 (March 1915), p. 4; "The Futility of the Woman's Peace Party," *Woman's Protest,* 7 (May 1915), pp. 5–6; and "Women Who Send Their Men into Battle," *Woman's Protest,* (October 1915), pp. 6–7.

46. "Woman's Peace Party, Preamble and Platform," WPP Papers, Box 1.

47. Conway, "Women Reformers and American Culture," p. 303.

48. Jane Addams, *Twenty Years at Hull House* (New York: New American Library, Signet Classic edition, 1961), p. 92.

49. Elizabeth Glendower Evans to Belle LaFollette, January 15, 1915, Robert LaFollette Family Papers, Series D, Box 14, LC.

50. Evans to LaFollette, January 24, 29, 1915.

51. Evans to LaFollette, February 1, 1915.

52. Alice Baxter to Lucia Mead, January 23, 1915, Lucia Ames Mead Papers, Box 6, SCPC.

53. Judith Douglas to Sophonisba Breckinridge, June 24, 1916, WPP Corr., Reel 12.7.

54. These activities included holding frequent meetings, providing peace speakers for community groups, distributing literature, watching state legislative actions, writing congressional representatives, and placing peace displays at state fairs. Thomas and Karsten were important sources of moral support for WPP leaders. For examples, see [Thomas] to Mrs. James Finch, November 26, 1915, June 19, 1916, WPP Corr., Reel 12.8; [Karsten] to Cooper, April 26, September 15, November 10, 1916, WPP Corr., Reel 12.8. The strongest branches, the Massachusetts and NYC-WPP, were the only ones that did not seek advice from the National WPP.

55. The differences between the Red Cross and the independent Surgical Dressings Committee illustrate the desire of women to maintain independent organizations and to receive

due notice for their efforts. Mabel Boardman to Maude Wetmore, October 15, 1915, Wetmore to Hopkins, n.d., Boardman to Hopkins, October 16, 1915, Mrs. Archibald Hopkins Papers, Box 3, LC.

56.   Potter was a student at both encampments of the first National Service School and Wickett attended the camp in Rhode Island. For their essays, see Dorothy Potter, "The Military Quality," *Sea Power,* 1 (October 1916), pp. 42–43; Potter, "And Then the Women," *Sea Power,* 2 (May 1917), pp. 15–16; and Emily Wickett, "Obedience and Team Work," *Sea Power,* 2 (February 1917), pp. 42–43. For more information on the camps: "When Woman Prepares," pp. 7, 9; and Barbara J. Steinson, "Sisters and Soldiers: The National Service Schools, Military Training Camps for American Women, 1916–1917," *The Historian* (forthcoming 1980).

57.   Potter, "And Then the Women," p. 16.

58.   Wickett, "Obedience and Team Work," p. 42.

59.   Lola Lloyd, notes on the WPP Annual Meeting, December 6–7, 1917, Lola Lloyd Papers, Schwimmer-Lloyd Collection, Box 028, New York Public Library, New York; *New York Times,* December 8, 1917; Adams to Margaret Lane, December 19, 1917, NYC-WPP, Reel 12.13.

60.   "Statement of the Executive Board of the National Woman's Peace Party," October 25, 1917, WPP Papers, Box 1.

61.   For examples of this sisterhood of belief, see Mrs. J. Hoper to WPP, October 1, 1917, WPP Corr., Reel 12.5; Laeticia Conard to Karsten, April 4, 1917, ibid.; Irene Knott to WPP, April 1, 26, May 23, 1916, WPP Corr., Reel 12.6; and Clara Laddey to Margaret Lane, March 16, 1917, NYC-WPP, Reel 12.14.

62.   Lerner, *The Female Experience,* p. xxiii.

63.   *Washington Post,* November 16, 1915; Poe to Marcy Tucker, February 16, 1916, Logan Family Papers, Box 143, LC.

64.   *Sea Power,* 2 (April 1917), 27–28; E. Frazer to Mrs. G. Noyes, May 11, 1917, John Mariner Family Papers, Box 6, Milwaukee Area Research Center, Wisconsin Historical Society; *New York Times,* June 24, 1917.

65.   The feud resulted from Navy League charges that Daniels was covering up information on an explosion at a naval yard in California. After Robert Thompson informed Daniels that he found it hard to respect the Navy Department when Daniels headed it, Daniels placed the ban on the organization. Rappaport, *The Navy League,* pp. 70–71; "To All Members of the Navy League," *Bulletin,* Josephus Daniels Papers (JDP), Navy League Subject File—1917, LC.

66.   Elizabeth Frazer to Daniels, September 11, 1917, JDP.

67.   Frazer to Members, September 13, 1917, JDP.

68.   *New York Times,* September 17, 18, 1917; Frazer, "Work of the Comforts Committee," *Sea Power,* 3 (October, 1917), p. 52.

69.   Navy League Executive Board, "Minutes," October 26, 1917, Navy League Headquarters, Washington, D.C.

70.   "Work of the Comforts Committee," *Sea Power,* 4 (February 1918), p. 135; "Comforts Committee Report," *Sea Power,* 6 (June 1919), p. 352.

71.   Crystal Eastman to Agnes Leach, February 21, 19167, NYC-WPP Corr., Reel 12.14.

72.   *New York Times,* April 16, 1915.

73.   Ibid., April 19, 1915.

74.   Ibid., April 23, 1915.

75.   Ibid., April 20, 1915.

76.   For more information on Shelly and Secor, see Steinson, "Female Activism," chaps. 3 and 6; and Barbara M. Florence, *Lella Secor: A Diary in Letters, 1915–1922* (New York: Burt Franklin, 1978).

77. Rebecca Shelly to Lola Lloyd, April 24, 1916, Lloyd Papers, Box 024.

78. Shelly to Lloyd, May 26, 1917, Lloyd Papers, Box 025.

79. Hamilton Holt to Jacob Schiff, August 1, 1916, WPP Corr., Reel 12.8.

80. Lella Secor to Laura Kelley and Lida Hamm, September 4, 1916, in *Lella Secor: A Diary*, p. 87.

81. Shelly to Lloyd, August 27, 1916, Lloyd Papers, Box 025.

82. The People's Council is discussed in Marchand, *The American Peace Movement*, pp. 266–322, and in Steinson, "Female Activism," chap. 7.

83. Louis Lochner to Shelly, September 7, 1917, Rebecca Shelly Papers, Box 1, Michigan Historical Collections.

84. Shelly to Lloyd, November 12, 1917, Lloyd Papers, Box 027.

Suggestions for Further Reading

The World War I peace movement is rich in autobiographical material, most of which pertains to mediation activities. Jane Addams, *The Second Twenty Years at Hull House* (New York: Macmillan, 1930) and *Peace and Bread in Time of War* (New York: Macmillan, 1922), reveal much about Addams' attitudes and personal problems during the war. Jane Addams, Emily Greene Balch, and Alice Hamilton, *Women at The Hague: The International Congress of Women and Its Results* (New York: Macmillan, 1915), maximizes the role of Addams at the congress; and Madeline Z. Doty, *Short Rations: An American Woman in Germany, 1915–1916* (New York: Century, 1917) discusses some of the generational differences among American delegates to The Hague conference. Emmeline Pethick-Lawrence describes her role in arousing the interest of American women in the peace cause in *My Part in a Changing World* (London: V. Collancz, 1938). Lella Secor discusses the Ford peace effort and other activities in which she and Rebecca Shelly were involved in "The Ford Peace Ship and After," in Julian Bell (ed.), *We Did Not Fight: 1914–1918 Experiences of War Resisters* (London: Cobden-Sanderson, 1935). A valuable new addition to this literature is Barbara M. Florence, *Lella Secor: A Diary in Letters, 1915–1922* (New York: Burt Franklin, 1978). Two other autobiographies of interest are Lillian Wald, *Windows on Henry Street* (Boston: Little, Brown, 1934), and Alice Hamilton, *Exploring the Dangerous Trades* (Boston: Little, Brown, 1943).

Of the several studies of Jane Addams, the most useful are Allen F. Davis, *American Heroine: The Life and Legend of Jane Addams* (New York: Oxford University Press, 1973), and James T. Farrell, *Beloved Lady: A History of Jane Addams' Ideas on Reform and Peace* (Baltimore: Johns

Hopkins Press, 1967). Biographies of some value are Mercedes Randall, *Improper Bostonian: Emily Greene Balch* (New York: Twayne, 1964) and R. L. Duffus, *Lillian Wald* (New York: Macmillan, 1938). A biographical essay on Crystal Eastman is contained in Blanche W. Cook, *Crystal Eastman on Women and Revolution* (New York: Oxford University Press, 1978). Some articles of interest are Jill Conway, "Women Reformers and American Culture, 1870–1930," *Journal of Social History* 5 (Winter 1971–2): 164–177; William Trattner, "Julia Grace Wales and the Wisconsin Plan for Peace," *Wisconsin Magazine of History* 44 (1961): 203–216; and Wiliam A. Linkugel and Kimm Giffin, "The Distinguished War Service of Dr. Anna Howard Shaw," *Pennsylvania History* (October 1961).

General studies of the Wilson administration and American neutrality worth consulting are Arthur Link, *Wilson: Campaigns for Progressivism and Peace, 1916–1917* (Princeton: Princeton University Press, 1964); and *Wilson: Confusion and Crises, 1915–1916* (Princeton: Princeton University Press, 1964); and Ernest R. May, *The World War and American Isolation, 1914–1917* (Cambridge: Harvard University Press, 1959). The suppression of civil liberties after the United States entered the war is discussed in William J. Preston, Jr., *Aliens and Dissenters: Federal Suppression of Radicals, 1903–1933* (Cambridge: Harvard University Press, 1963) and Harry N. Scheiber, *The Wilson Administration and Civil Liberties* (Ithaca: Cornell University Press, 1960).

The background on the pre-World War I peace movement, necessary for understanding the innovative nature of the World War I movement, is presented in a number of able studies: Robert Beisner, *Twelve Against Empire: The Anti-Imperialists, 1898–1900* (New York: McGraw-Hill, 1968); Peter Brock, *Pacifism in the United States, from the Colonial Era to the First World War* (Princeton: Princeton University Press, 1968); Sondra Herman, *Eleven Against the War: Studies in American Internationalism, 1898–1921* (Stanford: Hoover Institute Press, 1969); David Patterson, *The Travail of the Peace Movement* (Bloomington: Indiana University Press, 1977); Michael A. Lutzker, "The Practical Peace Advocates: An Interpretation of the American Peace Movement, 1898–1917" (Ph.D. diss., Rutgers University, 1969); and C. Roland Marchand, *The American Peace Movement and Social Reform, 1898–1918* (Princeton: Princeton University Press, 1972).

Charles Chatfield, *For Peace and Justice: Pacifism in America 1914–1941* (Knoxville: University of Tennessee Press, 1971) presents an overview of the development of the World War I peace movement and demonstrates the impact of the war on young pacifists who were important in later peace activities. A study of the mediation movement that recognizes the role of women is David S. Patterson, "Woodrow Wilson and the Mediation Movement, 1914–1917," *Historian,* 33 (August 1971), 535–556. Blanche Wiesen Cook, "Woodrow Wilson and the Anti-Militarists, 1914–1917" (Ph.D.

diss., Johns Hopkins University, 1970) and "Democracy in Wartime: Anti-militarism in England and the United States, 1914–1918," in Charles Chatfield, *Peace Movements in America* (New York: Schocken, 1973), 39–56 are valuable studies of the American Union Against Militarism. Marchand's *The American Peace Movement* is an invaluable source for the development of the peace movement after 1914. His chapter on women, "The Maternal Instinct," focuses on the connections between the suffrage movement and the women's peace movement. This concentration leads to overemphasis on the role of some suffragists who were not that active in the peace movement.

A durable study of the WPP is Marie L. Degen's *History of the Woman's Peace Party* (Baltimore: Johns Hopkins Press, 1939). Degen concentrates on the international activities of the WPP, which leads her to neglect domestic activities and differences within the organization. A recent study of the Ford Peace Ship is Barbara Kraft, *The Ford Peace Ship* (New York: Macmillan, 1978), which takes an especially critical view of Rosika Schwimmer. David Katz examines Catt's reaction to the women's peace movement in "Carrie Chapman Catt and the Struggle for Peace" (Ph.D. diss., Syracuse University, 1973). The WPP and other women's peace activities are discussed in Barbara J. Steinson, "Female Activism in World War I: The American Women's Peace, Suffrage, Preparedness and Relief Movements, 1914–1919" (Ph.D. diss., University of Michigan, 1977). The views of the WPP on the war referendum question are simplified in Ernest C. Bolt's comprehensive study of this issue, *Ballots Before Bullets: The War Referendum Approach to Peace in America, 1914–1941* (Charlottesville: University Press of Virginia, 1977).

The radical peace movement and its connection with the Socialist Party and the labor movement are discussed in Frank L. Grubbs, Jr., *The Struggle for Labor Loyalty: Gompers, the A.F. of L. and the Pacifists, 1917–1920* (Durham: Duke University Press, 1968), a study which makes the pacifists appear stronger than they were; and James Weinstein, *The Decline of Socialism in America, 1912–1925* (New York: Monthly Review Press, 1967).

Other books consulted for this paper were: Eleanor Flexner, *Century of Struggle* (Cambridge: Harvard University Press, 1959); Aileen Kraditor, *The Ideas of the Woman Suffrage Movement* (New York: Doubleday, Anchor Books edition, 1971); William O'Neill, *Everyone Was Brave* (New York: Quadrangle, 1969); Berenice Carroll, *Liberating Women's History* (Urbana: University of Illinois Press, 1976); Carol Ruth Berkin and Mary Beth Norton, *Women of America: A History* (Boston: Houghton Mifflin, 1979); Gerda Lerner, *The Female Experience* (Indianapolis: Bobbs-Merrill, 1977); June Sochen, *The New Woman* (New York: Quadrangle, 1972); J. Stanley Lemons, *The Woman Citizen* (Urbana: University of Illinois Press, 1973); Ida Clyde Clarke, *American Women and the World War*

(New York: Appleton, 1918); John P. Finnegan, *Against the Specter of a Dragon* (Westport, Conn.: Greenwood Press, 1974); John G. Clifford, *The Citizen Soldiers* (Lexington: University Press of Kentucky, 1972); Armin Rappaport, *The Navy League* (Detroit: Wayne State University Press, 1962).

Annotated Bibliography

In addition to the bibliographical notes provided by each contributing author, the following bibliography has been complied to assist the researcher on the topic of women in war and revolution. Listed first are the current bibliographic studies, which can be found in most research libraries. The most useful of these have been annotated; others of interest have been cited. Following this section on bibliographic source materials, the reader will find a bibliography of books, periodicals, and articles, specifically focused on the role of women in war and revolution but not mentioned in the bibliographic notes by the contributors. These are organized by country and then by chronology. The editors hope that the bibliographic efforts in this volume will assist younger scholars and those new to the field, and thus encourage the further, much needed work that is to be done.

I. Bibliographic Guides

Jacobs, Sue-Ellen. *Women in Perspective: A Guide for Cross-Cultural Studies.* Urbana: University of Illinois Press, 1974. This volume offers multiple entries under the subject-heading "Women and War." In addition, works are cross-listed by country or geographic region. Although citations are not annotated, the very specific subject groupings make this a useful and accessible tool. There is a general introduction focusing on the purposes of, and the need for, women's studies.

Knaster, Merl. *Women in Spanish America: An Annotated Bibliography from Pre-Conquest to Contemporary Times.* Boston: G. K. Hall and Company, 1977. This volume offers both author and subject indexes and a detailed listing by subject and country or region. Unpublished doctoral dissertations are listed separately. Many of the works are in Spanish.

Krichmar, Albert. *The Women's Movement in the Seventies: An International English Language Bibliography.* Metuchen, N.J., and London: The Scarecrow Press, 1977. This volume offers both an author and a subject index. Sources are arranged under geographic sections with topical subheadings. The introduction provides an excellent guide to the volume. Almost all entries are annotated. There is an additional reference section listing bibliographies, periodicals, polls, and statistical and media sources.

Rosenberg, Marie, and Bergstrom, Len. *Women and Society: A Critical*

Review of the Literature with a Selected Annotated Bibliography. Beverly Hills: Sage Publications, 1975. This a good reference source, with useful annotation. Author and subject indexes are combined and include a "War" entry. The table of contents divides entries by discipline. The history section lists "Women as Soldiers and Spies."

Rowbotham, Sheila. *Women's Liberation and Revolution.* Bristol, England. Falling Wall Press, 1973. This guide has no index; however, its table of contents is quite specific, with entries that include "Russian Revolution," "Women and the Puritan Revolution in England and America," and "The Eighteenth Century and the French Revolution." Subject sections are organized alphabetically by author. There is a general section, including miscellaneous periodicals, pamphlets, and articles. Each entry is annotated.

Women's Studies Abstracts: Volumes 1 (1972). P.O. Box 1, Rush, New York 14543. Each issue has subject and author index and a table of contents organized by subject (e.g., "education," "employment," "sexuality"). The periodical is published quarterly. It includes a book review index. Each abstract is accompanied by a paragraph summarizing the entries.

Al-Qazzaz, Ayad. *Women in the Middle East and North Africa: An Annotated Bibliography.* Austin, Texas: Middle East Monographs, Center for Middle Eastern Studies, University of Texas at Austin, 1977.

Friedman, Barbara; Greenstein, Emily; Pollack, Fannette, and Williamson, Jane. *Women's Work and Women's Studies.* New York: Barnard College Women's Center, 1975, Volumes 1972–1975.

King, Judith D. *Women's Studies Sourcebook: A Comprehensive Classified Bibliography of Books.* Grand Valley State College Library, Allendale, Michigan, January, 1976.

Krichmar, Albert. *The Women's Rights Movement in the United States 1848–1970. A Bibliography and Sourcebook.* Metuchen, N. J. and London: The Scarecrow Press, 1972.

Leonard, Eugenie; Drinker, Sophie, and Holden, Miriam. *The American Woman in Colonial and Revolutionary Times, 1565–1800: A Syllabus with Bibliography.* Westport, Connecticut: Greenwood Press, 1975.

Stanwick, Kathy, and Li, Christine. *The Political Participation of Women in the United States: A Selected Bibliography, 1950–1976.* Metuchen, N.J. and London: The Scarecrow Press, 1977.

II. General Works

Alsop, Gulielma Fell, and McBride, Mary F. *Arms and the Girl: A Guide to Personal Adjustment in War Work and War Marriage.* New York: Vanguard Press, 1943.

Fowler, William W. *Pioneer Women of America.* Hartford: S. S. Scranton & Co., 1891. See especially Chapter 5, "Captive Scouts—Heroines of the Mohawk Valley," Chapter 6, "Patriot Women of the Revolution," and Chapter 18, "Women in the Army."

Gribble, Francis G. *Women in War.* New York: Dutton, 1917. Accounts of women and their exploits from the time of Boadicea to Florence Nightingale.

Hanaford, Phoebe, A. C. *Daughters of America.* Augusta, Maine: True & Co., 1882. See especially Chapter 2, "Women of the Revolution," and Chapter 6, "Women during the Civil War."

Hanbrough, Henry Clay. *War and Women.* New York: Duffield, 1915. Maintains that women, in partnership with men, will eventually put an end to war.

Humphrey, Grace. *Women in American History.* Indianapolis: Bobbs-Merrill Co., 1919.

Hutton, J. Bernard. *Women in Espionage.* New York: Macmillan, 1972. A documented account of the female spy in Eastern and Western secret services.

Ibarruri, Dolores. *They Will Not Pass: The Autobiography of La Pasionaria.* New York: International Publishers, 1966.

———. *The Women Want a People's Peace.* New York: Workers' Library, 1941.

Jones, Katherine, ed. *Heroines of Dixie.* Indianapolis: Bobbs-Merrill Co., 1955.

Key, Ellen. *War and Peace and the Future.* New York: G. P. Putnam, 1916.

Lee, Kendrick. *Women in War Work.* Washington: Editorial Research Reports, 1942.

"Military Service: An Open Door to Learning for America's Young Women." *Adult Leadership* 14 (January 1966):229.

McConnell, Dorothy. *Women, War and Fascism.* New York: American League against War and Fascism, 1935.

Rowbotham, Sheila. *Women, Resistance and Revolution: A History of Women and Revolution in the Modern World.* New York: Pantheon Books, 1972.

Schaffter, Dorothy. *What Comes of Training Women for War.* Washington, D.C.: American Council on Education, 1948.

Taylor, Susie King. *Reminiscences of My Life in Camp with the 33rd United States Colored Troops, Late 1st South Carolina Volunteers.* New York: Arno Press, 1972. Reprint of 1902 edition.

Wakefield, Dan. *Supernation at Peace and War.* Boston: Little, Brown, 1968.

The Woman Question: Selections from the Writings of Karl Marx, Friedrich Engels, V. I. Lenin and Joseph Stalin. New York: International Publishers, 1970. Reprint of 1951 edition.

Women in War Industries. Princeton, N.J.: Princeton University Press, 1942.

III. Asia and Australia

Baron, V. O. "Personal Perspectives: Voices of Vietnam Era Women."
    Christian Century 93 (December 8, 1976): 1092–93.
Bergman, Arlene Eisen. *Women of Vietnam*. Rev. ed. San Francisco:
    People's Press, 1975.
Culhane, Clarie. "Women and Vietnam." *Canadian Dimension* 10 (June
    1975): 4–8. A description of women's role and activities in North
    Vietnam during the war and immediately after.
Dreifus, Claudia. "Women in Revolutionary China: An Interview with
    Suyin." *Evergreen* 16 (1972): 24–45.
"Daniel Ellsberg Talks about Women and War." *Ms.* (Spring 1972): 36–9.
Frenier, Marian Darce. "Aids and Barriers to Feminism in Modern China:
    The Effect of War and Economic Change on the Rate of Advance of
    Chinese Women's Status." *International Journal of Women's Studies*
    1 (May–June 1978): 133–40.
Grant, Zolin. "Mobilization of Women in Vietnam." *New Republic* 158
    (June 1, 1968): 11–13.
Grace, Paul, ed. *Vietnamese Women in Society and Revolution*. Cam-
    bridge, Mass.: Vietnam Resource Center, 1974.
Havens, Thomas R. H. "Women and War in Japan, 1937–1945." *American
    Historical Review* 80 (October 1975): 913–34.
Healy, Patricia. "Laos: Women in the Revolution:" *Refractory Girl* 12
    (September 1976): 36–37.
Hinton, William. *Fanshen: A Documentary of Revolt in a Chinese Village*.
    New York: Random House, 1968. Account of the revolution in one
    village, including new attitudes of women and their determination to
    struggle for a new life.
Le Duan, *On the Socialist Revolution in Viet Nam*. Vol. 3. Hanoi: Foreign
    Languages Publishing House, 1967. By the premier of North Vietnam
    on Vietnamese women and the Revolution.
Ma Hsin-teh. *Chinese Women in the Great Leap Forward*. Peking: Foreign
    Languages Press, 1960. Portraits of women in Communist China,
    including telephone operators, housewives, and farmers, and a dis-
    cussion of the part women have played in the Chinese Revolution.
Myrdal, Jan. *Report from a Chinese Village*. London: Penguin, 1967.
    Account of Revolution's effect on women.
Shute, Carmel. "Heroines and Heroes: Sexual Mythology in Australia,
    1914–1918." *Hecate* 1 (January 1975): 6–22. Australian women's
    participation in war efforts 1914–1918.
Turley, William S. "Women in the Communist Revolution in Vietnam."
    Asian Survey 12 (September 1972): 793–805.
Windschuttle, Elizabeth. "Women in the Vietnam War." *Refractory Girl* 12
    (September 1976): 4–10.

IV. Europe

England

McLaren, Barbara. *Women of the War.* London: Hodder & Stoughton, 1917. British women during World War I.

Newberry, Jo Velacott. "Anti-War Suffragists." *History* 62 (October 1977): 411–25. English women in World War I.

———, "Women and War in England: The Case of Catherine E. Marshall and World War I." *Peace and Change* 4 (Fall 1977): 13–17.

Tweedie, Ethel B. *Women and Soldiers.* London: John Lane, 1918. British women during World War I.

Weigall, David. "Women Militants in the English Civil War." *History Today* 22 (June 1972): 434–38.

France

Abray, Jane. Feminism in the French Revolution." *American Historical Review* 80 (Fall 1975): 43–62.

Aulard, Alphonse, ed. *Paris pendant la réaction thermidorienne et sous le Directoire.* 2 vols. Paris: L. Cerf, 1898–1902.

Bourdin, Isabelle. *Les Sociétés populaires à Paris pendant la Révolution française, 1789, jusqu'au la chute de la royauté.* Paris: Librairie du Recueil Sirey, 1937.

Bouvier, Jeanne, ed. *Les Femmes pendant la Révolution.* Paris: E. Figuiere, 1931.

Brice, R. *La femme et les armées dans la Révolution et l'Empire.* Paris: Librairie Ambert, n.d.

Brinton, Crane. *French Revolutionary Legislation on Illegitimacy, 1789–1804.* Cambridge, Mass.: Harvard University Press, 1936.

Chatelain, Abel, "Migrations et domesticité feminine urbaine en France, XVIIIeme siècle–XXeme siècle." *Revue d'histoire economique et sociale* 67 (1967): 506–28.

Cobb, Richard. *A Second Identity: Essays on France and French History.* London: Oxford University Press, 1969. Essays and reviews, including material on women's part in the French Revolution and later popular movements.

Duhet, Paule-Marie, *Les Femmes et la Révolution, 1789–1794.* Paris: Julliard, 1970.

Flandrin, Jean-Louis. *Familles, parenté, maison, sexualité dans l'ancienne société.* Paris: Hachette, 1976.

Goldsmith, Margaret. *Seven Women against the World.* London: Methuen and Co., Ltd., 1935. Short biographical essays on women, some of whom participated in the French Revolution.

Graham, Ruth. "Loaves and Liberty: Women in the French Revolution." In *Becoming Visible: Women in European History,* ed. R. Bridenthal and C. Koonz. Boston, 1976.

Kline, Rayna. "Partisans, Godmothers, Bicyclists and Other Terrorists: Women in the French Resistance and under Vichy." *Proceedings of the Annual Meeting of the Western Society for French History* 5 (1977): 375–83.

Levy, Darline Gay. "Feminism, Welfare and Subsistence: The Political Activism of Parisian Women during the French Revoltuion (1789–1795)." *Barnard Alumnae* 63 (Spring 1974): 9–12.

McCloy, Shelby T. "Charity Workshops for Women, Paris, 1790–1795." *Social Science Review* 11 (June 1937): 274–84.

Rudé, George. *The Crowd in the French Revolution.* London: Oxford University Press, 1959. Includes accounts of women in the revolutionary crowd during the French Revolution.

Schwartz, Bernard. *The Code of Napoleon and the Common Law World.* Westport, Conn.: Greenwood, 1956.

Stephens, Winifred. *Women of the French Revolution.* London: Chapman and Hall, 1922.

Thibault-Laurent, G. *La première introduction de divorce pendant la Révolution et l'Empire.* Clermont-Ferrand: Imprimerie moderne, 1938.

Germany

Blauel, Hans Peter. *Sex and Society in Nazi Germany.* J. Maxwell Brownjohn, trans. Philadelphia: Lippincott, 1973.

Stephenson, Jill. *Women in Nazi Society.* New York: Barnes & Noble, 1975.

Greece

Engle, Bernice Schultz. "The Amazons in Ancient Greece." *Psycho-Analytic Quarterly* 11 (1942): 512–54. The legendary race of Greek women warriors analyzed from a sociopsychological point of view.

Ireland

Servan-Schreiber, Claude. "Can Two Women Stop the Killing in Ireland?" *Ms.* 5 (December 1976): 62–65.

Poland

Kepińska-Bazylewicz, H. "Role of Women in the Piotrkow Resistance Movement." (Translated from the Polish). *Przeglad Lekarski* (Krakow) 19 (1972): 165–68.

Soviet Union

Bryant, Louise. *Six Red Months in Russia.* London: 1919. Journalistic account of life immediately after the Revolution, including information about women.

Clements, Barbara Evans. *Bolshevik Feminist: The Life of Alexandra Kollontai.* Bloomington: Indiana University Press, 1978.

Halle, Fannina. *Women in Soviet Russia.* London: 1933. Account of pre-revolutionary ideas about women's liberation and the position of women in revolution.

Levine, Isaac Don. *Yashka.* New York: Stokes, 1919. A transcription of the autobiography of Maria Botchkareva, commander of the Russian women's Battalion of Death.

Stites, Richard. *The Women's Liberation Movement in Russia: Feminism, Nihilism and Bolshevism, 1860–1930.* Princeton: Princeton University Press, 1978.

Whittaker, Cynthia H. "The Women's Movement in the Region of Alexander I. A Case Study in Russian Liberalism." *Journal of Modern History* 48 (June 1976): 35–69.

Yakovenko, A. "Unusual Fate." *Soviet Life* 12 (1975): 161–7.

V. Latin America

Azicri, Max. "Women's Development through Revolutionary Mobilization: A Study of the Federation of Cuban Women." *International Journal of Women's Studies* 2 (Jan.-Feb. 1979): 27–50.

Castro, Fidel. *Women and the Cuban Revolution.* New York: Pathfinder, 1970.

———. "Women as a Revolutionary Force." *Action Latin America* 1 1972: 12–13.

Guevara, Ché. *Reminiscences of the Cuban Revolutionary War.* London: Allen & Unwin, 1968. Numerous references to women guerrilla fighters.

Jacquette, Jane. "Women in Revolutionary Movements in Latin America." *Journal of Marriage and the Family* 35 (1973): 344–54.

Jenness, Linda, ed. *Women and the Cuban Revolution.* New York: Pathfinder, 1971.

Moore, Evelyn. "Girl of the Underground: La Pola, Heroine of Colombia's Struggle for Independence." *Americas* 5 (1953): 20–23, 27–28.

Plenn, J. H. "Forgotten Heroines of Mexico: Tales of the Soldaderas, Amazons of War and Revolution." *Travel* 66 (1936): 24–27.

"Revolution within the Revolution: Women in Latin America." *Action Latin America* 1 (1972). Special issue on women in revolutionary movements.

Rojas, Marta, and Rodriguez Calderon, Mirta, eds. *Tania. The Unforgettable Guerrilla.* New York: Randon House, 1971. Scrapbook of recollections and photographs concerning Tamara Bunke, an Argentine-born woman who worked for the revolution in Cuba and died with Ché Guevara in the Bolivian jungle.

Starrett, Vincent. "Soldier Women of Mexico." *Open Court. A Quarterly Magazine* 32 (1918): 376–82.

VI. United States and Canada

American Revolution

Berkin, Carol Ruth. "Remembering the Ladies: Historians and the Women of the American Revolution." In *The American Revolution: Changing Perspectives*, edited by William Fowler and Wallace Coyle. Boston: Northeastern University Press, 1979.

Blumenthal, Walter Hart. *Women Camp Followers of the American Revolution.* New York: Arno Press, 1974. Reprint of 1952 edition.

Booth, Sally. *The Women of '76.* New York: Hastings House, 1973.

Bunce, Oliver B. *The Romance of the Revolution.* New York: Bunce, 1854. Accounts of women who fought in the American Revolution.

Andrews, Matthew P. *Virginia, Old Dominion.* Garden City, N.Y.: Doubleday, Doran, 1937. Includes accounts of many colonial women who fought Indians, followed their husbands in the struggle for independence, and who died for freedom.

Campbell, Amelia D. "Women of New York State in the Revolution." *New York State Historical Association Quarterly* 3 (1922): 155–68.

Cometti, Elizabeth. "Women in the American Revolution." *New England Quarterly* 20 (1947): 329–46.

Coulter, Ellis M. "Nancy Hart, Georgia Heroine of the Revolution." *Georgia Historical Quarterly* 39 (1955): 118–151.

Darrach, H. "Lydia Darragh." *Pennsylvania Magazine of History and Biography* 23 (1899): 86–91. Story of a spy in the American Revolution.

Egle, William H. *Some Pennsylvania Women during the War of the Revolution.* Harrisburg, Pa.: Harrisburg Publishing Co., 1898.

Ellet, Elizabeth F. *Domestic History of the American Revolution.* New York: Lippincott Co., 1850.

———. *The Women of the American Revolution.* 3 vols. New York: Baker and Scribner, 1848–50. Includes accounts of Margaret C. Corbin, Lydia Darragh, Deborah Sampson Gannett, Nancy Hart, Rebecca Motte, Catherine Schuyler, and other women who participated in the Revolution.

Evans, Elizabeth. *Weathering the Storm: Women of the American Revolution.* New York: Scribner's, 1975.

Grant DePauw, Linda. *Four Traditions: Women of New York during the American Revolution.* Pittsburgh: KNOW, 1974.

Hassenchal, Fran. "Mary Hayes and Deborah Sampson: The Rhetoric of Neglect, Praise, and Expectation." ERIC Ed 102620. Focuses on rhetoric about two revolutionary war heroines.

Holden, James A. "The Influence of the Death of Jane McCrea on the Burgoyne Campaign." *New York State Historical Association Proceedings* 12 (1913): 249–94.

Hulton, Anne. *Letters of a Loyalist Lady, 1767–1776.* Cambridge, Mass.: Harvard University Press, 1927.

Kerber, Linda K. "Daughters of Columbia: Educating Women for the Republic, 1787–1805." In *The Hofstadter Aegis,* edited by Stanley Elkins and Eric McKitrick. New York: Knopf, 1974.

———. "The Republican Mother: Women and the Enlightenment—An American Perspective." *American Quarterly* XXVIII, 2 (special issue, summer 1976).

Lyman, Susan E. "Three New York Women of the Revolution." *New York Historical Society Quarterly* 29 (1945): 77–82.

Mann, Herman. *The Female Review: Life of Deborah Sampson, the Female Soldier in the War of the Revolution.* New York: Arno Press, 1972. Reprint of the 1947 edition.

McArthur, J. L. "Women of the Revolution." *New York State Historical Association Proceedings* 5 (1905): 153–61.

McLean (Ms.) D. "Baroness de Riedesel." *New York State Historical Association Proceedings* 3 (1905): 39–44.

Myers, Albert Cook, ed. *Sally Wister's Journal: A True Account of her Experiences with Officers of the Continental Army, 1777–78.* New York: Arno Press, 1972. Reprint of the 1902 edition.

Norton, Mary Beth. "Eighteenth Century Women in Peace and War: The Case of the Loyalists." *William and Mary Quarterly* 33 (July 1976): 386–409.

Parker, Amelia C. "Baroness Riedesel and Other Women in Burgoyne's Army." *New York State Historical Association Proceedings* 26 (1928): 109–119.

Parry, Edwin, S. *Betsy Ross, Quaker Rebel.* Philadelphia: Winston, Co., 1932.

Perley, S. "Moll Pitcher." *Essex Antiquarian* 3 (1899): 33–35.

Somerville, Mollie D. *Women and the American Revolution.* Washington: National Society, Daughters of the American Revolution, 1974.

Von Riedesel, Friederike C. *Baroness von Riedesel and the American Revolution: Journal and Correspondence of a Tour of Duty.* Marvin L. Brown and Marta Huth, eds. Chapel Hill: University of North Caroline Press, 1965.

Wilson, Joan H. "The Illusion of Change: Women and the American

Revolution." In *The American Revolution: Explorations in the History of American Radicalism.* De Kalb: Northern Illinois University Press, 1976.

Civil War

Goodrich, James W., ed. "The Civil War Letters of Bethiah Pyatt Mc-Known." *Missouri Historical Review* 67 (April 1973): 351–70.

Henle, Ellen Langenheim. "Clara Barton, Soldier or Pacifist?" *Civil War History* 24 (June 1978): 152–60.

Kondert, Nancy T. "The Romance and Reality of Defeat: Southern Women in 1865." *Journal of Mississippi History* 35 (1973): 141–52.

Jones, Katherine. *When Sherman Came: Southern Women and the "Great March."* Indianapolis: Bobbs-Merrill, 1964. How Southern women impeded Sherman's march to the sea during the Civil War.

Moore, Frank. *Women of the War: Their Heroism and Self-Sacrifices.* Hartford, Conn.: n.p., 1866.

Myers, Robert Manson. *The Children of Pride: A True Story of Georgia and the Civil War.* New Haven, Conn.: Yale University Press, 1972.

Quynn, D. M. "Flora MacDonald." *North Carolina Historical Review* 18 (1941): 236–58.

Simkins, Francis Butler. *The Women of the Confederacy.* New York: Garrett & Massie, 1936.

Velazquez, Loreta Janeta. *The Woman in Battle: A Narrative of the Exploits, Adventures, and Travels of Madame Loreta Janeta Velazquez, Otherwise Known as Lieutenant Harry T. Buford, Confederate States Army.* C. J. Worthington, ed. New York: Arno Press, 1972. Reprint of 1876 edition. Story of the battles she participated in as a Confederate officer, her career as a spy and blockade runner, her adventures as a miner, stockbroker, resident among the Mormons, and her numerous love affairs.

Wiley, Bell Irvin, *Confederate Women.* Westport, Conn.: Greenwood, 1975.

———. "Women of the Lost Cause." *American History Illustrated.* 8 (December 1973): 11–23.

World War I

"Are Many Women Replacing Soldiers in Industrial Work?" *Current Opinion.* 64 (January 1918): 60–61.

Baer, Clara Gregory. "Women and the War." *National Educational Association of the U.S. Journal of Addresses and Proceedings.* 56 (1918): 355–57.

Breen, William J. "Black Women and the Great War: Mobilization and Reform in the South." *Journal of Southern History* 44 (August 1978): 421–40.

———. "Southern Women in the War: The North Carolina Woman's Committee, 1917–1919." *North Carolina Historical Review* 55 (July 1978): 251–83.

Chenery, W. L. "The New Position of Women." *Survey* 45 (8 January 1921): 539–40. The economic status of women before, during, and after World War I and the need to give men the same safeguards as women rather than to tear down the laws set up for women. Also deals with the work of the U.S. Women's Bureau.

Fair, John D. "The Political Aspects of Women's Suffrage during the First World War." *Albion* 8 (Fall 1976): 274–95.

"Female Labor Arouses Hostility and Apprehension in Union Ranks." *Current Opinion* 64 (April 1918): 292–94. The problem of replacing men during the war by women working for lower wages.

Goldmark, Josephine. "Some Considerations Affecting the Replacement of Men by Women Workers." *American Journal of Public Health* 8 (April 1918): 270–76.

Goldmark, P. "Facts as to Women in War Industries." *New Republic* 13 (29 December 1917): 251–52.

Greenwald, Maureen. "Women Workers and World War I: The American Railroad Industry, A Case Study." *Journal of Social History* 9 (Winter 1975): 154–77.

Hobbs, M. A. "Wartime Employment of Women." *American Labor Legislative Journal* 8 (December 1918): 332–38.

Kelley, Florence. "The War and Women Workers." *Survey* 39 (March 1918): 628–31.

Malan, Nancy E. "How 'Ya Gonna Keep 'Em Down? Women and World War I." *Prologue: The Journal of the National Archives* 5 (Winter 1973): 203–39.

McFarland, C. K., and Neal, Nevin E. "The Reluctant Reformer: Woodrow Wilson and Woman Suffrage, 1913–1920." *Rocky Mountain Social Science Journal* 11 (April 1974): 33–43.

Norton, E. "Women in War Industries." *New Republic* 13 (15 December 1917): 179–86.

Secor, Lella. "The Ford Peace Ship and After." In Julian Bell, ed., *We Did Not Fight: 1914–1918. Experiences of War Resisters.* (London: Cobden-Sanderson, 1935).

Shorer, Michele J. "Roles and Images of Women in World War I Propaganda." *Politics and Society* 5 (1975): 469–86.

Thompson, W. Gilman. "Women and Heavy War Work." *Scribner's Magazine* 65 (January 1919): 113–16. The extent to which women can replace men in heavy industries and suggestions for accomplishing this.

Trattner, William. "Julia Grace Wales and the Wisconsin Plan for Peace." *Wisconsin Magazine of History* 44 (1967): 203–16.

Wolfe, A. B., and Olson, H. "War-Time Industrial Employment of Women in the United States." *Journal of Political Economy* 27 (October 1919): 639–69.

World War II

Amidon, Beulah. "Arms and the Women: From Now on, for the Duration, the Women of America Will Be Replacing Millions of Men at Jobs in War Production and Civilian Services." *Survey Graphics* 31 (May 1942): 244–48.

————. "Women's Place in the Defense Program." *Educational Record* 22 (July 1941): 403–13.

Anderson, Mary. "Women at Work: 'Woman Power' Can Be Used Effectively in the Defense Program when Health and Safety Measures Are Adequate." *National Safety News* 44 (July 1941): 10–11.

————. "Women in War Industry." *American Federationist* 49 (March 1942): 18–19.

————. "Women's Role in War Production." *Labor Information Bulletin* 9 (April 1942): 1–4.

Archibald, Katherine. "Women in the Shipyard." *Radical America* 9 (July–August 1975) 139–45. Author's work in a shipyard during World War II and problems encountered from men and trade unions.

Army Air Force Historical Office. "Women Pilots with the AAF, 1941–44." In *Army Air Force Historical Studies,* vol. 55. Washington, D.C., n.d.

Chun, Victor K. "The Origin of the WASPS." *Journal of the American Aviation Historical Society* 14 (Winter 1969): 259–62. The story of how women got into aviation during World War II.

Carson, John J. "Wasting of Manpower." *Atlantic Monthly* 170 (August 1942): 75–78. The necessity for married women to replace men in the armed forces.

Davenell, G. G. "When Johnny Comes Marching Home." *Independent Woman* 24 (July 1945): 182–3.

"Employment of Women in Peacetime and War Jobs in New York State." *Industrial Bulletin* 21 (October 1942): 346–48.

"Employment of Women in Wartime." *Monthly Labor Review* 55 September 1942): 441–45.

Flynn, Elizabeth Gurley. *Women in the War.* New York: Worker's Library, 1942.

Greenbie, M. B. "New Skills and How to Acquire Them: Women in Defense Industry." *Independent Woman* 20 (June 1941): 175–179.

Hartman, Susan M. "Prescriptions for Penelope: Literature on Women's Obligations to Returning World War II Veterans." *Women's Studies* 5 (1978): 223–40.

Hines, F. T. "The Ladies Want Post-War Jobs Too: Figures Show War Increase of Women Workers to Be Overrated." *Commerce* (June 1944): 18–19.

Kalisch, Philip A. and Beatrice J. "Nurses under Fire: The World War II

Experience of Nurses on Bataan and Corregidor." *Nursing Research* 25 (December 1976): 409–29.

McMillin, L. F. *The First Year: A Study of Women's Participation in Federal Defense Activities.* Washington: U.S. Bureau of Labor. Civil Service Commission, 1941.

Palmer, Gladys L. "Women's Place in Industry." *Current History* 6 (January 1944): 19–24. The economic status of women during and after the war.

Pidgeon, Mary Elizabeth. "Changes in Women's Employment during the War." *Monthly Labor Review* 59 (November 1944): 1029–30.

———. *Employment of Women in the Early Postwar Period with Background of Prewar and War Data.* Washington, D.C.: U.S. Bureau of Labor, Women's Bureau, 1946.

———. *Equal Pay for Women in War Industries.* Washington, D.C.: United Nations. Commission on the Status of Women, 1942.

"Policy of War Manpower Commission on Women Workers." *Monthly Labor Review* 56 (April 1943): 669–71.

Rupp, Leila J. *Mobilizing Women for War: German and American Propaganda, 1939–1945.* Princeton: Princeton University Press, 1978.

Schneider, Florence Hemley. "Defense and the Woman Worker." *Journal of Educational Sociology* 15 (January 1942): 260–71.

Seybold, Geneva. "Wartime Pay of Women in Industry." *Conference Board Management Record* 5 (October 1943): 402–5.

"Standards for Employment of Women in Defense Programs." *Monthly Labor Review* 51 (September 1940): 564–67.

Stitt, Louise. "Women's Wartime Employment: Expanding Needs; Increasing Problems." *American Association of University Women Journal* 35 (April 1942): 136–40.

Treadwell, Mattie. *The Women's Army Corps.* Washington, D.C.: Office of the Chief of Military History, Department of the Army, 1954.

Trey, Joan. "Women in the War Economy—World War II." *Review of Radical Political Economics* 4 (July 1972): 40–57.

Walsh, Mary Roth. "Women Physicians and World War II." *Journal of the American Medical Women's Association* 32 (May 1977): 189–93.

Walters, J. E. "Women in Industry." *American Academy of Political and Social Science Annals* 229 (September 1943): 56–62. Company policies on the employment of women during World War II.

Zapoleon, Marguerite Wykoff. "Women in Defense Occupations." *Occupations* 19 (April 1941): 509–11.

List of Contributors

Carol Ruth Berkin received her B.A. from Barnard College and her Ph.D. from Columbia University. She is Associate Professor of History at Baruch College of The City University of New York, where she teaches a course in the history of women in America. She is the author of *Jonathan Sewall: Odyssey of an American Loyalist* (Columbia University Press, 1974) and of *Colonists in Crisis: The Loyalist Experience of the American Revolution* (Columbia University Press, forthcoming). With Mary Beth Norton of Cornell University she had edited *Women of America: A History* (Houghton Mifflin, 1979) and has published articles in women's history, including "Within the Conjurer's Circle: Women in Colonial America," in *The Underside of American History*, volume 1 (ed. by Thomas Frazier; Harcourt Brace, 1978) and "Private Woman, Public Woman: The Contradictions of Charlotte Perkins Gilman" in *Women of America: A History*.

Clara M. Lovett holds an undergraduate degree from the University of Trieste (Italy) and graduate degrees from the University of Texas at Austin. She is Associate Professor of European History at Baruch College of The City University of New York. She has published *Carlo Cattaneo and the Politics of the Risorgimento* (Nijhoff, 1972) and *Giuseppe Ferrari and the Italian Revolution* (University of North Carolina Press, 1979) as well as eleven essays in American and Italian scholarly journals. She is also the author of *The Democratic Movement in Italy, 1830–1876* (Harvard University Press, forthcoming).

Harriet Branson Applewhite received her Ph.D. from Stanford University in 1972 and is now Associate Professor of Political Science at Southern Connecticut State College. Her publications include two collaborative efforts with Darline G. Levy and Mary D. Johnson: the anthology *Women in Revolutionary Paris, 1789–1795* (University of Illinois Press, 1979), and "Women: The Failure of Liberation," in *The French Revolution: Conflicting Interpretations* (ed. by Frank A. Kafker and James M. Laux; Random House, 1976). She has also published in the *Journal of Interdisciplinary History*. She is now at work on a book, "Political Culture in Revolutionary France, 1788–1791."

Lourdes Casal was born in Havana, Cuba, and has resided in the United States since 1961. She has a Ph.D. in social psychology from the Graduate Faculty of the New School for Social Research, and teaches at Rutgers University at Newark. In 1978–1979 she was a Fellow in the Latin American

Program at the Woodrow Wilson International Center for Scholars. Casal is the author or editor of several studies, among them *Los fundadores: Alfonso* (Miami: Ed. Universal, 1973) *Race Relations in Contemporary Cuba* (London: Minority Rights Group Monographs, 1979), and *The Cuban Minority in the United States*, which she co-authored with R. J. Prohias (Florida Atlantic University, Boca Raton, 1973).

Beatrice Farnsworth received her Ph.D. from Yale University. An Associate Professor at Wells College in Aurora, New York, she is the author of *William C. Bullitt and the Soviet Union* (1967). Her publications include "Bolshevism, the Woman Question and Aleksandra Kollontai," *The American Historical Review* (April 1976) and "Bolshevik Alternatives and the Soviet Family: the 1926 Marriage Law Debate," in D. Atkinson, A. Dallin, and G. Lapidus, *Women in Russia* (Stanford University Press, 1977). Most recently she has published the political biography *Aleksandra Kollontai* (Stanford University Press, 1979).

Judith Jeffrey Howard received her B.A. from the University of Rochester in 1970 and her Ph.D. from the University of Connecticut in 1977. Grants from the ACLS-SSRC and the Woodrow Wilson Fellowship Foundation helped her complete the essay in this volume. She is the author of several essays and papers on Italian women, including "The Feminine Vision of Matilde Serao," *Italian Quarterly* (Winter 1975) and "Widening Sex Roles and Social Transformation: An Overview of Women's Activism in the New Italian Nation," in *The Struggles of Eve* (ed. by Frances R. Keller; Clio Press, forthcoming). She is currently revising her dissertation, "The Woman Question in Italy, 1861–1880," for publication.

Mary Durham Johnson, a graduate of Skidmore College, received her Ph.D. from Washington University in 1972. She was Assistant Professor of History at Fontbonne College in 1972–73 and at Washington University in 1973–74. Since 1974 she has been Assistant Professor of History at Temple University. Between her undergraduate and graduate careers she spent three years in northern Nigeria as a Peace Corps Volunteer Teacher. The experience greatly interested her in the problem of social change for women, since she was living in Nigeria during its civil war and a period of rapid modernization. Her graduate work and research have concentrated on the history of French and American women in the late eighteenth and early nineteenth centuries. She has co-edited *Women in Revolutionary Paris* with D. Levy and H. Applewhite and has completed a forthcoming book, *Poissardes, Patriotes and Sans Jupons: A Study of the Women of the People during the French Revolution*. She is now doing research on women in the Franco-American community of the early nineteenth century.

Darline Gay Levy received her B.A. from Barnard College and her Ph.D. from Harvard University. She is Assistant Professor of History at Barnard College and the author of *The Ideas and Careers of Simon-Nicolas-Henri Linguet: A Study in Eighteenth Century French Politics* (University of

Illinois Press, forthcoming: 1980). She has edited, with Harriet Applewhite and Mary Johnson, the anthology *Women in Revolutionary Paris*, and with Applewhite, "The Concept of Modernization in the French Enlightenment," in *Studies on Voltaire in the Eighteenth Century.*

Joan M. Maloney served as a research consultant for Seton Hall University's Center for Asian Studies after completing her doctorate at Georgetown University. Since 1964 she has been Professor of History at Salem State College, where her course, "Women in Asia," is part of a minor in Women's Studies. She is the author of several articles on the women's movement in China and is currently completing a book on Maoism and the status of women.

Barbara Corrado Pope teaches courses in Women's Studies at the University of Oregon. She contributed an article to *Becoming Visible,* a book of twenty essays on European women's history (ed. by Renate Bridenthal and Claudia Koonz; Houghton Mifflin, 1977). She is now finishing her dissertation, "Mothers and Daughters in Early Nineteenth-Century Paris," in the History Department of Columbia University.

Leila J. Rupp is Assistant Professor of History and Women's Studies at The Ohio State University. She is the author of *Mobilizing Women for War: German and American Propaganda, 1939–1945* (Princeton University Press, 1978) and co-editor with Barbara Miller Lane of *Nazi Ideology Before 1933: A Documentation*. She is currently working on American feminism in the post-World War II period.

Marylynn Salmon is a doctoral student in early American social history at Bryn Mawr College. She is the author of "Equality or Submersion? *Feme Covert* Status in Early Pennsylvania," in *Women of America: A History* (ed. by Carol Ruth Berkin and Mary Beth Norton; Houghton Mifflin, 1979). She is now completing her dissertation, "Women's Property Rights, 1750–1820: A Comparison of the Law in Pennsylvania, Maryland and South Carolina."

Karen Beck Skold received her B.A. in Sociology from Oberlin College and is a Ph.D. candidate at the University of Oregon. Her essay in this volume is drawn from her dissertation, which won her a Woodrow Wilson Dissertation Fellowship in 1975. She has taught in the Women's Studies Program at San Diego State University and has read several papers on the sociology of women at professional conferences.

Barbara J. Steinson received her B.A. from Grinnell College and her Ph.D. from the University of Michigan. She is currently Assistant Professor of History at DePauw University. Among her essays on American women are "The Woman's Peace Party—New Departures and Old Arguments," in *The Role of Women in Conflict and Peace* (ed. by Dorothy McGrugan; University of Michigan Press, 1977) and "Sisters and Soldiers: The National Service Schools, Military Training for Women, 1916–1917," *Historian* (forthcoming).

Index